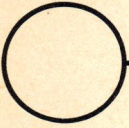

introduction
to linguistic concepts

BRUCE L. PEARSON
University of South Carolina

Alfred A. Knopf New York

for Mary R. Haas

THIS IS A BORZOI BOOK PUBLISHED BY ALFRED A. KNOPF, INC.

First Edition

9 8 7 6 5 4 3 2 1

Copyright © 1977 by Alfred A. Knopf, Inc.

Library of Congress Cataloging in Publication Data

Pearson, Bruce L   1932–
    Introduction to linguistic concepts.

    Bibliography: p.
    Includes index.
    1.   Linguistics.   2.   Language and languages.
I.   Title.
P121.P347   410   76-43012

ISBN 0-394-31122-1

Cover and text designed by Rodelinde Albrecht

Manufactured in the United States of America
Composed by Monotype Composition Co., Inc., Baltimore, Maryland
Printed and bound by R. R. Donnelley and Sons Co., Crawfordsville, Indiana

introduction
to linguistic concepts

Advisor
JOHN L. FISCHER
Tulane University

preface

Most books intended as introductions to linguistics present the subject as a unified discipline in terms of the insights that have been synthesized and are in common use at the time the book is written. This is useful for the beginning student, but it is deceptive for several reasons. These reasons must be set forth to justify a book that offers what some may consider a departure from tradition.

In linguistics, as in any discipline, there is never complete uniformity of viewpoint among all practitioners. There are, rather, different schools of thought—some large, some small. Whenever one school is sufficiently large and influential, its adherents may be in a position to define the issues both for themselves and for their opponents. To all outward appearances there may be consensus. But this consensus is merely tacit agreement as to the issues to be disputed. Being a linguist means coming to grips with the issues, however these are defined. Advances in scholarship come about as these issues are clarified and redefined until some new consensus emerges.

The purpose of this book is to present linguistics as a body of conceptual tools going back to the traditional grammar that originated in ancient Greece. These basic concepts were selectively elaborated and given an entirely new direction by the historical linguists of the nineteenth century. Their concepts, in turn, were applied to synchronic analysis by the structuralists. Transformational grammar has subsequently given structuralism a new direction. And at present, semantic analysis, in one version or another, seems likely to replace the standard transformational model.

Each new development has represented a break with its immediate predecessor but, at the same time, has been quite dependent on the conceptual apparatus of the school from which it developed. The conceptual apparatus has been elaborated at each stage, but its basic format still follows the same fundamental principles. Our intention, therefore, is not only to introduce the student to linguistic science as it is practiced today but to show why linguistics has developed as it has. If the conceptual tools that comprise linguistics are inadequate or inconsistent, it is largely because of their peculiar historical development.

We will attempt to recapitulate the history of linguistics by analyzing language data in terms of the concepts and analytical tools that have been available at different periods in the past. Awareness of the past is requisite to understanding the present. And, if linguists are to avoid expending their time in an independent discovery of knowledge already available on the reference shelf, it behooves them to study the past with care. A knowledge of where we are and why we are here is an inescapable part of charting the course linguistics will take in the years to come. The present, after all, is the only point of departure into the future.

The foregoing paragraphs are not intended as a disclaimer of any bias on my part. Obviously we all have some kind of bias. This being the case, it is only fair to give the reader an honest statement of the viewpoint that colors this presentation. Other scholars will no doubt have different ideas about the exact chain of events that has led linguistics to its present situation. Others may wish to define the current issues differently. Others will perhaps expect the new consensus to be quite different from what I envision. Either they or I—possibly both of us—will be wrong on specific details. But this much is certain: current notions about language will inevitably give way to a new synthesis. The notions that enjoy popularity at any given time are not an end point but merely a transition between what preceded and what will follow.

Looking back over the completed manuscript, I see in almost every sentence the need to write two or three additional sentences to clarify, modify, qualify, or elaborate what has been said. No book written today can be a definitive treatment of modern linguistics. The field is too complex and too rapidly changing to lend itself to definitive coverage in a single volume. A book like this can only hope to encourage serious readers to continue further study on their own and add their own marginal notes to clarify, modify, qualify, or elaborate the text in appropriate places.

The influence of one's colleagues, teachers, and friends is always important in the formation of an individual's ideas. I feel especially indebted to four of my former teachers, Mary R. Haas, Wallace L. Chafe, Raimo Anttila, and William O. Bright. It is often the case that "original" ideas are simply old ideas tried out in a new setting, and I suspect this is true of anything that may seem original in this book. Of course, the juxtaposition of familiar ideas, the analysis of trends, and the interpretation of different points of view are matters for which I accept full responsibility. I hope that those whose influence I acknowledge will be satisfied with the presentation, but I have no wish to implicate them in the final form of this book.

Several persons have helped with manuscript preparation at various stages—Holly Hook, Mary Anne Webber, Anna Dixon, Kathy Helms, and Janice Pryor. A number of colleagues have read portions of the manuscript and offered helpful comments. These include William Ayres, Judi Breuggemann, Gale Coston, George Dorrill, Stephen Durham, Richard Gunter, Erika Lindemann, Greta Little, Barry Loewer, Robert Oakman, Raymond O'Cain, Ted Rathbun, and Richard Scoville. Among colleagues at other institutions I would like to thank Karen Dakin, who examined an early version of the manuscript; John L. Fischer, Richard Morrill, and Robert A. Palmatier, who read the manuscript at the request of Barry R. Fetterolf of Alfred A. Knopf, and whose comments were forwarded to me; John L. Fischer, again, who served as consultant throughout the preparation of the book; and Helen D. Litton of Knopf, who served as production editor, and her staff of eagle-eyed assistants. I am grateful for their many suggestions, which have enabled me to correct errors of fact and clarify the presentation at many points. Needless to say, no one except myself should be held accountable for defects that remain.

Port Royal, S.C.   BRUCE L. PEARSON

contents

Colorless green ideas are emerging from hibernation,
Hungry, but otherwise unharmed.
What is the half-life of a grammar?

I find I can open my hand
  but I can't beat my heart.
Now I ask you, is that fair?

A Mexican jumping bean is an agent,
  but not a very good one,
    bridging the lexical gap as it does
    between grapenut and hornet.

God is an ambient noun,
Dead is a patient verb,

$$\begin{bmatrix} process \\ action \end{bmatrix} \;\;—\!\!—\!\!>>\;\; pointless.$$

—MOLLY DANIEL

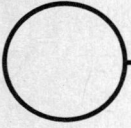

introduction
to linguistic concepts

1 the nature of language

1.1 LANGUAGE AS A HUMAN TRAIT

Nothing sets human beings apart from the other creatures with whom they share the earth as decisively as does language. Language is a uniquely human activity, a defining characteristic of *Homo sapiens*. Other animals have fairly elaborate communication systems, but in their complexity or flexibility, these systems do not approach human language. It was the development of language as much as any other single trait that marked the transition from nonhuman primate to human being. Language made possible the accumulation of knowledge and the transmission of culture. Humanity's survival has always depended on the extra advantage given by this versatile tool.

A shared language is a cohesive force binding individuals to other members of their community. But that which is shared inevitably has its counterpart in that which is not shared, and the language that binds one group together simultaneously sets that group apart from all other groups. One's language is thus a badge of one's group identification and, as such, is inseparable from attitudes and thought patterns that are constantly being expressed in the language of the group. Within large groups there may be varied numbers of subgroups and even subgroups within subgroups, each using a slightly different variety of the common language. At the individual level each person is distinguished from other individuals by personality qualities and mannerisms that are virtually inseparable from speech traits, among them, voice quality, rate of speech, favored expressions, and the like.

In short, language is omnipresent in human activities and experiences and is an inextricable part of what every individual is, does, perceives, and believes. Yet for the most part everyone uses language without conscious effort or thought. The fact that language can be so pervasive and at the same time so unobtrusive is one of the compelling reasons for studying it.

1.2   LANGUAGE DEFINED

Everyone has a fairly clear idea of what language is. But in any formal study it is always useful to define the subject to avoid any misunderstanding. If the subject is clearly defined, we can reduce the twofold risk of misdirecting attention to unrelated subjects on the one hand or excluding proper parts of the subject on the other.

Language can be defined in various ways depending on the features one wishes to emphasize. The subject could be defined broadly enough to include all forms of communication or narrowly enough to focus on a particular type of grammatical rule. A middle course between these two extremes is likely to prove the most fruitful.

> **Language is a system of human communication based on speech sounds used as arbitrary symbols.**

It will be helpful to consider in detail just what this definition does and does not include.

1.3   A SYSTEM OF COMMUNICATION

Certainly the communicative function of language deserves prime emphasis. It is true that humans use language for other purposes. The stock greetings and small talk exchanged by acquaintances serve to reinforce social ties rather than communicate vital information. Songs and rhymes are a pleasant form of motor activity, enjoyable apart from any potential communicative function. But these are certainly peripheral uses of language. The central purpose of language is communication.

Communication implies the transmission of meaningful data from one organism to another. There is no way that two nervous systems can be directly linked to each other, but language provides a means of encoding messages that can be transmitted in such a way that two or more nervous systems can for all practical purposes achieve a linkup. The study of language must therefore involve the study of meaning.

1.4   SPEECH VERSUS WRITING

Language is based on speech sounds. These are sounds produced in the vocal tract as the airflow from the lungs is restricted in various ways and then resonated through the oral and nasal cavities. Speech was the only form of language used by humans for the greater part of a history going back more than a million years. For many people in the world today, language still exists only in its spoken form. From the standpoint of the linguist, therefore, language is sound and not print.

Writing is a way of representing language, but writing always represents something that could be spoken. Writing is therefore a secondary way of representing language; it is not an alternative way. Written forms cannot exist apart from the spoken forms on which they are based; spoken forms can exist whether or not they are written. This is not intended to deny the usefulness of writing. It is simply intended to emphasize the proper relationship between speaking and writing.

In our own culture, with its emphasis on literacy, it is sometimes easy to forget that writing is based on speech and not the other way around. This is particularly true of people whose education extends over many years and who spend a relatively large proportion of their time dealing with written representations of language. Because the written representation is normally the form we deal with on a conscious level, it is all to easy to fall into the trap of looking only at written forms when we begin to think consciously about language. Then too, when we praise someone for having a good command of the language, we most often are thinking of the written evidence of this command rather than the spoken form represented by the written record. Linguists of course deal with written forms, but in doing so they are careful to distinguish between language, the spoken system they are studying, and writing, a visible medium used to represent language.

Laymen occasionally suppose that the Chinese writing system is independent of spoken forms or that the sign language of the Plains Indians is a "natural" communication system not dependent on the spoken word. It is true that a written Chinese word can be understood by anyone who knows its meaning, but it is understood primarily because the reader equates the written symbol with a linguistic form that could also be pronounced if desired. The situation is comparable to the use of arabic numerals that signify *one, two, three* or *uno, dos, tres*, depending on whether the reader speaks English or Spanish.

The sign language of the Plains Indians is an arbitrary system devised primarily for communication between tribes speaking different languages. Some signs, such as the hand-to-mouth gesture for 'eat,' are imitative of familiar actions, but other signs were devised quite consciously by bilingual individuals and taught to others through the medium of conventional language. Other symbolic systems, such as traffic signals or the sign language used by deaf persons, have been devised in the same way and should not be misconstrued as latter-day remnants of prelinguistic communication systems.

1.5 AN ARBITRARY SYSTEM

The speech sounds used in language are employed as arbitrary symbols. That is, the meaningful values assumed by speech sounds in language are arbitrarily fixed. There is nothing about the sound of the word *house* that requires it to have the meaning that it has in English. It could just as easily have different sounds, such as *casa* (in Spanish), *maison* (in French), *uchi* (in Japanese), and so on. To say that the relationship between sound and meaning is arbitrary does not, of course, imply that the speakers of a language sit down at a conference table to agree on the forms they will use. It is impossible even to imagine such a conference taking place without a language already available. It means simply that in any language there are certain sequences of sounds that have a conventionally accepted meaning. These words are customarily used by all speakers with the same intended meaning and understood by all listeners in the same way.

The fact that a given sequence of sounds is used repeatedly with the same meaning is one reason that language is a system. If language lacked systematic qualities, it could not function as an instrument of communication. Everything would be random. Speakers and listeners would be reduced to guessing at the intended content of messages. But the meaning of individual units is fixed, and the possibilities for combining these units are also fixed in a systematic way. As a result, language is not random but is constrained within predictable limits. This is not to suggest that the content of any given message can be predicted in advance. But since the possible form of a message is strictly limited, the encoding and interpretation of messages must follow fixed patterns. A speaker and listener must use the same conventions—the same system—if they are to succeed in communicating.

Because of the importance of systematic patterning in language, linguists have generally concentrated their energies on identifying and describing these patterns. The kinds of patterns that have interested linguists have varied from one time to another and from one school to another, but the focus of attention has invariably been on language as system.

1.6   HUMAN VERSUS ANIMAL COMMUNICATION

It was noted at the outset that many animals besides human beings have communication systems. Some of these systems are fairly elaborate and have various attributes in common with human language. For example, much of the communication system of vervet monkeys is based on speech sounds used as arbitrary symbols. The same is true of communication systems used by more familiar animals, such as the domestic dog or cat. These systems are organized very differently from human language, however. This fact can be appreciated by the casual observer even though it may not be at all obvious how the different organizational principles should be described. Our purpose after all is to determine the organizational principles of human language. Once this has been accomplished, it should be fairly simple to see how the human communication system differs from animal systems.

This is why we have begun with a definition that restricts language to the type of communication system used by human beings. We could of course start with a definition that would direct our attention to various attributes of language regarded as making it uniquely human. Such an approach, however, would predispose us to find what we were invited to look for. A better procedure is to start without firm predispositions, hoping that the attributes of human communication identified in the process will lead us inductively to a clearer understanding of language. If so, we should have little difficulty in identifying the features that distinguish human language from animal systems of communication when we return to this topic in Chapter 7.

1.7 COMPONENTS OF LANGUAGE

We have already indicated that language can be thought of as speech sounds that represent meanings. We might therefore expect that it will be necessary to investigate at least the two subsystems of language represented in Figure 1–1. The diagram is a schematic representation of a possible model of language. It consists of a meaning component, the output of which is processed by a sound component. The output of this component is what we hear as language.

FIGURE 1–1   A Tentative Model of Language

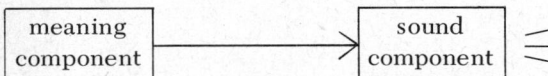

Actually the facts of language are a good bit more complicated. For one thing, the properties of the sound-processing component and the meaning component, at least in terms of their output, are entirely different. Sound occurs in a continuous stream along a dimension of time. It is therefore appropriate to speak of sound as linear. The linearity of sound along the time dimension corresponds to the linearity of print, in which the left-to-right sequence of letters matches the temporal sequence of the sounds these letters represent. It is by no means clear, however, that meaning involves linearity at all.

Imagine a situation in which one is looking out the living room window of one's home. The scene is a familiar one. Cars pass along the street in the background. A few children are playing. The roses are blooming, and the lawn needs mowing. The postman, a regular visitor at this time each day, starts across the lawn, busy shuffling a pile of envelopes. As he does so a dog comes running from behind a neighbor's house and takes a solid bite of the postman's trousers—and the postman as well. The person watching all this may wish to report the event to someone else in an adjoining room. There are many ways the message could be expressed, but let us suppose it comes out:

A dog bit the postman!

The message is typical in that it is highly selective. Nothing is said about the backdrop against which the action occurs. The message focuses exclusively on an action of biting involving a dog as **agent,** or actor, and the postman as **patient,** or recipient. This relationship is made clear in English by the fact that *dog* is the subject of the sentence and precedes the verb *bit.* The fact that *postman* is the object of the verb (and patient of the process) is clear from its position following the verb.

Interchanging *dog* and *postman* would lead to an entirely different sentence: *The postman bit a dog!* The sentence is just as grammatical as the one cited above, although much less probable. The point is that the arrangement of elements in a linear order constitutes an important part of the message. The question we must consider is whether the arrangement is a natural expression of the relationship or is itself an arbitrary part of the message. To a person familiar only with English, the subject-verb-object (SVO) arrangement may seem natural enough to be attributed to a logical progression of thought or to the order in which the elements being discussed were perceived.

But recall that the postman in the episode actually appeared on the scene before the dog. And in the specific event singled out for encoding in the message, the postman, the dog, and the act of biting are all part of a single event. There is no way we can attribute temporal or logical priority to one part over another. The linear arrangement of elements in the final message is an arbitrary part of the language system.

We can of course find languages, such as Spanish, that follow the same SVO order as English:

Un perro mordió al cartero.   'a dog bit the postman'

But we can also find languages, such as Japanese, in which the normal arrangement is SOV:

inu-ga yūbinya-o kanda   'dog-(subj.) postman-(obj.) bit'

In translating the above we have made a point of glossing each element of the Japanese sentence. The portions in parentheses are grammatical markers that do not have a direct translation into English but that are nevertheless a conventional part of the Japanese message. A great variety of sentence structures can be identified by checking other languages to see how the same basic meaning would be encoded. In Bulgarian the order of elements is basically the same as in English and Spanish; but the definite article follows the noun instead of preceding it, and the counterpart of the indefinite article is the absence of any overt marker at all:

> kuče xapi poštadjiya-ta   'dog bit postman-the'

In Arabic the arrangement of sentence elements is VSO:

> add-a kalb murasil-al-bariid   'bit-he dog carrier-the-mail'

Speakers of English, Spanish, Japanese, Bulgarian, or Arabic witnessing the attack on the postman would be exposed to the same visual impressions, but the speakers would report the event according to the conventions of their own language. Of considerable importance among these conventions is the arrangement of the elements into an arbitrary linear order.

We are forced to conclude that the units of meaning within the meaning component in Figure 1–1 have no natural linear order. This must be supplied by an additional component, as shown in Figure 1–2.

FIGURE 1–2   An Elaborated Model of Language

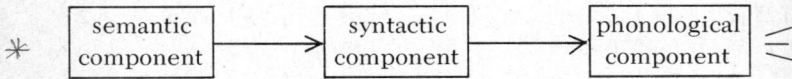

The technical term in common use for the arrangement of linguistic units in an arbitrary linear order is **syntax.** We can therefore think of language as containing a **syntactic component.** In Figure 1–2 we have substituted the technical terms **semantic component** for "meaning component" and **phonological component** for "sound component."

At this point the diagram may appear complete, but it is not. We have indicated by the three lines emanating from the phonological component that the output of this component is a part of the real world—that is, physical sounds. The semantic component also serves as a bridge to the real world—although in a slightly different way. We assume that the semantic component contains units of meaning somehow associated with objects and actions of the real world. To be more precise we should say that these units are associated with the world as perceived by the individual speaker. Whether or not the perceived world corresponds systematically to the real world is a philosophical question that we will not attempt to answer in these pages. Most speakers assume that their perceptions of the world have objective validity, and we will beg the question by making the same assumption.

If, as we assume, the semantic component contains units of meaning, it is important to make a distinction between these units of meaning on the one hand and words on the other. Meaning is essentially language-independent; words are always part of a specific language. In the English, Spanish, Japanese, Bulgarian, and Arabic sentences cited above, the meaning was the same throughout. Only the words (and their arrangement) were different. It seems reasonable to say that in all five sentences the semantic structure, which is based on an event in the real world, is essentially the same. Differences in the final output of the five languages can be attributed in part to different syntactic arrangements dictated by the conventions of each language. But by far the most conspicuous difference is found in the fact that each language uses a different set of words to convey the same meaning. It is therefore useful to think of each language as having a vocabulary list, or lexicon, containing words that can be matched with the meanings provided by the semantic component. Words are selected from the lexicon to express the intended meanings, and these words are inserted in positions provided by the syntactic component. We can therefore propose a final revision in the model considered thus far.

It is important to emphasize again the independence of meanings and words. Nearly everyone has had the experience of being ready to say something and having the right word on the "tip of the tongue" but being unable to remember the word at the crucial moment. Many persons who are bilingual know the names for objects in one language but are embarrassed to discover that they have never learned names for the same objects in the other language. Probably we all can think of familiar objects that we never have occasion to name. People are able to think about such objects without difficulty, but if forced to vocalize, they must often resort to terms like "thingamajig" or "whajamacallit."

If it is possible to conceive of meanings and words as separate entities, there may still be doubt as to whether words should be drawn from the lexicon before or after meaningful units are given a linear arrangement by the syntactic component. Words are so closely related to their meanings, it may seem, that they should be put in place as soon as the semantic structure itself is available. But Figure 1–3 is unequivocal in placing the reference to the lexicon after syntactic arrangement, and there is a good reason for this.

Given whatever semantic structure underlies A *dog bit the postman,* it is important to determine which noun is to precede the verb and which is to follow. This depends on a knowledge of which noun is agent and which is patient—information provided by the semantic component. This information must still be present at the time of linearization—and it would not be present if the word *dog* or *postman,* drawn from the lexicon, had already replaced the semantic complex 'dog as agent' or 'postman as patient.' (Notice that we are following a convention of citing linguistic forms in italic type and meanings in single quotation marks. This is a standard practice among linguists and will be followed throughout the book.) Once linearization has taken place, the part of the semantic structure relating to 'agent' and 'patient' is signaled by the syntactic arrangement. At this point the meanings 'dog' and 'postman' can be replaced by the words *dog* and *postman* without further complications. All that remains is for the phonological component to assign the actual pronunciation to the resulting sentence.

1.8   LANGUAGE AND A MACHINE MODEL OF LANGUAGE

Figure 1–3 shows the semantic component as a bridge to the real world. Semantic configurations, we have said, give rise to syntactic arrangements, each unit of which can be replaced by an item drawn from the lexicon. The string thus created is given a pronunciation by the phonological component. The physical sound waves that constitute the output are again part of the real world and therefore part of the perceptual world of other speakers. Since these sound waves are the end product of a symbolic system in which they represent other elements in the real world, listeners can allow the sound waves impinging on their ears to substitute for quite different portions of the real world. In effect language allows sound waves heard by one person to transmit the perceptions and conceptualizations of another person. Language thus greatly extends the perceptual world of the individual and, for all practical purposes, links the nervous system of one organism to that of another.

FIGURE 1–3   A Fully Developed Model of Language

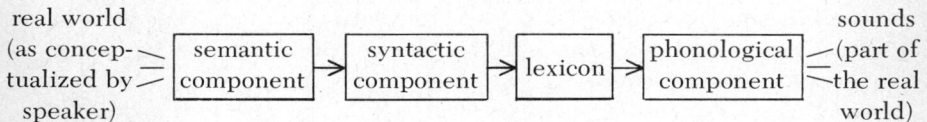

real world
(as concep-
tualized by
speaker)
→ | semantic component | → | syntactic component | → | lexicon | → | phonological component | → sounds
(part of
the real
world)

The diagram given in Figure 1–3 is both a model of language and a model of a language-using machine. If we wished to construct a robot capable of using language or to endow a computer with language-using ability, we would have to build into it at least the four components represented in the diagram. Actually much more would need to be included because we have said nothing about the way in which sensory perception—sight, hearing, and the like—leads to a conceptualization of the real world. For present purposes we are interested chiefly in the way that language mediates between this conceptualization and the sounds that symbolize it. In the chapters to come, we shall therefore need to investigate the workings of the four components posited as essential to language. And to do this we shall consider how concepts relating to the four components have taken shape as linguistics itself has developed as a science.

The four components of Figure 1–3 are related to separately describable parts of language. The four components take conceptualizations as their input and produce speech as their output. Each component, as just noted, represents a describable stage in the process of language use. The arrow connecting the semantic component with the syntactic component represents the conversion of meanings into linearized sequences of words (actually morphemes, but this is a technical term that will not be defined until Chapter 4). The arrow connecting the lexicon with the phonological component represents the various processes that lead to modified pronunciation of words under certain circumstances. The remaining arrow, which connects the syntactic component with the lexicon, represents the conversion of a sequence of meaningful units into a sequence of pronounceable units. For this reason we will speak of this arrow as the **symbolization arrow**—that is, the arrow that represents the symbolization of certain meanings by sounds conventionally associated with those meanings. The importance of language as a process of symbolization is something that will be emphasized repeatedly in later chapters.

The preceding discussion has been couched in machine terms not only because language can fruitfully be analyzed in a very mechanical way but also because thinking in mechanical terms is useful as a problem-solving device. In this case it has led us to an understanding of the organization of language and given us an idea of the capabilities that would have to be built into a hypothetical language-producing machine. It would be interesting to build such a machine, particularly if we could program it to translate from one language to another by taking the sounds of one language (or some written representation of them), analyzing these into their underlying semantic structure, and converting this structure into the sounds (or a written representation) of a second language.

But it is not really necessary to cast about in our imaginations to conjure up a language-using machine. Machines do not have to be made of metal, nor do they need to contain transistors or the like. Flesh-and-blood language-using machines exist all around us. The study of languages and the science of linguistics is, ultimately, the study of man.

summary

Language is a system of human communication based on speech sounds used as arbitrary symbols. Although other species have communication systems that sometimes employ vocal sounds, these sounds invariably occur in conjunction with body postures that carry an important part of the message. Only the vocalisms of human beings have been elaborated to the point that they constitute an independent communication system—one that can be analyzed in terms of its own structure, with or without reference to accompanying postures, situational settings, and the like. In recent years linguists have tended to view language as consisting of several subsystems: (1) the semantic component, which allows for the arrangement of units of meaning; (2) the syntactic component, which provides for the arrangement of words within a sentence and also the arrangement of formative units within individual words; (3) the lexicon, a list of vocabulary items available to express meanings symbolized in the language system; and (4) a phonological component, which modifies the pronunciation of words or word parts according to the context. This view of language as a device consisting of four components is useful because it reduces language to systems that can be analyzed in a rather mechanical way. It is also useful as a model because it duplicates the automatic use of language that is typical of ordinary speech acts, and the different subsystems seem to correspond to different kinds of data processing that are involved in the act of speaking.

② traditional grammar

2.1 HEBREW CURIOSITY ABOUT LANGUAGE

Human beings are curious about everything in their environment, and it seems likely that their curiosity about language goes back a long time before the formal study of language began in ancient Greece. The traditional Hebrew story of Adam and Eve relates the Creation and tells that God empowered humankind to select names for everything that had been created previously. Another ancient Hebrew story tells of efforts to build a tower that would reach the very heavens and God's punishment of this arrogance by creating a sudden diversity of languages among the laborers, thus thwarting their ability to work cooperatively. Both stories offer explanations of language. The former suggests how language came about in the first place, and the latter accounts for the differences among languages spoken by different communities—differences that the nomadic Hebrews must have noticed early in their history.

Both stories were committed to writing about 850 B.C., long after the Hebrews were well established in Judah, but it is certain that they represent a much older oral tradition. It is largely a matter of chance that the Hebrew stories have been preserved. There is no way of knowing how many comparable legends were repeated around Stone Age campfires through history without ever being recorded. The Hebrew tales were preserved with uncommon care because they were part of a cultural tradition valued for religious reasons. But Greek philosophers only a few centuries later became interested in language for broader philosophical and practical motives. The work of the Greeks marks the start of the Western grammatical tradition. Although scholars in India and China had begun independent investigations of language even before the Greeks, the Eastern tradition remained unknown in Europe until the nineteenth century.

2.2 GREEK AND ROMAN INTEREST IN LANGUAGE

The Greeks were quick to recognize that persons who spoke persuasively commanded authority and assumed positions of leadership. The earliest formal study of language—rhetoric—focused on the principles of effective language use in public speaking. The Sophists, who initiated the study of rhetoric, developed an elaborate terminology, much of which remains in use to the present day. They distinguished the various sentence types (statement, command, question, etc.) and noticed such properties of language as tense and gender. But their interest was chiefly practical. They analyzed the speeches of skilled orators and developed a terminology suitable for instructing their students in the art of persuasive speech. The foundation they laid for the formal study of grammar was largely a coincidental by-product.

Later Greek philosophers directed their attention to broader issues —the question of whether words have meaning because of their natural properties or simply because of arbitrary conventions. This controversy is the subject of Plato's dialog *Cratylus,* in which Cratylus argues for natural meaning and Hermogenes for conventional meaning. As might be expected, each is able to find persuasive evidence to support his own point of view. Socrates, as usual in the Platonic dialogs, clarifies the issues for both discussants and finally concludes that meaning in language is largely a matter of convention despite occasional instances of words that seemingly have some kind of "natural" relationship with their referents.

In his other dialogs Plato builds on the groundwork already laid by the earlier Sophists. In *Theatetus* Plato has Socrates define language in terms very much like the definition presented in Chapter 1. Socrates describes language as the expression of one's thoughts by means of words and phrases that reflect these ideas in the stream of air passing through the mouth.

Plato was also concerned with the way in which the meaning of words can be defined. The method he proposed—one still widely used by linguists, anthropologists, and lexicographers today—involves a hierarchical classification. The object to be defined is placed in the largest class of which it is a member, and this class is progressively subdivided into mutually exclusive subclasses having different attributes until the object can be placed uniquely in relationship to the larger class.

Of the later Greek philosophers, Aristotle was to remain the most influential through the Middle Ages and into the beginning of the modern period. But in fact the grammar developed by Aristotle and his predecessors was elaborated and modified in various ways by later Greek scholars and by the Roman grammarians, who adopted Greek rhetoric virtually intact.

The Stoic philosophers, for example, drew a distinction between meaning and form—the signified and the signifier—a distinction that has also figured prominently in the thinking of modern linguists. Roman scholars made few original contributions but wrote lengthy texts applying existing concepts to their own language in painstaking detail. Scholars in the Middle Ages continued the tradition inherited from Rome and added to it the notion of a universal grammar based on logic. This notion, cherished in traditional grammar, was rejected by modern structuralists but has since been revived by transformational grammar.

The fact that Greek and Latin are closely related in their overall structure made it fairly easy for the Romans to adopt Greek rhetorical scholarship so readily. Scholars in the Middle Ages continued to use Latin as an international language. When they attempted to apply the Greco-Latin model to their own languages, they generally encountered little difficulty because their languages were also related to Greek and Latin and exhibited much the same structure. The result is that the approach handed down to the present day under the banner of traditional grammar is a model developed originally for Greek, later adapted to Latin, and subsequently applied to other European languages that were quite similar in form to Latin.

We are indebted to traditional grammar for the modern notion of sentence; the parts of speech; and for numerous technical concepts, such as subject and predicate. Moreover, we are indebted to traditional grammar for certain basic procedures that are an inescapable part of any approach to language analysis. At the same time it is only fair to acknowledge that modern practitioners of traditional grammar have often gone about analyzing and describing languages in ways that have evoked criticism and led to the development of competing schools of grammar.

2.3   PARADIGM ANALYSIS: "SAME" OR "DIFFERENT"

It is common in learning a foreign language to study noun or verb paradigms of the language being learned. A paradigm is a set of linguistic elements in which one part remains constant while another part is different in each member of the set. The basic analytical procedure is to classify the elements in question as either "same" or "different." This simple procedure is an implicit part of traditional grammar and, as we shall see, lies at the very heart of any approach to linguistic analysis. Indeed, all of human experience seems to be classified in just this way. Every new experience is classified either as same or different with respect to previous experience.

Corpus 2–1 contains two examples of a Latin verb paradigm. Considering both as a single paradigm, it is possible to identify the component parts and to formulate a simple but complete statement of the rule (i.e., principle) for constructing the present tense forms of Latin verbs of this type.

Much of the presentation of linguistic concepts throughout this book will be based on data problems similar to Corpus 2–1. Analyzing such bodies of data (i.e., the corpus) and developing a statement that accounts for the data (i.e., a grammar) is exactly what linguistics is all about. Although a detailed discussion will accompany each corpus, serious students should try working out an acceptable solution on their own and then compare their solutions with the one offered in the text. Additional data problems are presented in the accompanying volume, *Workbook in Linguistic Concepts*, in which exercises of varying complexity are provided for each section of the present text.

Several words of caution should be offered before turning to Corpus 2–1. If you have studied Latin previously, be careful to avoid terminology that is not self-explanatory. Take care also to avoid making unwarranted assumptions about the data. Treat the data as though this is the only information available about Latin, and analyze it on that basis. Bear in mind that an analysis based on this limited data will not lead to a complete grammar of Latin and will, in fact, produce certain distortions because certain bits of relevant data are intentionally omitted from the corpus. The task at this point is simply to deal with the data at hand.

Finally, take nothing for granted. Make the statement explicit enough so that it could be correctly applied by a mindless robot (e.g., a computer) to produce the appropriate verb forms—the twelve given in the corpus and, with sufficient additional data, an indefinite number of Latin verb forms belonging to this paradigm.

CORPUS 2–1

amō	'I love'	laudō	'I praise'
amās	'you (sg.) love'	laudās	'you (sg.) praise'
amat	'he, she, it loves'	laudat	'he, she, it praises'
amāmus	'we love'	laudāmus	'we praise'
amātis	'you (pl.) love'	laudātis	'you (pl.) praise'
amant	'they love'	laudant	'they praise'

The bar over certain vowels, called a **macron,** denotes length. Vowels so marked occupy roughly twice the duration of vowels lacking a macron. The macron is therefore part of the spelling of these vowels. Other questions of the phonetic value of these letters will be taken up in Chapter 4. For the present we can conduct the analysis in terms of spelling even if we are uncertain of the pronunciation represented by the spelling.

There are at least two ways to describe the data of Corpus 2–1. One obvious approach is to offer no analysis at all but simply to say that each verb contains six forms, and each of the six forms must be learned separately. The implications of this approach are far from satisfactory, however. For each verb the learner of the language, whether an infant born into the language community or an outsider studying the language as an adult, would be expected to master six separate items. This makes twelve items to be learned for the two subparadigms, and the number of items to be mastered increases in multiples of six for each additional verb.

This solution also runs counter to an intuitive feeling that speakers of a language are able to make use of some general principle to construct forms they have not actually encountered personally. This is actually more than an intuitive feeling. It is something that can be verified empirically by observing small children, who make use of their limited control of language to construct linguistic forms that fit into a pattern they have come to expect even though they have had no opportunity to hear the particular form before. Sometimes children produce forms, such as *I goed,* that do not occur in their language at all. This is unmistakable evidence that they are applying a general rule to construct an expected form that, by chance, does not actually occur.

A better analysis of Corpus 2–1, one that is both comprehensive and brief, can be worked out by comparing the twelve forms to determine which parts are the same and which are different. In the first column we note that all six forms carry the meaning 'love.' All six forms also begin with the same letters *am-.*

(Notice that we continue the convention of citing meanings in single quotation marks and linguistic forms in italics. When a portion of a word is cited as a linguistic form, it is customary to precede or follow this with a hyphen denoting that the element is not a free form but a bound form—that is, it must occur with some other element to be an independent form. These conventions are widely used by linguists and should be fixed in mind at this point.)

In the second column the six forms sharing the meaning 'praise' have in common the letters *laud-.* By comparing the two columns, we find that the following elements can be classified as the same:

-ō	'I'	-āmus	'we'
-ās	'you (sg.)'	-ātis	'you (pl.)'
-at	'he, she, it'	-ant	'they'

This reduces the total inventory from twelve to eight. The corpus contains six person markers and two verb stems. Each verb **stem** symbolizes the meaning associated with the verb, while each person marker appears in the form of a **suffix** following the verb stem. This statement, in effect, constitutes a rule for the formation of the verb forms of Corpus 2–1.

The significant point about the approach adopted here is that we no longer need to think of storing twelve separate bits of information. We need to store only eight bits of information and one simple rule. If we wish to account for additional verbs of this type, the number of items to be memorized will not increase in multiples of six; it will simply require the addition of a single item—the verb stem—for each new verb. The suffixes and the rule for adding suffixes to the verb remain the same.

Students who are already familiar with Latin may be inclined to view the verb stems *am-* and *laud-* as derived from the infinitives *am-āre* 'to love' and *laud-āre* 'to praise,' which were deliberately omitted from Corpus 2–1. The forms are written here with a hyphen to emphasize that the infinitive actually contains two elements: the verb stem and an infinitive ending. The infinitive itself is thus seen as built on the verb stem in a manner exactly like the twelve forms in Corpus 2–1. Latin verb forms can be explained without reference to the infinitive, but the infinitive is customarily taken as the starting point in traditional presentations of Latin or other languages having a similar structure. The reason is that the infinitive is the only independent form that contains no reference to person or tense. It is the most neutral form and therefore has traditionally been used as the citation form; the verb stem is then treated as derived from the infinitive rather than the other way around.

The solution we have arrived at still has certain defects. But, as far as it goes, it is a solution within the spirit and framework of traditional grammar. That is, it embodies just those insights into language that were developed in Greece, transmitted to Rome, and subsequently incorporated into European culture. It would be possible to devise a similar analysis for Latin verbs whose infinitives take the form *-ēre*, *-ere*, or *-īre*, but these were intentionally excluded from Corpus 2–1. Their inclusion would complicate the analysis in some respects even though it would lead to simplification in others.

Let us now consider the data in Corpus 2–2 from the standpoint of restating the Latin stems and affixes. An ideal solution is virtually impossible, given the meager conceptual apparatus at our disposal thus far. But it will still be instructive to examine the data merely to clarify the issues.

CORPUS 2–2

monēre	'to advise'	regere	'to rule'	audīre	'to hear'
moneō		regō		audiō	
monēs		regis		audīs	
monet		regit		audit	
monēmus		regimus		audīmus	
monētis		regitis		audītis	
monent		regunt		audiunt	

The forms originally given in Corpus 2–1 belong to what is traditionally called the first conjugation. The forms given in Corpus 2–2 belong to the second, third, and fourth conjugations. Except for certain irregular verbs, these four conjugations cover all types found in Latin. Glosses are not given for individual forms because these can be inferred from what is already known from Corpus 2–1.

If we follow the approach adopted for describing Corpus 2–1, we would set up the following:

stem *mon-* 'advise' plus endings *-eō, -ēs, -et, -ēmus, -ētis, -ent*
stem *reg-* 'rule' plus endings *-ō, -is, -it, -imus, -itis, -unt*
stem *aud-* 'hear' plus endings *-iō, -īs, -it, -īmus, -ītis, -iunt*

The difficulty is that we are forced to posit four separate sets of endings even though the four sets are similar enough that they clearly represent a single set. We could therefore reexamine the solution to Corpus 2–1 and propose the following set of endings, which could apply to all four paradigms:

-ō 'I'   -mus 'we'
-s 'you (sg.)'   -tis 'you (pl.)'
-t 'he, she, it'   -nt 'they'

Such a solution would work nicely if we could reanalyze the verb stems to include the vowel that was previously assigned to the endings. The only problem is that sometimes the vowel in question is long and sometimes short, as in *amās* and *amat*. And sometimes the vowel is dropped altogether, as in the first person singular forms of the first and third conjugations.

We can now seen another reason that the infinitive was taken as the base form in traditional grammar. The infinitive ending contained the theme vowel that served to match each verb stem with the appropriate set of endings. It has always been obvious that the four conjugations somehow belong to a single overall pattern, although it is not clear how this pattern can best be described. Traditional grammarians adopted the practice of presenting a paradigm of a typical verb from each conjugation and letting it serve as a model for other verbs in the paradigm. Such an approach did not deny the similarity of the four patterns, and it neatly side-stepped the question of describing alternations of vowel length and the like. Techniques for describing such variations did not become part of the linguistic arsenal until the nineteenth century and have only recently come into widespread use.

Formal notions of set theory were not available to scholars before the present century either, but paradigm analysis involves the implicit use of sets. The stem meaning 'love' is represented by the set *am-/am-/am-/am-/am-/am-*, but we instinctively reduce this six-member set to the equivalent single-member set *am-*. Separate occurrences of the stem are not treated as something novel but as manifestations of a previously identified unit. This is a fairly obvious fact when the stem remains the same throughout the paradigm, but the analysis would still be valid if there were variations in the stem occurring in a regular pattern within the paradigm. Such stem variation in fact occurs in Spanish, a modern descendant of Latin, where we have *vengo* 'I come' and *viene* 'he comes.' In this case the stem is *v(i)en-*, with the parenthesized element occurring in predictable contexts. In like manner the first person suffixes in the four Latin paradigms clearly belong to a set characterized by *-ō* even though there are problems in analyzing the vowel that precedes the suffix.

The introduction of set theory at this point may seem gratuitous, but the concept of a set will become more and more important in subsequent chapters, where the identification of sets will depend on increasingly subtle factors.

2.4 IMPLICIT VERSUS EXPLICIT DESCRIPTION

The customary approach in traditional grammar, as we have just seen, was to present paradigms for each conjugation as separate patterns to be learned, with the learners left on their own to somehow deal with the underlying unity of the patterns. Just as traditional grammarians avoided citing such forms as the verb stem, which do not occur independently, they found it difficult to deal with individual sounds that varied in length or that were only sometimes present. In the first case it was easier to turn to the infinitive as the citation form, and in the second it seemed easiest to present an individual paradigm as a model of the grammatical pattern and in so doing let the paradigm exemplify the pattern. The description of the pattern is thus implicit rather than explicit.

This approach was required in part because certain linguistic concepts were not available to traditional grammar. There was no convenient way to cite units smaller than a word. And there was no standardized procedure for discussing the phonological modification of words. But the approach was also eminently suited to the purposes of the time. In the ancient world the study of grammar was related to effective public speaking. The need was for terminology that would provide labels for grammatical structures that students of public speaking needed in dealing with language on a conscious level. During the Middle Ages, when Latin served as the international language of the European scholarly community, the need was for a means of teaching Latin grammar to students whose native language was Italian, German, French, Spanish, English, or the like. The study of grammar was not an end in itself but rather a means to learning Latin.

All children, barring gross physiological or mental defects, manage to learn their native language rather quickly and with no formal instruction. They are exposed to the data in a random fashion, and from the raw data they abstract the principles for constructing grammatical sentences. The approach of traditional grammar, to a large extent, was to present the data of the language to be learned—Latin—and trust the pupils to master the data much as they had already mastered their native language. Rather than being random, however, the presentation was systematic, typically in the form of paradigms; and it was often accompanied by statements of grammatical rules in the learners' native language. Because the languages of Europe were related to Latin, and during the Middle Ages were quite similar to Latin in their overall structure, bright students would have no real difficulty finding structural parallels between Latin and their native languages and somehow mastering the details of Latin grammar that they were not taught explicitly. Naturally, individual students varied considerably in their ability to do this. The academic career of any who failed to catch on was doubtless brief, and the return to the stable or sty no doubt came as welcome relief from what must have seemed like a torture contrived by the devil himself.

2.5   INTEREST IN NATIONAL LANGUAGES

During the Middle Ages, and well into the modern period, Latin was highly regarded as a language of special excellence. It was widely believed that Latin was ideally suited to expressing logical, abstract thought. At the same time it was felt that the various national languages were not so well suited for such purposes. The national languages, like humankind itself, seemingly had fallen from a state of original grace and were somehow corrupt and degenerate versions of what they might have been. This attitude had much less to do with the intrinsic merits of individual languages than with the fact that Latin had always been used for scholarly purposes while the others had not.

But it was also true that Latin had a formal grammar, available in textbooks, while the national languages did not. It was commonly thought, because of this, that Latin was an "organized" language while other languages were not. The simple truth was that scholars had not troubled to compose grammars of languages other than Latin. Nor was there any need for such grammars in an age when anyone with anything serious to communicate would write it in Latin. The need, and the compelling interest, was the study of Latin grammar.

It was not until after Dante in Italy, Chaucer in England, and similar innovators in other countries began to produce literature in their national languages that scholars developed an interest in the grammar of these languages at all. Factors such as the development of printing and the rise of a literate middle class contributed to a growing interest in the national languages. As grammars of these languages were written, it was rather natural that they should be patterned after the grammars of Latin that were already available. To the extent that the languages of Europe resembled Latin, it was a simple matter to apply Latin terms and assign Latin categories to their counterparts in other languages. But by the end of the Middle Ages, all of the European languages were quite different from Latin in certain respects. Spanish and Italian verb paradigms remained similar to the Latin paradigms given in Corpus 2–1 and Corpus 2–2, but this was no longer true of English:

I love	we love
you love	you love

$$\left\{ \begin{array}{l} \text{he} \\ \text{she} \\ \text{it} \end{array} \right\} \text{loves} \qquad \text{they love}$$

Modern English, essentially the same as the English spoken at the end of the Middle Ages, would not be adequately described by a verb paradigm listing merely the verbs themselves. Only the third person singular forms retain a special suffix; all other forms are distinguished by the pronoun rather than by a distinctive verb ending. The distinctive ending in the third person forms, which occurs only in the present tense, is now largely redundant because the form is always accompanied by the pronoun as well. In fact the paradigm cited above is really a pronominal paradigm rather than a verbal paradigm. Despite this, there has been a continuing tendency in traditional grammar to follow Latin models even when they are no longer appropriate. The crucial point here is not the Latin model itself but the appropriateness of the Latin model.

2.6 PRESCRIPTIVISM

Traditional grammar had as its primary purpose the teaching of Latin to those unfamiliar with Latin. This of course involved teaching correct Latin—that is, teaching students to avoid constructions that would stand out as deviant. The teaching of grammar and the teaching of correctness became inseparable in the minds of many, and when the study of grammar was directed to English and other modern European languages, it was often undertaken from the standpoint of establishing rules for the "correct" use of the language. In other words the grammars were not intended simply to describe the language but were set up as normative and prescriptive. Because language, as noted in §1.1, is often a badge of one's social station, it is easy to understand why upwardly mobile people have always flocked to buy handbooks purporting to instruct them in the "correct" use of their language. But from the standpoint of scientific inquiry, it is difficult to justify the practice of passing judgment on competing linguistic forms instead of simply describing them and relating them to the circumstances in which each is used—an approach known today as sociolinguistics. Nonetheless, traditional grammar as practiced up to the present time has remained strongly prescriptive in its approach.

These implied criticisms of traditional grammar are aimed more at the way in which traditional grammar is practiced than at any real or imagined weaknesses inherent in traditional grammar itself. All modern approaches to grammar are heavily indebted to traditional grammar for basic terminology and methodology. There is really nothing about traditional grammar to prevent it from incorporating relevant insights into language that have come from more recent schools, and indeed many practitioners of traditional grammar have been influenced in varying degrees by recent grammatical studies.

2.7   PARSING

One method used in traditional grammar to describe sentence structure is **parsing.** Parsing involves classifying every word in the sentence so that its relation to the sentence as a whole and to every other word in the sentence is clear. Traditionally this has involved (1) identifying the structural components of the sentence; (2) stating the part of speech to which each word in the sentence belongs; (3) describing the inflectional form of all inflected words in the sentence; and (4) explaining the relationship of each word to other words or relevant sentence components. When a sentence has been parsed, the structure of the sentence is said to have been described. If the parsing is done exhaustively, there is presumably nothing more to be said about the sentence.

2.8   SENTENCE COMPONENTS

It is customary in traditional grammar to begin with notional definitions of the sentence and its components. A sentence is typically defined as an independent group of words expressing a complete thought, as for example, *The boy went to the store.* The phrase *to the store*—which could occur quite naturally in answer to the question *Where did he go?*—is not regarded as a sentence because it is not independent. That is, it cannot occur except as the answer to a question.

Another way of defining the sentence is to say that a sentence is a statement containing a **subject** and a **predicate.** A subject is the element about which a statement is made, and a predicate is the statement made about a subject. Thus *The boy* is a subject, and *went to the store* is a predicate. The structure *to the store* is not a sentence because it lacks a subject and predicate.

A sentence containing a single subject and predicate is said to consist of one clause. A clause is therefore the equivalent of a sentence, but a distinction between the two becomes useful when a sentence consists of two or more clauses joined together. It is then possible to use the term **sentence** for the larger unit and reserve **clause** for the sentencelike units that make up the larger structure. A sentence containing a single clause is a simple sentence. Other sentence types will be discussed in connection with conjunctions in §2.9.

Elements occurring within both the subject and predicate can also be further classified. Thus, *to the store* is a prepositional phrase, a structure consisting of a preposition followed by an object, which is always a noun or noun substitute. In this case the prepositional phrase is said to have an adverbial function because it is associated with the predicate. A prepositional phrase associated with a noun, as in *He read a book of poetry*, functions as an adjective.

An object may of course be associated with a verb instead of a preposition, as was the case with *the postman* in the earlier example *A dog bit the postman*. A verbal object, necessarily part of the predicate, is ordinarily subclassified either as a direct object or as an indirect object. In the sentence *The librarian gave Mary the book*, the direct object is *book* and the indirect object is *Mary*. The rationale for this distinction is that *book* actually undergoes the action while *Mary* benefits from the action indirectly. If the sentence is rephrased as *The librarian gave the book to Mary*, the structure *to Mary* is classified as a prepositional phrase rather than an indirect object.

Some verbs occurring with direct objects require the presence of an additional word that completes the action expressed by the verb and simultaneously refers to the direct object.

> The committee appointed Leonard chairman.
> The fraternity painted the town red.

In the above sentences *chairman* and *red* serve this function and are termed **objective complements** because they complete, or further specify, the role of the object within the predicate. Forms of the verb *be* also require complements.

> Leonard is the chairman.
> The paint is red.

These are termed **predicate nouns** or **predicate adjectives** for fairly obvious reasons. Each occurs within the predicate and refers back to the subject, either by naming it or describing it.

The terminology of traditional grammar provides a useful framework for describing the outward structure of sentences and continues to serve as the point of departure for all schools of grammatical analysis. It is important to emphasize that the terminology is directed to outward structure rather than semantic content. An indirect object and prepositional phrase frequently are alternative vehicles for carrying the same semantic information, as noted above. Traditional grammar, by focusing on outward structure, emphasizes the difference of these units rather than their similarity.

Finally it should be noted that the terms presented here are technical terms. That is, they are specially defined for purposes of technical use, and their meaning in technical discussions is not to be confused with their meaning in conventional circumstances. This is a point that has been needlessly obscured by the notional definitions traditionally used. To define a subject as the element about which a statement is made invites the literal minded to look for the subject anywhere in a sentence, for indeed a statement is made about both *postman* and *dog* in *A dog bit the postman*, although only *dog* is the grammatical subject. Later we will see how other schools of grammar have attempted to define such terms with greater precision.

2.9   PARTS OF SPEECH

Like the components of sentences, the parts of speech have customarily been given notional definitions. Thus a **noun** is defined as the name of a person, place, or thing. The definition is broad enough to include all nouns and possibly some words that are not nouns. Although *red,* for example, can be regarded as a "thing" in a sentence like *Red is the color of my true love's hair,* it is traditionally classed as an adjective.

Nouns can be subclassified in various ways—as common or proper, concrete or abstract, count or mass, and the like. Of these, only the last two are likely to be unfamiliar. A count noun is one that can be counted and therefore has a plural form. Mass nouns are those lacking plurals—for example, *rice, wheat, flour, iron, water, milk.*

Because Latin nouns were inflected to show their grammatical function, it has often been the practice in traditional grammar to speak of the cases of nouns—even though most of these cases are no longer marked inflectionally in Modern English. Nominative case is the form used as the subject of sentences. Genitive, or possessive, case is the form showing possession. Dative is the form showing the indirect object, and accusative is the form denoting the direct object. Because these last two are not formally distinguished in English, they are often classed together as the objective case.

A **pronoun** is a word that substitutes for a noun, and pronouns can be classified in basically the same ways as the nouns they replace. Overt case distinctions show a greater number of contrasts in the pronouns of Modern English than in the nouns, as seen in the following paradigm of third person forms. Note that English has no formal distinction between dative and accusative. The two are frequently treated as a single category: objective. But the distinction is sometimes maintained, partly on grounds that the two are functionally distinct, although formally identical, and partly (one suspects primarily) because the two were distinct in Latin.

	Noun		*Pronoun*	
	singular	*plural*	*singular*	*plural*
nominative	man	men	he	they
genitive	man's	men's	his	their
dative	man	men	him	them
accusative	man	men	him	them

An **adjective** is a word used to modify a noun. Adjective subclasses include descriptive adjectives (*popular song, new dress*), quantificational adjectives (*some people, any money, three suitcases*), and demonstratives (*this movie, that house*). Pronominal adjectives (*my car, his pencil*) are sometimes treated as a separate class, sometimes as a class of demonstratives. The definite article *the* is a kind of demonstrative, and the indefinite article *a/an* is basically a quantifier; but the definite and indefinite articles together are often treated as a special subclass of adjectives.

Verbs are words that express an action or state of being. Finite forms of the verb are characteristically inflected for tense. Other verbal categories include mood, aspect, and voice. Mood (or mode) in English is indicated by the various modal auxiliaries *may, might, can, could, would, should, must,* and *ought*. Textbooks usually distinguish among indicative, imperative, and subjunctive modes, although these are no longer inflectionally distinct in Modern English. (**Indicative** refers to factual statements, **imperative** to commands, and **subjunctive** to hypothetical statements.) Aspect has to do with the status of the verbal action. In English the **perfective** (*Beverly has sung*) and the **progressive** (*Beverly is singing*) aspects are sometimes termed compound tenses. A verb whose subject performs an action (*Pablo painted the picture*) is said to be in the **active voice,** while a verb whose subject undergoes an action (*The picture was painted by Pablo*) is in the **passive voice.** If the subject of a verb performs an action which is carried over to a direct object, the verb is said to be **transitive,** a category which is further classified as active or passive, as just noted. The verb remains passive even if explicit reference to the agent of the action is omitted (*The dancer was acclaimed*). Verbs having no direct object are said to be **intransitive** (*The dancer is graceful; The audience cheered*).

As already suggested a verb may be classified as either the main verb or an auxiliary verb in any given sentence. Verbs such as *be* may be used either way (*He is tall. He is running*). The nonfinite forms of the verb, those that do not show true tense, include the **infinitive** (*He likes to write*), the **present participle** (*a writing instrument*), the **past participle** (*a written message*), and the **gerund** (*an instrument for writing*). The present participle and gerund are alike in form but different in function. The former serves as an adjective and the latter as a noun. The infinitive may function as either a noun (***To write** is difficult*), an adjective (*a letter **to write***), or an adverb (*The food is ready **to eat***).

Adverbs, like adjectives, are modifying words. Adverbs modify verbs, adjectives, or other adverbs (*He ran **quickly**. He was **unusually** tall. She sang **quite** softly*). Adverbs can be classified as relating to time, place, direction, manner, validity, and degree. In addition, negatives such as *not* and interrogatives such as *why, when, where, how* are classed as adverbs.

Prepositions are function words, sometimes called particles, that link a noun or pronoun (the object of the preposition) to some other part of the sentence. As noted in §2.8 the resulting prepositional phrase functions as either an adjective or adverb, depending on whether the phrase as a whole modifies a noun or either a verb, adjective, or adverb. Prepositions are sometimes compound (*He jumped **out of** the boat*); but compound prepositions should not be confused with a simple preposition that happens to follow an adverb (*She came up **on** the bus*), which in turn is distinct from a simple preposition formed from the same elements (*She came **upon** it unexpectedly*). Nor should a preposition be confused with an ordinary adverb, even if the same word is sometimes used as a preposition (*He ran **down** the hall. He sat **down***). A special problem involves "prepositions" that come at the end of a sentence (*It was a good house to live **in***). Unless the word can clearly be classed as an adverbial particle, the usual practice is to analyze the sentence as representing an underlying structure in which the preposition has some kind of object (*It was a good house **in which** to live*).

Conjunctions are particles that join words, phrases, or clauses. Coordinating conjunctions, such as *and, but, or,* can join clauses to form compound sentences. Subordinating conjunctions, such as *if, when, since, because, although,* join two clauses to form a complex sentence. In a complex sentence the clause containing the conjunction is subordinate to the main clause—that is, structurally dependent on it. Thus it is common to speak of dependent and independent clauses in these sentences. The clauses of a compound sentence are structurally autonomous.

The coordinating conjunctions *and* and *or* also join words and phrases within clauses. A clause attached to no other clause remains a simple sentence even though it may contain a compound subject or predicate.

Relative pronouns have the attributes both of conjunctions and pronouns. These particles take the place of a noun in the clause they introduce, and at the same time they serve to relate the clause to the rest of the sentence (*He is the man who came to dinner*).

Interjections, emotive words ranging from *well* and *oh* to *damn* and other more emphatic expressions, are generally regarded as a separate category unrelated to other parts of the sentence in which they occur.

The foregoing discussion, by no means exhaustive, is intended chiefly as a review of basic terminology. By and large these are the terms that remain in use in all schools of language study.

2.10 ROOTS, STEMS, AFFIXES, AND DERIVATION

In any language it is sometimes necessary to use a verbal form of a word that is basically nominal or adjectival. Traditional grammarians were aware of this, and it was customary to speak of the Latin verb *albēre* 'to be white' as derived from the adjective *albus* 'white.' The two forms have in common a **root** *alb-* 'white' and are differentiated by the verbal affix *-ēre* and the adjectival affix *-us*. Both **affixes** in this case can be classified as suffixes because they follow the root. In the case of *ad-mon-ēre* 'to remind,' it is possible to speak of the prefix *ad-* 'at' being added to the root *mon-* 'advise' to create a new **stem** that is then subject to the usual verbal inflections. Such an analysis has always been implicit in traditional grammar, although, as noted previously, it was often considered awkward to cite forms that were not independent words.

The process of derivation can also allow verbs to be converted into nouns—as in the case of gerunds, which were recognized as a special class of verbs in §2.9. Inflectional endings are quite systematic in most languages, but derivational processes often involve considerable idiosyncratic variation. As a case in point, consider the regular plural or past tense formations in English compared with the various ways of deriving verbs. These include, among others, the addition of *-ate* (*activate*) or the addition of *-ize* (*legalize*); change in pronunciation from *s* to *z* (*to house* from *house*); or no change at all—sometimes called zero derivation—(*to plow* from *plow*). As a result the analysis of derivational processes has often been neglected even though its importance has been widely recognized.

2.11 PARSING REVISITED

Given the Latin sentence *Flaccus et Pomptīnus meritō laudantur* 'Flaccus and Pomptinus are deservedly praised,' we can parse it by observing that *Flaccus et Pomptīnus* is the subject. The structure consists of the two nouns *Flaccus* and *Pomptīnus* joined by the conjunction *et*. Both nouns are in the nominative case. The predicate *meritō laudantur* consists of the verb *laudantur* formed from the stem *laud-* (which is also a root), with a suffix marking the third person plural indicative mode of the passive voice. The verb is modified by the adverb *meritō*.

For the English sentence A *dog bit the postman,* a similar treatment is possible. We can observe that *a dog* is the subject and *bit the postman* the predicate. Within the predicate, *the postman* is the direct object. The subject noun *dog* is modified by the indefinite article *a,* while the object noun *postman* is modified by the definite article *the.* The verb *bit* is the past tense of *bite,* formed irregularly by vowel change.

It is sometimes noted that *dog* is nominative and *postman* accusative (or objective), but this observation is superfluous because the case relationships are marked by the syntactic arrangement rather than by an inflectional affix. Note that in Latin the presence of inflectional markers allows for considerable freedom in syntactic arrangements. A typical Latin SOV sentence, such as *pater puerum amat* '(the) father loves (the) boy' could in principle be rephrased with the words in any order because subject and object are identified by inflectional endings, and the verb is marked as agreeing with its subject. Varied syntactic arrangements would have the effect of focusing attention on whatever element might be placed first for purposes of contrast or emphasis.

2.12 DIAGRAMING

A latter-day approach to parsing has involved diagraming. In this procedure the structural relationship of sentence components is represented graphically. Diagraming can best be explained by letting the following diagram types illustrate the basic format.

As we see in diagram 1, subject and predicate, the basic constituents, appear on a horizontal base line bisected by a vertical line. A predicate noun or predicate adjective (mutually exclusive possibilities) follows the verb, separated from it by a line slanting back toward the subject. Diagram 2 shows that a direct object follows the verb, separated from it by a vertical line extending above the base line. An indirect object, if present, appears under the verb. If a direct object is accompanied by a predicate complement rather than an indirect object, as in diagram 3, the complement follows immediately after the verb, separated from it by a line slanting toward the complement.

Modifiers of various kinds are represented by a slant line placed under the component being modified. Adjectives, adverbs, and prepositions appear on the slant line; nouns appear on a horizontal line extending from this line. An adverb modifying an adjective is placed under the adjective's slant line on a parallel line, and the two are connected by a horizontal line. Conjoined elements, of which only one possibility is illustrated here, require a bifurcation of the base line. The conjoined elements are connected by a broken line, and the conjunction is placed on this line.

The sentences diagramed below as 1a through 3a are representative of the foregoing sentence types.

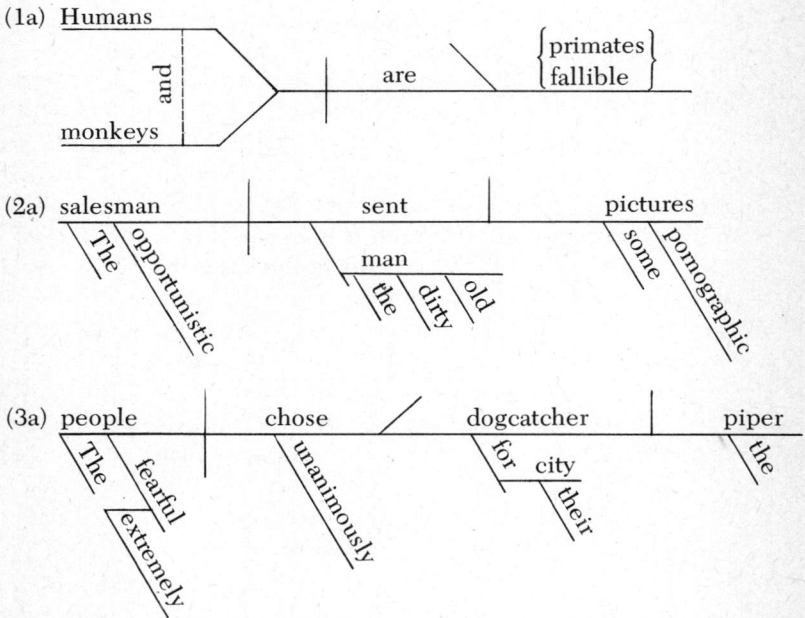

(1a) Humans / and / monkeys — are — primates / fallible

(2a) The opportunistic salesman sent the dirty old man some pornographic pictures

(3a) The extremely fearful people unanimously chose dogcatcher for their city the piper

A diagram unfailingly shows the structure of the entire sentence, provided of course that the conventions for constructing the diagram are understood and applied correctly. Ability to construct a diagram naturally depends, first of all, on understanding the structure of the sentence being analyzed. Diagraming itself is no substitute for grammatical insight that is otherwise lacking. But diagraming is useful for two reasons: (1) a diagram is a convenient way of displaying the structure of a sentence once the structure has been ascertained and (2) construction of a diagram requires that each word in the sentence be accounted for. And because the format of the diagram is **isomorphic** (i.e., has a point-by-point correspondence) with the structural categories of traditional grammar, a diagram can provide a framework for testing and eventually arriving at a suitable analysis.

The principles involved in diagraming are fairly simple. Positions on or attached to the base line count as slots for various sentence components, or constituents. These slots are filled by specified parts of speech. The subject is filled by a noun (or noun equivalent), the predicate by a verb, and so forth. Nouns and verbs may be modified in various ways and may take various kinds of complements. Adjectives serve to modify nouns, while adverbs modify verbs, adjectives, and other adverbs. Complements are typically the nouns that function as direct objects, indirect objects, objective complements, or the like. The substitution of a noun equivalent for a noun opens various possibilities for structural elaboration. A noun slot may be filled by a gerund or infinitive, which may itself have one or more complements; or a noun slot may be filled by a whole clause. In addition, each constituent of the sentence may be compounded. That is, a noun slot or verb slot may be filled by a pair (or series) of nouns or verbs, each of which can be modified and elaborated in numerous ways. Because of the varied combinations of sentence constituents that are possible, and the fact that there is no upper limit on the length of grammatical sentences, the actual number of sentences in English (or any other language) is unlimited. This fact has seldom been emphasized in traditional grammar, although it is implicit in an analytical procedure such as diagraming, which is designed specifically as a device for displaying the structure of numberless sentences of indefinite complexity.

As one might expect, the diagrams used in traditional grammar analyze no units smaller than whole words. Traditional diagraming thus avoids having to deal with abstract units, such as roots and affixes, that never occur as independent words. In other areas, however, traditional diagraming has shown a surprising willingness to use abstract forms. This can be illustrated by considering declarative and interrogative forms of a single sentence:

Noel did read the book.
Did Noel read the book?

Both sentences are represented by the same diagram because the auxiliary-verb unit *did read,* even though discontinuous in the interrogative sentence, counts as a single unit in both sentences. The declarative sentence, in effect, is taken as the form underlying both sentences, and the question is seen as a transformed variant derived from it.

We have made no effort here to present in exhaustive detail the conventions for diagraming sentences in traditional grammar. The conventions, although still taught in many textbooks and available in standard reference works, are less important than the concepts on which they are based. It is these underlying principles that are important. The fundamental principle is that all sentences, no matter how complex, are composed of structures that can be identified and assigned a place in the overall structure of the sentence. The ability of the analytical method to account exhaustively for every element within a sentence—and the structural property of sentences that makes this possible—is taken as a fundamental attribute of language and of the grammatical system for describing language. The kind of diagrams that modern linguists use are different in appearance and sometimes purport to describe structural units that are different from those of traditional grammar, but the goal of providing an exhaustive analysis of a potentially infinite corpus remains unchanged.

summary

The traditional approach to language study that developed in Europe continues to exercise a powerful influence over the teaching of language skills in public schools. This approach can be traced back to the work of Greek and Roman scholars. The basic technique—which continues to be used in all modern approaches to linguistics—is paradigm analysis, a technique that involves the examination of related forms and the analysis of these forms into elements that are "same" and "different." Thus, the paradigm *walk, walked, walking* can be analyzed as consisting of a constant *walk*, to which may be added variables, the suffixes *-ed* and *-ing*. Concepts such as the parts of speech, subject, predicate, and the like are all the heritage of traditional grammar.

In principle traditional grammar is an analytical and descriptive science, but in practice it has often been associated with pedagogical approaches that stress the supposed correctness of certain constructions and incorrectness of others, often on the basis of Latin models. Many modern linguists have therefore criticized traditional grammarians for adopting a prescriptive rather than descriptive approach to language study. It would be a mistake, however, to downplay the importance of traditional grammar simply because it has sometimes been put to use in ways that are open to question. It is important to distinguish between the methodology and a resulting body of knowledge on the one hand and a totally extraneous attitude about "correctness" on the other. The fact is that traditional grammar had much the same goals that are now proclaimed by modern linguists. For example, traditional grammarians sought through parsing to develop a framework that would make possible the exhaustive description of every possible sentence, a goal that has sometimes been implemented through schemes for the diagrammatic representation of sentence structures. Modern linguists continue to set for themselves the task of accounting exhaustively for the structure of all possible sentences. They differ with traditionalists primarily in the kind of diagrams they use in working toward this goal and in the claims they make about what the diagrams represent.

further reading

Books and articles suggested for further reading at the end of this and subsequent chapters are listed by the author's last name and the year of publication. Complete information is given in the bibliography, together with a brief annotation indicating the technical level of each selection. If more than one work is given, the selections are listed in the order that students are advised to read them. This is sometimes a chronological order but is often influenced by the importance of a work or the relative difficulty of selections.

References appearing in the text will be presented in the same format. If a page number is included, this will follow the year of publication and will be separated from it by a colon. Thus Teeter 1971:213 means page 213 of Teeter's publication dated 1971.

General: Dineen 1967, Robins 1967, Waterman 1963, House and Harmon 1950, Willis 1972, Laird and Gorrell 1971, Hungerford, Robinson, and Sledd 1970. **2.1** Jespersen 1922 (§11.2). **2.2** Dineen 1967 (Chap. 4), Robins 1951. **2.5** Dineen 1967 (Chap. 5). **2.7** Lees 1960a. **2.12** House and Harmon 1950.

3 historical grammar

3.1 THE NINETEENTH CENTURY

The traditional view expressed in the Hebrew Scriptures, that language was a divine gift, was not seriously questioned in the West until the nineteenth century. The intellectual atmosphere that had developed at the beginning of this century made a reeaxmination of language almost inevitable.

By the beginning of the nineteenth century, scholars had come to realize that the manuscripts produced during the Middle Ages were not equally reliable. Before the development of printing, all manuscripts had been hand copied from originals or from other copies. With the advent of printing, it became possible to publish definitive editions of the classics. But to do this scholars had to resolve discrepancies among the existing manuscripts and establish a reliable text. Scholars soon realized that discrepancies among manuscripts resulted from scribal errors in the process of copying. If the same error was found in several manuscripts, it was simpler to explain these errors by assuming a single error—that is, an innovation—that was faithfully recopied, rather than assuming independent commissions of the same error. By a careful comparison of manuscripts, it was possible to establish a probable line of transmission. What appears at first to be a welter of differences among manuscripts that are otherwise the same is seen, on close examination, to represent a sequence of historical events. The comparative method as applied to the study of manuscript tradition provided a model that was soon to prove useful in the comparative study of language.

With the renewal of interest in classical literature following the Renaissance, scholars increasingly turned their attention to reconstructing the life of classical times from clues found in the language and literature of the people. This study, called philology, also uses information about the life of the period, gained from archeology or history, as an aid in interpreting texts. Close examination of the texts of the Homeric poems led to the startling conclusion that different portions of the *Iliad* and the *Odyssey* were written in different literary styles. By the end of the eighteenth century, scholars recognized that the poems were not the work of a single author, as traditionally supposed. Instead, they were a compilation of tales composed at different times and places. The author was not one person but a number of unknown poets whose individual identities were overshadowed by their work.

Having made this discovery about Homer, scholars applied the method to the Bible, with similar results. The first five books of the Old Testament, traditionally attributed to Moses, were seen as a compilation of five principal sources—which did not, however, correspond to the five books of the modern Bible. During the first half of the nineteenth century, the method was applied to the New Testament as well. The first three gospels, for example, were seen as compilations based on common source material, while the fourth gospel was viewed as representing a somewhat divergent tradition.

Meanwhile, the Romantic movement in literature had directed attention to the commonplace elements of life. Urbanization and the beginnings of industrialism had already created a yearning for the simple life of the countryside. City people began to view rural life, traditions, and speech as something having intrinsic value rather than something to be looked down on. Folk tales preserved in oral tradition were seen as possessing literary merit on a par with printed literature. Scholars like the Grimm brothers set about collecting the oral literature of their countries while they could, mindful that changing life styles threatened its continuance. In the process they became increasingly aware of regional speech differences.

During the Middle Ages scholars in Europe had contact with relatively few non-European languages. Churchmen were of course familiar with Hebrew, and scholars knew of Arabic through the work of Muslim scientists and mathematicians. But this did nothing to disturb prevailing notions about language. As long as there was no reason to doubt the historical accuracy of Genesis, it could be assumed that the human species was a recent creation, that Hebrew was the original language, and that other languages dated from the Tower of Babel.

But with the Bible already subject to critical reexamination, it became possible to question old and cherished notions in all areas of life. Archeologists and geologists were undertaking studies that would push the human horizon much farther back in time than the 6,000 years assumed on the basis of the Biblical record. The intellectual climate in which these studies took place impelled scholars to take a new look at language. By the time Darwin published his *Origin of Species* in 1859, he was able to refer to studies on the evolution of language and cite the concept of genetic relationships among languages as a model for his own work.

Beginning in the sixteenth century, explorers and colonists had come in contact with an increasing number of diverse languages. By the nineteenth century descriptions of varying quality were available for Chinese as well as several languages of the New World. It was now clear that the number and variety of languages in the world was much greater than once supposed. At the same time it was known that certain languages bore a more-than-chance resemblance to one another. This is true, for example, of Hebrew and Arabic, of Spanish and Portuguese, of Dutch and German—although each pair seems quite different from the other pairs. The observable facts were not satisfactorily accounted for by the traditional Biblical account.

3.2 THE DISCOVERY OF SANSKRIT

The real breakthrough came with the European discovery of Sanskrit, an ancient language of India. Sir William Jones, a jurist in the British colonial administration in India, studied Sanskrit manuscripts and published a paper in 1786 noting that the language "bears a stronger affinity to Latin and Greek both in the roots of verbs and in the forms of grammar, than could possibly have been produced by accident; so strong, indeed, that no philologer could examine them all three without believing them to have sprung from some common source, which, perhaps, no longer exists."

Jones, who died at the age of 48, was never able to follow up his remarkable discovery. It is clear from his remarks, however, that he was working within the framework of traditional grammar. In fact it is fair to say that the earliest advances in historical grammar would not have been possible without a thorough grounding in traditional grammar. Although Jones himself did not undertake a systematic study of the precise relationships among Latin, Greek, and Sanskrit, he did notice similarities that served as the point of departure for those who followed.

The kind of similarities first noticed by Jones and other early scholars can be exemplified by the following set, in which German and English have been added to Latin, Greek, and Sanskrit. Even a cursory inspection is enough to reveal similarities too far-reaching to be attributed to chance. As long as only Latin and Greek were known to Europeans, their similarity could be attributed to the fact that they represented some kind of linguistic Golden Age—that is, they were true to what languages should be, while English and German represented a latter-day stage of degeneracy. But as soon as Sanskrit was placed beside Latin and Greek, it became clear that a more sophisticated explanation was required. The observable facts called for a dynamic explanation, and scholars of the time sought this in the dynamics of history.

The verb illustrated in Figure 3–1 is *be,* a common verb that might be expected in almost any language. The fact that we find a verb with this meaning in the five languages shown here is not surprising in itself. But it happens that this is an irregular verb in Latin and Greek, and the surprising thing is that it is irregular in Sanskrit as well. Even more striking is the fact that the irregularities are essentially the same in all three languages. The consonants are virtually identical, with only a loss here and there. There is also extensive similarity between vowels. Greek and Latin *e* is regularly matched by *a* in Sanskrit. Where we find a *u* in Latin, we find a zero (i.e., no vowel at all) in Greek and Sanskrit.

FIGURE 3–1   **Present Tense Forms of 'Be'**

Latin	Greek	Sanskrit	German	English
sum	emmí	ásmi	bin	am
es	essi	ási	bist	are
est	estí	ásti	ist	is
sumus	esmén	smás	sind	are
estis	esté	sthá	seid	are
sunt	entí	sánti	sind	are

We could assume that one of these languages is the "original" and that the other two developed from it somehow. Or we could assume, with Jones, that all three developed from a common source. It is the latter assumption that was eventually accepted by linguists.

If we include German and English in the comparison, we see that they share some of the irregularities found in the three classical languages. Certainly English *am* agrees well with the others, as does German *bist* and the third person singular forms in both languages. But we notice that the modern languages are much more regular than the classical languages. The initial *b* in two of the German forms looks like a recent innovation, as does the use of *sind* at two places in the plural set. English has gone even farther because *are* is used for all the plural forms and for the second person singular as well. This is what modern linguists have come to call **analogical leveling:** the original differences are leveled out by the analogical substitution of a form occurring elsewhere in the paradigm.

Notice that these conclusions are supported by a knowledge of history. We know that the classical languages were spoken over 2,000 years ago, and we can assume that they represent a still earlier stage with some degree of faithfulness. The divergencies found in the modern languages must therefore be relatively recent innovations.

The innovations, we notice, are in the direction of simplicity and regularity. They reduce the amount of complexity rather than introduce new complexities. This is generally the tendency in language change, although, as we shall see, new irregularities are sometimes introduced as a by-product of other changes.

3.3   THE COMPARATIVE METHOD

The foundation was now laid for an approach to language study so different from what had preceded it that the nineteenth century is still widely regarded as ushering in the modern period of scientific linguistics. This is not to suggest that whimsy was forever banished. Indeed, it reigned supreme in many of the schemes proposed during the century for classifying languages. Moreover, the novelty of Sanskrit led scholars to suppose for many years that it was much closer to the original language than either Latin or Greek. Scholars eventually recognized that the classical languages were equally distant from the common source—by this time called Proto-Indo-European—and sensed that it would be fruitless to look for this language spoken in unchanged form in some remote part of the world. The protolanguage was not preserved anywhere without change; rather, it was preserved with regular modifications in each of the languages that had developed from it.

By 1818 the Danish scholar Rasmus Rask had published a description of the regular "letter" (i.e., sound) correspondences in the various Indo-European languages. However, it was the description of these correspondences in 1822 by the German scholar Jakob Grimm that received wider circulation and led many to speak of the sound changes involved as Grimm's law.

Grimm, caught up in the Romantic movement at the beginning of the nineteenth century, spent a number of years with the help of his brother, Wilhelm, collecting folk tales from different parts of Germany—a project for which the brothers are still best known to the general public. But the exposure to various German dialects was important for another reason. Grimm rejected the notion that rural dialects were somehow defective versions of the prestige dialect spoken in urban areas. He approached each dialect as equally worthy of study. It was hard not to notice the systematic similarities and differences among the different dialects, and for the first time it became possible to think of all German dialects as deriving from a common source. This was not the insight, however, that was to make Grimm famous. Even more intriguing to him was the possibility that Sanskrit, Greek, Latin, and German had their beginnings as dialects of a single language. The different Indo-European languages were simply dialects made grossly dissimilar through the passage of time. The

·kinds of differences found among languages and dialects are the same. Only the time depth is different.

In Figure 3–2 data from four Indo-European languages is presented to call attention to the systematic relationship noted by Rask, Grimm, and others in the early nineteenth century. Words from the languages are arranged so that corresponding consonants are aligned vertically. The languages in descending order are Sanskrit, Greek, Latin, and English—the last of these serving to represent the Germanic branch of the Indo-European family. Each set of words represents the meaning indicated by the English word—or a closely related meaning. Modern English is used in all but three cases where the modern word has undergone further development that would obscure the pattern; in these cases a form from Old English is substituted, and the modern form is given in parentheses.

Even casual inspection of the data is enough to reveal systematic regularities. In 1 the initial consonants match in a pattern *p/p/p/f*. This **matching** is not merely a coincidence because in 2 we find the same pattern repeated. Repeated matchings of this kind are **correspondences**—that is, recurring instances of the same matching letters (i.e., sounds) in analogous positions in words of the same or similar meaning. Such word sets are called **cognates**.

For the set *p/p/p/f* we assume development from a protoform **p*, which is marked here and in Figure 3–2 by an asterisk to show that it is a reconstructed form, one posited by inference based on the comparative method and not a form attested by documentary records. To say that the protoform **p* develops into the set *p/p/p/f* is to say that the Germanic family, as exemplified by English, represents an innovation. By abstracting the patterns from the data, we can say that the following correspondences are found in the four languages:

*p	p/p/p/f	(exemplified in 1, 2)
*t	t/t/t/th	(exemplified in 1, 8)
*k	k/k/k/h	(exemplified in 3, 4)
*b	b/b/b/p	(exemplified in 4)
*d	d/d/d/t	(exemplified in 2, 5)
*g	g/g/g/k	(exemplified in 6, 7)
*bh	bh/ph/f/b	(exemplified in 5, 8)
*dh	dh/th/d/d	(exemplified in 9, 10)
*gh	h/kh/h/g	(exemplified in 11, 12)

With one exception, all of the above occur more than once and therefore count as true correspondences. Additional data would show that the same correspondences occur in numerous other word sets as well. The correspondence posited here on the basis of a single occurrence presents a special problem because we have no cognate set from

FIGURE 3–2   Word Sets from Sanskrit, Greek, Latin, and English

1	2	3	4
p i t á r	p a d	k r a v í h-	– ‖ –
p a t ế r	p ó d a	k r é a s	k á nn a b i s
p a t e r	p e d e m	c r u o r	c a nn a b i s
f a th e r	f oo t	h r ē a w (raw)	h æ n e p (hemp)
*p *t	*p *d	*k	*k *b

5	6	7	8
bh i n á d	y u g á -	g é r a n o s	bh r ā́ t a r
ph e í d	z u g ó n	g r ū s	ph r ā́ t ē r
f i n d ō	i u g u m	c r a n e	f r ā́ t e r
b i t e	y o k e		b r o th e r
*bh *d	*g	*g	*bh *t

9	10	11	12
v i dh á v ā	d á dh ā t i	h á r i	v á h a t i
ēí th e o s	t í th ē m i	kh ó l o s	ó kh o s
dī- v i d ō	ab - d e r e	h e l vus	v e h ō
w i d o w	d o	g o l d	w e g (way)
*dh	*dh	*gh	*gh

all four languages. This can be termed a **discontinuous correspondence.** To make a discontinuous correspondence usable, we must find enough of the pattern attested in available data to infer the overall pattern and thus eliminate the property of discontinuity. In this case there are two additional cognate sets that prove helpful. Set 13, which has no English representative, means 'strong,' although the prefixed Latin form has the meaning 'without strength.' Set 14, found only in Latin and English, refers to a dwelling place. The Latin form means 'beam' or 'timber.' The English form, meaning 'village,' occurs in the modern language only in place names.

13	14
b á l a m	–
b e l tíōn	–
de- b i l is	t r a b ē s
–	th o r p
*b	*b

By considering sets 4, 13, and 14 together, we can see that each constitutes a discontinuous part of an overall pattern *b*/*b*/*b*/*p*, for which we posit the protoform *b*. It happens that these three cognate sets are the only evidence to support this particular correspondence. But the correspondence receives additional support from the fact that the overall pattern of relationships seems to require just such a correspondence to fill what would otherwise be a gap in the pattern.

3.4   RECONSTRUCTION

We have already seen that a correspondence reflects the continuation of an element from the original speech community. Early scholars spoke in terms of letter correspondences, although it is now customary to speak of sound correspondences, recognizing that letters merely represent sounds. It happens that the letters used in Figure 3–2 to represent sounds are used with enough consistency that it has been necessary to make only one substitution in presenting the table of correspondences. This is the letter *k*, which replaces the *c* used in Latin and English spelling.

When we say that the correspondence *p*/*p*/*p*/*f* reflects proto *p*, or is a **reflex** of *p*, we are making an inference about the protolanguage and at the same time offering an explanation for the attested correspondence. All things being equal, the sound that is reflected most frequently in the attested correspondence is the most probable protoform. We say this assuming that language systems tend to be conservative and change slowly. If one language diverges from several others, it is more reasonable to assume that the one language has undergone innovation than to suppose several languages have independently made the same innovation while only one preserved the original form. But considerations of overall patterning often require the linguist to posit a form attested only sparsely or not at all. Thus *gh* fits best into the overall pattern and provides the best basis for explaining the attested correspondence *h*/*kh*/*h*/*g* even though it is not preserved intact in any of the languages under study.

We have noted the importance of similarity in both form and meaning in establishing a cognate set. In most cases the forms given in Figure 3–2 agree in meaning with the English word. If the meaning is not identical, it must be closely enough related to be at least plausible. Thus the English word in set 11 means 'gold,' while the Sanskrit meaning is 'yellow,' the Greek meaning is 'bile,' and the Latin meaning is 'honey-yellow.' All of these have in common a reference to yellowishness and could presumably derive from the same source.

Associating a correspondence with a proto-sound constitutes a claim about the historical development of the sound involved. This can be illustrated diagrammatically:

```
        *p              *b              *bh
      /|\ \           /|\ \           /| \
     p p p f         b b b p         bh ph f b
```

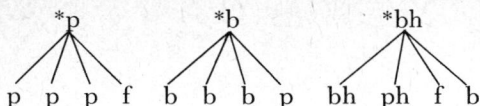

Only three of the Proto-Indo-European sounds are illustrated here, but this is enough to reveal the pattern of development. Moreover, the three diagrams together suggest that the Germanic innovation was not a series of isolated changes but was something that involved the entire system. As *bh* became *b* it did not fall together with *b*, because this sound was already in the process of changing to *p*. The same can be said of *b* > *p* (the symbol > is used to denote a change through time) because, while this change was taking place, original *p* was leaving a position vacant by shifting to *f*. The result is that English preserves the original system, but each token within the system is now different.

It should be clear by now that the process of sound change is regular. When it occurs, it occurs in all words containing the affected sound or sounds. The comparative method is wholly dependent on this principle.

The Indo-European correspondences that have been cited are actually much more complicated than the material presented here would indicate. Because of the great time depth involved, there have been numerous secondary developments to obscure the basic relationships expressed in these correspondences. The full complexity of the relationships was not understood at the very outset. Indeed, linguists spent the greater part of the nineteenth century working out the major problems, and work on details is still continuing. We can anticipate the findings by noting that the principal members of the Indo-European family of languages are represented in Figure 3–3 (p. 44).

3.5 APPLICATION OF THE COMPARATIVE METHOD

It is fairly obvious even to the untrained observer that the languages spoken today in the United States and Great Britain must once have been part of a single language community. We know this to be the case from independent historical evidence anyway. But if for some reason historical documentation were lacking, the common origin of American English and British English could be inferred from the linguistic evidence alone. The common origin of two speech communities, in turn, implies a common origin for the two people themselves.

The similarities between English and German are not so conspicuous, but the common origin of the two languages could still be inferred by trained specialists. In this case, also, documentary evidence of a migration from Germany to England is available. But the

FIGURE 3–3   Major Branches of the Indo-European Language Family

Approximate years before present

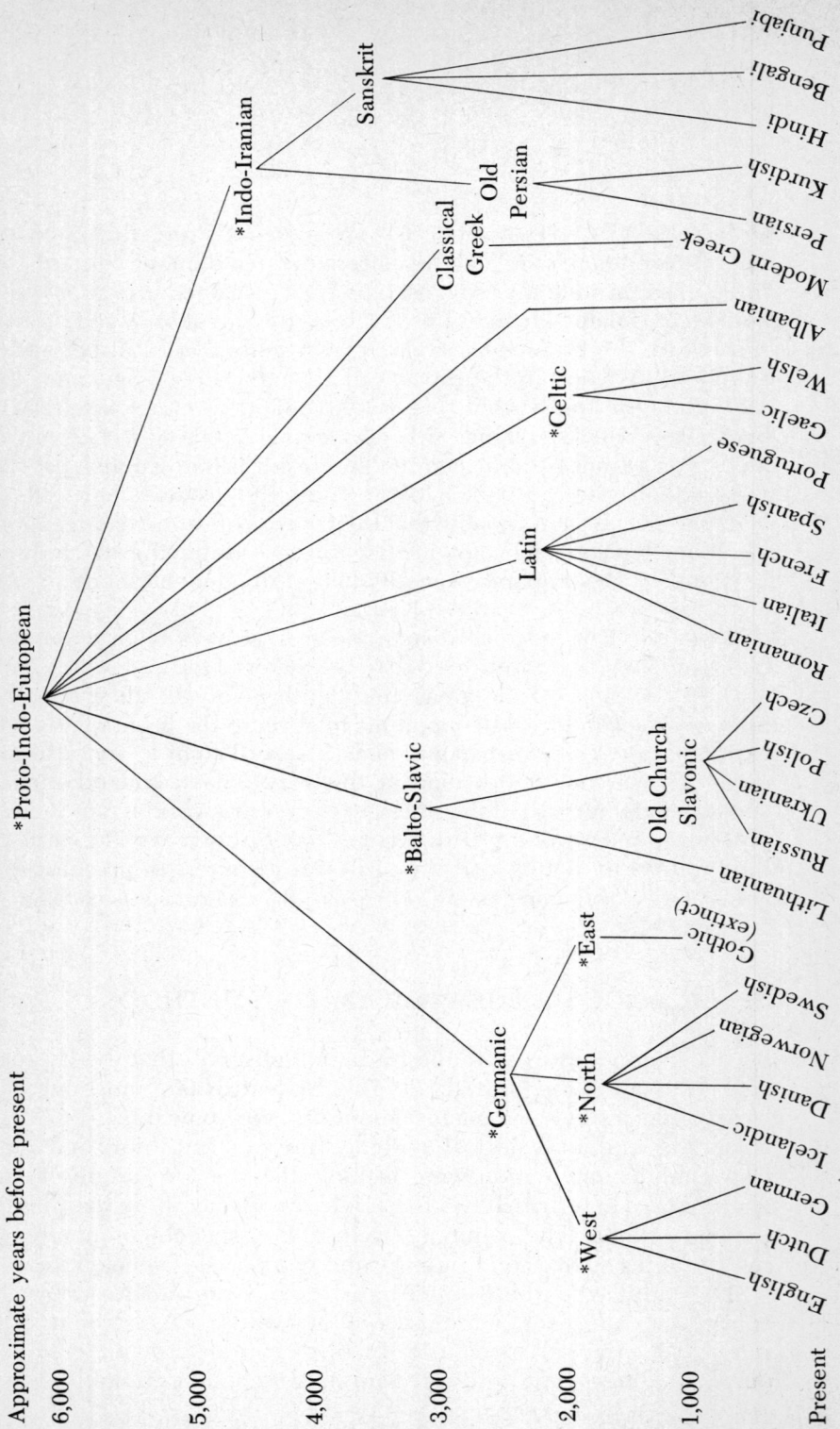

6,000   *Proto-Indo-European

5,000

4,000

3,000

2,000

1,000

Present

migration could be inferred from the linguistic evidence alone. As far as the linguist is concerned, the documentary evidence simply confirms the reliability of the linguistic evidence.

In the case of English and Sanskrit, the similarities are so tenuous that considerable skill is required to recognize the languages as related. But as we have seen from Figure 3–2, it is possible to detect a web of systematic resemblances that can be explained only as a shared heritage from a common source. Because this evidence is of exactly the same type that is supported by historical records for more recent migrations, we have no doubt of the reliability of the linguistic evidence applied by itself to a period for which there are no written records. The inescapable conclusion is that the modern Indo-European languages are descended from a protolanguage spoken by a single tribe that expanded into the area now reaching from India to northern Europe.

For many years linguists believed that the comparative method would work only for European languages, where we had access to documentary records for the earlier stages of certain languages. Thus it is possible to trace the development of the modern Romance languages century by century from the time of Latin. And the existence of Latin manuscripts serves to confirm the results of the comparative method as applied to the Romance languages. It was thought that the comparative method would not yield equally reliable results when applied to unwritten languages. One would be forced to conclude by implication that sound change is regular only in written languages, not in languages lacking a writing system.

But in 1925 the American linguist Leonard Bloomfield published a paper in which he reconstructed Proto-Algonkian using data he had collected from four North American Indian languages. In a famous footnote he proclaimed that the principle of regular sound change "is either a universal trait of human speech or nothing at all. . . ." Linguists have since then applied the method to numerous languages in all parts of the world with justifiable confidence in the results.

Not only does the comparative method cast light on linguistic forms spoken in the past, but a reconstructed vocabulary provides information about the culture of an earlier period. And by verifying genetic relationships among languages, the method contributes to an understanding of prehistoric population movements.

Because material drawn from real languages tends to be fairly complex, we can best illustrate the comparative method by using hypothetical data. The material presented in Corpus 3–1 resembles actual language data in every respect except that it is simplified for the benefit of the beginner.

The data consists of ten cognate sets that have been numbered for convenience. The correspondences to be abstracted from the data could be presented in any order, but it is usually best to begin with those that present the fewest difficulties. Members of each corre-

CORPUS 3–1

	Language A	Language B	Language C	Language D	
(Cog–1)	piga	biga	pik	piha	'bowl'
(Cog–2)	tumi	dumi	tum	tumi	'water'
(Cog–3)	kanu	ganu	kan	hanu	'fire'
(Cog–4)	wira	wila	wir	wira	'man'
(Cog–5)	tubi	dubi	tup	tupi	'leaf'
(Cog–6)	mawu	mawu	maw	mawu	'woman'
(Cog–7)	kida	gida	kit	hita	'tree'
(Cog–8)	nubi	nubi	nup	nupi	'child'
(Cog–9)	ragu	lagu	rak	rahu	'smoke'
(Cog–10)	pira	bila	pir	pira	'fishnet'

spondence set are listed in the order A/B/C/D, and each set is numbered for reference.

(Cor–1)	m/m/m/m	(attested in cognate sets 2, 6)
(Cor–2)	n/n/n/n	(attested in 3, 8)
(Cor–3)	w/w/w/w	(attested in 4, 6)

These three correspondences are the simplest because they are not only completely regular but the four members of each set are identical. Such sets can be called **identity correspondences**. Another correspondence, equally regular, is more complicated only in the sense that one member of the set differs from the other members.

(Cor–4)	r/l/r/r	(attested in 4, 9, 10)

The remaining correspondences present a special complication, and a fairly sophisticated technique is required to determine which correspondence sets are to be classified as same and different. We call these **overlapping correspondences** because the various sets share certain members.

(Cor–5a)	p/b/p/p	/	word initial	(attested in 1, 10)
(Cor–5b)	b/b/p/p	/	elsewhere	(attested in 5, 8)

To determine if the sets are the same or different, we must analyze their **distribution**—that is, the environment where each occurs. This information is noted following the slash after each correspondence. Cor–5a occurs in word-initial position. Cor–5b is found elsewhere—that is, in noninitial position. The term "elsewhere" covers all possible environments not previously mentioned. In this case there is only one other possibility (for consonants), but "elsewhere" is still the most convenient way to describe it. We could say "non-word-initial position," but this is awkward. We might say "between vowels," but such a description would not apply to Language C. "Elsewhere" is therefore an extremely useful term, but its utility depends on careful use because the term acquires meaning only with reference to what has been mentioned previously.

Since sets 5a and 5b have members in common and occur in mutually exclusive environments, we say that they are in **complementary distribution** and treat them as environmentally conditioned subsets of a single set, which we can call Cor–5. This was anticipated by assigning them numbers 5a and 5b—numbers that cannot actually be assigned until the distribution of the sets is determined.

Note that the slash in the above presentation is used in two different ways. In one instance it separates members of the correspondence set; in the other instance it separates the correspondence set from its environment. The two functions are themselves an example of complementarity.

Another notable example of complementary distribution is the use of capital letters and small letters in writing. Capitals occur at the beginning of sentences and proper names; small letters occur elsewhere. Elements in complementary distribution are not likely to be confused with one another even though they may be similar in appearance. If the environment is purely functional (e.g., word position, a preceding or following sound, etc.), the elements are normally classed as "same." If the environment is meaningful (as in the case with the two uses of the slash mentioned above), the elements are normally classed as "different."

Notice that there is no way of knowing in advance what the relevant environment is likely to be in any given case—or even whether overlapping sets can be associated with mutually exclusive environments at all. The linguist must be alert to the various possibilities and test alternate hypotheses until the overall picture emerges.

If we wished to be extremely methodical, we could apply a distributional analysis to Cor–1, identifying subsets Cor–1a *m/m/m/m* in word initial position and Cor–1b *m/m/m/m* elsewhere. But in this case the procedure is unnecessary because both sets are identical—not merely overlapping—and there is no real restriction on the distribution at all.

The other consonant sets with overlapping members can be stated as follows:

(Cor–6a)	t/d/t/t	/	word initial	(attested in 2, 5)
(Cor–6b)	d/d/t/t	/	elsewhere	(attested in 7)
(Cor–7a)	k/g/k/h	/	word initial	(attested in 3, 7)
(Cor–7b)	g/g/k/h	/	elsewhere	(attested in 1, 9)

As before, the two sets in each pair can be classified as conditioned variants of a single set. The same approach can be applied to the vowels.

(Cor–8a)	i/i/Ø/i	/	word final	(attested in 2, 5, 8)
(Cor–8b)	i/i/i/i	/	elsewhere	(attested in 1, 4, 7, 10)
(Cor–9a)	a/a/Ø/a	/	word final	(attested in 1, 4, 7, 10)
(Cor–9b)	a/a/a/a	/	elsewhere	(attested in 3, 6, 9)
(Cor–10a)	u/u/Ø/u	/	word final	(attested in 3, 6, 9)
(Cor–10b)	u/u/u/u	/	elsewhere	(attested in 2, 5, 8)

The treatment here is the same as before, and the pattern is just as clear. All languages have *i, a,* and *u* except that the vowel is absent in final position in Language C. This absence is represented in the correspondences by Ø, a symbol called canceled zero, or simply zero. The diagonal through the zero is useful to distinguish it from the capital letter *O*.

Notice that in each statement the most general environment—that is, the one having the fewest restrictions or no restrictions at all—is always given last. Those having the most restrictions are given first; and if more than two sets are involved, the sets can be arranged in the order of increasing generality. This may seem like a trivial point, but it is an important principle of linguistic analysis and will figure repeatedly in the remaining examples to be presented in this chapter and in subsequent chapters.

It is clear from the distribution of the seven consonant sets that we are dealing with a seven-way contrast. That is, all seven sets occur in the same environments and therefore are in **contrastive distribution.** Simply stated, the sets contrast. Each is different. The same observation may be made of the three vowel sets. The vowels and consonants themselves are in complementary distribution, but they are units of such different types that they are conventionally regarded as distinct by definition. (Note that the vowel sets and consonant sets never have overlapping membership. This is one indication of their distinctness. Moreover, their distribution is such that *all* consonants are complementary to *all* vowels; no *individual* consonant set is uniquely complementary to any *individual* vowel set.)

3.6   RECONSTRUCTION OF PROTOFORMS

Once the correspondences are identified and grouped into contrasting sets, it is possible to infer the likely shape of the protoforms—the forms that existed before the division of the protolanguage into separate language communities. Because the four "daughter" languages have exactly the same material in Cor–1 through Cor–3, we can assume that the daughter languages have preserved the form of the protolanguage without change in each case. Accordingly we can say that Cor–1 represents, or continues, the sound *m of the protolanguage. Notice that even though this seems to be an open-and-shut case it remains customary to place the asterisk before a form that is not directly attested. Similarly we can say that Cor–2 continues *n and Cor–3 continues *w.

In the case of Cor–4, there is disagreement among the daughter languages. In these circumstances we must posit the protoform that offers the simplest explanation for the forms found in the daughter languages. Following the reasoning of §3.4, we can posit *r. This implies that Languages A, C, and D preserved the original form while Language B made the change *r > l.

Following the same line of reasoning, we can posit *p as the form underlying Cor–5, containing the subsets 5a and 5b. This hypothesis implies that Language B made the change *p > b, and Language A made the change *p > b / V __ V. The change in Language B took place in all environments; it was not conditioned by word position or by adjacent sounds. The change in Language A, however, took place only between vowels. The shorthand notation used here is the same as that used in the statement of correspondences themselves. The change indicated took place in the environment shown to the right of the slash, that is, between vowels. The symbol V stands for any vowel (just as C can be used to stand for any consonant), and the blank shows the locus of the change in question.

The same reasoning leads us to posit *t as the protoform for Cor–6 with its two subsets. Notice that the sound change assumed here parallels that assumed in the previous case. Anticipating the phonetic terminology to be introduced in Chapter 4, we can say that both the change *p > b and the change *t > d involve changing a voiceless stop to one that is voiced without changing the pronunciation in any other way. (A stop is a sound that involves complete stoppage of the air flow through the oral tract; a voiced sound is one accompanied by vibration of the vocal folds, popularly called "vocal cords." A diagram of the vocal tract is given in Figure 4–1.)

Cor–7 shows still greater variety. Considering both subsets of Cor–7 together, we have three candidates for the protoform instead of two. But we should expect this change to parallel those we have seen previously, and this leads us to posit *k. Language B voices this to g in all cases, and Language A voices it between vowels—exactly the changes we would expect on the basis of Cor–5 and Cor–6. The only new element is the change in Language D *k > h, a change that occurs in all environments.

The three vowel sets, each containing two subsets, can be considered together. We can reconstruct Cor–8 as *i, Cor–9 as *a, and Cor–10 as *u. The only change to be explained is in Language C, where *V > ∅ / __#. That is, any vowel becomes zero in word final

position. The symbol # represents word boundary, and the blank preceding it denotes the position immediately before this boundary,
hence word final position.

3.7 FURTHER DATA

As a further test of the method, it will be useful to consider additional
data from the same four languages. This material, presented in Corpus
3–2, contains much that is already familiar—for example, the set t/d/t/t
found in Cog–11. In addition to the familiar material, a number of new
sets will be encountered; but these can now be considered in the light
of what is already known about the four languages. The corpus also
contains a strange symbol ɣ, which is not part of the English—or
Latin—alphabet. The symbol seems to pattern with both h and x, and
that is all we need to know at present. It is important to realize that
the comparative method can be applied to symbols in a mechanical
way even if we are not sure of the phonetic content involved. Dealing
with an unfamiliar symbol at this point will set the stage for additional
symbols to be introduced in the next chapter. It will also serve as a
reminder that we are still in the position of linguists in the early nineteenth century who dealt clumsily with "letter" correspondences.
Like them, we sense that letters represent phonetic content and we
are handicapped by a lack of knowledge about phonetics, but the
handicap need not interfere with application of the method.

CORPUS 3–2

	Language A	Language B	Language C	Language D	
(Cog–11)	tiba	deba	tip	tepa	'dwelling'
(Cog–12)	nami	name	nam	name	'lightning'
(Cog–13)	kuɣi	goɣi	kuh	hohi	'magic'
(Cog–14)	huru	ɣulo	hur	huro	'earring'
(Cog–15)	waga	waga	wak	waha	'body'
(Cog–16)	piɣa	biɣa	pih	piha	'fish'
(Cog–17)	hiri	ɣeli	hir	heri	'necklace'
(Cog–18)	ɣanu	ɣano	xan	ɣano	'face'
(Cog–19)	puɣi	boɣe	pux	poɣe	'mouth'
(Cog–20)	dego	dego	tik	dewih	'spirit'

Before proceeding, it may be helpful to review the premise on
which the comparative method is based. The hypothesis is that the
languages being compared were once spoken by a single community
that, for some reason, divided into separate communities. At the time
of division, each community continued to speak the language of the

original community, but with the passage of time, each language developed independent of the others. Eventually the languages became quite different from one another (and from the original language), although they continue to show systematic traces of their common heritage.

Establishing proof of a genetic relationship among languages depends on recognizing a web of systematic resemblances, and this in turn depends on the recognition of cognates—those words in the daughter languages having similarities in form and meaning by reason of common descent. The selection of cognates is thus a screening process that involves at the very outset a commitment to a hypothesis about the historical development of the languages. The identification of true cognates requires both positive identification and the elimination of what are sometimes called **false cognates.** This boils down to a matter of classifying elements as either the same or different.

Sets of words exhibiting similarities in both form and meaning may be presumed to be cognates, given that the languages involved are assumed to be related. This of course is quite circular. We need a list of cognates to show that languages are related, but we first need to know that the languages are related before we may safely look for cognates. In actual practice, therefore, the hypothesis builds slowly, and there may be a number of false starts along the way. But gradually certain correspondence patterns begin to emerge. These patterns point to unsuspected cognates that reveal additional correspondences until eventually a tightly woven web of interlocking evidence is developed.

False starts occur primarily because words originally thought to be cognates turn out on investigation not to be true cognates. To eliminate false cognates it is often necessary to compare words within a single language (rather than between languages) to identify those words that deviate from the normal patterns of that language. Thus in Corpus 3–2 it is apparent that *dewih* 'spirit' in Language D is "different" with respect to the other words of that language. The word exhibits a CVCVC pattern while all other words in the list are patterned CVCV. Moreover, it contains a sound represented by the letter *d* that is not found elsewhere in the langauge. Most important, the word simply does not exhibit an arrangement of letters that enters into a correspondence pattern with the word of the same meaning in the other three languages. The word cannot be regarded as a cognate.

A more subtle—and therefore more insidious—deviation from the expected pattern is found within Language A, again with the word meaning 'spirit.' In this case the word exhibits the expected CVCV form; but it has initial *d*, which is not found elsewhere in this language, and it has the vowels *e* and *o*, which do not belong. The sounds of this word can be matched with sounds found in the word for 'spirit' in Languages B and C, but the matching will not be a correspondence. It will be a unique pattern; a correspondence must be a recurrent pattern. The word does not fit into the expected pattern for Language A, although it fits perfectly into the pattern expected for Language B.

These two discrepancies can be explained as **borrowings.** The inherited word for 'spirit' has been replaced in Language A by a word borrowed from Language B. In Language D it has been replaced by a word borrowed from some unrelated language. Such borrowing is a common occurrence in language history. Perhaps the speakers of A were impressed by the ceremonies of their neighbors, the speakers of B. They may have copied some of these ceremonies, including a term that eventually displaced their own word. The same must have happened with the speakers of D, the only difference being that the source language in this case was different enough to make the borrowed word more conspicuous. The words for 'spirit' in both A and D must be eliminated from the comparison. We can use only the words from B and C. This will yield discontinuous correspondences that we must key to recognized correspondences, using the procedure outlined in §3.3.

We find that much of the new data simply confirms correspondences that have already been identified from Corpus 3–1. New correspondences can be stated as shown below. Note that reference to Cog–20 is valid only for Languages B and C because members of this set in Languages A and D have been eliminated as noncognate.

(Cor–11)	ɣ/ɣ/x/ɣ			(attested in 18, 19)
(Cor–12a)	h/ɣ/h/h	/	word initial	(attested in 14, 17)
(Cor–12b)	ɣ/ɣ/h/h	/	elsewhere	(attested in 13, 16)
(Cor–13a)	i/e/Ø/e	/	word final	(attested in 12, 19)
(Cor–13b)	i/e/i/e	/	elsewhere	(attested in 11, 17, 20)
(Cor–14a)	u/o/Ø/o	/	word final	(attested in 14, 18, 20)
(Cor–14b)	u/o/u/o	/	elsewhere	(attested in 13, 19)

Cor–11 occurs in all environments and therefore contrasts with all of the previously identified consonant sets. Sets 12a and 12b overlap and are in complementary distribution. Note that both subsets of 12, as well as the union of the sets, overlap with Cor–11; the final classification depends on the distribution of the sets, following the procedure shown in Figure 3–4. The procedure for distributional analysis has already been described in detail but is here reduced to a mechanical procedure. The mechanics of this procedure are important because it remains the basis for distributional analysis in structural grammar (Chapter 4) and continues to influence transformational grammar and semantic analysis as well.

The four vowel sets consist of two overlapping pairs. Sets 13a and 13b are complementary, as are sets 14a and 14b. Each pair constitutes a larger set, with Cor–13 and Cor–14 contrasting. These sets also contrast with the previously identified vowel sets.

FIGURE 3–4   **Procedure for Classifying Correspondence Sets**

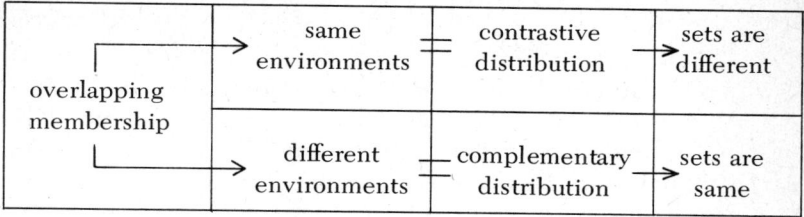

overlapping membership	→ same environments	⊣ contrastive distribution	→ sets are different
	→ different environments	⊢ complementary distribution	→ sets are same

The new correspondences reflect four additional sounds in the protolanguage. Cor–11 in all likelihood continues *ɣ. Cor–12 is almost equally divided between occurrences of ɣ and *h;* but with *ɣ pre-empted by Cor–11, we must posit *h for Cor–12. This is probable for another reason, because *h* is voiceless while ɣ is voiced. The implied change *h > ɣ in A and B parallels other sound changes already identified. Since the vowel sets contrast with the previously identified vowel sets, Cor–13 cannot be a continuation of *i, nor can Cor–14 reflect *u. We therefore posit *e for Cor–13 and *o for Cor–14. Languages A and C have undergone changes *e > i and *o > u, leading to **merger** with original *i and *u respectively. This can best be shown by a diagram in which the top line represents the situation in the protolanguage (PL) and the bottom line represents the situation in the modern languages.

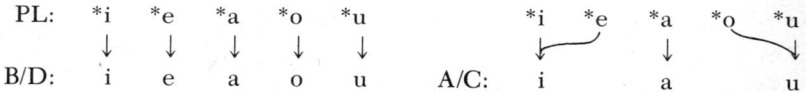

```
PL:   *i   *e   *a   *o   *u          *i   *e   *a   *o   *u
       ↓    ↓    ↓    ↓    ↓            ↘        ↓      ↘
B/D:   i    e    a    o    u    A/C:    i         a        u
```

The protolanguage had five vowels, and the situation is continued unchanged in B and D. But in A and C *e merges with *i, and *o merges with *u. The result is that the original five-vowel system is replaced by a three-vowel system.

The protolanguage had nine consonants. Language A has expanded this inventory to ten; B has reduced it to eight; C retains a nine-place system, although one token in the system is now different; and D has developed an eight-place system, although not the same system as B. The protosystem and that of the daughter languages can be compared as follows:

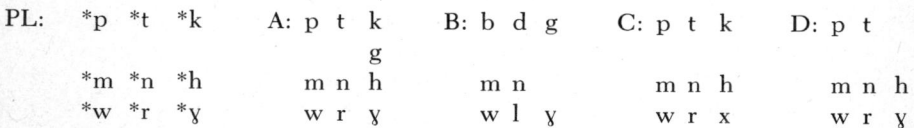

```
PL:   *p *t *k      A: p t k      B: b d g      C: p t k      D: p t
                          g
      *m *n *h         m n h         m n           m n h         m n h
      *w *r *ɣ         w r ɣ         w l ɣ         w r x         w r ɣ
```

The changes can be explained as mergers in some cases and as **splits** in others, as diagramed below.

PL: *k   *h   *ɣ   *k   *h   *ɣ   *k   *h   *ɣ   *k   *h   *ɣ

A: k g h   ɣ   B: g   ɣ   C: k   h   x   D: h   ɣ

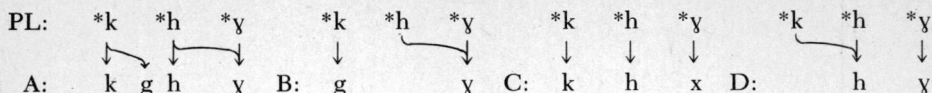

The simplest picture is presented by Language C, where all three sounds of the protolanguage are continued as independent units. The only difference is that *ɣ now appears as x. In both B and D, the original three units are now reduced to two. In B the change *h > ɣ results in a merger; the reflexes of *h become ɣ and are indistinguishable from ɣ resulting from *ɣ. In D the change *k > h leads to a merger with h. The most complex situation is presented by Language A. Original *k has split into two units k and g. Original *h has also split, with one variant remaining h and the other merging with ɣ.

The complete history of the languages can be summed up in the following table, which shows each unit of the protolanguage and the correspondences that have developed from it.

(Cor–1)	*m	m/m/m/m	
(Cor–2)	*n	n/n/n/n	
(Cor–3)	*w	w/w/w/w	
(Cor–4)	*r	r/l/r/r	
(Cor–5a)	*p	p/b/p/p /	word initial
(Cor–5b)		b/b/p/p /	elsewhere
(Cor–6a)	*t	t/d/t/t /	word initial
(Cor–6b)		d/d/t/t /	elsewhere
(Cor–7a)	*k	k/g/k/h /	word initial
(Cor–7b)		g/g/k/h /	elsewhere
(Cor–8a)	*i	i/i/Ø/i /	word final
(Cor–8b)		i/i/i/i /	elsewhere
(Cor–9a)	*a	a/a/Ø/a /	word final
(Cor–9b)		a/a/a/a /	elsewhere
(Cor–10a)	*u	u/u/Ø/u /	word final
(Cor–10b)		u/u/u/u /	elsewhere
(Cor–11)	*ɣ	ɣ/ɣ/x/ɣ	
(Cor–12a)	*h	h/ɣ/h/h /	word initial
(Cor–12b)		ɣ/ɣ/h/h /	elsewhere
(Cor–13a)	*e	i/e/Ø/e /	word final
(Cor–13b)		i/e/i/e /	elsewhere
(Cor–14a)	*o	u/o/Ø/o /	word final
(Cor–14b)		u/o/u/o /	elsewhere

3.8 RECONSTRUCTION OF WORDS AND MEANINGS

Reconstruction of whole words is a fairly mechanical procedure once the individual correspondences have been determined and identified with protoforms. Starting with the first word in Corpus 3–1 (p. 46), we notice that the correspondences involved are 5a, 8b, 7b, and 9a—in that order. Arrangement of the appropriate protoforms in the same sequence yields *pika, the presumed form of this word in the proto-language. A complete list of reconstructed proto-words follows:

(1)	*pika	'bowl'	(11)	*tepa	'dwelling'
(2)	*tumi	'water'	(12)	*name	'lightning'
(3)	*kanu	'fire'	(13)	*kohi	'magic'
(4)	*wira	'man'	(14)	*huro	'earring'
(5)	*tupi	'leaf'	(15)	*waka	'body'
(6)	*mawu	'woman'	(16)	*piha	'fish'
(7)	*kita	'tree'	(17)	*heri	'necklace'
(8)	*nupi	'child'	(18)	*ɣano	'face'
(9)	*raku	'smoke'	(19)	*poɣe	'mouth'
(10)	*pira	'fishnet'	(20)	*teko	'spirit'

The process of sound change, which differentiates the daughter languages from their common starting point, is completely regular and takes place without regard to the meaning of words. One consequence of this can be seen in Language D, where the words for 'bowl' and 'fish,' through the process of regular sound change, fall together as *piha*. The two words were of course distinct in the protolanguage. It is exactly such processes of merger that give rise to homonyms in languages.

We have no difficulty in reconstructing the meaning of these words because all four languages are in agreement. This probably means that each language preserved the original meaning, but we cannot always be sure. If archeological evidence suggests that clay bowls have replaced wooden bowls in all four communities, we might assume that *pika referred to a wooden bowl rather than the clay bowls now in use. If we find that the modern reflexes of *kita mean 'tree' in some languages and 'bush' in others, we might be hard pressed to infer the original meaning unless we key this data to other nonlinguistic evidence.

From even a word list of twenty items, we can make certain inferences about the culture of those who spoke the protolanguage. They had terms for 'man,' 'woman,' 'child,' and various body parts—things we would expect to be named in any culture. They possessed fire; they practiced net fishing; they had earrings and necklaces. We can infer a belief in magic. Probably the proto-community built dwellings of some kind, but caution is required here. We cannot assume that earlier dwellings were exactly the same as those built today. It is always possible that all four communities adopted modern building styles from some neighboring community. In such circumstances the original word for 'dwelling' would quite naturally be applied to the new type of building. This would involve a simultaneous shift of meaning in all four languages.

We can assume that at least two communities have been influenced by the religious practices of their neighbors. These are Languages A and D, which have replaced the original word for 'spirit' with a borrowing. Since we can reconstruct the protoform of this word, we know what form it would take if it had been preserved in these languages. Often such a word will turn up in the language with a different meaning. Thus if we should find the missing word associated with the meaning 'ancestor' in Language A or D, it would hardly be surprising. Indeed, it would provide additional insight into the community's cultural history.

3.9   CUMULATIVE RESULTS OF CHANGE

The basic principles of the comparative method are reasonably simple and can be applied to language data in a very mechanical way. At least this has been true of the examples considered thus far. In real languages it often happens that the results of change accumulate in such a way as to obscure underlying regularities and complicate the analysis. We turn now to such an example, again using hypothetical data to simplify matters. (See Corpus 3–3.)

Analysis of the data involves three steps. First, we can identify eighteen correspondences and reduce this to thirteen distinct sounds of the protolanguage by grouping together those correspondences that have overlapping members and are in complementary distribution. This will be done by presenting the correspondences in tabular form and including the posited protoform in the table.

CORPUS 3–3

	A	B	C	D	
(Cog–1)	tasip	tasip	tasip	tašip	'house'
(Cog–2)	wanut	wanut	wanut	onut	'sun'
(Cog–3)	nilak	ninak	nilak	nilak	'boat'
(Cog–4)	tisup	tisub	čisub	tisub	'spoon'
(Cog–5)	winat	wined	winad	winad	'water'
(Cog–6)	nuluk	nunug	nulug	nulug	'dream'
(Cog–7)	tusip	tusip	tusip	tušip	'dog'
(Cog–8)	wunat	wunet	wunat	wunat	'food'
(Cog–9)	tilip	tinib	čilib	tilib	'fire'
(Cog–10)	walat	wanad	walad	olad	'moon'

Second, we can reconstruct the protoform for each of the ten words in the list.

Third, we can state the sound changes that took place in each language. Working out the exact history of the sound changes is the most challenging part of the problem—and the part that is crucial to a thorough analysis.

Again it is wise to begin with the correspondences presenting the fewest difficulties—in this case vowels rather than consonants.

	PL	A/B/C/D
(Cor–1)	*i	i/i/i/i
(Cor–2)	*u	u/u/u/u

Both correspondences occur without environmental restrictions. The separate steps of first identifying the correspondence and then positing a protoform are presented together. Correspondences involving *a* are postponed because they present a more complex pattern.

	PL	A/B/C/D
(Cor–3)	*p	p/p/p/p
(Cor–4)	*b	p/b/b/b
(Cor–5)	*k	k/k/k/k
(Cor–6)	*g	k/g/g/g

Sets 3 through 6 are limited to word final position, but because all occur in that position, they clearly contrast with one another and must therefore represent different protoforms. The pattern of contrast in these four sets leads us to look for a similar distribution of the sets involving *t* and *d*. These sets, however, overlap with another set containing *č* and parallel the previous sets only in part.

(Cor–7a)	*t	t/t/č/t	/	before *i*
(Cor–7b)		t/t/t/t	/	elsewhere
(Cor–8)	*d	t/d/d/d		

Sets 7a and 7b are in complementary distribution. Both occur word initially and word finally, but the significant point is that 7a occurs only before *i* while 7b occurs elsewhere, including of course word final position. This is the position where Cor–8 is found. This means that set 8 contrasts with part of set 7 and, therefore, with the whole set.

At this point we may dispose of several consonant sets having distributional peculiarities but posing no real difficulties.

(Cor–9)	*n	n/n/n/n		
(Cor–10)	*l	l/n/l/l		
(Cor–11a)	*s	s/s/s/š	/	before *i*
(Cor–11b)		s/s/s/s	/	elsewhere

Sets 9 and 10 overlap because both contain *n*. Set 9 occurs word initially and medially—that is, in a position that is neither initial or final. Set 10 occurs medially, where it contrasts with 9. The two sets are consequently assigned to different protoforms. Set 11a is complementary to 11b, having undergone special development before *i*, the same environment that figured in set 7a.

The remaining correspondences are the ones that present the greatest difficulty, but it is possible to attack them now in the light of what is already known about the family we are dealing with. Part of the difficulty is that the occurrence of each set is conditioned in some way by the occurrence of another set. Therefore, each set must be stated in terms of the other. This seems circular, but it is a perfect example of how the solution to linguistic problems requires each piece of evidence to be related to every other piece. When all the pieces fit neatly together, with nothing left unaccounted for, the problem is solved.

In the remaining sets, we note that *w* and *a* are the two units that occur most frequently. It seems reasonable to suppose that these units might continue the protoforms, but we cannot be sure until we can show that the correspondence sets found in the modern languages can be explained by positing these two units for the protolanguage. The words *onut* 'sun' and *olad* 'moon' in Language D deviate from the expected pattern—but only in part. We have already seen that the last three elements of these words fit into the correspondences that have been identified up to this point. It therefore seems likely that *w* has been lost and that *o* occurs instead of *a* in a special environment in Language D. We can state this in the following way:

(Cor–12a)	*w	w/w/w/Ø	/	before Cor–13b
(Cor–12b)		w/w/w/w	/	elsewhere
(Cor–13a)		a/e/a/a	/	after Cor–9
(Cor–13b)	*a	a/a/a/o	/	after Cor–12a
(Cor–13c)		a/a/a/a	/	elsewhere

The statements presented above tie together nicely. The statements were difficult to formulate because it was not possible to identify environments in terms of simple sounds. On the contrary, environments had to be identified in terms of sounds as represented by correspondence sets—that is, in terms of a pattern rather than individual sounds. Of course, since each correspondence set is equated with a single sound of the protolanguage, we are speaking of individual sounds in a sense. We are saying that Cor–12a (*w*/*w*/*w*/Ø) developed from *w* when *w* preceded *a*, that Cor–13b (*a*/*a*/*a*/*o*) developed from *a* when *a* followed *w*, and that Cor–13a (*a*/*e*/*a*/*a*) developed from *a* when *a* followed *n*. These interdependencies have important implications for ascertaining the historical sequence of sound changes, a matter we will turn to shortly. Notice that we have started with eighteen correspondences and reduced them to thirteen distinct units in the protolanguage by grouping together those that are in complementary distribution. It would also be possible to posit sixteen sets by eliminating 12a and 13b and substituting a special statement about the matching of *wa* in A, B, C with *o* in D:

PL   A/B/C/D

*wa   wa/wa/wa/o

This alternative approach would still recognize thirteen distinct units in the protolanguage. The statement about the special development of *wa* would be presented separately rather than being included in the presentation of correspondences. The alternative approach has the effect of treating *w* and *a* in Language D as the normal reflex, or continuation, of *w* and *a*, with the stipulation that *wa* > *o* in this language.

Once the sounds of the protolanguage are determined, it is a simple matter to reconstruct the ten words.

(1)	*tasip	'house'	(6)	*nulug	'dream'
(2)	*wanut	'sun'	(7)	*tusip	'dog'
(3)	*nilak	'boat'	(8)	*wunat	'food'
(4)	*tisub	'spoon'	(9)	*tilib	'fire'
(5)	*winad	'water'	(10)	*walad	'moon'

It is possible to make other inferences as well. It would appear that the typical form of words was CVCVC, a pattern that is preserved virtually intact in the daughter languages. A pattern such as this is called the canonical form of words, or simply the **word canon**. Notice that the word canon of these languages differs from that of the languages in Corpus 3–1 and Corpus 3–2, where the pattern was CVCV. Of course, in that case one language had developed a different canon, CVC, through the loss of final vowels.

It also appears, at least on the basis of the limited data at our disposal, that certain sounds in the protolanguage of Corpus 3–3 were restricted in their occurrence. There was no restriction on vowels, but the consonants seemingly fit into the following pattern:

CVCVC

w s p
t l t
n n k
      b
      d
      g

In many ways the most interesting part of Corpus 3–3 involves tracing the history of sound changes in the individual languages. For Language A this is fairly simple. We can say that all stops became voiceless. This of course led to a merger of *b, *d, *g with the reflexes of *p, *t, *k. Language C also shows a fairly simple change:

*t > č / ___ i

Language D has a similar change:

*s > š / ___ i

But Language D has another sound change that can be described either as a single step or as a sequence of two steps:

(a) *wa > o   (b) *a > o / w___
                       *w > ∅ / ___ o

The one-step approach seems simpler at first, but most linguists would probably prefer the second approach because the two steps form a logical sequence and each is well motivated—that is, each can be explained as a natural modification of pronunciation in a specific context. When we consider that sounds overlap one another to some extent in actual speech, it is understandable that *a* might take on certain *w*-like qualities following *w* and develop into a sound like *o*. Once this happens, the continued presence of *w* becomes redundant because *o* itself implies a sequence of *wa;* and *w* is quite easily dropped. Notice that the steps must take place in this order; if *w* is lost first, the environment that would change *a* to *o* is effectively destroyed.

Another ordering problem arises in Language B. It is fairly easy to see that *l has become n. It also appears that *a has become e following *n. The catch is that this change does not occur after every n—only after those instances of n belonging to Cor–9, that is, those that derive from *n in the protolanguage. The change does not occur after those instances of n belonging to Cor–10, those that derive from original *l. There is nothing anomalous about this. It is a simple question of the order in which the changes took place.

(1) *a > e / *n___   (2) *l > n
     *l > n   *a > e / n___

Unless both changes took place simultaneously, they must have occurred either in sequence (1) or (2). If in sequence (2), the result would be first a merger of *l with *n and then a change of *a to e following every n regardless of the ultimate source of n. This is not the actual situation in Language B. Therefore, the sequence must have been as in (1). First *a changed to e following *n. After this change took place, *l merged with *n, creating several instances of n preceding un-changed a. This is exactly the situation we find in Language B.

Such an inference leads to **relative dating.** There is no way to ascertain the exact year of the change in question, but it is still important to know the relative order of the changes. In conjunction with information from other sources, it is often possible to reconstruct significant facts about cultural history using data of this kind. This is particularly true when we consider the form of words borrowed into one language from another. The evidence of borrowings often provides the anthropologist or cultural historian with information not available from any other source. We know, for example, that the English word *chair* is a borrowing. English also has the word *stool,* which is the expected cognate for German *Stuhl.* We know from documentary evidence that in French r > s, and we conclude therefore that *chair* is an early borrowing from French antedating this change. The modern French word is *chaise,* and because this word has also been borrowed into English, we know it must have been borrowed after the French sound change.

Relative order is also important in language because the individual changes take place in a haphazard way with no ultimate goal in mind. Hence, any language may be viewed as a unique collection of random changes through history even though each change is part of no overall purpose. For comparison imagine a house with four doors and eight windows:

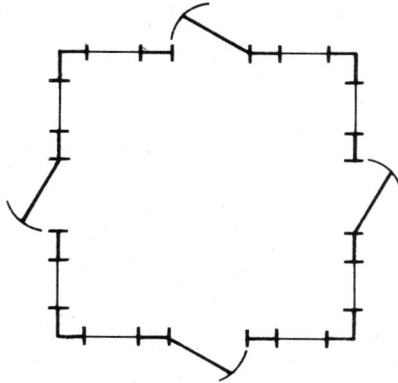

Imagine that a computerized robot capable of doing carpentry work is brought into the house and given the following instructions to be carried out in the order given:

(1) place shutters on each window
(2) convert the two side doors to windows

The result will be that the two side doors emerge as windows—but without shutters. If the renovations are carried out in the opposite order, both doors will be windows at the time shutters are installed, and both will receive shutters. The situation is comparable to the different results that would occur in Language B depending on the order in which the sound changes took place.

Human beings of course are accustomed to thinking in terms of a desired end result. Automatons—even robots capable of carpentry—are concerned only with a mechanical following of the instructions given them. Language as it changes through time is an automaton.

3.10 THE REGULARIST HYPOTHESIS

Recognition that change in language is cumulative is important for two reasons. First, it enables the linguist to trace the changes that have taken place and, by taking them into account, uncover relationships and reconstruct underlying forms that would otherwise be hopelessly obscured. In effect the linguist can reverse the direction of change by peeling away its results layer by layer. And second, the concept of ordered change has had far-reaching consequences for twentieth-century linguistics. Although the principle was certainly recognized by many linguists in the latter part of the nineteenth century, its implications were not fully appreciated until quite recently.

The concept of ordered change was only one of several important conceptual tools developed in the latter part of the nineteenth century. Grimm and his immediate followers believed that, although sound change was basically regular, there were always unexplained "sporadic" changes that were not themselves regular. In the latter part of the century, a new generation of scholars had come on the scene in Germany. These young scholars had the advantage of being able to build on the accomplishments of their predecessors, and they were quick to recognize that many seeming irregularities could be explained as subregularities consistent with the overall pattern if only the proper factors were taken into consideration. The factors they noted included the effects of cumulative change, the influence of adjacent sounds, the position of word accent, and the like.

These scholars, brashly calling themselves *Junggrammatiker* (usually translated "neogrammarians"), loudly proclaimed that "all sound changes take place according to laws that admit no exceptions." Some put it in milder terms: "There must be a rule for exceptions; the only question is to discover it." By insisting on a statement in terms of regular rules, the *Junggrammatiker* were simply carrying on in the tradition of their predecessors. But in noisily asserting that the scientific study of language had not begun until they arrived on the scene, they set themselves apart from the older generation of scholars and created the impression that there was a greater difference between the two schools than was actually the case. In retrospect the interests and objectives of both the earlier and later nineteenth century seem very much the same.

3.11 INTERNAL RECONSTRUCTION

Another important technique for analyzing the historical development of language can be traced to the latter part of the nineteenth century. The technique, known as **internal reconstruction,** is based on the use of internal evidence found within a single language. The approach has many points in common with the comparative method, however—as we can see from analyzing the following data in Corpus 3–4.

CORPUS 3–4

file	vile	wife	wives	book	books
fat	vat	leaf	leaves	cliff	cliffs
fail	veil	elf	elves	hat	hats
waif	wave	hoof	hooves	harp	harps

The basic task is to determine which elements are to count as same and which are to count as different. Beginning with the first two columns, it is evident that each word in the first column differs from each word in the second column. In each case the only element (as far as pronunciation is concerned) that differs is the set f/v. We therefore conclude that f and v are different. This conclusion may seem to be a trivial confirmation of something that all native speakers of English know anyway, but the important thing here is to realize how it is that speakers of English know this.

When we compare the third and fourth columns, we uncover data that appears to conflict with the conclusion we have just reached. Each word in the third column is a singular form, and each word in the fourth column is the corresponding plural. We naturally want to say that the plural suffix occurring throughout column four is a constant. And by all rights we would expect this suffix to be added to the singular root that has already been identified in column three. But in each case we have a variation, or **alternation,** in the form of the word. An alternation of this type, as we saw in columns one and two, normally counts as different; but in this case we instinctively feel that it must somehow be counted as same. The pattern in columns three and four is in conflict with the pattern found in columns one and two. Moreover, it conflicts with the pattern found in the last two columns, where we find no such variation in the singular and plural forms—even in the case where f is involved. Additional examples would show that the pattern of the last two columns is without question the usual pattern for English.

One further point must be noted before we can make an inference about the history of these forms that will enable us to reconcile the conflicting patterns. The final e of *wife* is a spelling convention and does not represent a separate sound that is pronounced. We may therefore regard all the words in column three as ending in the consonant *f*. We also notice that the plural suffix is spelled *-es* in each example in column four. (This statement includes the spelling of *wiv-es* if we equate the final *e* of *wife*, which serves to indicate the value of the preceding vowel, with a null element.) The only thing left to account for is the *f/v* alternation.

Although the plural suffix is spelled *-es*, the vowel *e* is not actually pronounced—nor is it really necessary as a spelling convention. In this respect it is different from the final *e* of *wife*. One possible explanation for the presence of a vowel in *-es* is that this vowel was once pronounced as a separate sound and has been retained in the spelling system from force of habit. If so, we can see that members of the *f/v* set are in complementary distribution: *f* occurs in word final position, and *v* occurs between vowels. This apparently was once an automatic alternation in English.

Given the two positions—word final and between vowels—we must ask which is the more restricted. Is there anything about one of these environments that would naturally cause a consonant occurring in it to be modified? The difference between *f* and *v* can be explained by saying that *f* is voiceless and *v* is voiced—terms that will be defined with precision in Chapter 4. When a consonant is preceded and followed by vowels, it is surrounded by voiced sounds, and it might seem natural for the consonant to undergo voicing in this environment. Possibly this is what happened to *f* in this case. Speakers found it easier to pronounce *f* as *v* when it was preceded and followed by voiced sounds than to expend the effort required to pronounce it without modification.

However, it is also natural for the last sound of a word—a sound followed by silence, or the absence of voicing—to be voiceless. We could apply a similar argument to sounds in word initial position, where the preceding sound is silence, the absence of voicing. We must reexamine our original conclusion (1) by comparing it with another possible explanation (2):

    (1) *f* became *v* between vowels
    (2) *v* became *f* in word final position and word initial position

Several factors favor (1) over (2). We are likely to regard the singular form as somehow basic and the plural a modification of this basic form rather than the other way around; thus, the sound that occurs in the singular form would be taken as the basic unit. We can observe that words in modern English end in both voiced and voiceless sounds, and we might assume, tentatively at least, that this was also the case at an earlier period. But perhaps most important we can readily see that (2) is more complicated than (1).

The simplest and most natural conclusion, the hypothesis that fits best with the known facts, is that at some stage of English the set *f/v* alternated in the pattern:

v / between vowels
f / elsewhere

What could happen then to introduce a second, conflicting pattern? All that is required is that a few words be introduced into the language containing *v* in word initial position or word final position, where its occurrence would not be automatic. This would force a reinterpretation of *f* and *v* as belonging to different sets. But long-established alternations between these sounds in words like those of columns three and four could still be expected to continue from force of habit, thus introducing a conflict between two patterns.

These conclusions are all inferential. For most languages we have no certain way of confirming the accuracy of inferences based on internal reconstruction; but in the case of English, there is a long history of documentation, and we can often find confirming evidence from documentary sources. This is a great help because it strengthens our confidence in internal reconstruction when applied to languages without a writing tradition.

In the case of English, it happens that we have documents from the Old English period (ca. A.D. 500–1100) in which only *f* is used. Following the Norman conquest in 1066, numerous French words were introduced into English. Many of these began with *v: veal, very, victory,* and so on. This led to just the kind of pattern conflict we have inferred through internal reconstruction. Originally the contrast between *f* and *v* involved relatively few words, and the basic alternation between the two sounds continued undisturbed. With the passage of time, however, the *f/v* contrast became more and more pervasive until in modern English the original alternation is preserved in a mere handful of words. But because of its anomalous position in the modern language, it furnishes valuable insight into the nature of language and of language change.

We turn now to a problem in internal reconstruction involving the identification of a pattern using hypothetical data:

CORPUS 3–5

tak	'salt'	tal	'man'	tap	'gourd'	mat	'belly'	lat	'breast'
čik	'earth'	čil	'cloud'	čip	'fish'	mač	'foot'	lač	'path'
cuk	'sun'	cul	'woman'	cup	'thunder'	mac	'arrow'	lac	'milk'

A comparison of the columns and rows reveals that certain elements remain constant while others are systematically different. Data that linguists collect in field situations does not come already organized, of course. It is often necessary to spend long hours sorting and considering the data from many angles before a pattern begins to emerge. Once the analysts detect a pattern, they can look for other words that fit into the pattern or even ask native speakers of the language with whom they are working if such words exist. Often, arrangement of the data to form a pattern, recognition of the pattern, and formulation of a statement describing the pattern occur simultaneously as linguists gain insight into the language they are studying.

In Corpus 3–5 the paradigm involves individual letters, standing for sounds. The distribution of sounds can be analyzed much the same as in the comparative method. We are still concerned about the distribution of sets. The only difference is that the sets in this case have but a single member each. The composition of the sets is different, but the analysis of distribution remains the same.

Beginning with the first column, we note three occurrences of k. Presumably these are three separate occurrences of the same set, namely, the set k. However, the vowels preceding k are different: a, i, and u. These are the only vowels found in the data, and it seems safe to assume that these constitute three separate sets. In the second and third columns, we find additional consonants l and p. These, like k, can apparently follow any vowel. But the remaining consonants are restricted in their distribution: t occurs only before a; $č$ occurs only before i; and c occurs only before u. These appear to be in complementary distribution, and we can therefore assign them to a single set that we can label, noncommittally, *T. The cover symbol *T represents the set $t/č/c$, a correspondence set of a special kind. Members of the set are found, not in different languages, but in specified environments within a single language.

We have focused on distribution of the set *T in the first three columns, where the distribution pattern is unambiguous. In the last two columns, members of the set all occur in final position, where they are not dependent on a following vowel. If we considered only the last two columns, we would be forced to conclude that members of the set are contrastive, rather than complementary. The two patterns seem inconsistent, but they can be reconciled if we assume that words in the last two columns formerly ended in a vowel that is now lost. If this was the case, it must have been that t occurred before a, $č$ before i, and c before u—the same pattern of distribution that we find in the modern language. Accordingly we can reconstruct the words in the last two columns as follows:

*maTa	'belly'	*laTa	'breast'
*maTi	'foot'	*laTi	'path'
*maTu	'arrow'	*laTu	'milk'

If we assume that all words in the language at some time in the past followed a CVCV canon, we would expect the other words in the list to exhibit the same pattern. However, the final consonants in the first three columns bear no imprint that would enable us to reconstruct the now-missing final vowel. We can reconstruct an earlier form of these words by using the cover symbol *T, but we can do nothing more than indicate the original word canon without specifying the exact nature of the vowel:

*TakV	'salt'	*TalV	'man'	*TapV	'gourd'
*TikV	'earth'	*TilV	'cloud'	*TipV	'fish'
*TukV	'sun'	*TulV	'woman'	*TupV	'thunder'

In the reconstruction we have used the cover symbol *T for the larger set. We could just as easily choose one of the individual members of the set to serve as the cover symbol. In that event the logical choice would be *t. The choice is based on the fact that t is very common in languages of the world, whereas č and c are not so common. Moreover, it is common for t to develop into č before i and into c before u, but the reverse development is rather unusual. We have seen an example of t > č / ___ i in Corpus 3–3, but there has been no opportunity as yet to discuss overall tendencies in sound change or to fit individual examples into a broader frame of reference. Awareness of the universal tendencies comes gradually as one encounters an increasing number of examples.

Notice that we still have not actually identified the letters č and c with any definite sound. This has been done intentionally to emphasize the fact that the method depends solely on analyzing the distribution of elements in terms of mutually exclusive, hence complementary, environments or the opposite, that is, contrasting or conflicting environments. In the history of linguistics, the principle of distribution was recognized first; the fact that letters represent sounds and that sounds themselves form intricate patterns was recognized only later.

3.12 CONCLUSION

Both the comparative method and internal reconstruction enable the linguist to reconstruct earlier forms by factoring out the results of change. The linguist searches for alternations occurring in predictable environments. These alternations indicate a unity between ostensibly different forms and allow one to infer an earlier pattern that was completely regular. The alternations examined in the comparative method involve sets of corresponding sounds drawn from two or more languages. The alternations examined in internal reconstruction involve sets of individual sounds that occur in related forms of the same word or otherwise form a distribution pattern within a single language.

The comparative method leads to reconstruction of protoforms that can be attributed to the stage immediately preceding separation of the daughter languages from one another. Internal reconstruction leads to the reconstruction of earlier forms that may be quite recent or extremely archaic. That is, the reconstructed forms may be more recent than the separation of sister languages, may coincide with forms immediately preceding separation, or may go back to a period long before separation.

The comparative method was developed early in the nineteenth century, and internal reconstruction was developed in the later part of the century. The comparative method has often been considered the more powerful of the two tools, but in actual fact the two approaches complement each other; and in the hands of the skilled practitioner, both are used together. It is true that the comparative method often seems to provide more information, but it depends on the availability of matching data from at least two languages. Internal reconstruction provides scattered details, but these details are often important. And the most advantageous point is that it can be applied even to limited data from only a single language.

Both methods have certain limitations. Both require positive evidence and are stymied in the face of negative evidence. For example, in Corpus 3–5 we can reconstruct the now-missing final vowel for words in the last two columns, and we can infer that at one time the words in the first three columns also ended in a vowel. But because there were no distributional restrictions on the consonants preceding these vowels, the vowels are forever lost if we must depend on internal reconstruction alone. If comparative evidence is available, it can of course fill the gap in such a case.

But the comparative method is completely powerless to reconstruct a form that is lost from all the daughter languages. In fact a word must ordinarily be preserved in at least two languages to be attributed to the protolanguage. If a word occurs in only one language, even if the sounds enter into recognized correspondences, there is no way of being sure that the word is preserved from the protolanguage. It is always possible that the word is a postseparation innovation formed from existing phonetic material.

If by chance all the daughter languages have made exactly the same sound change following separation, the comparative method will attribute the outcome of this change to the protolanguage. Offhand it may seem unlikely that this would happen, but parallel sound changes are indeed attested in the loss of final sounds. This is a universal tendency that could easily occur independently in two related languages following their separation. In such cases internal reconstruction may serve as a check on the comparative method.

At present something in excess of 3,000 languages are spoken in the world—many of them by small groups of speakers threatened with extinction as their community struggles to maintain ethnic identity in a larger, culturally dominant community, where the pressure to conform can be enormous. There is no way of knowing how many languages, once spoken, are already extinct. Neither the comparative method nor internal reconstruction can recover data of this kind.

It is worth emphasizing that language is a highly structured system involving an intricate network of relationships. This makes the task of describing language much more complicated than it might seem at first. But at the same time it guarantees a number of built-in checks. Everything must be expected to tie together. If it does not, something is wrong—somewhere—with the analysis.

The ideal language would be perfectly regular. But we have seen that there are natural historical forces constantly at work tending to introduce new irregularities. At the same time there are natural forces at work tending to eliminate irregularities in favor of regular patterns. Thus, language is constantly subject to countervailing forces pulling in opposite directions. Inherited irregularities tend to be regularized, but even as this happens new irregularities are unwittingly introduced. Both the comparative method and internal reconstruction enable the linguist to look beyond present irregularities to reconstruct an idealized earlier stage where everything was completely regular.

As scholarly attention in the nineteenth century focused on historical studies, the assumption was gradually abandoned that languages should be described in terms of the traditional model developed for Greek and Latin. Scholars now felt that the best way to describe a language was in terms of its historical development and its relationship to other languages. But even as this viewpoint was gaining general acceptance, the knowledge of sounds and sound systems that had accumulated during the century was already leading linguists to see language in a new light. The foundations of structuralism had already been laid, but the full story belongs in the next chapter.

---

summary

Similarities in form and meaning in two or more languages are not simply matters of curiosity but are the raw material for establishing historical connections between the languages. The comparative method looks for cognates—that is, words showing similarities in both form and meaning—in different languages. Repeated matchings of similar sounds occurring in analogous positions in cognates are described as sound correspondences. The assumption is that correspondence sets continue individual sounds of the protolanguage. This assumption in turn is based on the assumption that the protolanguage was spoken by a unified community that later split into separate groups, each of which underwent independent changes. The changes in each group are presumed to be quite regular, so that a given sound in the protolanguage will always be represented by the same correspondence set in the successor languages. Correspondence sets that have overlapping membership and that occur in complementary environments are assigned to the same set and regarded as conditioned variants of a single proto-sound.

Internal reconstruction involves the identification of sound alternants in related forms of the same word within a single language. The sets yielded by this method are, in effect, language-internal correspondences; and each of these sets, like those of the comparative method, constitutes a set representing an original unity. Many internal correspondence sets are associated with transparent phonological environments, suggestive of recent innovation; others, which occur in environments that must be stated partly in terms of phonology and partly in terms of grammar, may be quite archaic.

Historical analysis is complicated by several factors. Borrowed vocabulary items can lead to discontinuous correspondences if the borrowings replace inherited words. Borrowings can even introduce contradictory correspondences when related languages borrow from each other, and these "borrowed" correspondences cannot be used in the comparative method. Another form of borrowing, the analogical replacement of one form for another within a paradigm, can also lead to discrepancies among cognates. Finally, since sound changes are cumulative, each change is based on the output of previous changes. The passage of time, with its build-up of successive changes, can therefore obscure the sequence and scope of individual changes. This complication can be overcome by testing different hypotheses about the sequence of changes since some sequences will lead to the attested outcome and others will not.

further reading

General: Arlotto 1972, Anttila 1972, Hoenigswald 1960, Lehmann 1962, 1967, Haas 1969, Keiler 1972. **3.1** Jespersen 1922, Pedersen 1959. **3.2** Leh-mann 1967. **3.5** Bloomfield 1925, 1946. **3.10** Jespersen 1922, Pedersen 1959. **3.11** Anttila 1972, Chafe 1959, 1968b, Haas 1966, 1969.

4

structural grammar

4.1 SAUSSURE'S INFLUENCE

By the latter part of the nineteenth century, the basic relationship of
the Indo-European languages had been worked out. The principal
sound correspondences—and the sound changes they imply—had
been recognized quite early. And in the 1870s the *Junggrammatiker*
were dealing with the seeming irregularities that they found could be
stated as subregularities within the broader pattern. One of the most
brilliant efforts of this period came from the pen of a young Swiss
undergraduate, Ferdinand de Saussure. His paper, *Mémoire sur le
système primitif des voyelles dans les langues indo-européennes,*
which appeared in 1878, combined the comparative method and internal reconstruction. This paper remains one of the most sophisticated examples of linguistic reasoning ever written. The summary
that follows, although greatly simplified, may still contain details
that the beginning student will find difficult to follow. These details,
however, are less important than a general appreciation of the broad
principles involved: the reasoning process Saussure followed, the
assumptions he made about the nature of language and language
change, and the implications of these assumptions for the nonhis-
torical study of language.

One of the characteristic features of Indo-European is a process
known as **ablaut,** which involves vowel change as a grammatical device. In English the process is continued by such forms as *swim,
swam, swum.* Because ablaut is found in numerous correspondences
in nearly every Indo-European language, the process must be attributed to the protolanguage. The most common pattern involves a
series of five vowels: *e, o, Ø, ē, ō.* Except as noted, the examples that
follow are drawn from Greek. Roots are set off by hyphens. The

earliest attested form of Greek has introduced the short vowel *a* where other evidence points to an original absence of any vowel.

e	kl	é	p-to	'I steal'
o	ké-kl	o	p-ha	'I have stolen'
∅	*e-kl		p-ēn > e-kláp-ēn	'I stole'
ē	hl	ē	f-um	'we stole' (Gothic)
ō	kl	ṓ	p-s	'thief (nom. sg.)'

In a number of roots, the alternating vowel is followed by an additional vowel, which can be termed a glide—that is, a nonvocalic element that accompanies a vowel. Saussure's term was "sonant coefficient." In roots where the vowel is followed by a glide, the pattern of vocalic alternation is the same as that shown above except that the two lengthened vowels have not been preserved systematically in attested languages.

e	p	é	ith-omai	'I obey'
o	pé-p	o	ith-a	'I trust' (perfective of 'obey')
∅	e-p		ith-ómen	'I obeyed'

It appears that in their underlying form both roots shown here ('steal' and 'obey') contain *e*. This is suggested by the second form in each case, where the root vowel is *o* but the prefix contains *e*. These are reduplicating prefixes—that is, a prefix that repeats the first consonant and vowel of the root. Because the reduplicated vowel is *e*, this vowel must have been present in the root before the alternation to *o* within the root developed as a signaling device.

A limited number of Greek forms show a different kind of ablaut that, because of its grammatical distribution, appears to match the *e, o, ∅* of the main class. However, the vowels in these subclasses are *ē/ō/a, ā/ō/a,* and *ō/ō/a.*

ē	rh	é	g-nūmi	'I break' (r > rh /#____)
ō	ér-r	ō	g-a	'I have broken'
a	er-r	á	g-ēn	'I was broken'
ā	hí-st	ā	-mi	'I stand'
ō	st	ō	-ía	'hall of columns'
a	hé-st	a	-men	'we are standing'
ō	dí-d	ō	-mi	'I give'
ō	d	ô	-ron	'gift'
a	d	a	-t	'he gives' (Latin)

The three subclasses appear at first to be aberrations. The vocalism is wrong. The vowel length is wrong. And in certain respects the word canon is wrong. The basic form of Indo-European roots, taking *klep-* and *peith-* as the main class, is CVC, where C is used to represent either a single consonant or consonant cluster. We have already seen, however, that a root vowel may be followed by a vocalic glide. Saussure realized that by positing a different kind of glide—one not directly attested in any surviving language—he could account simultaneously for vowel mutation, vowel length, and deviation from the expected canon, and in so doing he could merge the subclass with the main class.

Schematically the new glide can be represented by the cover symbol R (for **resonant,** a sound having vowel-like qualities), allowing among other possibilities roots having the shape CVC, CVR, and CVRC. Because there are three distinct subclasses, we must actually assume three varieties of R, which can be represented as E, A, and O. (The symbols and certain details of presentation differ from those of Saussure, but the substance of the argument remains the same.) We can now say that sequences of *eR* emerge as a long vowel with the phonetic quality of the specific resonant: $eE > \bar{e}, eA > \bar{a}, eO > \bar{o}$. All the sequences of *oR* emerge as $\bar{o}$. All instances of R without a preceding vowel emerge as a short vowel (*ə in the protolanguage, *a* in the Greek and Latin examples). The development of the three stems (omitting irrelevant details) can now be shown as follows:

*reEg-	>	*rēg-
*roEg-	>	*rōg-
*rØEg-	>	*rəg-
*steA-	>	*stā-
*stoA-	>	*stō-
*stØA-	>	*stə-
*deO-	>	*dō-
*doO-	>	*dō-
*dØO-	>	*də-

The comparative method alone leads to the forms given in the second column. Internal reconstruction in this case carries us a step farther, to the forms shown in the first column, which represent Pre-Proto-Indo-European. The reconstruction is not merely a fictive convenience. The *a* of *errágēn* belongs to a paradigm containing an otherwise unexplained long vowel, and this paradigm never contains a zero in place of *a*. The *a* of *eklápēn* belongs to a paradigm based on a short vowel, and the *a* of this paradigm is replaced by zero in certain contexts. In short, $a < *ə < *R \neq a/\emptyset < *\emptyset$.

Saussure was able to arrive at this insight because he was willing to assume that the language he was trying to reconstruct was a self-contained system consisting of structures entering into relationships in which each part was dependent on every other part. Saussure's guiding assumption was that the protolanguage was a system essentially no different in its makeup than languages spoken in the nineteenth century, a radical suggestion in 1878. Indeed, the implications of this assumption were not fully appreciated for another fifty years, when in 1927 Hittite tablets were analyzed in which a direct continuation of the posited element in the protolanguage was found. Nonetheless, the seeds of what later came to be called structural grammar were planted in Saussure's 1878 paper, and all modern reconstructions of the Indo-European vowel system stem directly from the resonants posited by Saussure.

The consequence of Saussure's insight was a drastic revision in ideas held about the structure of Proto-Indo-European. Scholars had been prone to think in terms of periods of "development" and "decay" in language. Many had believed that Proto-Indo-European had been a "primitive" language consisting entirely of monosyllabic roots. Roots were combined in various ways during the time of the protolanguage —a period of "development." More recently there had been a period of "decay." This view tied in nicely with the notion of a golden age followed by a period of decline; but it was refuted by Saussure's findings, which indicated that processes of decay were already at work in the Pre-Proto-Indo-European period. The notion of a "primitive" language had to be discarded. All languages, whether modern or reconstructed, are subject to countervailing tendencies of development and decay.

In some respects, Saussure suggested, language is like a game of chess. It is ever changing, but at any given stage it can be described as a static system with the various pieces entering into specified relationships with other pieces. A development in one direction is balanced by a move in a different direction. A build-up of one piece leads to a similar build-up of others. A shift away from one square may lead to the shift of other pieces from related squares and a later build-up of a different type. But at any given moment there is equilibrium. The structural organization of language is like this too. Language is a system.

4.2   THE ENGLISH CONSONANT SYSTEM

The last quarter of the nineteenth century and the first third of the twentieth century saw continued interest in historical studies but ever-increasing interest in the study of language as a system. Because the greatest achievements in historical grammar had been stated in terms of sound correspondences, it was only natural that linguists should turn with accelerated interest to the study of speech sounds themselves. The concept of sound correspondences implies that certain sounds are more closely—perhaps more naturally—related than others. Likewise, the notion of sound change implies that changes from one sound type to another can be expected as a natural process.

People have long been aware of the phonetic nature of language. The earliest writing systems—the cuneiform of Mesopotamia and the hieroglyphs of Egypt as well as the logographs of China—all began as picture writing but incorporated various phonetic principles at a very early stage. Our own alphabet is based on the Phoenician adaptation of Egyptian hieroglyphs. The Phoenicians adopted a limited number of symbols, using them only for their phonetic value rather than their meaning. These symbols were gradually stylized until all resemblance to the original pictures was lost.

From Phoenicia the alphabet was diffused to Greece and later to Rome. It was first used for English by Christian missionaries from Rome during the Old English period. The process used by the monks was simple. They transcribed each English sound with the letter used for that sound in Latin, improvising a few letters for English sounds having no Latin counterpart. The process involved two steps—first identifying a unique set of discrete sounds and then matching these sound types with fixed reference points, in this case the Latin alphabet.

The standard writing system used for modern English does not maintain a one-to-one relationship between sounds and letters. For this reason linguists have often preferred to use a notational system in which each sound is systematically represented by a single letter and each letter always represents the same sound. The first step in devising such a notational system is to identify a finite number of discrete sound units. Once identified, these sounds can be described in terms of their **articulation**—that is, the manner in which they are produced by the vocal apparatus. There is general agreement among linguists that the consonants of English can be described in terms of twenty-four discrete units.

We have already seen examples of how sound units are identified in languages, including the example of *fat* and *vat*, which establishes *f* and *v* as contrasting units because they occur in contrasting environments. Such word pairs as *fat/vat*, which are the same except for a single contrasting sound, are called **minimal pairs.** The distinctive sound units themselves are called **phonemes.** Native speakers of any language can ordinarily recognize the phonemes of their language. For English the list of consonant phonemes accepted by most speakers will contain twenty-four sounds, each of which can be represented by a single symbol. The English consonant phonemes are listed below with the ordinary spelling given first—except in the case of one sound that has no "ordinary" spelling. The conventional spelling is followed by the phonemic symbol enclosed in diagonals and one or more key words in which the consonant in question is exemplified in various positions. A few sounds, however, do not occur in all possible positions.

p	/p/	*p*in, su*pp*er, s*p*it, ta*p*
b	/b/	*b*in, a*b*le, ru*b*
t	/t/	*t*ile, bi*tt*er, s*t*op, hi*t*
d	/d/	*d*ial, un*d*er, la*dd*er, ba*d*
k	/k/	*c*lock, see*k*ing
g	/g/	*g*row, lo*gg*ing, clo*g*
ch	/č/	*ch*urch, bu*tch*er
j	/ǰ/	*j*udgment, we*dg*e
f	/f/	*f*at, o*ff*er, loa*f*
v	/v/	*v*at, o*v*er, sie*v*e
th	/θ/	*th*ink, e*th*er, wrea*th*
th	/ð/	*th*ese, ei*th*er, wrea*the*
s	/s/	*s*ue, awe*s*ome, mo*ss*
z	/z/	*z*oo, o*z*one, ro*s*e
sh	/š/	*s*ure, wi*sh*ing, wa*sh*
	/ž/	mea*s*ure, rou*g*e
h	/h/	*h*all
m	/m/	*m*ean, si*mm*er, so*m*e
n	/n/	*n*ice, ru*nn*er, si*n*
ng	/ŋ/	ha*ng*er, si*ng*
l	/l/	*l*ake, a*l*imony, sou*l*
r	/r/	*r*ake, o*r*ifice, soa*r*
w	/w/	*w*ent
y	/y/	*y*outh

Of the twenty-four phonemic symbols used for consonants, seventeen are standard letters of the English—or Latin—alphabet. As phonemic symbols, however, they always represent the same sound unit; and each sound unit is always represented by the same symbol. There is a fixed one-to-one correspondence between sound and symbol. The system is entirely free of spelling variations.

The unfamiliar symbols are used in exactly the same way. Four of them, /č, ǰ, š, ž/, are familiar letters with a **wedge** placed above the letter. These are customarily referred to by a compound consisting of the conventional name of the letter and the suffix *wedge,* for example, *C-wedge,* and so on. The two representing *th* sounds form a pair. The symbol /θ/, called theta, is borrowed from the Greek alphabet. The symbol /ð/, called eth (pronounced with the /ð/ sound itself), was an innovation of the monks who first transcribed English. The letter is a manuscript *d* with a cross like that of *t* through the ascender. The final symbol /ŋ/ is a transparent combination of *n* and a printed version of *g*. This is often called eng, pronounced of course with the /ŋ/ sound.

The next step, describing these sounds in articulatory terms, is difficult for the average speaker, who produces the sounds with unconscious effort. As one becomes consciously aware of the sounds themselves, it is not at all difficult to associate them with specific regions of the vocal tract and the movable organs within the tract (Figure 4–1). Sounds can then be classified in terms of their point of articulation within the vocal tract and their manner of articulation at each point (Figure 4–2).

FIGURE 4–1   The Vocal Tract

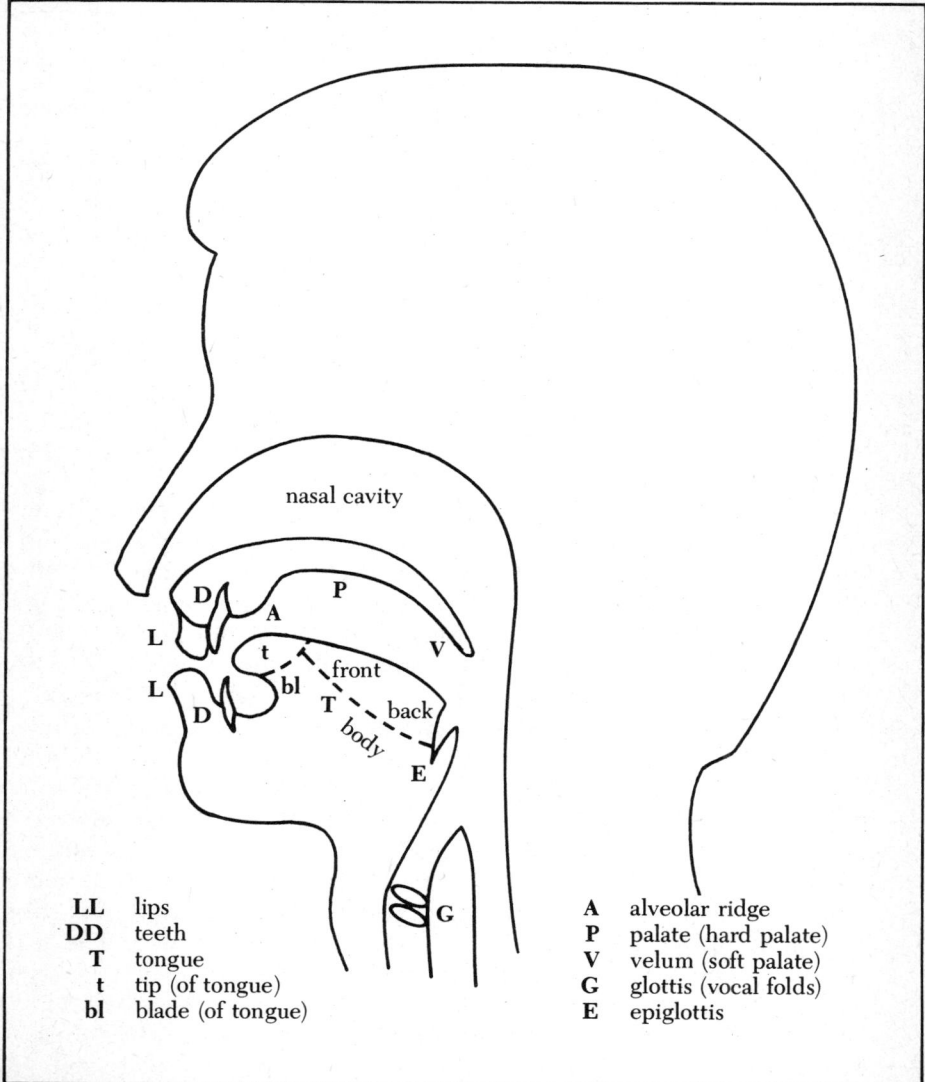

LL	lips	**A**	alveolar ridge
DD	teeth	**P**	palate (hard palate)
T	tongue	**V**	velum (soft palate)
t	tip (of tongue)	**G**	glottis (vocal folds)
bl	blade (of tongue)	**E**	epiglottis

FIGURE 4-2   English Consonant Chart

Articulation point / manner		Labial		Dental	Alveolar	Palatal	Velar	Glottal
		bilabial	labio-dental					
Stops	voiceless	p			t		k	
	voiced	b			d		g	
Affricates	voiceless					č		
	voiced					ǰ		
Fricatives	voiceless		f	θ	s	š		h
	voiced		v	ð	z	ž		
Voiced	nasals	m			n		ŋ	
	lateral				l			
	retroflex				r			
	semivowels	w					y	

In addition to the parts marked in Figure 4–1, it is useful to be able to refer to other regions: the oral cavity is the chamber extending from the lips to the velum; the pharyngeal cavity extends from the velum to the glottis; and the nasal cavity extends from the nasal opening to the velum. The trachea is the tube connecting the lungs with the pharyngeal cavity, and the esophagus is the tube leading from the pharyngeal cavity to the stomach. The epiglottis, which plays no direct part in the production of speech sounds, blocks off the trachea during swallowing to prevent the aspiration of foreign objects into the lungs.

As air is expelled from the lungs, it is constricted in various ways by the lips, tongue, teeth, and other articulators. If the air stream is completely blocked, the resulting sound is called a **stop** and is described in terms of the point at which the stoppage occurs. If the vocal tract is constricted so that the escaping air stream produces friction without actual stoppage, the resulting sound is called a **fricative.** The term **spirant** is sometimes used for the same type of sound. The exact type of fricative can be specified in terms of the point of articulation. A sound type combining features of both stop and fricative—that is, a stop released as a fricative—is called an **affricate.**

In addition, English has three **nasals.** These are consonants resonated through the nasal cavity while the oral cavity is blocked off by tongue or lip closure. The **lateral** involves contact between the tongue and the alveolar ridge with the air stream escaping around either side of the tongue. The **retroflex** is roughly a mirror image of the lateral. That is, the sides of the tongue are retracted so that they make contact with the gums while the air stream continues to escape through the center of the oral cavity. In addition, the retroflex is accompanied by lip rounding and a high degree of muscular tension in all parts of the vocal tract, making this an extremely complex sound. The **semivowels** are so designated because of their peculiar structural status. Preceding vowels, they function as consonants, but following vowels, they function as part of the vocalic nucleus.

4.3   PHONETICS AND PHONEMICS

In discussing the English consonants, we have attempted to identify only those units that are structurally significant. Thus, for example, we have recognized /č/ as a unit even though it could just as well be analyzed as a sequence of /t/ followed by /š/. Using only /t/ and /š/ would eliminate the need for /č/ as a separate symbol but would obscure the fact that the supposed sequence actually functions as a unit. In this respect /č/ is fundamentally different from the sequence of /t/ followed by /s/, which occurs in English only in the plural of nouns or the third person singular form of verbs in the present tense: *hat-s, sit-s,* and so on. The sequence *ts* can be represented /c/ in a language like Japanese, where it patterns as a unit: *cunami* 'tidal wave.'

While striving to recognize units that are structurally significant, we have systematically ignored sounds that have no significance. These are of two types: (1) random noise such as the sound of air being inhaled in preparation for speaking and (2) variant speech sounds that might be structurally significant in another language but that do not figure into the English consonant system. For example, Hindi distinguishes two varieties of *t,* one plain and one followed by a puff of air, which can be represented in transcriptions by a superscript *h*:

tām	'copper'	tʰām	'pillar'
tāpnā	'to warm oneself'	tʰāpnā	'to tap, pat'
tāl	'pond, pool'	tʰāl	'metal dish'

English has both varieties of *t,* but the difference in English is not significant. The set *t/tʰ* does not serve to differentiate words in English as it does in Hindi.

How is it possible then that both members of the set *t/tʰ* can occur in English without leading to confusion? The two occur in complementary environments (see Figure 4–3), and since they are phonetically similar, speakers of the language come to regard them as equivalent. Each variant is associated with its characteristic environment, and most speakers with no training in phonetics have difficulty detecting a difference at all. Part of learning to speak English involves learning to overlook this perceptible, but nonfunctional, difference while automatically using each variant in the proper environment. Members of the set *t/t*ʰ constitute a single structural unit /t/ in English. In Hindi they constitute two contrasting units /t/ and /tʰ/.

FIGURE 4–3   Distribution of Members of the Set /t/ in English

Symbol	Description	Examples	Environment
[tʰ]	⎡voiceless⎤ aspirated alveolar ⎣stop⎦	*t*ip, *t*ake, at*t*ack	before stressed vowels
[č]	⎡voiceless⎤ aspirated palatal ⎣affricate⎦	*t*ree, *t*raveler, at*t*rition	before /r/ (for some speakers; others use tʰ)
[t]	⎡voiceless⎤ unaspirated alveolar ⎣stop⎦	s*t*and, as*t*ound	following /s/
[T]	⎡voiced⎤ unaspirated alveolar ⎣flap⎦	li*tt*le, a*tt*ic, bu*tt*er	between vowels or between a vowel and syllabic /l, r/
[ʔ]	⎡voiceless⎤ unaspirated glottal ⎣stop⎦	bu*tt*on, mi*tt*en	before syllabic /n/
[tʰ, t, ʔ]	[variable]	hi*t*	

In the comparative method, sets with overlapping membership that occur in complementary distribution are classed as a single set. In internal reconstruction, otherwise contrasting sounds that occur in a pattern representing earlier complementarity can also be taken as belonging to the same set. In determining the significant sound units— the **phonemes**—of a language without reference to their historical development, a similar observation is possible: **Phonetically similar sounds that occur in complementary environments, or that exhibit free variation in a particular environment, are classed as members of the**

same structural unit, the phoneme. An explicit statement of the rationale for structural classification may not seem necessary in analyzing English *t/t*ʰ, since every speaker of the language will intuitively think of the two sounds as constituting a single unit. English-speaking linguists, however, must rely on an explicit analytical procedure when they encounter a language such as Hindi. Otherwise they will find themselves imposing English categories on Hindi structure.

In actuality the variants that comprise the English phoneme /t/ are more numerous than the two thus far singled out for identification. A more complete analysis would include at least the six alternate forms given in Figure 4–3. A careful analysis could be expected to produce still further variants, depending on such factors as the skill of the observer, the dialect of English being studied, and so on.

Certain basic terminology is essential at this point. Sounds without reference to their structural status are called **phones.** The phones that constitute a structural unit are termed a **phoneme** (§4.2) and are transcribed between slashes, for example, /t/. Members of the set of phones classified as a phoneme are called **allophones** of the phoneme. Individual allophones, as well as unclassified phones, are enclosed in brackets, for example, [t, tʰ]. Since phonemes and their allophones are structural classes that must be described in terms of the distributional patterns of a particular language, these units must be defined anew for each language studied. Thus, it is possible to speak of the phones [t] and [tʰ] in both English and Hindi, but classification of these units as either separate phonemes or allophones of a single phoneme is valid only with reference to the distributional pattern of one language or the other.

Allophonic variation, as seen in Figure 4–3, is normally quite systematic. That is, each allophone occurs in a specified environment where its distinguishing characteristics involve some kind of phonetic compromise with an adjacent sound. This kind of subphonemic variation is known as **conditioned variation.** In some cases, however, nonsignificant variation may occur in a way that cannot be attributed to environmental conditioning. This is true of English /t/ in word final position, as seen in Figure 4–3. It is convenient in such cases to think of a sound unit as having an articulatory target but straying from that target in a random fashion. Nondistinctive variation of this kind is termed **free variation.**

4.4 THE ENGLISH VOWEL SYSTEM

Having identified the English consonants, we can do the same for the English vowels. Again we will want to describe the articulation of the vowels in terms of tongue position as each vowel is pronounced. While there is general agreement among linguists on the identification of English consonants, there is some disagreement about the proper identification of vowels. Eventually we must deal with the issues here, but let us begin by looking for minimal pairs to establish the basic contrasts. Since the spelling of vowel sounds varies from one English word to the next, we will adopt the practice of presenting the standard phonetic symbol followed by a key word illustrating each sound.

[i]   b*ea*t

[ɪ]   b*i*t

The first pair establishes a contrast between two varieties of *i*. Notice that the practice among linguists is to use the phonetic value of letters from the Latin alphabet, supplementing standard symbols as necessary with specially invented letters. We can rather easily find another pair of sounds related to each other in much the same way.

[e]   b*ai*t

[ɛ]   b*e*t

Two additional pairs exhibit a parallel contrast.

[u]   b*oo*t
[ʊ]   b*oo*k

[o]   wr*o*te
[ɔ]   wr*ou*ght

Still another pair seemingly pattern together, although in this case the difference between them does not appear to parallel the difference involved in previous pairs.

[æ]   h*a*t   [a]   h*o*t

The remaining vowel involves enough variety that it might be useful to distinguish three principal variants within this unit—that is, three subsets within the larger set constituting this unit.

[ɨ]   b*u*rner, und*e*r
[ʌ]   *u*nder, b*u*t, ab*o*ve
[ə]   *a*bove, *a*bsent, *a*bility, philos*o*phy, *u*mbil*i*cal

We are dealing here with three phones—that is, three sound types that are perceptibly different. However, as far as English is concerned, the three phones are in complementary distribution and therefore constitute a single phoneme—that is, a structural unit within the

language consisting of phonetically similar sounds that pattern together in a regular way. Members of this structural unit are allophones. Each allophone occurs in its own characteristic environment,
and each environment is complementary to the other environments—
that is, the environments are mutually exclusive.

In the case under discussion, we will find it convenient to use /ə/ as
a cover symbol for the set containing [ɨ, ʌ, ə]. We can describe the
distribution of allophones by saying that [ɨ] occurs before /r/ (actually
many linguists prefer to think of this variant as a syllabic form of /r/,
writing it [r̩]); [ʌ] occurs in stressed syllables; and [ə] occurs elsewhere. Accordingly, ə will be written either [ə] or /ə/, depending on
whether it refers to the allophone or to the cover symbol for the set of
allophones that constitute the phoneme. We could also state the distribution using a kind of shorthand notation:

$$/\text{ə}/ \rightarrow \left\{ \begin{array}{ll} [\text{ɨ}] & / \underline{\quad} /\text{r}/ \\ [\text{ʌ}] & / \quad \text{in stressed syllables} \end{array} \right\}$$

The symbol > , used to denote sound change through time, is modified by having a shaft added so that it now has the form of an arrow →.
This arrow is conventionally used to denote sound variation observable at any given stage of a language—that is, variation that does not
involve change through time but is dictated by environmental differences. The braces indicate that there are two options that must apply
in the given order. In other words [ɨ] will always take precedence
over [ʌ], as can be determined from the word *further* [fɨrðɨr],
where the first *ɨ* is stressed, but nevertheless assumes the phonetic
form appropriate to the environment preceding *r*. The shorthand notation contains no instructions for ə itself. But this presents no problem
because ə is left unaltered in the absence of explicit instructions to the
contrary. This is exactly what "elsewhere" means. In the example
above, the diagonals and brackets have been used to emphasize the
difference between phones and phonemes. These are often omitted
in shorthand notation of this type. Since one purpose of this kind of
notation is to specify the allophones of a phoneme, the proper placement of diagonals and brackets is always implicit in the notation itself.

At this point we have identified eleven basic phones. In terms of
tongue position, they can be represented as shown in Figure 4–4,
which is a conventionalized representation of the vocal tract as pictured in Figure 4–1. Note that the terms *high, mid,* and *low* refer to
tongue height. The terms *front, central,* and *back* refer to tongue advancement. Thus the terms *mid* and *central* refer to different articulatory properties and can be kept distinct.

Since we are attempting to identify the contrasting structural units

—phonemes—we have parenthesized the various allophones of the central vowel, placing [ɨ] in the intersection of *high* and *central* and [ʌ] in the intersection of *low* and *central*.

Front and back vowels are paired, with one of each pair labeled *tense* and the other *nontense*. This attribute has to do with the relative degree of muscular tension involved in producing the sounds. The low vowels /æ/ and /a/ are not distinguished in this way, and since they are not explicitly specified as tense, they may be regarded as nontense.

FIGURE 4–4   English Vowel Chart

		Tongue advancement					
		front		central	back		
		tense	nontense			nontense	tense
Tongue height	high	i		(ɨ)			u
			I			U	
	mid	e		ə			o
			ɛ			ɔ	
	low		æ	(ʌ)		a	

The distinction between tense and nontense vowels is a peculiar feature of English and has no counterpart in many of the world's languages. The distinction is manifested by a difference in phonetic quality ([i] vs. [ɪ]), but it is also manifested by a difference in duration and—more important—by the fact that tense vowels in English are always followed by a **glide,** or vowel-like sound, to form a **diphthong.** This glide is the semivowel /y/ in the case of front vowels and the semivowel /w/ in the case of back vowels. (A semivowel is a sound that functions sometimes as a consonant and sometimes as a vowel.) A complete phonetic transcription of the key words given earlier in this section will therefore be as follows:

beat	[biyt]	boot	[buwt]
bit	[bɪt]	book	[bʊk]
bait	[beyt]	wrote	[rowt]
bet	[bɛt]	wrought	[rɔt]
hat	[hæt]	hot	[hat]

All allophones of the central vowel will be transcribed /ə/.

Three other glides are formed by taking a nontense vowel, which ordinarily is not followed by a glide, and placing a glide after it.

boy	[bɔy]		
eye	[ay]		
house	[haws]	or	[hæws]

These glided vowels are never confused with the glides that automatically follow the tense vowel in each pair for a fairly obvious reason: The tense vowel [o] is automatically followed by the glide /w/, which is the consonantal counterpart of [u], hence a back glide. But [ɔ] is followed by /y/, the counterpart of [i], and is therefore a front glide. Thus the choice of glide serves to reinforce the basic phonetic distinction between the original vowels.

Since /æ/ and /a/ are both nontense, they do not contrast with another vowel that is automatically followed by a glide. This means that either a front glide or back glide is possible for those vowels. Moreover, there is little danger of confusion regardless of which vowel is used before either semivowel. In practice, however, all speakers use /a/ before /y/. Some speakers use /a/ before /w/, while others habitually use /æ/, but the usual contrast between these two vowels is neutralized in this environment.

The vowel scheme presented here is applicable to a variety of American English spoken in all parts of the country and ordinarily used by radio and television announcers or by film actors unless there is a clear intention to represent a regional dialect. This widely spoken dialect commands enough social prestige that it is often described as the "standard" dialect. The term is perhaps unfortunate since it suggests that there are other dialects that are somehow "substandard." To describe this as the "prestige" dialect or "neutral" dialect presents other difficulties; so there is no perfect label for this dialect. The terms "standard" and "nonstandard," widely used by linguists, are intended as nonjudgmental labels, although this is not always understood by laymen.

In any event, it is likely that most individuals will find that their own speech diverges in some details from the vowel system described here. If this is the case, it will be necessary to modify the basic vowel system until it is adequate for describing one's own pronunciation. Then it will be a fairly simple matter to extend the system to the pronunciation of others.

To take a few examples, we can observe that many Southerners in the United States lack the diphthong /ay/ as in *eye*. For these speakers the vowel has the same starting point /a/, but it is not followed by the glide /y/. Instead of gliding to a high front position, the diphthong glides to a point much closer to the central vowel /ə/. The pronunciation of *eye* could therefore be represented as [aə̯] for this dialect. (The mark under /ə/ identifies the symbol as a glide; without such a mark the sequence [aə] would be interpreted as two vowels, both having equal prominence.) Many linguists adopt the convention of transcribing the centering glide with /h/, thus representing *eye* in this dialect as /ah/. The important point is that this dialect makes the same structural distinctions that are made in the "standard" dialect even though the phonetic details of the distinction may differ.

Similarly, the word *path*, pronunced /pæθ/ by many, is often pronounced /pæyəθ/ by Southern speakers. There is no "correct" phonemic transcription apart from the pronunciation that one is trying to represent. Most people in any language community are aware of dialect differences, but we are seldom troubled by them because we are able to set up equivalences between the sounds of other dialects and the sounds of our own. These equivalences are essentially the same as sound correspondences discussed in connection with historical grammar. The only difference is that we are speaking now of correspondences between mutually intelligible dialects instead of correspondences between totally different languages.

It is worth emphasizing that the different dialects of English maintain essentially the same contrasts even if the contrasting units differ from one dialect to another. If we can imagine a game of baseball in which each player rides a unicycle or wears roller skates instead of running by foot, the outward appearances would be noticeably different; but we would still be constrained to say that the underlying system represented by the players, each functioning in a particular way with respect to the others, is unchanged. This is what linguists mean when they say that the different dialects of English are simply different manifestations of the same system.

4.5   ELIMINATION OF REDUNDANCY

We have taken pains to examine English vowels as a structural system. The discussion has thus far included three central vowels that are in complementary distribution and therefore constitute a single functional unit. These three vowels [ɨ, ə, ʌ], we observed, are allophones of a single phoneme /ə/. Such an analysis is generally favored by linguists on the grounds that it views the system in terms of structural units. That is, it recognizes only the units that are functional within the system and ignores those that could perhaps be identified but that are not functional. There is still another way in which the system presented in §4.4 can be streamlined. This system, containing full phonetic detail, is presented below as A and is restated as B and C.

A

iy	I		U	uw
ey	ɛ	ə	ɔ	ow
æ				a

B

i	I		U	u
e	ɛ	ə	ɔ	o
æ				a

C

iy	i		u	uw
ey	e	ə	o	ow
æ				a

Each of the above maintains the necessary eleven contrasts between vowel units, not counting the nontense glided vowels [ɔy, ay, aw], which must be represented separately anyway. Phonetically the contrast must be described in terms of two features: (1) vowel quality and (2) the presence or absence of a glide. The two features are systematically related so that certain vowels imply the presence of a glide, and glides always imply the presence of certain vowels. It is not really necessary to represent both the differences in vowel quality and the presence of a glide since either one implies the other. This **redundancy** can be eliminated if we represent one dimension of contrast and let it imply the other.

System B simplifies A by relying on the difference of vowel quality to predict glides:

/i/ = [iy]
/ɪ/ = [ɪ]
/ay/ = [ay] etc.

This approach saves having to write the glides that automatically follow these vowels. The system still requires an inventory of eleven vowel symbols. But since the glides that follow the nontense vowels must still be represented, the economy is negligible. There are distinct advantages to system C, where the presence or absence of a glide is used to predict vowel quality:

/iy/ = [iy]
/i/ = [ɪ]
/ay/ = [ay] etc.

System C has the added advantage of reducing the inventory of vowel symbols to seven since the same cover symbol can be used for the paired tense/nontense vowels, and the distinction between them is carried by the presence or absence of a glide:

    i   u
  e   ə   o
  æ   a

Both B and C contain exactly the same information as A, but the redundancies are eliminated in such a way that native speakers will automatically associate any vowel or diphthong in either system with a unique phonetic output.

Linguists attach high regard to such tightly knit schemes as system C, often describing them as economical, efficient, systematic, or symmetrical. These functional considerations often merge with esthetic considerations; and a compact, well-organized, descriptive statement will be praised as "elegant."

Linguists are willing to tolerate loss of redundancy because they are accustomed to working with rules that systematically fill in redundant details on the basis of a compact, redundancy-free system. Speakers of a language also can tolerate considerable loss of redundancy—witness the fact that in English we can write such words as *bow* /bow/ and *bow* /bæw/ with the same spelling and depend on readers familiar with both words and the context in which each is used to know which is intended. The use of such a nonredundant phonemic system as B or C places even less of a demand on the speaker or reader.

Of course the same assumption cannot be made for non-native speakers of a language—that is, outsiders trying to learn the language. Non-native speakers lack any prior knowledge of the sound system they are trying to learn, and for such people a transcription containing redundancies such as A may actually be a great help. Learners of a foreign language, however, are often expected to deal with the standard writing system of the target language from the outset. This presents few difficulties in the case of a language like Spanish, where most significant contrasts are represented in the spelling system. It is something more of an obstacle in the case of English.

4.6   THE ENGLISH STRESS AND PITCH SYSTEM

In addition to contrasting sounds, English is distinguished by differences of **stress,** or prominence of certain syllables. Stress may be absent or present in varying degrees in any syllable. And since each syllable may be defined as a segment of speech containing a vowel, we can associate stress with individual vowels. To understand the English stress system, we can think initially of stress as being either present or absent. If absent, it requires no special mark. If present, it is denoted by the acute accent (´) placed over the appropriate vowel:

/bə́kəl/ 'buckle'   /ménšən/ 'mention'

In many words we can detect a reduced degree of stress intermediate between **primary stress** (described above simply as "stress") and the complete absence of stress:

/éləvèytər/   'elevator'   /ápərèytər/   'operator'

This can be marked with a grave accent (ˋ). It would seem at this point that we have identified the basic contrasting units of stress. However, there is another peculiar fact of English that must be noted. When two words containing a primary stress occur together, only one primary stress is assigned to the word group. The other primary stress is reduced to **secondary stress.**

/éləvèytər   âpərèytər/   'elevator operator'

Secondary stress can be denoted by a circumflex (ˆ), as done above. The previously identified intermediate stress now can be called **tertiary stress** (ˋ). For words cited in isolation, primary and tertiary stress marks are often the only units needed. Secondary stress becomes important only when larger units are cited.

Although the absence of a mark is normally sufficient to indicate absence of stress, it is sometimes convenient to note absence of stress in some explicit way. For this purpose the breve (˘) is customarily used:

/éləvèytər   âpərèytər/   'elevator operator'

As a rule experienced linguists and neophytes alike will have no trouble agreeing on the stress patterns of words cited in isolation. For longer utterances there will often be disagreement. This can be attributed largely to the fact that any string of words can usually be stressed in more than one way, depending on which word is given contrastive emphasis. Linguists must train themselves to hear what other speakers say rather than hearing what they themselves would say in the same situation.

Much the same observation can be made of the English **pitch** system. All observers are inclined to agree that a normal level of pitch can be identified and that this contrasts with a low pitch, a high pitch, and an extra high pitch used occasionally for contrastive purposes. If we think of these pitch levels as something like tones on a musical scale, we can represent each level by a number from one through four:

4 extra high pitch
3 high pitch
2 normal pitch
1 low pitch

It then becomes an easy matter, in principle at least, to use superscript numbers to represent the pitch contour within a sentence. In practice, of course, there are often complications. Since the pitch levels are relative and not absolute, one person's high pitch may overlap another's normal pitch, and so on. Skill in dealing with problems of this sort can come only from practice with relatively clear-cut examples like those below:

^{2}He ^{3}came.^{1}	(normal contour)
^{2}He came?^{3}	(question)
^{2}He ^{3}came?^{4}	(surprise, disbelief)
^{2}John ^{3}came, ^{2}and ^{3}Mary left.^{1}	(The contrast between the behavior of John and Mary is emphasized.)

By convention, the pitch level denoted at the beginning of the utterance is understood to continue until a different pitch is noted. If a word begins on one pitch and ends on another, it is understood that the transition is associated with the vowel. In words of more than one syllable, the transition typically is associated with the syllable receiving greatest stress. If there is any possibility of ambiguity, it is acceptable to break the word to show where the transition occurs.

Students are well advised to become aware of pitch contours. Like many other features of language that we normally deal with unconsciously, pitch can usually be omitted from transcriptions without danger or ambiguity. But if students fall back on this as an excuse for not learning to recognize different pitch contours, they will be at a loss when finally forced to deal with a subtle contrast depending on pitch.

It should be noted in passing that pitch contours in English are associated with the sentence. In many languages having pitch as a structural unit, pitch is assigned to the individual word, and this word retains a fixed pitch regardless of how it is used in the sentence. Such languages—usually called tone languages—include those spoken in China and Southeast Asia, certain languages in Central America, and a number of languages in Africa.

4.7   RISE OF STRUCTURALISM

Between the years 1933 and 1957, structural grammar placed great emphasis on analyzing the sound systems of language. This emphasis developed primarily for three reasons: (1) interest in descriptive rather than historical studies; (2) the accessibility of sounds and the availability of techniques for analyzing and describing them; and (3) practical applications of linguistics. Each of these developments will be discussed in turn.

4.8 SYNCHRONY VERSUS DIACHRONY

The rise of historical studies in the nineteenth century had introduced a new way of looking at language. Like any new idea, it was fresh and exciting; and when the *Junggrammatiker* were at their zenith, it was widely believed that the historical approach was the only valid way to study language at all. This view seemed superficial to Saussure, who had relied on the assumption that the protolanguage was a self-contained structural system in working out a solution to a difficult problem in Indo-European vowel alternation (§4.1).

In lectures before his classes at Geneva shortly after the beginning of the present century, Saussure drew a distinction between historical and descriptive studies. His basic premise was that, at any point in time, a language may be viewed as a self-contained system—that is, a set of interrelated structures. The study of language at one point in time is a **synchronic** study. The study of changes in a language from one point in time to a subsequent point is a **diachronic** study. Saussure described synchronic study as slicing through the trunk of a tree to study the arrangement of rings. Diachronic study was then seen as tracing the development of the rings by comparing two synchronic slices. Saussure saw synchronic studies as logically prior to diachronic studies and as vastly more important. He died without putting his views in print; but students, working from his lecture notes and from notes they had taken in class, published his theories in 1916 under the title *Cours de Linguistique Générale.*

Saussure's views proved influential in redirecting the course of linguistics in the twentieth century. Interest in historical studies declined and was replaced by efforts to describe previously unexamined languages in terms of their own structural systems. The trend represented a reaction to the earlier obsessive interest in historical studies and a return to the descriptive emphasis of traditional grammar. The difference was that traditional grammar had tended to see all languages in terms of Latin categories; the focus now was on describing each language as a self-contained structural system. This approach required no reference to related languages or to presumed historical development, and it involved no reference to Latin.

4.9 STUDY OF SOUNDS

We have already seen (§4.2–4.3) how historical grammar led inevitably to the detailed, careful study of speech sounds. In the late nineteenth century, the goal of phoneticians (scholars specializing in the study of speech sounds) was to identify every possible speech sound and devise a symbol for it so that each time this sound was encountered in a language of the world it could be transcribed. The difficulty with this objective is that there is no upper limit to the number of possible speech sounds. No two sounds are exactly alike. To deal with this problem, phoneticians developed two kinds of notation, or transcription. **Narrow** notation was intended to record all discernible phonetic information. **Broad** transcription was intended to record only the most important distinctions. The concept of the phoneme was the logical outgrowth of broad transcription, a development that has been anticipated in the organization of this chapter. The concept was formalized by Leonard Bloomfield in his book *Language*, published in 1933.

Language is of course much more than sound. But sounds are accessible to observation. That is, they can be heard, and one can judge whether two successive sounds are the same or different. Sounds could be recorded by early mechanical devices and later by electronic devices. The acoustic and articulatory properties of sounds could be analyzed and described. It seemed natural to say that sounds were the basic building blocks of language. Words could be described as composed of sounds, sentences as composed of words, and larger units as composed of sentences. This approach developed as the basic descriptive format of structural linguistics.

4.10 PRACTICAL APPLICATIONS

The practitioners of historical grammar had come to their study from literature and philology. Phonetics and the methodology that was to become structural grammar had no such orientation. But since the new methodology was oriented toward the spoken word, it was ideally suited for use by the fledgling science of anthropology, which was striving in the early twentieth century to collect information about tribal peoples living on the fringes of Western culture. These people had no written language, and almost without exception their cultures were facing extinction as they competed with the technology of expanding Western culture for the same ecological niche.

In the United States, Franz Boas (1858–1942), a German-born geographer, taught himself linguistics in order to learn about the culture of Eskimos living in Baffin Land. He began his study of these people in the latter part of the nineteenth century, at a time when Europeans still believed that geography was the main force for shaping a people's culture. Boas quickly saw that it was the cultural tradition itself that shaped people's lives, and he perceived that efforts to understand a people's culture without a knowledge of their language would be of little avail. Boas, who became the founder of American anthropology, spent his life studying the language and culture of

North American Indians. His students, among them Edward Sapir and
Alfred Kroeber, continued this line of study.

Boas discovered great variety among North American languages
and was quickly convinced that each language had to be described in
terms of its own structural system—the same conclusion that Saussure
had reached independently at about the same time. An important part
of the work of Boas was collecting lengthy texts in native languages.
For this a knowledge of phonetics was necessary. The objective was
to transcribe as much detail as possible because one could never be
certain which phonetic distinctions would prove to be structurally significant in a new language. Many of the linguists who followed Boas
and his students were interested in developing writing systems for
native people, especially in cases where a sizable population could
be expected to maintain itself and benefit from literacy programs in
their native language. A writing system presupposes a phonemic
analysis.

4.11 PHONETICS

Anyone who has tried to use a dictionary that indicates pronunciation
of words by supplementing the original spelling with diacritics can
appreciate the simplicity of a phonetic alphabet. In a system using
diacritics, the same sound is usually represented by several different
letters (or combinations of letters), and each letter (or combination) is
used in various ways depending on the diacritic used with it. It is
much easier to see the one-to-one relationship between sound and
symbol in a phonetic alphabet.

The phonetic symbols introduced thus far are widely used, especially by American linguists. European linguists have usually preferred to stick closer to the system originally devised by the International Phonetic Association. But linguists using either system
generally adapt it to the needs of whatever language they are transcribing. Thus, [d] ordinarily represents a voiced alveolar stop. If
necessary to contrast this with a similar sound produced more forward
(i.e., in a dental position), a fronting diacritic can be added: [d̪]. If the
sound is produced farther back (i.e., in the palatal position), a backing
diacritic can be added: [d̠]. But in a language having only a dental
variant, the ordinary symbol [d] can be redefined as a dental and used
without a diacritic.

Figure 4–5 provides the basic framework for articulatory description of the sounds most commonly encountered in the world's languages. But since no language utilizes all possible sounds, linguists
tend to use a familiar symbol (often one available on a typewriter) for
unfamiliar sounds as long as no confusion will result. Thus, [d] is

likely to be used for either [ḍ] or [ḍ] as long as only one variety of *d* occurs in the language. Similarly, [r] is often used to represent a flapped *r* or trilled *r,* provided the language has only a single variety of *r.* For these reasons the student must pay close attention to the articulatory description accompanying the symbols used in any particular language.

FIGURE 4–5   Basic Consonant Chart

Articulation point / manner		Labial		Dental	Alveolar		Palatal	Velar	Uvular	Glottal
		bilabial	labio-dental							
Stops	*voiceless*	p	p̣	t̪	t		ṭ	k	q	ʔ
	voiced	b	ḅ	d̪	d		ḍ	g	ɢ	
Affricates	*voiceless*	pφ	pf	tθ	ƛ	c	č	kx	kx̣	
	voiced	bβ	bv	dð	λ	ʒ	ǰ	gɣ	gɣ̣	
Fricatives	*voiceless*	φ	f	θ	s		š	x	x̣	h
	voiced	β	v	ð	z		ž	ɣ	ɣ̣	ɦ
Nasals	*voiceless*	M	Ɱ	N̪	N		Ñ	Ŋ		
	voiced	m	ɱ	n̪	n		ñ	ŋ		
Laterals	*voiceless*				ɫ		ʎ̥	Ł		
	voiced				l		ʎ	L		
V o i c e d	*retroflex*				ɹ					
	trills				r̃				R	
	flap				ɾ					
	semi-vowels	w					y			

In describing the consonants of a language, the simplest approach usually is to construct a chart, such as Figure 4–5, and fill in the appropriate intersections as was done for the English consonants in Figure 4–2. But it is possible to use articulatory descriptions alone, as illustrated below:

ɸ	voiceless bilabial fricative
β	voiced bilabial fricative
x	voiceless velar fricative
ɣ	voiced velar fricative
q	voiceless uvular stop
ɢ	voiced uvular stop
ʔ	glottal stop (always voiceless; voicing would be a physical impossibility in this case)

For languages having voiceless nasals, semivowels, and laterals, capital letters are often used. If a language has only one variety of [r], the standard letter can be used. If a distinction must be made between variants, a capital and small letter can be used or various diacritics employed. Thus, if a language has only two laterals, one voiced and one voiceless, the simplest approach might be to use [l] and [L] respectively.

Most of the symbols in Figure 4–5 should be reasonably clear since their placement in the grid specifies both the point and manner of articulation. Note, however, that four alveolar affricates are listed. These differ in the manner of release. All four represent a series of stop plus fricative in which the stop is [t] or [d]. The symbols [ʎ] and [λ] represent the release as [ɫ] and [l]; the symbols [c] and [ʒ] represent the release as [s] and [z] respectively.

In some languages a rounding of the lips accompanies the stops [k, g] in such a way that the resulting labialized stops constitute units rather than sequences. These units are usually written [kʷ, gʷ], although some linguists find it more convenient to transcribe them as [kw, gw]. Similarly the aspiration following stops such as [t] may be transcribed either [tʰ] or [th]. Some languages, especially those of the Pacific Northwest of North America, have glottalized consonants—that is, consonants whose articulation is accompanied by simultaneous glottal closure. Such consonants are given a raised comma as a diacritic to denote glottalization: [k̓, č̓, ṅ] or [k', č', n'].

Most of the sounds discussed here do not occur in English, but they do occur frequently in the languages of Europe and other parts of the world. The sound [x], for example, occurred in Old English and Middle English and is found in modern German in words such as *Buch* [bux] 'book.' For most American speakers the glottal stop occurs as an allophone of /t/ in the pronunciation of words like *button* /bə́tən/, which is phonetically [bʌ́ʔn̩]. The diacritic under the *n* denotes that the nucleus of the syllable in this case is a consonant rather than a vowel.

It is possible to distinguish other variants of /t/ (§4.3), as in the pair *top* [tʰap] and *stop* [stap]. In this case the sound is aspirated in word initial position if immediately followed by a stressed vowel, but not aspirated in other environments. Since these variants are in com-plementary distribution, native speakers of English automatically re-gard them as belonging to the same structural unit—that is, they are regarded as allophones of a single phoneme.

Similar fine distinctions can be made for vowels, although, as we have already seen (§4.5), the essential structural distinctions in English can be represented by seven vowel symbols used in conjunc-tion with two semivowels that must be part of the consonant inventory anyway. Thirteen vowel symbols (the eleven in Figure 4–4 plus [ɨ] and [ʌ]) are sufficient for many languages. Some languages, how-ever, systematically distinguish between rounded and unrounded vowels. English has two rounded vowels /u, o/, with a total of four rounded allophones [u, ʊ, o, ɔ], but these vowels are part of a system in which the overall contrasts depend on tongue position rather than lip rounding or its absence. In languages where front vowels may be rounded as well as unrounded, the rounded variant may be given a special marking: [ï] or [ı]. If a similar contrast is required for back vowels, it is the unrounded variant that is given the special marking: [ü] or [ʉ]. This use of diacritics assumes that rounding is typical of back vowels and lack of rounding is typical for front vowels. Anything deviating from this pattern is treated as requiring special marking. Note that this scheme is different from the one to be described immediately below. The refinements of any notational system are like the ground rules of a game and may vary slightly from one playing field to another.

English has only oral vowels in its basic system. If a language has a contrast between oral vowels and nasalized vowels (i.e., vowels reso-nated through the nasal as well as the oral cavities), the nasalized variant can be given a special marking: [ã, ɔ̃], and so on.

Figure 4–6 provides the basic framework for analyzing the vowels of any language in terms of tongue height and advancement. It differs from Figure 4–4 by omitting *tense* as a distinctive feature since this feature is functional only in terms of the English vowel system.

The basic grid provides for seven degrees of tongue height, three degrees of tongue advancement, and two possible lip positions—forty-two vowel possibilities altogether. Only thirty intersections are ac-tually filled in Figure 4–6, providing in effect for only five degrees of tongue height. This allows a narrow enough transcription for most purposes. If finer discriminations are required, it is a simple matter to devise symbols for the unfilled intersections.

The empty square in the higher mid row can be filled by [ė]. The empty square in the lower low row can be filled by a small capital digraph [Æ]. The unfilled squares in the mid mid row are filled by variants of small capital *E* and the upper-case form of omega: [ɛ, Ω̇, Ω̣, Ë, Ω]. The unfilled squares in the higher low row are filled by variants of lower-case omega and digraph: [ö̇, ä̇, ω̇, ä, ω]. The student may find it helpful to add these symbols to Figure 4–6 using a colored pencil to distinguish them from the more commonly used vowel symbols.

FIGURE 4–6   **Basic Vowel Chart**

Lip rounding or unrounding			Tongue advancement				
			front		central		back	

Tongue height			U	R	U	R	U	R
high	higher	i	ü	ɨ	u̇	ï	u
	lower	ɪ	Ü	ɫ	U̇	Ï	ᴜ
mid	higher	e	ö		ȯ	ë	o
	mid			ə	˙		
	lower	ɛ	ɔ̈	ɜ	ɔ̇	ʌ	ɔ
low	higher	æ					
	lower		ɒ̈	a	ɒ̇	ɑ	ɒ

Certain symbols drawn from the International Phonetic Alphabet are preferred by some linguists over symbols presented in Figure 4–6:

Front rounded	Back unrounded	/r/-Sequences
ü = y	ï = ɯ	ɨr = ɚ
ö = ø		ɪ́r = ɝ
ɔ̈ = œ		ar = aɚ etc.

The best advice concerning symbols is to repeat what has already been said several times. The use of consonant and vowel symbols presented in this section is by no means uniform among linguists. The student must therefore be prepared to deal with new symbols whenever they are introduced and must pay careful attention to the articulatory description accompanying them.

4.12 PHONEMICS

As already noted, the interest of linguists in the late nineteenth century and early twentieth century was in narrow phonetic description. This was replaced after 1933 by an interest in describing sound systems in terms of their phonemic structure. To do this it remained necessary to first secure a narrow phonetic transcription and then systematize the notation by determining which phonetically similar sounds were in complementary distribution and could be construed as constituting a single unit. Phonemic analysis therefore became one of the chief goals of structural grammar between the years 1933 (publication of Bloomfield's *Language*) and 1957 (publication of Chomsky's *Syntactic Structures*).

   The following corpus (Bowen 1965) contains data from Tagalog, also known as Pilipino, one of many Austronesian languages spoken in the Philippines. The language has a large body of speakers and is used as an official national language. Vowel and consonant symbols are drawn from the lists presented in §4.11. Word stress is marked by an acute accent (´). Stress in Tagalog involves a lengthening of the stressed vowel, but without the heightened pitch associated with stress in English.

CORPUS 4–1   (Tagalog)

(1)	bátah	'bathrobe'	(12)	báta?	'child'
(2)	bátɪk	'spot'	(13)	bátɪ?	'greeting'
(3)	ʔɪtúro?	'point'	(14)	ʔʊmágah	'morning'
(4)	púno?	'chief'	(15)	ʔɪtóh	'this'
(5)	paʔálam	'good-bye'	(16)	táʔoh	'person'
(6)	húlah	'hula dance'	(17)	húla?	'prediction'
(7)	bágah	'ember'	(18)	bága?	'lung'
(8)	káhɪt	'although'	(19)	kahón	'box'
(9)	bʊkód	'separate'	(20)	takót	'frightened'
(10)	gahíh	'night'	(21)	hɪlɪ?	'a kind of fish'
(11)	túboh	'pipe'	(22)	pʊláh	'red'

We notice at once that phonetically similar back consonants [h, k, ?] are found in the data, and we must determine whether they occur in contrastive or complementary environments. Similarly, we may wonder about the status of phonetically similar pairs [i, ɪ] and [u, ʊ]. Since there is no way of knowing in advance what the relevant environment is likely to be in any given case, we must consider all possibilities. The most fruitful approach is to run through a checklist like the following:

	Occurs initially	*Occurs finally*	*Occurs medially*
[h]	yes	yes	yes
[k]	yes	yes	yes
[?]	yes	yes	yes

It appears that all three consonants occur in all environments without restriction. It is possible of course that the conditioning factor is not word position but rather an adjacent sound. However, a closer examination of each positional environment fails to produce evidence of such a pattern. In fact, a careful look at individual words shows that items 1 and 12 are a minimal pair establishing *h* and *?* as contrasting units. Several other minimal pairs for the *h/?* set occur in the data. Items 2 and 13 are a minimal pair for *k* and *?*. The data contains no minimal pair for *h* and *k,* but since these units occur in the same environments and each contrasts with *?,* it follows that they contrast with each other. The fact that *k* and *?* occur in the same environment can be established by taking items 8 and 20 to show that both sounds follow *a* and taking 19 and 20 to show that both sounds precede *o* in medial position. If sounds contrast in any one position, they must be regarded as potentially contrastive in all positions. Our conclusion is that all three consonants are independent phonemes.

In the case of phonetically similar vowels [i, ɪ] and [u, ʊ], we must pay special attention to possible conditioning factors in medial position. The checklist can therefore be constructed to pinpoint the relevant information:

	Occurs initially	*Occurs finally*	*Occurs medially*	*Occurs after*	*Occurs before*	*Attestation*
[i]	no	no	yes	h	h, l	10, 21
[ɪ]	no	no	yes	t, ?, h, l	k, t, ?	2, 3, 8, 13, 15, 21
[u]	no	no	yes	t, p, h	r, n, l, b	3, 4, 6, 11, 17
[ʊ]	no	no	yes	b, ?, p	k, m, l	9, 14, 22

Since no vowels occur in initial or final position, we are concerned only with medial position. Since all four phones occur in this position, it is evident that the conditioning environment cannot be stated in terms of word position alone. We notice that both [i] and [ɪ] occur after *h*. Each occurs before different sounds, but it is not clear whether this is significant or the result of chance in the compilation of a corpus containing only twenty-two items. In the cases of [u] and [ʊ], it appears that both phones occur after *p* and before *l*. If we look no farther, we might suppose that the phones contrast. At this point it is well to ask if any untested hypotheses remain. Since all words in the corpus contain either two or three syllables, we might consider whether occurrence in a particular syllable affects vowel quality. This apparently is not the case, as can be determined by comparing such items as 6 and 9 or 8 and 10.

The one factor that has not yet been considered is word stress. Each word has one stressed vowel, occurring in either the first or second syllable. The occurrence of stress is not predictable and must be specified in the transcription of each word. It happens that [i] and [u] are associated with stress; [ɪ] and [ʊ] are associated with the absence of stress. Since these are complementary environments, we can regard each pair as constituting a single phoneme with two allophones each:

/i/   [i]   occurring under stress
      [ɪ]   occurring elsewhere (i.e., not under stress)
/u/   [u]   occurring under stress
      [ʊ]   occurring elsewhere

The distributional pattern is straightforward enough that an experienced linguist would recognize it quickly without going through each step that has been described above. For the beginning linguist, a logical program is a necessity—just as it is for an experienced investigator dealing with a problem of great complexity. Linguistic analysis is largely a matter of hypothesis construction and testing. If the initial hypothesis fails to stand up, it must be replaced by a new hypothesis that can be tested in its turn, and so on until the investigator is finally satisfied. The investigator must always be open to the possibility that an expanded corpus will force revisions in the original hypothesis.

The form of phonetic transcription that is used by the field investigator can of course contribute to a solution or complicate the analysis. In Tagalog, stress is represented by a lengthening of the stressed vowel, a feature that can be indicated by placing a raised period after the vowel to denote length: $a\cdot$, $i\cdot$, and so on. (This notation is roughly equivalent to the use of a macron in Latin: $\bar{a}$, $\bar{\imath}$, etc.) A retranscription of items 8, 10, 17, and 22 focusing on length rather than stress would appear as follows:

(8) ka·hɪt   'although'   (17) hu·la?   'prediction'
(10) gahi·h 'night'   (22) pʊla·h   'red'

It is now clear that the phonetically higher vowel in each pair is associated with length, while the lower vowel is associated with the complementary environment of nonlength. The analysis remains the same, although the basis for it may be slightly different.

A listing of phonemes and the allophones associated with each, as given above, is typical of the descriptive statements used in structural grammar. The same distribution could be expressed in shorthand notation as follows:

/i/ → [ɪ]   / in unstressed syllables
/u/ → [ʊ]   / in unstressed syllables

Since the two patterns occur in the same environment, the statements can be consolidated by enclosing the parts that differ in brackets.

$$\begin{bmatrix} /i/ \\ /u/ \end{bmatrix} \rightarrow \begin{bmatrix} [\text{ɪ}] \\ [\text{ʊ}] \end{bmatrix} \quad / \text{ in unstressed syllables}$$

Use of this convention implies that the item on the first line to the left of the arrow is related to the item on the first line to the right of the arrow, and so forth. The convention differs from the use of braces, which was introduced in §4.4. Braces indicate a choice of items must be made; brackets serve to consolidate similar statements. Because this notation implies the conversion of phonemic units into phonetic units, the diagonals and brackets that enclose phonemes and phones respectively can be eliminated. The result is a reduction of visual clutter without material change in the statement itself:

$$\begin{bmatrix} i \\ u \end{bmatrix} \rightarrow \begin{bmatrix} \text{ɪ} \\ \text{ʊ} \end{bmatrix} \quad / \text{ in unstressed syllables}$$

Although the quasi-mathematical shorthand notation is usually associated with transformational grammar rather than structural grammar, it is important to recognize that it makes precisely the same distributional statement as a listing of phonemes and their allophones in ordinary prose. If the prose statement and notational statement differ at all, it is in their conception of the system they are describing, not their analysis of the data.

The prose statement is based on a static view of language. Phonemes are viewed as a significant structural unit having a number of allophones, each assigned its own place in the system and each having approximately the same status. The shorthand notation leans toward a more dynamic view of language. One allophone is taken as basic, and the other is seen as a contextual variant. Relatively little attention is given to the status of the phoneme as such.

Whether the two viewpoints are to be regarded as diametrically opposed or as only slightly different but fully equivalent ways of looking at the same thing is largely a matter of taste. This ultimately becomes a question of what one happens to believe about the nature of language. Structural linguists vacillated between the two approaches, but for the most part they leaned toward a static view of language.

Sapir's view of language had been dynamic, but in the 1920s and 1930s, when he was active, the shorthand notation used for describing language in dynamic terms had not been developed. Sapir's prose descriptions of language were dynamic in their orientation, but the prevailing fashion was to focus on synchronic studies, and the methodology developed for synchronic analysis tended toward the static approach.

The most influential figure of the period was Leonard Bloomfield, whose book *Language* (1933) gave a precise definition of the phoneme and stimulated synchronic studies aimed at describing languages in terms of the phoneme and similar structural units. Bloomfield himself was aware of both the static and dynamic aspects of language, but linguists who followed him tended to focus exclusively on the static aspects. It is noteworthy that Bloomfield studied historical linguistics in Germany under the leading neogrammarians of the day. His concept of the phoneme as a set of phonetically similar units in complementary distribution is essentially the same as the concept developed earlier in historical grammar to classify the distribution of correspondence sets.

In historical grammar the relevant sets are matchings drawn from two or more languages. In phonemic analysis the relevant sets are individual phones occurring in a single language. The distributional analysis is the same in either case.

4.13 MORPHEMICS

The phonemes of a language can be taken as the basic building blocks. But since phonemes by themselves convey no meaning, it is customary to define an additional level of structure consisting of **morphemes**, units associated with meaning and consisting of various arrangements of previously defined phonemes. To examine the procedure for identifying morphemes, we turn to an example from Kongo (Bentley 1967), a member of the Bantu subfamily of the Congo-Kordofanian languages spoken in Africa. The transcription is phonemic.

CORPUS 4–2   **(Kongo)**

bakama	'to get caught'	mbakami	'one who is caught'
boŋga	'to bring'	mboŋgi	'one who fetches'
vaŋga	'to make'	mvaŋgi	'maker'
kaya	'to distribute'	ŋkayi	'a generous person'
kiya	'to travel'	ŋkiyi	'traveler'
kumba	'to slander'	ŋkumbi	'slanderer'
landa	'to follow'	nlandi	'follower'
leŋga	'to flatter'	nleŋgi	'flatterer'
sumba	'to buy'	nsumbi	'buyer'
taŋga	'to learn'	ntaŋgi	'student'

The forms in column one appear to be the basic units out of which those in column two are built. Each form in column one seems to be a verb, while those in column two are apparently nouns formed from the verbs. If we disregard the final vowel in both columns for the time being, we can say that the nouns in column two are formed from the verbs in column one by the prefixation of a nasal phoneme, either /m-/, /ŋ-/, or /n-/. Since this prefix represents a unit of meaning (i.e., 'one who performs the action specified by the related verb'), each phone is a **morph.** Each morph is an **allomorph** of the morpheme identified with the meaning that each allomorph represents. The allomorphs in this case are phonologically conditioned—that is, each occurs in a phonological environment that is complementary to the environments occupied by the co-allomorphs. The allomorph /m-/ occurs before labials; the allomorph /ŋ-/ occurs before velars; the allomorph /n-/ occurs elsewhere. Thus, a morpheme is a set of morphs that are associated with the same meaning and that occur in complementary distribution. At the level of meaning, the concepts of morph, allomorph, and morpheme are exact parallels of the concepts of phone, allophone, and phoneme, which apply at the phonological level.

The material, of course, is more complicated than the analysis thus far would indicate. Since the final vowel differs in the verb set and noun set, we are forced to say that the verb morpheme (i.e., the verb root) consists of the forms in column one, without the final vowel included. Thus, /bakam-/ is the morpheme meaning 'get caught,' /boŋg-/ is the morpheme meaning 'bring,' and so forth. The final vowel in column one /-a/ appears, on the basis of this corpus at least, to be an infinitive marker. We can therefore classify it as a **function morpheme,** distinguishing it from a **content morpheme** such as /boŋg-/, which is associated with lexical content rather than a grammatical function:

/boŋg-/ 'bring' /-a/ 'INFINITIVE'

It is sometimes convenient to gloss content morphemes using small letters and function morphemes using small capitals, but the practice is by no means uniform among linguists.

The one remaining morpheme is /-i/, which occurs along with the nasal prefix to mark derived nouns. On the basis of the data at hand, it appears that the nasal prefix and the /-i/ suffix together constitute a discontinuous morpheme that we might label 'NOMINALIZER.' However, it is probable that an expanded corpus would provide evidence for associating each morph with a separate meaning not discernible from the limited data presented here. A reminder is in order that the analysis must always be considered tentative until all available data has been accounted for and each part of the analysis is consistent with every other part. The remarks on linguistic analysis as hypothesis construction, made in connection with phonemics, apply here as well. A small corpus, carefully selected to illustrate a particular phonological or morphological pattern, is bound to yield an incomplete, and therefore distorted, view of the complete language.

To recapitulate, we can say that the data in Corpus 4–2 consists of a number of morphemes used as verb roots: /bakam-/ 'get caught,' /boŋg-/ 'bring,' and so on. Each morpheme has an invariable form, which is to say that each consists of a single allomorph, namely itself. There is an infinitive marker /-a/, which happens to consist of a single phoneme. The number of phonemes in a morpheme is immaterial, but note the importance of clearly identifying the structural level that is being analyzed: The same unit may be either a phoneme or morpheme depending on whether its phonological or morphological status is being considered. The morpheme /-a/, like the verb roots, has only one allomorph. The nasal prefix, which marks derived nouns, has three allomorphs: /m-/ before labials, /ŋ-/ before velars, and /n-/ elsewhere. Finally there is the morpheme /-i/, which accompanies the nasal prefix and has but a single allomorph.

In the foregoing discussion we have followed what is now the prevailing practice of citing morphemes in their phonemic transcription and using hyphens to mark morpheme boundaries. Many structuralists have preferred to use braces to enclose morphemes and diagonals to enclose individual allomorphs. Such a practice would entail citation of the morpheme {bakam-} and its one allomorph /bakam-/, the morpheme {N-} and its three allomorphs /m-, ŋ-, n-/, and so forth. Capital letters are commonly used as cover symbols for a set of phonologically conditioned allomorphs. The use of braces requires an additional bit of notational apparatus that can be omitted without ambiguity. Its use served nicely to emphasize the parallelism between morpheme and allomorph at one level of analysis and phoneme and allophone at another. Braces are found in grammatical sketches published through the 1950s and occasionally since then.

4.14 ENGLISH PLURALS

Disregarding irregular plurals, we can say that the English plural morpheme has three allomorphs: /-z, -s, -əz/ as in /glæsəz, geymz, kæts/. We can regard this data as the nucleus of a corpus that would enable us to make a comprehensive statement about the distribution of these allomorphs in English.

Analysis of the corpus involves collecting and arranging data so that it takes on the appearance of data problems that have been presented earlier. It may seem strange at first to solve a problem by constructing a problem, but the simple fact is that identification of a problem, arrangement of the data to form a pattern, and solution of the problem are inseparable. This is why linguists are constantly shuffling their data, literally or figuratively. The intention is always to consider the data from some new angle that will lead to a better interpretation of it.

Words chosen to illustrate distribution of the plural allomorphs are transcribed below using the phonemic system presented in §4.2 and §4.5.

s	/glǽsəz/	p	/mæps/	b	/slæbz/	ŋ	/soŋz/
z	/rówzəz/	t	/hæts/	d	/bidz/	l	/holz/
š	/díšəz/	k	/strayks/	g	/pigz/	r	/barz/
ž	/gərážəz/	f	/klifs/	v	/gruwvz/	w	/šuwz/
č	/čə́rčəz/	θ	/miθs/	ð	/leyðz/	y	/boyz/
ǰ	/ǰə́ǰəz/			m	/ruwmz/	o	/soz/
				n	/rənz/	a	/spaz/

Familiar words have a way of appearing quite strange in transcription, but it is important to use the system until one is able to think in terms of sounds automatically.

In the first column are arranged words that take the /-əz/ allomorph. These words end in sibilants, a small class of sounds having an *s* quality. Since some of these are affricates and some are fricatives and since the point of articulation is either alveolar or palatal, there is no way to list these sounds in terms of a natural class short of listing the six phonemes individually.

In the second column are found words that take the /-s/ allomorph. It happens that these words involve fewer actual phonemes than the first group, but it is fairly easy to describe this group as a natural class since it consists of all voiceless sounds not already listed. We therefore conclude that this environment is less restricted (i.e., less specialized, therefore more general) than the first group.

The remaining two columns contain words that take the /-z/ allomorph. This is by far the largest group. It happens that the words in this group end with voiced sounds not included in the first group, but it is not even necessary to specify this detail. We can simply say that this allomorph occurs elsewhere—that is, following all sounds not previously mentioned. The sounds left over at this point are all voiced, but they include many different sound types—stops, fricatives, nasals, lateral, retroflex, semivowels, and two vowels. Semivowels occur in word final position because they follow tense vowels and form glides with certain nontense vowels. This means that tense vowels themselves can never occur in word final position. Nontense /a/ is rare in final position and so is /o/, where it of course is phonetically [ɔ]. Other nontense vowels do not occur in word final position at all. At least this is true if we exclude marginal words, such as pause filler *huh* /hə/, and a few onomatopoeic words ending in /æ/, such as *baa*

/bæ/. Nor does the consonant /h/ occur in word final position. These gaps account for the presence of twenty-five rather than thirty-one sounds illustrated above.

To sum up, we can state the distribution of the plural morpheme in English in the following terms:

/-əz/   occurs after words ending in /s, z, š, ž, č, ǰ/
/-s/   occurs after words ending in voiceless sounds not included above
/-z/   occurs elsewhere

This is the kind of statement favored in structural grammars. It neatly accounts for the data. It has predictive power in the sense that it will apply to additional forms, including nonsense words, not included in the original data corpus. There is a parallelism between the kinds of statements that can be made about phonemes and their allophones and the kinds of statements that can be made about morphemes and their allomorphs.

In the foregoing we have another example of allomorphs whose distribution is **phonologically conditioned.** If we included irregular plural formations, we would quickly discover that a number of additional allomorphs of the English plural suffix are **morphologically conditioned.** That is, their distribution is determined not by a phonological environment but must be stated in terms of a morphological environment. For example, the plural suffix /-ən/ is restricted to three words: *child, ox,* and *brother.* It remains strong in the first, a word of everyday usage, and has been preserved in the second mainly because oxen were important draft animals until quite recently. The third form, *brethren* (which occurs with a special allomorph of the morpheme 'brother'), exists alongside the regular formation *brothers.* The two are complementary since the /-ən/ formation occurs in the context of religious or fraternal organizations, while the regular formation occurs elsewhere.

A complete listing of other irregular plural morphs would show that they are also morphologically conditioned. The list would include a number of replacives, at least one suppletive, and a zero allomorph. A **replacive** is a morph that occurs not as an affix but as a replacement for some part of the morph undergoing modification. Thus, the singular/plural set *man/men* involves the replacive morph /æ → e/, which can also be symbolized /(æ) → e/ or /e ← (æ)/. Comparable replacives are found in *goose/geese, mouse/mice,* and the like. **Suppletives,** as the name implies, occur in the process of suppletion, the replacement of an entire morph by another morph unrelated in form. For some speakers *people* is a suppletive plural for *person.* Suppletives are perhaps more common in verbs (*went* as the past of *go*) and adjectives (*better* and *best* as the comparative and superlative of *good*). A **zero morph** is the significant absence of an overt form—

that is, a null element that occurs in a paradigm where it must be classed as an allomorph of some morpheme having overt properties:

dog	cat	deer	sheep
dog-s	cat-s	deer-∅	sheep-∅

4.15 DERIVATION AND INFLECTION

Analysis of derivational morphology (§2.10) was an important element in traditional grammar. Derivational morphology was of interest to historical linguists because semantically similar affixes exhibiting sound correspondences provide strong evidence for genetic relationships among languages, and because similarities of this type are not likely to result by chance or even from borrowings. However, the development of one form from an earlier form (or a succession of earlier forms) is also called derivation, and it was the tracing of this kind of derivation that actually received more attention in historical linguistics.

Structural grammar inherited an interest in phonology from historical linguistics and combined this with an interest in word morphology that differed from traditional grammar only in detail. The morpheme was defined as the formal unit, and the traditional distinction between derivational and inflectional morphology was embraced almost without change. Derivational affixation involves the conversion of a form belonging to one class into a form belonging to a different class—for example, conversion of the verb *run* into the noun *runner.* Inflectional affixation involves a modification without changing from one form class to another—for example, inflection of the singular noun *bird* as the plural *birds* or inflection of the unmarked verb *stop* for past tense *stopped.*

Derivational affixes typically form an inner layer of affixation, while inflectional affixes form an outer layer. Thus, the English adjective /æktiv/ forms the derived verb /æktiv-eyt/, which is then inflected in the usual manner: /æktiv-eyt-s, æktiv-eyt-əd/. The inflectional pattern remains the same for the related derived negative: /diy-æktiv-eyt/. The verb /rən/, mentioned above, yields the derived noun /rən-ər/, which takes the usual plural inflection: /rən-ər-z/. Similarly we can say that the form /beys-rən-ər/ is derived by compounding the nouns /beys/ and /rən- ər/. The derived compound is then treated inflectionally like any other noun: /beys-rən-ər-z/. In general the derivational patterns of a language tend toward diversity, while the inflectional patterns tend toward regularity.

In Malecite-Passamaquoddy, an Algonkian language spoken in New Brunswick, Canada (Teeter 1971:213), a series of derivational affixes can be described as forming an inner layer, while a number of inflectional affixes form an outer layer:

```
n-tə-lap-əm-ək-w-ən-en-ol
|  1  2  3  4  | | | |
6  ‾‾‾‾‾‾‾     7 8 9 10
       5
```

The morphemes can be described as follows: (1) semantically empty morph required in a particular phonological environment; (2) verb root 'look'; (3) derivational affix denoting the formation of a transitive verb involving an animate participant; (4) derivational affix denoting that the flow of action is from suffix to prefix rather than from prefix to suffix; (5) verb stem incorporating the foregoing meanings; (6) inflectional prefix denoting first person; (7) inflectional suffix denoting third person; (8) inflectional suffix denoting that the preceding morpheme refers to an inanimate entity; (9) inflectional suffix that pluralizes the prefix; (10) inflectional suffix that pluralizes the first of the suffixes. The complete word means 'they (inanimate) look at us (not including the listener or listeners),' a statement that might be made with reference to inanimate devices such as cameras.

Derivational and inflectional morphology can of course be distinguished on the basis of function alone when the two types of affixation occur without layering. This is clearly seen in Tzeltal (Slocum 1948), a Mayan language spoken in Central America.

CORPUS 4–3   (Tzeltal)

(1) -šiw   'be afraid'   (VERB)
(2) -yakub   'get drunk'   (VERB)
(3) šiw-el   'fright'   (NOUN)
(4) yakub-el   'drunkenness'   (NOUN)
(5) ʔinam   'wife'   (NOUN)
(6) mamlal   'husband'   (NOUN)
(7) aw-inam   'your wife'   (NOUN)
(8) a-mamlal   'your husband'   (NOUN)
(9) lah   'end'   (NOUN)
(10) -lah-in   'finish'   (VERB)
(11) -ʔinam-in   'take a wife'   (VERB)
(12) ya h-lah-in   'I finish'   (PRONOUN + VERB)
(13) ya k-inam-in   'I take a wife'   (PRONOUN + VERB)

The corpus can be described as consisting of nine morphemes: two verbs, two nouns, one pronoun, and four affixes. The verbs are /-šiw/ 'be afraid' and /-yakub/ 'get drunk,' each having a single allomorph. The nouns are /ʔinam/ 'wife' and /mamlal/ 'husband.' The former has allomorphs /ʔinam/ occurring in initial position and /inam/ occurring in noninitial position, while the latter has but one allomorph. The pronoun is /ya/ 'I.' The affixes include two derivational suffixes /-el/ 'NOMINALIZER' and /-in/ 'VERBALIZER' along with two inflectional prefixes /AW-/ 'your' and /K-/ 'I.' The inflectional affixes consist of two

allomorphs each: /aw-/ occurs before vowels and /a-/ before consonants; in parallel manner /k-/ occurs before vowels and /h-/ before
consonants.

To present a morpheme inventory like the foregoing is to make certain implicit statements about productive grammatical patterns as
well. A nominalizing suffix presumably must be attached to verb roots,
and a verbalizing suffix presumably must be attached to noun roots.
If there are restrictions on the class of noun or verb roots with which
these affixes may occur, the restrictions must be included somewhere
in the statement. Similarly, the listing of inflectional prefixes implies
rules for inflection. These are fairly straightforward matters that are
specified as a by-product of listing the morphemes and describing the
distribution of allomorphs.

The analysis, however, remains unsatisfactory in two respects. One
problem has to do with the scheme for describing allomorphs, and the
other has to do with syntax. Both are important enough to receive additional discussion. Each in its own way contributed to the development
of transformational grammar, the subject of the next chapter.

4.16 MORPHOPHONEMIC VARIATION

In listing the morphemes occurring in Corpus 4–3, it was necessary to
include the allomorphs of each morpheme. For morphemes having a
single allomorph, the listing of allomorphs amounted to a perfunctory
statement that the morpheme in question had but one allomorph. For
morphemes having more than a single allomorph, two approaches are
possible. Both were in fact used in describing the corpus.

In one instance it was convenient to speak of the morpheme
/ʔinam/ 'wife' as having allomorphs /ʔinam/ in initial position and
/inam/ in noninitial position. The description selects one form as
"basic" and describes allomorphs as either preserving the basic form
or deviating from it in some particular. In another instance it seemed
convenient to speak of the morpheme /K-/ 'I' with allomorphs /k-/ before vowels and /h-/ before consonants. In this case a nonoccurring
abstraction /K-/ is selected as a cover symbol and the allomorphs that
actually occur are treated as derived from it in specified environments.
Another possible way of describing the morpheme would be to list it
as /k- ~ h-/ and explain the distribution of the two allomorphs in an
auxiliary statement. The linguistic facts are reasonably clear; the problem is finding the best way to describe the facts.

Variation of the phonemes within a morpheme can be called **morphophonemic variation.** (The term as used in structural grammar takes
on a rather broad meaning, quite different from the use of this term as
redefined in §7.20.) A morphemic description assumes the availability
of a phonemic analysis so that morphemes can be described as composed of these predefined units. Moreover, since phonemes and mor-

phemes belong to separate levels of analysis, it is possible for two units to contrast as phonemes and yet be complementary as morphemes. This is true of the phonemes /s/ and /z/ in English (*Sue/zoo*), which are complementary as allomorphs of 'PLURAL': /-s ~ -z/ (*hat-s, bag-z*). Phonemes and morphemes are seen as units of a different kind and subject to different rules of arrangement.

In historical grammar a conflict of this type would be resolved by internal reconstruction—a possibility to which we shall return in later chapters. In structural grammar, with its emphasis on synchronic analysis, it was enough to identify the relevant structures at each level of analysis. Historical statements were regarded as out of place, and indeed, any description that relied on underlying forms and process rules for converting these to actually occurring forms was regarded as suspect. Language was viewed as consisting of static units or, rather, sets of units—phonemes and morphemes—and rules for selecting and arranging these units. Since grammatical description was seen as consisting of units and rules for arranging these units, the descriptive approach was often called the **item-and-arrangement model** of language description.

However, language developed for purposes of communication, not for the convenience of linguists. And in its changes through time, language invariably develops phonological alternations that require some kind of dynamic descriptive statement. In the item-and-arrangement approach, data such as that presented in §3.11 could still be described in terms of allomorphs:

/wayf-/   occurs before 'SINGULAR'
/wayv-/   occurs before 'PLURAL'

This statement would take priority over the description of plural allomorphs since the allomorph /-z/ would be assigned to the allomorph /wayv-/ made available by this statement. In other words, assignment of the appropriate plural allomorph depends on the availability of the appropriate allomorph of the noun itself.

Thus, each allomorph is actually dependent on the other. This can be viewed either as circularity or as a tidy example of the interdependence of linguistic units. In structural linguistics it was of course given the latter interpretation. The system was workable, and in many respects the years from 1933 to 1957 look like a remarkably stable period in which all linguists held a common point of view and used the same analytical approach. This is largely an illusion. The developments in linguistics since 1957 have been so profound that, in comparison, the issues that divided linguists in the 1930s, 1940s, and 1950s seem less controversial; and the earlier era looks deceptively uniform. This appearance is reinforced by the practice of labeling the principal approach to grammar since 1957 as transformational grammar and designating the earlier approach structural grammar. In actual fact the unresolved issues of structural grammar were simply attacked from a different angle in transformational grammar. The individual points of difference between the two schools are quite small, but added together the differences have amounted to a major shift in the tradition of grammatical analysis.

4.17 SYNTAX

In principle, the item-and-arrangement model of structural grammar can provide a comprehensive description of any language. Phones are classified into phonemes. These basic units are arranged to form morphemes, and these in turn are arranged to form words. Once words are described, it is a simple matter, in principle, to state the rules for arranging words to form sentences. A simple matter, that is, until one starts to do it. In practice the variety of sentence patterns occurring in any language has seemed to defy exhaustive description.

In Corpus 4–3 we had only two examples of constructions involving more than a single word:

/ya h-lah-in/ 'I finish' (PRONOUN + VERB)
/ya k-inam-in/ 'I take a wife' (PRONOUN + VERB)

It is evident that we have here an example of a subject + predicate construction constituting a possible sentence pattern in the language. The arrangement of words to form sentences is traditionally termed **syntax,** and the relevant descriptive units at this level can be termed syntagmemes or simply **tagmemes.**

A tagmeme is a unit of grammatical arrangement that can be described in terms of **slots,** that is, grammatical functions or positions within a sentence, and **fillers,** the class of items grammatically acceptable in each slot. For the Tzeltal examples cited above, we might say that a sentence or clause (C) consists of a subject (S) and predicate (P). The subject slot may be filled by a pronoun (pr) and the predicate by a verb (v). A verb in turn may consist of a personal prefix (p) and a verb stem (St), which in turn may consist of a noun root (R) and a verbalizing suffix (s). These relationships can be expressed by a series of formulas:

C = +S:pr +P:v
v = +pSt
St = ±Rs

The equal sign denotes that the units that follow comprise the unit to the left of the sign. A colon denotes the class of fillers that occupies the slot identified to the left of the colon. Symbols for slots and fillers can be devised as appropriate for the morphological and syntactic categories of each language. Obligatory categories can be marked by a plus sign, and optional categories can be marked by a plus-or-minus sign (±). Variations of the basic system can easily be imagined. For a language having numerous verbal affixes, it might be convenient to devise a formula for verbs that would include numbers to differentiate the various affix positions:

V-1-2-3-4 . . . n

Such a scheme was in fact used by Bloomfield (1962, 1958) in his descriptions of Menomini and Eastern Ojibwa.

The system is well suited for describing morphology, and it is adequate for describing syntactic patterns that have been identified in data the linguist has collected. But the scheme is incapable of going beyond the immediate corpus. In the Tzeltal example we can determine only that the subject slot may be filled by a pronoun. If an expanded corpus shows that this slot can also be filled by nouns, we must either revise the original statement, formulate an additional statement, or somehow redefine nouns and pronouns so that both are members of some larger class that can be taken as filler for the subject slot.

Because of the great variety of alternative patterns available in the syntax of most languages, any system of tagmemic notation quickly becomes quite complex. The question of course is not really the complexity of the descriptive system as such. If a language has complexities, a description of it will also have complexities. The problem therefore is to find a way to describe syntactic structures so that systematic patterns are discernible in the maze of variety that engulfs the investigator.

Although many structuralists have approached syntax in terms of tagmemic description, it has often seemed just as reasonable to offer a simple description of a few typical sentence patterns, either in formulaic notation or in ordinary prose augmented perhaps with diagrams of one kind or another. A few examples, often in the form of a sample text, have served to illustrate the most common sentence types. The goal has been to exemplify the typical rather than to provide an exhaustive account of all possible sentence types. The typical grammar has usually contained a listing of phonemes, an extensive discussion of morphology, and a mere hint of syntax. The notion that an exhaustive account of syntax was even attainable did not come until publication of Chomsky's *Syntactic Structures* in 1957. But when it came, it arrived with a kind of revolutionary impact that quickly eclipsed structuralism and gave rise to a new school scorning the work of structuralists and asserting for itself an exclusive claim to scientific methodology. This twentieth-century *Junggrammatiker* movement, led by Noam Chomsky, became known as transformational grammar.

summary

Nineteenth-century insights into the nature of language as a dynamic system gave rise in the twentieth century to an analytical approach that emphasized the study of individual languages at a single point in time as self-contained structural systems. The distributional analysis of correspondence sets was replaced by the distributional analysis of individual phones within a language. Phonetically similar sounds that occur in complementary environments are classed as allophones of the same structural unit, the phoneme. Phonetically similar sounds that occur in the same environment without affecting word meaning are classed as free variants of the same phoneme. Sounds that occur in the same environment and are related to differences in word meaning are classed as different phonemes.

The morpheme is a structural unit parallel to the phoneme except that the morpheme is a unit of meaning rather than a unit of sound. Morphs associated with the same meaning but occurring in complementary environments are classed as allomorphs of the same morpheme. Allomorphs may be conditioned by phonological environments or by the co-occurrence of another morpheme on which they are dependent. Content morphemes are associated with lexical meaning, such as /buk/ 'book,' while function morphemes are associated with grammatical functions, such as /-z, -s, -əz/ 'PLURAL.'

In structural grammar, distributional analysis is used to define phonemes, which are taken as the basic building blocks. Phonemes are arranged to form morphs, and distributional analysis at this level yields the morphemes of the language. The morphemes in turn constitute items that can be arranged to form words and ultimately sentences. These larger structures can be described as consisting of tagmemes, slots that can be filled by specified classes of morphemes.

further reading

Primary sources: Boas 1911, Saussure 1959, Sapir 1921, Bloomfield 1933, Bloch and Trager 1942, Fries 1952, Harris 1951, Joos 1958. **Secondary sources:** Wells 1947a, Whitehall 1951, Hockett 1958, Francis 1958, Gleason 1961, Landar 1966, Leichty 1964. **4.1** Anttila 1970 (Chap. 12). **4.2** Trager and Smith 1951. **4.3** O'Conner 1973. **4.4** Trager and Smith 1951. **4.5** Trager and Smith 1951. **4.6** Whitehall 1951, Trager and Smith 1951. **4.7** Dineen 1967. **4.8** Saussure 1959. **4.9** Sapir 1921, 1925, 1949. **4.10** Boas 1911. **4.11** Pike 1943, O'Conner 1973. **4.12** Bloomfield 1933, Pike 1947b, 1948, B. Bloch 1948, Bowen 1965. **4.13** Bloomfield 1933, Nida 1946, Bentley 1967. **4.14** Gleason 1961. **4.15** Slocum 1948, Teeter 1971. **4.16** Harris 1942, Hockett 1947, 1954b. **4.17** Bloomfield 1933, Elson and Pickett 1960, Longacre 1964, Pike 1967, Cook 1969, Brend 1973.

(5) transformational grammar

5.1 STATUS OF THE MORPHEME

Once the phoneme is defined as the minimal structural unit of a language, it is available as a building block for use in forming larger units. We have already seen how morphemes can be described as composed of phonemes. Morphemes in turn can combine to form words. The logical next step is to think of larger units as composed of words. The units at this next level of analysis are phrases, clauses, and sentences.

In principle there should be no difficulty in moving on to this level. In practice, however, there are several serious obstacles to describing language at the sentence level. The most serious is the inescapable fact that morphemes and phonemes behave in significantly different ways in spite of their seeming parallelism. The allophones of a phoneme never contrast. Thus, in English [t] and [tʰ] are allophones of /t/; each occurs in its own characteristic environment and never contrasts with the other. The phonemes /s/ and /z/, however, are contrasting units and occur in the same environments, accounting for the difference in a pair such as /rays, rayz/ 'rice, rise.' But as allomorphs of 'PLURAL' these normally contrasting phonemes are in complementary distribution, as in /buk-s, boy-z/ 'books, boys.'

Since the morpheme is by definition a unit of meaning, each allomorph of a morpheme has the same meaning. Thus, the morpheme has an extra dimension, a constant factor, that is lacking in the phoneme. The allophones of a phoneme are not associated with any similar constant value. Each allophone counts as the same structural unit: the phoneme. But this structural unit has significance only as it enters into a pattern of contrasts with other phonemes in the structural system. It is not a token of something outside the system, as is the case with a morpheme.

The central problem in dealing with morphemes is the phonemic variation that occurs in allomorphs of a morpheme. The most efficient communication system would have a one-to-one relationship between meaning and form, but in actual practice the relation is often one-to-many or many-to-one:

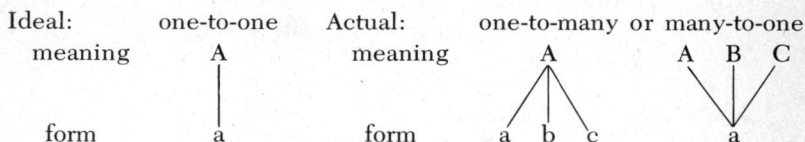

Ideal:	one-to-one	Actual:	one-to-many	or	many-to-one
meaning	A	meaning	A		A B C
			/\		|/
form	a	form	a b c		a

The vast majority of meanings stand in a one-to-one relationship with the forms that express them. The meaning 'house' is represented by the word /haws/, the meaning 'rose' by /rowz/, and so forth. A familiar example of the one-to-many relationship between meaning and form is 'PLURAL,' represented as /-z, -s, -əz/. An example of a many-to-one relationship would be the meanings 'vane,' 'vein,' and 'vain,' all expressed as /veyn/.

Many-to-one relationships have seldom been regarded as a problem: homophony need not prevent the homophonous forms from being regarded as different morphemes. Nor do one-to-one relationships present a problem. But when different forms associated with the same meaning occur, each must be regarded as an allomorph of the same morpheme—even if the difference among allomorphs is great enough to constitute a structural difference at the phonemic level. Such is the case with the allomorphs of 'PLURAL.'

In structural grammar, problems of this sort were most commonly handled in terms of the distribution of allomorphs—an approach discussed in the preceding chapter. But there was a second approach that also developed within the framework of structural grammar. In this approach allomorphic variation was treated under the heading of **morphophonemics,** and morphemes whose phonetic make-up varied to the point of involving replacement of one phoneme by another were said to exhibit morphophonemic variation, or **alternation.** The process of morphophonemic alternation is essentially dynamic in character. The variants /-z, -s, -əz/ exist side by side in modern English, and efforts to describe their distribution in static item-and-arrangement terms can scarcely hide the dynamic process by which a single unit of meaning has three different manifestations. One can treat this as a matter of the distribution of variants, but to do so leaves basic questions unanswered. What is the difference, if any, between a statement describing the distribution of variants and a statement describing the process of converting a single underlying form into two or more actually occurring forms?

5.2   MORPHOPHONEMIC ANALYSIS

One method devised by structural linguists to handle morphophonemic variation by means of distributional statements was to posit morphophonemic units that were like phonemes but that had the property of encompassing two different phonemes in different morphological environments. Thus, the stem *wife* could be transcribed /wayF/. The unit /F/, which contrasted with both /f/ and /v/, required a special statement:

$$F \rightarrow \begin{Bmatrix} \text{v} & / & \text{before 'PLURAL'} \\ \text{f} & / & \text{elsewhere} \end{Bmatrix}$$

At the same time 'PLURAL' was designated as /-Z/ and was accompanied by a descriptive statement of the form:

$$Z \rightarrow \begin{Bmatrix} \text{-əz} & / & \text{following s, z, š, ž, č, ǰ} \\ \text{-s} & / & \text{following other voiceless sounds} \\ \text{-z} & / & \text{elsewhere} \end{Bmatrix}$$

To define the above as statements of distribution does little to disguise their process function. These are still process statements, of course, but they were accepted as compatible with the overall item-and-arrangement approach of structural grammar. A form like /wayF/ clearly contrasts with forms like

    /klif/   'cliff'
    /gruwv/ 'groove'

since these stems remain the same in singular and plural. The contrast between alternating /F/ and nonalternating /f/ and /v/ could be incorporated in the grammar—but at the cost of adding another unit to the inventory of phonemes. This unit, /F/, was called a **morphophoneme** because of its special status. Structurally a morphophoneme can be described as a set of phonemes in complementary distribution —an approach that emphasizes the parallelism with other structural units like the phoneme and morpheme.

The alternative would have been to take either /wayf/ or /wayv/ as the basic variant and accompany it by a statement describing its alternation—too patently a process approach to be acceptable in structural grammar.

5.3   SYNCHRONIC CONSEQUENCES OF DIACHRONIC CHANGE

At this point it is appropriate to ask just why a language tolerates irregularities of the type we have been discussing. The answer should already be clear from the discussion of historical linguistics in Chapter 3. Languages change through time. The change takes place slowly enough that speakers are seldom conscious of significant change from one generation to the next, but the cumulative results are great enough that after the passage of a thousand years speakers of a language would not be able to communicate with other speakers of the "same" language if some mystical time machine could bring them together.

One result is that the optimal one-to-one relationship between meaning and form is frequently converted to a one-to-many relationship. This is not the only kind of change, but it is one of the most convenient to study because it lends itself readily to analysis by internal reconstruction. We will return to this in a moment.

While historical changes often lead from a one-to-one to a one-to-many relationship between meaning and form, this is frequently offset by a countervailing tendency to restore the ideal one-to-one relationship. This can be done either by eliminating all but one variant or by associating different variants with slightly different meanings so that a new one-to-one relationship emerges.

It would be a mistake to assume that any language was completely regular at some point in the remote past and that it developed all irregularities after that time. All known languages contain some irregularities such as morphophonemic variation. Some of these irregularities are eliminated through time, but new ones arise elsewhere in the language. Thus, there is an ongoing tug of war with forces on one side pulling toward greater variation and forces on the other pulling toward greater regularity. Undoubtedly this has been the situation as long as humanity has had language.

If we apply internal reconstruction to the allomorphs of 'PLURAL' in English, we attempt to show that these three members of a set expressing a single meaning can also be shown to have developed from a single form. In the case of English, the writing system, which tends to be more conservative than actual pronunciation, provides additional evidence that the variation between /s/ and /z/ in 'PLURAL' is nondistinctive. The writing system points toward some form of *s* as the earlier variant of the modern plural suffix, and this hypothesis is supported by the fact that in another case we have examined—the *f*/*v* alternation in words like *wife*—it was the voiceless fricative that was taken as the underlying form.

We must still ask whether the earlier form of 'PLURAL' contained ə, which was lost in certain environments, or whether this was originally lacking and was later inserted in certain environments. The difficulty of pronouncing a sequence consisting of a sibilant followed by /s/ or a sequence consisting of a voiced consonant followed by /s/ suggests that /ə/ must have been present at the outset. We can therefore say that the protoform for 'PLURAL' was *əs, and we can say that the modern allomorphs developed because of the following sound changes:

(1)   ə > Ø / after all sounds except s, z, š, ž, č, ǰ
(2)   s > z / after voiced sounds

We can show the derivation of modern forms from presumed earlier forms in the following way:

Protoform	*glæ-əs	*dog-əs	*buk-əs
step 1:	——	dogs	buks
step 2:	glæsəz	dogz	——
Modern form	glæsəz	dogz	buks

Notice that, as before, we must assume the changes took place in the specified order. If the order of these sound changes were reversed, we would have the form /bukz/ in modern English for the plural of *book.* Since the actual form is /buks/, we can be certain that the steps took place as shown above.

Internal reconstruction was carried out in this case without reference to actual historical documents—although we did allow ourselves a glance at the modern English spelling system on the assumption that it might reflect an earlier pronunciation. It is always interesting to see if the results of internal reconstruction can be confirmed by available documents. Extant manuscripts of Old English show a much more complicated set of plural allomorphs than the set of three found in Modern English, but one of these allomorphs was written *-as* and was undoubtedly pronounced /-əs/. Old English nouns had different plural allomorphs depending on whether the noun was masculine, feminine, or neuter and depending on whether the noun was used in one of four cases: nominative (i.e., subject), accusative (i.e., direct object), dative (i.e., indirect object), or genitive (i.e., possessive). The single form /-əs/ displaced the others, and to this extent the language moved toward a one-to-one relationship between meaning and form. But at the same time the surviving morph developed three phonologically conditioned allomorphs with the end result that the Old English one-to-many relationship was merely simplified and not completely eliminated.

There is yet another curious wrinkle to the whole matter. From the standpoint of modern English, the basic variant of the plural morpheme is not /-əs/ (or its modern counterpart /-əz/), which has a restricted distribution, but /-z/, which occurs in the least restricted environment. We can therefore say that in modern English 'PLURAL' is represented by /-z/. We term the basic variant, from which other variants can be derived, an **underlying form.** The actual pronunciation is determined by two rules:

$$(1) \quad \emptyset \to \text{ə} \ / \left\{ \begin{array}{c} \text{s} \\ \text{z} \\ \text{š} \\ \text{ž} \\ \text{č} \\ \text{ǰ} \end{array} \right\} \underline{\quad} \text{z}$$

$$(2) \quad \text{z} \to \text{s} \ / \ \text{following voiceless sounds}$$

If the rules apply in the order given, the voiceless sounds affected by rule 1 will be removed automatically from the domain of rule 2, and the two rules will apply as follows:

Underlying form	glæs-z	dog-z	buk-z
rule 1:	glæsəz	——	——
rule 2:	——	——	buks
Actual form	glæsəz	dogz	buks

The above approach differs both from the classical structuralist analysis and from the historical analysis. There is no recourse to an abstract morphophoneme /-Z/ underlying both /-s/ and /-z/, as in one version of the structuralist approach. A single base form is adopted, and ordered rules are used to explain the derivation of the actually occurring forms from this underlying form, as in historical grammar. But the form chosen is not the historical form, and the rules are the exact reverse of the historical sound changes. The approach, while ostensibly historical, is quite different from the actual history, and at the same time the use of out-and-out process rules makes this solution unacceptable in the usual framework of structural grammar.

In fact this approach to language analysis sets the stage for a completely different way of looking at language. Historical grammar would be content to trace the history of the plural suffix in English. But this is unsatisfactory from the standpoint of a synchronic analysis of modern English because speakers born in the twentieth century have no knowledge of the history of the language before their birth. Structural grammar would be content to analyze structural units found synchronically in modern English and describe their distribution. But this too is less than satisfying because there is no way of knowing how closely the resulting grammar actually corresponds to the way speakers of the language organize their internal grammar.

The process approach, sometimes called the **item-and-process model** to distinguish it from the item-and-arrangement model (§4.16), assumes that speakers of a language organize their grammar in the most logical way. There is a one-to-one relationship between meaning and form. And if this one-to-one relationship is replaced by a one-to-many relationship, it is simply the result of general processes that apply automatically in certain environments. These processes are in most cases the result of historical changes. But the form they assume in a synchronic grammar may either be a direct recapitulation of history or a restructuring that differs from actual history.

The process approach to analyzing phonological variation in language is important for two reasons. It led linguists to posit abstract units such as /Z/ that were viewed as underlying more concrete units such as /s/ and /z/, thus paving the way for adopting a similar approach in the analysis of syntax. And once the process approach was adopted in syntax, it seemed quite natural to develop a model of language that integrated the process analysis of syntax with the process analysis of phonology.

5.4   THE ITEM-AND-PROCESS MODEL

Before attempting to see how process rules provide an effective framework for describing syntax, it will be helpful to see more clearly how the process approach is applied in phonology by examining data from Japanese:

CORPUS 5–1

oyogu	'swim'	oyogimas	'swims'	oyogimašita	'swam'	oyogimašō	'will swim'
aruku	'walk'	arukimas	'walks'	arukimašita	'walked'	arukimašō	'will walk'
tacu	'stand'	tačimas	'stands'	tačimašita	'stood'	tačimašō	'will stand'
macu	'wait'	mačimas	'waits'	mačimašita	'waited'	mačimašō	'will wait'

By applying the same/different test, it is fairly easy to identify the stems *oyog-* 'swim' and *aruk-* 'walk.' Because of alternation of the final consonant, it is not so easy to identify the stems meaning 'stand' and 'wait,' so we shall return to these later. We notice that immediately following the stem we find one of two suffixes, *-u* or *-imas*. The first of these seems to denote 'INFINITIVE' or 'NONFINITE,' that is, a verb form that is neutral with respect to tense. The second seems to denote present tense, but in fact it merely forms a base to which past and future markers are added. Strictly speaking it is the absence of these markers that denotes 'PRESENT,' and the suffix *-imas* itself simply denotes 'FINITE' as opposed to 'NONFINITE.'

The choice of *-imas* as the underlying form for 'FINITE' is deliberate, based on the assumption that it is the presence of a following *i* that modifies *s* to *š*. Such modification under the influence of a following *i* is fairly common; we have already encountered one such example in Corpus 3–3 (§3.9). To check out the hunch, though, we can look at additional Japanese words:

sabišii	'lonely'	tecudai	'assistance'
secumon	'explanation'	tōkyō	'Tokyo'
sensō	'war'		

It appears that *s* can occur before any vowel except *i*, when it is regularly modified to *š*. At the same time we notice that, while *t* may occur before *a, e, o*, we find only the affricate *c* (stop *t* released as fricative *s*) before *u* and *č* before *i*. These patterns of alternation are the key to analyzing the corpus. The palatalization of *t* to *č* by a following *i* is something already familiar from Corpus 3–3 and Corpus 3–5 (§3.11); the process of affrication before *u* occurred in Corpus 3–5.

One problem remains. It would seem that both *s* and *š* can occur before *o*. If so, the two phones would be in contrastive rather than complementary distribution, and it would be impossible to attribute both to the same underlying unit—even though the alternation of *s* and *š* elsewhere points in that direction.

Evidence bearing on this question can be assembled by considering the canon of the Japanese syllable. Typically the syllable begins with a consonant and ends with a vowel. The only exceptions are a few cases where the initial consonant is lacking and one case where a syllable ends in *n*. (Final *s* in Corpus 5–1 is actually followed by an underlying *u*, which has been omitted to simplify the problem.) But we also have one example of *y* intercalated between the consonant and vowel; so this is also apparently an acceptable syllable type. Since *y* is phonetically similar to *i*, we could assume that the problematic sequence *šo* is actually derived from an underlying sequence *syo* (which would be an acceptable syllable), with the *y* behaving like *i* in palatalizing the preceding *s* and disappearing as a separate segment in the process.

The foregoing assumptions allow us to posit an underlying one-to-one relationship between meaning and form for the morphemes making up the Japanese verb paradigm under consideration. The morphemes can be listed as follows:

Stems		*Position 1*		*Position 2*	
oyog-	'swim'	-u	'NONFINITE'	-ita	'PAST'
aruk-	'walk'	-imas	'FINITE'	-yō	'FUTURE'
tat-	'stand'				
mat-	'wait'				

We assume further that certain phonological processes modify these underlying units according to systematic rules that apply generally throughout the language. In other words the rules that we posit are not limited to the few words under consideration but can be expected to apply without exception to all Japanese words. The sound alternation is so systematic that speakers of the language need to learn only a single underlying form for each morpheme and a small number of automatic rules for modifying these underlying forms. This is clearly more economical then having to learn two or more allomorphs for a large number of morphemes.

The phonological rules required in the present case can be stated as follows:

$$(1a) \quad s \rightarrow š \; / \; \underline{\quad} \; \begin{Bmatrix} i \\ y \end{Bmatrix} \quad and \quad (1b) \quad t \rightarrow č \; / \; \underline{\quad} \; \begin{Bmatrix} i \\ y \end{Bmatrix}$$

Since the two rules apply in exactly the same environment, they can be viewed as two manifestations of a single process and consolidated into a single rule:

$$(1) \quad \begin{bmatrix} s \\ t \end{bmatrix} \rightarrow \begin{bmatrix} š \\ č \end{bmatrix} \; / \; \underline{\hspace{1em}} \; \begin{Bmatrix} i \\ y \end{Bmatrix}$$

In the restatement of this rule, we follow a convention for the use of square brackets that was introduced in §4.12. The convention requires the topmost element in brackets on the left of the arrow to be matched with the topmost element on the right, and so on. Thus, the two versions of rule 1—one given in two parts and one given as a consolidated statement—are fully equivalent. Given the two alternatives, linguists generally prefer the consolidated rule on the grounds that it constitutes a more revealing statement about the overall processes found in the language. The fact that the two rules can be combined is regarded as a linguistically significant generalization.

$$(2) \quad t \rightarrow c \; / \; \underline{\hspace{2em}} u$$

$$(3) \quad y \rightarrow \emptyset \; / \; \begin{Bmatrix} š \\ č \end{Bmatrix} \; \underline{\hspace{1em}}$$

Since the environments for rules 1 and 2 are different, the two rules can apply simultaneously, or either one can precede the other. Rule 3, however, must follow rule 1 since the presence of *y* is required for the operation of 1. Rules 2 and 3 are not inherently ordered with respect to each other. Derivatives of the four forms given for 'stand' are shown below; a similar procedure will confirm the validity of the rules for the remaining forms.

Underlying form	tat-u	tat-imas	tat-imas-ita	tat-imas-yō
rule 1:	——	tačimas	tačimašita	tačimašyō
rule 2:	tacu	——	——	——
rule 3:	——	——	——	tačimašō
Phonetic form	tacu	tačimas	tačimašita	tačimašō

In the above examples the rules are shown as though they applied in linear order, although the actual ordering relationship, as already noted, is somewhat more subtle.

Notice that we have posited an abstract sound segment /t/ as the final consonant of a verb stem even though we have not as yet seen any verb form in which this sound occurs in that position in a stem. The inference was made solely on the basis of the overall patterning of *t*, *c*, *č*, a patterning that requires the three sounds to be grouped together. Moreover, we have made no claims about the actual historical development of these sounds—even though there are obvious historical implications. The analysis was developed entirely in terms of a synchronic description. A similar approach is possible, also with Japanese data, focusing on slightly different problems.

CORPUS 5–2

ikkai	'first floor'	ičiban	'first'
nikai	'second floor'	niban	'second'
saŋgai	'third floor'	samban	'third'
yoŋgai	'fourth floor'	yomban	'fourth'
gokai	'fifth floor'	goban	'fifth'
rokkai	'sixth floor'	rokuban	'sixth'
nanakai	'seventh floor'	nanaban	'seventh'
hakkai	'eighth floor'	hačiban	'eighth'
kyūkai	'ninth floor'	kyūban	'ninth'
jūkai	'tenth floor'	jūban	'tenth'

Both columns contain the Japanese numerals from one to ten. In the first column the numerals are followed by a morpheme meaning 'floor' and in the second by an ordinal formative. The ordinal is regularly symbolized *-ban*. The morpheme meaning 'floor' has two allomorphs *-kai* and *-gai*. The numerals for two, five, seven, nine, and ten are invariable, but the others exhibit alternations that should be explainable in terms of natural phonological processes that occur when certain sounds come together. The alternations are the following:

$$
i\;\boxed{\begin{matrix}č&i\\k&\emptyset\end{matrix}}\;\begin{matrix}\text{-ban}\\\text{-kai}\end{matrix}\quad sa\;\boxed{\begin{matrix}m\\ŋ\end{matrix}}\;\begin{matrix}\text{-ban}\\\text{-gai}\end{matrix}\quad yo\;\boxed{\begin{matrix}m\\ŋ\end{matrix}}\;\begin{matrix}\text{-ban}\\\text{-gai}\end{matrix}\quad rok\;\boxed{\begin{matrix}u\\\emptyset\end{matrix}}\;\begin{matrix}\text{-ban}\\\text{-kai}\end{matrix}\quad ha\;\boxed{\begin{matrix}č&i\\k&\emptyset\end{matrix}}\;\begin{matrix}\text{-ban}\\\text{-kai}\end{matrix}\quad and\quad -\boxed{\begin{matrix}k\\g\end{matrix}}\begin{matrix}ai\\ai\end{matrix}
$$

Individual alternations can be abstracted from the data and presented in any order. The order chosen below is related to the order in which the alternations affect each other, as will be apparent in the accompanying discussion.

(1) V/Ø

(2) č/k

(3) ŋ/m

(4) k/g

The alternations can be restated as processes by including the environment that presumably conditions the change:

(1) $\left\{\begin{matrix}i\\u\end{matrix}\right\} \rightarrow \emptyset\ /\ \#(C)VC\_\_\_k$

The rule appears fairly complex, but it amounts simply to saying that a high vowel (i or u) is lost before k if the vowel in question comes in the second syllable of a word. At least some restriction of this sort is required since a similar vowel is not lost in *ni-kai* 'second floor.'

> (2)   č → k / ____ k

That is, č becomes k when it occurs immediately before another k. Notice that this rule is dependent on the preceding rule, which creates the conditioning environment by deleting the vowel that would otherwise separate č and k.

> (3a)   nasal → $\begin{cases} \text{m /\_\_\_\_bilabial} \\ \text{ŋ /\_\_\_\_velar} \end{cases}$

That is, a nasal assimilates to a following sound, becoming m before labials and ŋ before velars. We note that the only nasal other than m or ŋ in the data is n, which occurs as the final sound in *-ban*. Since the sound in this environment is not influenced by a following sound, it appears that a nasal would normally occur as n in Japanese. This factor suggests a possible restatement of the rule for nasals:

> (3b)   n → $\begin{cases} \text{m / \_\_\_\_bilabial} \\ \text{ŋ / \_\_\_\_velar} \end{cases}$

Finally we can state the rule for the k/g alternation, working on the assumption that the voiced variant occurs in the more restricted environment:

> (4)   k → g / nasal____

Of the four rules, the first two are crucially ordered. The last two are not ordered with respect to each other and together are completely independent of the first pair.

At this point it would be interesting to know the form of Japanese numerals when they occur by themselves. The forms are:

iči	'one'	roku	'six'
ni	'two'	nana	'seven'
san	'three'	hači	'eight'
yon	'four'	kyū	'nine'
go	'five'	jū	'ten'

These, together with *-kai* as the underlying form for 'floor,' are exactly the forms required to establish a one-to-one relationship between meaning and form using the process rules posited above. The derivation can be illustrated with the following examples:

Underlying form	iči	iči-ban	iči-kai	san	san-ban	san-kai
rule 1:	——	——	ičkai	——	——	——
rule 2:	——	——	ikkai	——	——	——
rule 3:	——	——	——	——	samban	saŋkai
rule 4:	——	——	——	——	——	saŋgai
Phonetic form	iči	ičiban	ikkai	san	samban	saŋgai

5.5 PROCESS RULES IN SYNTAX

To see how the process approach can be applied to syntax, it is necessary to backtrack. Traditional grammar had given considerable attention to syntactic categories. Sentences were analyzed as consisting of a subject and a predicate. These components, or constituents, were in turn analyzed as consisting of various syntactic types—nouns, verbs, and the like. The practice of parsing, common in traditional grammar, consisted of analyzing each constituent of the sentence in terms of its part of speech and function. This practice, in one form or another, is still widely used in teaching grammar today.

Although the scholars who developed historical grammar were thoroughly steeped in traditional grammar, their interests were quite different from those of their predecessors, and they devoted relatively little attention to syntax. Structuralists, as we have seen, were preoccupied with analyzing and describing structural systems in language, with much of their attention focusing on sound systems. The structure of morphological systems was then described in terms of previously described phonemic units. This was a workable approach for the most part, although, as we have seen, the description of phonological alternation remained an unresolved issue in structuralism. Some structuralists used process rules, but most preferred an item-and-arrangement approach in which allomorphs were treated as distinct entities rather than as the result of process rules acting on underlying forms.

Syntax received relatively little attention from structuralists. Structural grammars were written without reference to syntax at all, or syntax was described very briefly—almost as an afterthought. A few examples of typical sentence patterns would be presented, along with the statement that there was much more to the subject that remained to be worked out.

There is a simple enough reason for this. The number of phonemes in a language is strictly limited. Hawaiian has thirteen, and some languages of the Caucasus are reported to have in excess of eighty.

But most languages have an inventory about midway between these two extremes. Similarly the number of morphemes in a language—although very great—is finite. Even the possible ways of arranging morphemes to form words is strictly limited. But the possibilities of arranging words to form new sentences conveying novel meanings is without limit. A list of all the possible sentences in a language would be an infinite list and therefore impossible to construct.

Even a list constructed in terms of all the words that could possibly begin a sentence, followed by lists of all the words that could follow each of these words would be an impossible task. For it too would have to provide for an infinite set of possible sentences.

Structuralists who tackled syntax at all approached the problem in one of two ways. Either they sought to catalog the possible **sentence types** found in a language or they adopted some modification of the traditional approach aimed at an exhaustive identification of the **constituent structure** of sentences. Both approaches can be practiced within the framework of an item-and-arrangement model, but both imply processes as well. Both require the existence of certain units that occur in varying patterns. These units may consist of a single word (subject, predicate, etc.) or its replacement by a larger phrase that is structurally equivalent to the one-word unit. In complex structures a unit may occur with its components arranged in different ways and still count as the same unit (e.g., *The student put away the book/The student put the book away,* to be discussed in §5.9). The question arises, are we discussing the arrangement of syntactic units or the processing of such units? Indeed, is there a genuine difference between arranging and processing? And even if there is, could it be that a blend of both approaches is required in the description of syntax?

5.6   SENTENCE TYPES

Efforts to classify the sentence types found in a language reveal certain recurring patterns. Seven basic types can be identified for English. These are presented below with the structural components identified as follows (S = subject; D = direct object; N = predicate noun; V = verb; I = indirect object; A = predicate adjective):

SV	Henry swam.
SVD	George ate the salami.
SVID	Betty gave Eloise the tickets.
SVN	That man is the new choir director.
SVA	The goldfish are friendly.
SVDN	The voters elected him dogcatcher.
SVDA	The rescuers found him already dead.

The limitation of this approach is that it is not always easy to determine whether certain sentences should count as new patterns or be classified as variants of more common patterns. For example, *Up the street came John* could be viewed as a variant of the SV type (*John came up the street*) or as a completely new VS type. It is perhaps significant that in traditional diagraming (§2.12) both sentence variants would be analyzed by the same diagram despite their superficial dissimilarity. Structuralism, however, attached greater importance to surface appearances and never really came to grips with problems of this sort.

5.7 CONSTITUENT STRUCTURE

Analysis of constituent structure was an adaptation of the traditional method of analyzing a sentence into its major components and subdividing these constituents until every morpheme was accounted for. In effect this is a form of parsing—although as applied in structural grammar it normally involved bracketing or boxing of constituents without labeling their function, as would have been the practice in traditional grammar.

Taking the simple sentence *The boy saw the dog* as an example, we can show in successive steps how parentheses can be used to "cut" the sentence into its parts. The process is called **immediate constituent analysis** since each component is analyzed in terms of its own constituents:

(The boy saw the dog.)	sentence
((The boy) (saw the dog.))	subject/predicate
((The boy) ((saw) (the dog.)))	verb/object
(((The) (boy)) ((saw) ((the) (dog.))))	article/noun

The same analysis can be expressed by enclosing the constituents completely to create a **box diagram:**

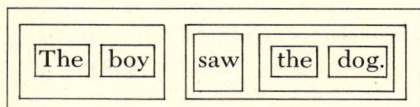

Since both of the foregoing diagrams involve intricate patterns of lines and are difficult to interpret without labels, it is sometimes more convenient to use a **labeled constituent analysis,** which conveys equivalent information:

The	boy	saw	the	dog.
			article	noun
article	noun	verb	object	
subject		predicate		
sentence				

Sentences like *The boy saw the dog* can be classed as SVD types. It is possible to imagine an indefinite number of similar sentences, all having the same structure: *The lion ate the lamb; The postman delivered the letter;* and so forth. In each case the constituent structure of the sentence will be the same. Constituent structure therefore not only provides a way of analyzing sentences already known to be grammatical but also offers a means of predicting the form of previously unattested sentences that will also be grammatical.

Speakers of a language are not limited to analyzing sentences produced by others. They can distinguish grammatical sentences from ungrammatical sentences. And more important, speakers of a language can produce grammatical sentences of their own. Most of these sentences have never been encountered before but are constructed for the occasion on the basis of patterns—or rules—that speakers have abstracted from previous linguistic material and that they know will lead to grammatical sentences that other speakers of the language will accept and be able to understand.

5.8 PHRASE STRUCTURE RULES

What exactly are the patterns that recur in sentences of the SVD type? It seems clear that in every case a sentence consists of a subject and predicate. In SVD sentences the predicate includes an object. Subjects and objects both consist of a noun preceded by an article. By adopting the arrow notation that is already familiar from its use in phonological rules, we can state these rules in a precise way:

sentence	→	subject	predicate
predicate	→	verb	object
subject	→	article	noun
object	→	article	noun

Notice that these rules, for obvious reasons, must apply in the order given. The sentence is taken as the starting point, and a predicate is a constituent of the sentence. A rule applying to the predicate must therefore follow the rule that introduces the predicate as a constituent.

Although not exhaustive, the list of rules as given above is basically correct for the **phrase structure** of English sentences. However, the rules can be streamlined considerably. For example, it appears that both a subject and object have exactly the same internal structure, a structure built around a noun. We might therefore call both the subject and object a noun phrase and let a single rule cover both types. In a parallel fashion we might redesignate the predicate a verb phrase since its basic component seems to be a verb. We can then reduce the original four rules to three:

$$
\begin{array}{lll}
(1) & S \to NP\ VP \\
(2) & VP \to V\ \ NP \\
(3) & NP \to ART\ \ N
\end{array}
$$

The abbreviations used here should be self-evident: S = sentence; NP = noun phrase; VP = verb phrase; V = verb; ART = article; N = noun. (Note that these abbreviations, which will be used from this point on, differ from those presented in §5.6.) The rules can be viewed as subdividing a sentence into constituents until slots are defined in such a way that each slot is reserved for words of a certain class. When words of the appropriate class are then inserted in each slot, the result should be a grammatical sentence. The application of the three rules is shown below, with the resulting **tree structure** equivalent in every detail to the labeled constituent diagram used earlier.

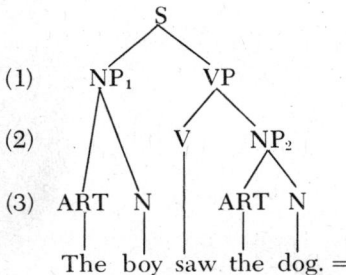

The	boy	saw	the	dog.
			article	noun
article	noun	verb	object	
subject		predicate		
sentence				

(1) NP_1 VP
(2) V NP_2
(3) ART N ART N
The boy saw the dog. =

In the revised rules the terms subject and object have been eliminated in favor of the single abstract symbol NP; however, the concepts of subject and object remain viable. The subject is the NP dominated by S—that is, the NP appearing as an immediate constituent of S. This is NP_1 in the tree structure diagram. The object is the NP dominated by VP, which is NP_2 in the tree structure diagram.

Several observations can still be made about the rules. The noun phrases illustrated thus far have all contained articles, but any speaker of English knows that the article can be omitted in sentences like *Slaves built the pyramids*. We can incorporate this fact by restating rule 3 to make the article an optional element. This is done below by enclosing ART in parentheses. We must also provide for the introduction of prepositional phrases and predicate adjectives. It will also be useful to distinguish between prepositions and a class of adverbial particles that resemble prepositions—a conclusion made necessary by sentences like the following:

The boy ran *over the hill*.   (preposition + noun phrase)
The car *ran over* the pedestrian.   (verb + particle)

Finally it will be necessary to provide for the inclusion of subsidiary sentences within the main sentence—a requirement that will be discussed in detail presently.

As a revision of rules 1 through 3, we therefore adopt the following phrase structure (PS) rules, which will remain in use until we see substantial reasons for further modification and elaboration.

(PS–1)   S $\rightarrow$ NP VP

(PS–2)   VP $\rightarrow$ V (PART) $\left(\left\{\begin{array}{c} NP \\ ADJ \end{array}\right\}\right)$ (PP)

(PS–3)   PP $\rightarrow$ PREP NP

(PS–4)   NP $\rightarrow$ (ART) N (S)

(PS–5) lexical insertion

Again, the new abbreviations should be largely self-explanatory: PART = adverbial particle;   ADJ = adjective;   PP = prepositional phrase; PREP = preposition.

Several facts are worthy of mention. A noun phrase is introduced in several different ways, but regardless of how it is introduced, a noun phrase is subject to the same expansion rule, PS–4, which specifies its possible internal structure. The one essential constituent of the noun phrase is the noun. A preceding article is optional, as is a following sentence. Examples of a subsidiary sentence within a noun phrase will be given in §5.10.

The one essential constituent of the verb phrase is the verb itself.

The verb may be followed by any or all of the following: PART, either NP or ADJ (but not both), and PP—in that order. In this formulation of the rules, the final step, which heretofore has been taken for granted, is stated explicitly. This is the process of lexical insertion, which provides for the introduction of actual words in the positions defined by the phrase structure rules. Notice that even though PS–5 is now included as a formal step, we are still taking for granted the existence of a list from which the appropriately labeled words may be drawn.

5.9 TRANSFORMATIONS

A number of sentence pairs can be found that appear to have exactly the same meaning, although their structure is clearly different:

> The student put away the book.
> The student put the book away.

Facts like this pose a considerable problem in describing English and other languages. We have seen that in principle it is desirable to maintain a one-to-one relationship between meaning and form. It is not only esthetically satisfying to do so, but it is also extremely awkward to be in the position of saying that certain words in the sentence may move freely from one place to another without affecting the meaning. Yet this is apparently what actually happens.

The phrase structure rules that we have adopted at this point provide nicely for sentences like *The student put away the book*, where the particle immediately follows the verb. To account for *The student put the book away*, we could adopt one of two possible solutions. One approach would be to modify the phrase structure rules to allow an alternative formulation of the verb phrase in which the particle follows the noun phrase instead of coming immediately after the verb. This seems attractive at first, but it would complicate the phrase structure rules. The other approach would be to stick to the original phrase structure rules, which require the particle to come immediately after the verb, and have an entirely different rule to shift the position of the particle. We could state this **particle shift rule** as follows:

(T–1) V PART NP ⇒ V NP PART

This rule, a **transformational rule,** or transformation, says that a structure consisting of a verb followed by a particle followed by a noun phrase may be transformed into a structure in which the positions of the particle and noun phrase are permuted. Transformational rules are customarily written with a double-shafted arrow. The number T–1 (for transformational rule 1) is intended to simplify subsequent reference to the rule.

The rule is interpreted as applying to a tree structure in which a configuration is found bearing labels in the exact arrangement given to the left of the arrow. The double-shafted arrow is used to distinguish rules of this type from phonological rules or phrase structure rules. The arrangement to the right of the arrow represents the tree structure that results from application of the transformation. The complete derivation of such a structure can be represented as shown in Figure 5–1. Rule T–1 applies to the entire tree structure, replacing the original structure with a derived structure.

FIGURE 5–1 Transformational Derivation. Underlying structure on left; derived structure on right.

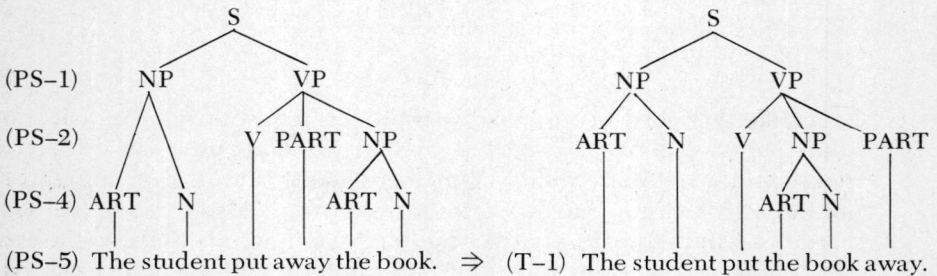

(PS–1) / (PS–2) / (PS–4) / (PS–5) The student put away the book. ⇒ (T–1) The student put the book away.

In Figure 5–1 the expected phrase structure rules have applied to produce the underlying structure *The student put away the book.* This is an **underlying structure** in precisely the same sense that underlying forms, discussed earlier in connection with phonology (§5.4), were underlying structures. Transformational rule T–1 applies to the underlying form in exactly the same way that phonological rules apply to underlying forms. The output of transformational rules is a **surface structure.** Thus, in both phonology and syntax a parallelism seems to exist. Both contain underlying forms that are subject to process rules, the output of which are surface forms.

It happens that in the example of Figure 5–1 both the underlying structure and the **derived structure** constitute acceptable surface structures. This is paralleled in phonology by such examples as *cannot* and *can't,* where we would want to say that *cannot* is somehow the underlying form for both surface forms. We have already seen examples in phonology where the underlying form is always modified and is never directly attested but only inferred on the basis of surface variations that would otherwise be difficult to explain. We shall soon see comparable examples involving syntax.

To return to the mechanics of applying the particle shift transformation (T–1), it should be noted that the rule will apply to a tree structure in which a configuration of V PART NP is found at the lowest level of the tree. This is the pattern in Figure 5–1 since ART N counts as a possible manifestation of NP. The rule therefore applies to the two elements taken as a unit. The application of the rule can be shown in a format similar to that used previously for phonological rules. This is a convenient format and in most cases is the practice that will be used to illustrate transformational rules, rather than the format of Figure 5–1.

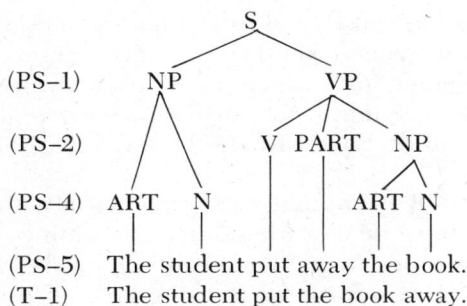

```
                              S
(PS–1)        NP                       VP

(PS–2)       /  \          V   PART    NP

(PS–4)   ART    N                    ART   N
          |      |      |     |        |    |
(PS–5)   The student put away the book.
(T–1)    The student put the book away.
```

In the diagram of the derived structure in Figure 5–1, we omitted indication of the phrase structure rules since these rules are not directly responsible for the structure. There is no phrase structure rule that produces the sequence V NP PART. This structure can be interpreted only as the result of the particle shift rule acting on an underlying sequence of V PART NP. The structurally similar patterns V NP PART and V PART NP overlap semantically and are in complementary distribution. Thus, it is the familiar principle of complementary distribution that enables us to assign them to the same structure.

The phrase structure rules presented in §5.8 are adequate for the immediate purpose of illustrating the constituent structure of elementary sentences and showing the operation of certain transformations. It is important to bear in mind, however, that these rules will need further revision as we try to extend them to more complex data. To take just one example, we might very well ask if we should not introduce an element VB (standing for verbal) that could be a constituent of VP and have as its constituents V and an optional PART. This would require an extra step in the derivation of verb phrases, but it might be a desirable step since V and PART form a logical unit. In principle, it should be possible to decide such questions empirically. That is, it should be possible to determine on the basis of actual language data that one formulation will work better than the other to account for the data.

Notice that the particle shift transformation itself was proposed and justified on the basis of observed syntactic behavior—on the basis of sentence pairs that differ only in the placement of the particle. Such pairs could well be called **allosentences.** This term has never been used in transformational grammar largely because it is reminiscent of a structuralist approach that was consciously rejected. But just as individuals often adopt the behavioral patterns of their parents even while denouncing their philosophy, transformationalists have clearly made use of a structural concept even though they have refrained from giving it the expected label. Transformational grammar attaches great importance to observing syntactic behavior in sentences and using this behavior to posit formal rules that account for patterns in the behavior. Two sentences, similar in meaning but exhibiting patterns that are complementary to each other, are regarded as alternate forms of a single underlying structure. Transformational rules are posited to convert the underlying structure into actually occurring structures.

For present purposes it is enough merely to call attention to the kinds of problems that must be considered in determining the proper form of phrase structure rules. We will concentrate for the present on identifying and formulating additional transformational rules before returning to the question of phrase structure rules. It should be mentioned, however, that we have not as yet said anything about such important elements as plural as a unit associated with the noun or tense as a unit associated with the verb. Eventually we must make explicit provision for these categories, but for the present we will represent nouns and verbs as either inflected or uninflected without dealing directly with the question of how the appropriate inflection must be accounted for in the grammar.

5.10 RELATIVE CLAUSES

As yet we have considered only one transformation: the particle shift. It is relatively easy to think of sentence pairs where the relationship could be described in terms of a transformation. Affirmative and negative sentences constitute such a pair. Declarative and interrogative sentences form another. Actives and passives form still another. Transformations accounting for these relationships can be set up, although their precise formulation is rather complex. And since the data can be interpreted in different ways, there is considerable disagreement among linguists as to just how these rules should be stated.

A less obvious but, if anything, more important use of transformations within sentences is in accounting for the clauses, phrases, and even individual words that seem to convey the same information that could be contained in a separate sentence. For example, a statement like *The lucky coach praised the player who sank the basket* can be analyzed as making three separate assertions:

(1)   The coach praised the player.
(2)   The coach is/was (= BE) lucky.
(3)   The player sank the basket.

The first of these, in traditional terminology, is the main sentence. In transformational terminology it is called the **matrix sentence,** and the two remaining sentences are said to be **embedded sentences.** The logic of this terminology is apparent from a glance at Figure 5–2.

FIGURE 5–2   Derivation of Relative Clauses and Adjectives

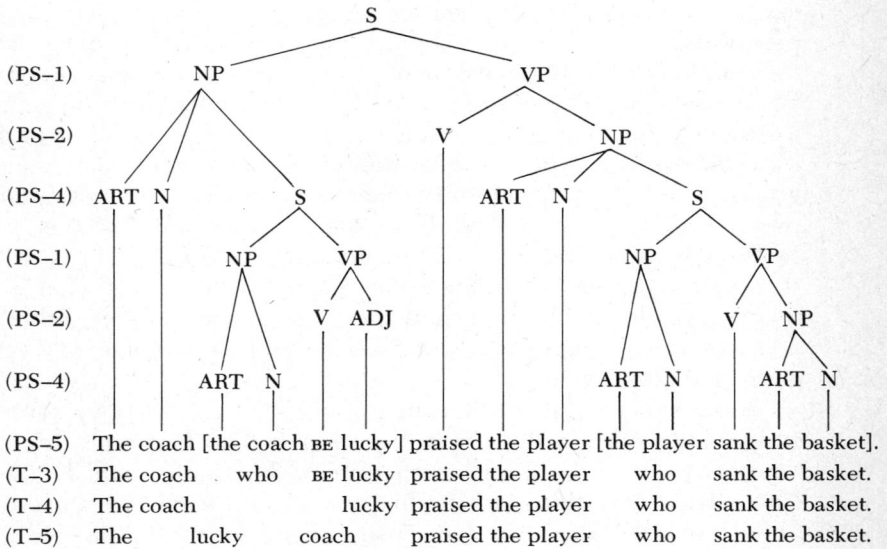

(PS–5)   The coach [the coach BE lucky] praised the player [the player sank the basket].
(T–3)   The coach   who   BE lucky   praised the player   who   sank the basket.
(T–4)   The coach   lucky   praised the player   who   sank the basket.
(T–5)   The   lucky   coach   praised the player   who   sank the basket.

The matrix sentence provides the overall structural framework, while the two subsidiary sentences are incorporated within this matrix. A speaker could of course make three separate statements, but speakers generally find it less time-consuming, less demanding of energy, and therefore more natural to combine related assertions into a single sentence. The significant point is that there is no loss of information in this process of consolidation.

It appears, therefore, that some mechanism is required for introducing subsidiary sentences within a main sentence. This of course was the purpose of allowing S as an optional element following N within the noun phrase, presented as PS–4 in §5.8. A sentence so introduced triggers reapplication of the phrase structure rules applying to S, and the renewed application of the rules leads to the development of a sentence having the same kind of structure as any other sentence. This fully developed underlying structure is of course considerably reduced in surface structure so that an embedded sentence may assume the form of a modifying clause or may even be reduced to a single word.

In principle there is nothing to prevent an embedded sentence from serving as the matrix for a second embedded sentence, with that sentence serving as a matrix for still another embedded sentence, and so on. One example of such sentence types is found in a children's story: *This is the dog that chased the cat that chased the rat that lived with the mouse that ate the cheese.* . . . Such a sentence could continue indefinitely. For every sentence of this type that would be grammatical, we can imagine a similar sentence with one additional clause that would also be grammatical. Such sentences are not commonly used—not because they are ungrammatical but because they are cumbersome. It is customary to say that producing and understanding such sentences is part of the **competence** of the speakers of a language but that such sentences are avoided because of **performance** factors. A distinction between competence and performance is also useful in accounting for the fact that actually occurring linguistic data is often "ungrammatical" in the sense that it contains incomplete sentences, false starts, hesitations, interruptions, and even examples where a speaker begins with one sentence but finishes with another. Children learning their native language are exposed to such data yet still manage to abstract the correct rules for forming grammatical sentences.

In the sentence illustrated in Figure 5–2, we have two sentences embedded within a third matrix sentence. The first embedded sentence is reduced in surface structure to the single word *lucky,* and since there is nothing about this word to indicate the tense of the underlying sentence, we have used an abstract form BE that is unmarked for tense. The use of an abstract form has ample precedent in our earlier discussion of morphophonemics—for example, the choice of /F/ to represent an actually occurring *f/v* in words like *knife/knives.* The whole question of tense is one to which we shall return in Chapter 6. For the present, it is enough to call attention to the concept of **unmarked** versus **marked.** As this concept applies to tense, we can observe that certain forms are marked (e.g., *-ed* for past tense) and other forms are not specifically marked to designate a tense. The notion of marked versus unmarked will be explored more fully when we return to the question of tense, but it will have other applications as well.

Three transformational rules are involved in the derivation in Figure 5–2. The first of these, T–3, is **relativization.** (Rule T–2, which precedes this rule, will be introduced in §5.11.) Since the formulation of T–3 is fairly complex, we will describe its operation in ordinary prose rather than attempting a statement in arrow notation. Relativization looks in an embedded sentence for a noun phrase that is identical with the noun phrase immediately preceding it. (The notion "identical" in this context is basically a semantic notion, that is, 'having the same referent.') The embedded noun phrase is replaced by a relative pronoun. If the noun being replaced is inanimate, the pronoun is *which*. If it is human, the pronoun *who* may be used, especially in formal speech. *That* is used informally for humans as well as for inanimate things. For animate but nonhuman beings, *that* is the most common replacement, but *which* is widely used in formal circumstances, and *who* is occasionally used for animals viewed anthropomorphically. In addition, *whose* is used with both animate nonhumans and inanimates when a possessive form is required. This tendency apparently has to do with the awkwardness of *which's* as a possessive. For some reason *whose* also occurs rather than *that's* even though the latter form occurs as a contraction of *that is.* Thus, we have *the man whose coat . . . the dog whose paw . . . the book whose cover. . . .*

Rule T–4 is **relative reduction.** The rule applies under several different circumstances, but the context that is relevant in the present case is a sequence consisting of a relative pronoun followed by a form of the verb BE followed by an adjective. The rule deletes the relative pronoun and BE.

It is important to note that relativization is an **obligatory rule** since it applies to a structure that would otherwise be an unacceptable surface structure. Relative reduction, on the other hand, is an **optional rule** since it applies to a structure that is already acceptable. The output of relative reduction is not itself an acceptable surface structure since adjectives in English must precede rather than follow the words they modify. In English this requires the operation of another obligatory rule. In languages like French and Spanish, where adjectives customarily follow the nouns they modify, relative reduction by itself would lead to a grammatical surface structure.

Rule T–5 is **adjective inversion.** The rule is simple enough that it can be stated using arrow notation without any great difficulty:

(T–5) N ADJ ⇒ ADJ N

The rule requires that a sequence of a noun followed by an adjective be permuted so that the adjective precedes the noun. The output of T–3, T–4, and T–5 can be represented by the derived structure shown in Figure 5–3.

As before, we have made no effort to show the application of phrase structure rules in this tree. The final structure is the result of transformational rules rather than phrase structure rules alone, and certain parts of the structure (e.g., ART ADJ N as constituents of NP) are not attributed directly to any phrase structure rule.

FIGURE 5–3   Derived Surface Structure for Figure 5–2

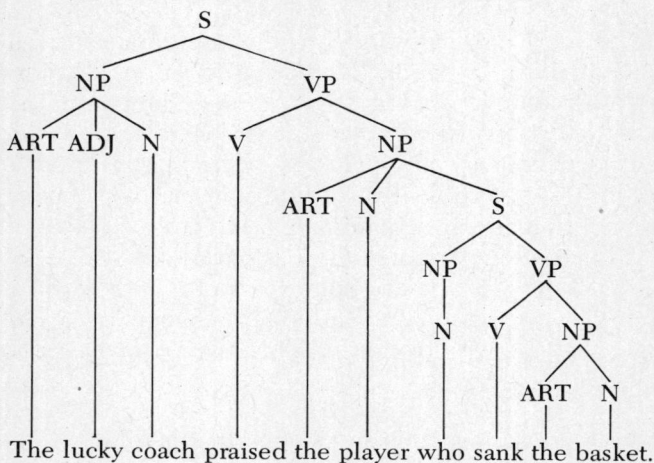

The lucky coach praised the player who sank the basket.

The three transformational rules (T–rules) that have just been discussed include one optional rule and two rules that are obligatory, provided the conditions for their application occur in a particular derivation. All three rules, however, must apply in sequence if they apply at all. With respect to sequential application, T–rules are exactly like phonological rules (P–rules) that have been discussed earlier. T–rules are also like P–rules in that they can apply wherever the requisite structural conditions are met. Thus, T–3 (relativization) applies at two places in the underlying structure in Figure 5–2 because the structural conditions for its application are met at two different places. Rules T–4 and T–5 apply in only one place because the structural conditions are found in only one place. Both T–rules and P–rules are process rules, and both act on underlying forms to produce a series of **intermediate forms,** leading eventually to a surface form.

In both phonology and syntax, the underlying form may be an abstraction that never occurs as a surface form but that is posited on the basis of surface alternations. In many cases the underlying forms posited in both phonology and syntax are the same as actual surface forms and are modified only under certain circumstances. In phonology, intermediate forms are seldom acceptable as surface forms: they are always subject to all applicable rules. The only exceptions are a few forms where optional modification is a matter of formality or stylistic preference, such as *cannot/can't.* In syntax, however, the transformational rules often seem to be optional. Consequently many "intermediate" forms are acceptable as surface structures without further modification, but these same forms may equally well be subject to further modification by additional T–rules.

5.11 NOUN PHRASE ADVANCEMENT

In the examples of relative clauses that have been considered so far, the relativized noun phrase has been the subject of the embedded sentence. But in a sentence like *The President vetoed the bill which Congress enacted,* we would want to represent the relativized noun phrase as the object of *enacted,* as in Figure 5–4. Since the relative pronoun that actually symbolizes *the bill* comes at the beginning of the relative clause in surface structure, it is necessary to posit an additional transformation, one that precedes relativization. This transformation, known as **NP advancement,** looks for the noun phrase in the embedded sentence that is identical with the noun phrase immediately preceding the embedded sentence and moves the embedded noun phrase to the front of the embedded sentence. This process is designated T–2 in Figure 5–4.

FIGURE 5–4   Noun Phrase Advancement

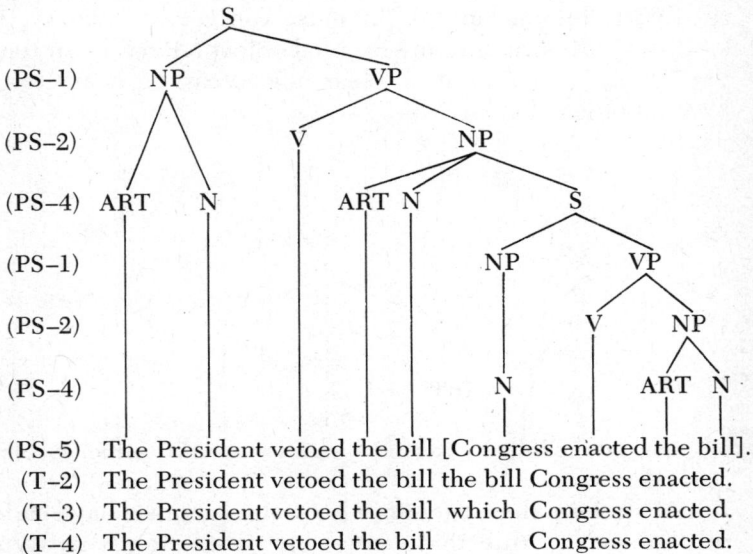

(PS–5)	The President vetoed the bill [Congress enacted the bill].
(T–2)	The President vetoed the bill the bill Congress enacted.
(T–3)	The President vetoed the bill which Congress enacted.
(T–4)	The President vetoed the bill Congress enacted.

We have already seen how relative reduction may apply optionally to sequences of relative pronouns followed by BE followed by an adjective. Since we can say *The President vetoed the bill Congress enacted,* it appears that relative reduction is also applicable in this context. We may therefore add the following condition to T–4: A relative pronoun symbolizing an original object noun phrase may optionally be deleted. This constitutes a separate instance of the relative reduction rule originally presented in §5.10. Notice that both instances of the rule are optional.

It is important to specify that relative reduction in this case is restricted to noun phrases that originate as objects. This condition makes the rule inapplicable to subject noun phrases, an analysis confirmed by the ungrammaticality of a sentence like *The President signed the bill became law.* The foregoing sentence would be grammatical only if a relative pronoun is retained between *bill* and *became.* (Notice that in transformational grammar the asterisk, which was used in historical grammar to denote unattested forms, is now used to denote ungrammatical forms. These two uses of the asterisk should lead to no confusion since they occur in different contexts.)

It is interesting that the variety of relative reduction we have just considered must apparently be stated in terms of a grammatical function that is not operative at the time the rules applies. The terms *subject* and *object* are not primitive terms in transformational grammar—that is, they are not introduced by phrase structure rules as part of the formal system. Instead, they are implied by tree configurations. The noun phrase dominated by S is the subject, and the noun phrase dominated by the verb phrase is the object. But at the time relative reduction applies, it must apply to a substructure like (c) below. In this structure the original object NP has been removed from the VP, and it is not at all clear how it can be characterized as "an original object NP."

(a)   (b)   (c)

Congress enacted the bill   the bill Congress enacted   which Congress enacted

We are here dealing with what some linguists have called a **global rule**—that is, a rule that cannot be stated simply in terms of local conditions in force at the time the rule applies but that requires some knowledge of an earlier state of affairs. (Note how, in a synchronic description using process rules, it is virtually impossible to avoid terminology reminiscent of historical grammar.) Just how such knowledge is to be incorporated into the rule format is at present an unresolved question in transformational grammar. One arbitrary suggestion is to propose that, at the time NP advancement applies, the noun phrase is somehow marked as having originated in a verb phrase. This would serve to distinguish it from noun phrases that originated as sentence constituents—that is, as subject noun phrases.

An objection that many linguists would raise to this proposal is that it relies on information that is just as much semantic as syntactic. Some linguists of course would regard this as a strength rather than a weakness, but transformational grammar has traditionally focused on syntax and has attempted to justify rule formations entirely in terms of syntax. In keeping with this approach, we could note that derived structures (b) and (c) above differ from underlying structure (a) in that two noun phrases appear as sentence constituents within the embedded sentence. This is structurally distinct from the usual NP VP pattern found within an embedded sentence (or any sentence). We could therefore formulate relative reduction to apply to the first of the two noun phrases occurring together within an embedded sentence. This solution is certainly the most satisfying if we wish to state the rules as purely mechanical processes. In this approach meaning is treated as irrelevant. Eventually, of course, we will have to return to the question of how meaning is to be treated within transformational grammar. But it is significant that syntactic patterns can be analyzed to a very large extent without reference to meaning.

5.12 PREPOSITIONAL PHRASES

There is still one complication concerning NP advancement that must be cleared up. Consider the following sentences:

> The knife with which the workman cut the rope was dull.
> The knife that the workman cut the rope with was dull.
> The knife the workman cut the rope with was dull.

The three sentences have essentially the same meaning and logically should be derived from the same underlying structure. If so, the surface differences can be attributed to the choice of different transformational rules. The logical underlying structure for the three sentences can be represented as in Figure 5–5 (p. 143).

To account for the three sentences, we must modify the NP advancement rule (§5.11) by saying that if the noun phrase that would otherwise be subject to the rule is located in a prepositional phrase, the noun phrase may either be advanced by itself or it may be accompanied by the preposition—which is to say, the entire prepositional phrase is advanced. If the latter option is exercised, the following intermediate structure will be produced within the embedded sentence:

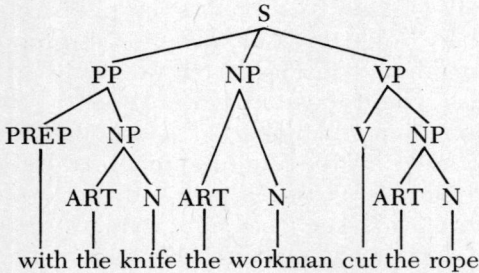

with the knife the workman cut the rope

If only the noun phrase itself is advanced, the following intermediate structure will be produced:

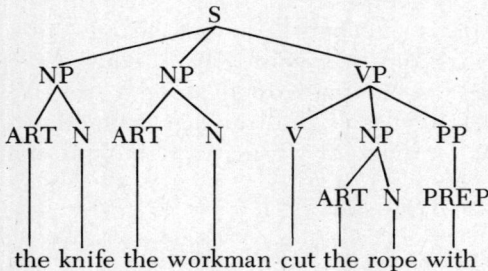

the knife the workman cut the rope with

When relativization is applied to the first structure, the outcome for the sentence as a whole will be *The knife with which the workman cut the rope was dull.* Relativization applied to the second leads to *The knife that the workman cut the rope with was dull.* Relative reduction may subsequently be applied to the last sentence to yield *The knife the workman cut the rope with was dull.*

Some stylists would prefer the formal expression *with which,* especially in writing. A few would go so far as to say that a preposition cut off from its logical object is "incorrect." But transformationalists, like structuralists, are not interested in prescribing usage. They view their task as simply describing the forms that actually occur. If speakers use a form, that form is grammatical and must be provided by the rules of the grammar.

FIGURE 5–5   **Underlying Structure with an Embedded Prepositional Phrase**

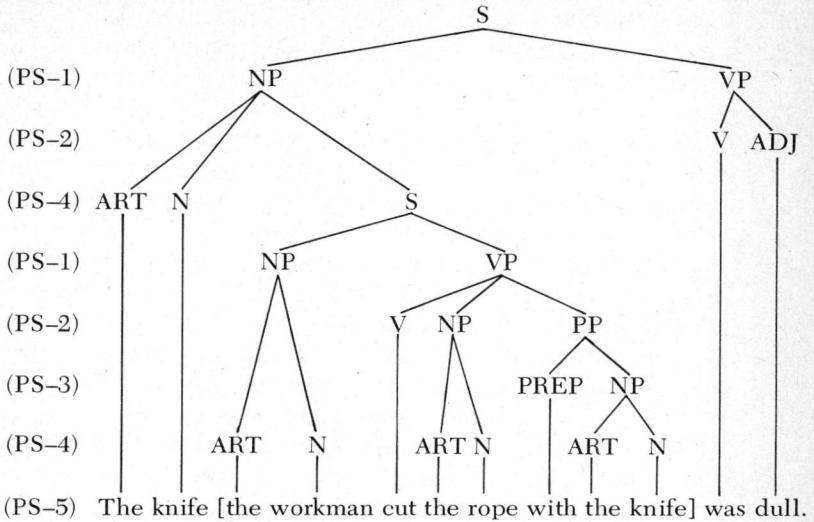

                                    S

(PS–1)   NP   VP

(PS–2)   V ADJ

(PS–4) ART N   S

(PS–1)   NP   VP

(PS–2)   V NP   PP

(PS–3)   PREP NP

(PS–4)   ART   N   ART N   ART   N

(PS–5) The knife [the workman cut the rope with the knife] was dull.

5.13 THE CONCEPT OF GENERATIVE GRAMMAR

If a form is provided by the grammatical rules, it is said to be **generated** by the grammar. The goal of transformationalists is to construct grammars that will generate all grammatical sentences and only the grammatical sentences of a language. Thus, a grammar of English should generate sentences ending with prepositions, since these actually occur in the language; it should avoid generating sentences in which articles follow nouns, since these do not occur in English. The notion "grammatical" is therefore understood as referring to forms that occur or do not occur in a language and is not to be confused with questions of stylistic preference for one grammatical form over another.

The notion "generate" is borrowed from mathematics, where rules are said to generate infinite sets. For example, the set of positive whole numbers is generated by a simple process that requires the numerical concept of one as a primitive, together with the operation of addition. The operation can be applied to one and reapplied to the sum of one plus one, then reapplied to that sum, and so on. Each number produced by the rule is a whole number, and the rule may be applied indefinitely to produce an infinite set. Since a language contains an infinite set of possible sentences, the grammar of a language must operate on the same principle as a formal system in mathematics. That is, it must contain a finite set of rules capable of generating an infinite set of sentences.

No linguist has yet succeeded in constructing a grammar that actually generates all the grammatical sentences and only the grammatical sentences of a language. Such a grammar would be a **generative grammar.** When linguists speak of a generative grammar, they usually are referring to a grammar constructed with this goal in mind —or to a hypothetical grammar that would be generative—rather than to any existing grammar. Since transformational grammars always attempt to be generative, it is fairly common to hear the term "transformational-generative" as though the terms "transformational" and "generative" are synonymous. Technically, a transformational grammar is simply a grammar using transformational rules. Such grammars were the first to be constructed with the generative goal in mind, but in principle other kinds of grammars could also be generative.

It is only fitting to note that, although linguists have not yet achieved the elusive goal of constructing a generative grammar, every native speaker of a natural language has in fact internalized such a grammar. (A natural language is one spoken by human beings; an artificial language is one used by computers.) The accomplishment is the more remarkable because it is completed within the first few years of life, at a time when a child's intellectual powers have traditionally been regarded as not yet fully developed.

Many additional transformations are required in a complete grammar of English, but our purpose is not to discuss all these transformations. Numerous volumes have been written on the subject since 1957; yet there is by no means complete agreement among linguists on the exact transformations that must be posited for English or any other language.

The purpose of this chapter therefore is to present the conceptual apparatus so that readers will be in a position to understand the more detailed discussions available elsewhere and to apply the methodology in dealing with language data on their own. Before closing the discussion, however, it will be useful to consider a few other important transformations. This will serve four purposes: It will (1) cast light on the origin of transformational grammar; (2) lead to a consideration of ways in which the rules we have been using can be elaborated; (3) clarify the issues raised by disagreements among linguists over the analysis of certain structures; and (4) lead to an examination of recent trends in transformational theory.

5.14 COMPLEMENTATION

Since the sentences below are related both structurally and semantically, it seems reasonable to attribute them to the same underlying structure.

(1) I know Mary painted the picture.
(2) I know that Mary painted the picture.

The question is whether we should assume that *that* is present in the underlying structure and subsequently deleted or whether it is not present in the underlying structure and is subsequently inserted. At least four possible underlying structures could be posited, as indicated in Figure 5–6.

FIGURE 5–6   **Complementation**

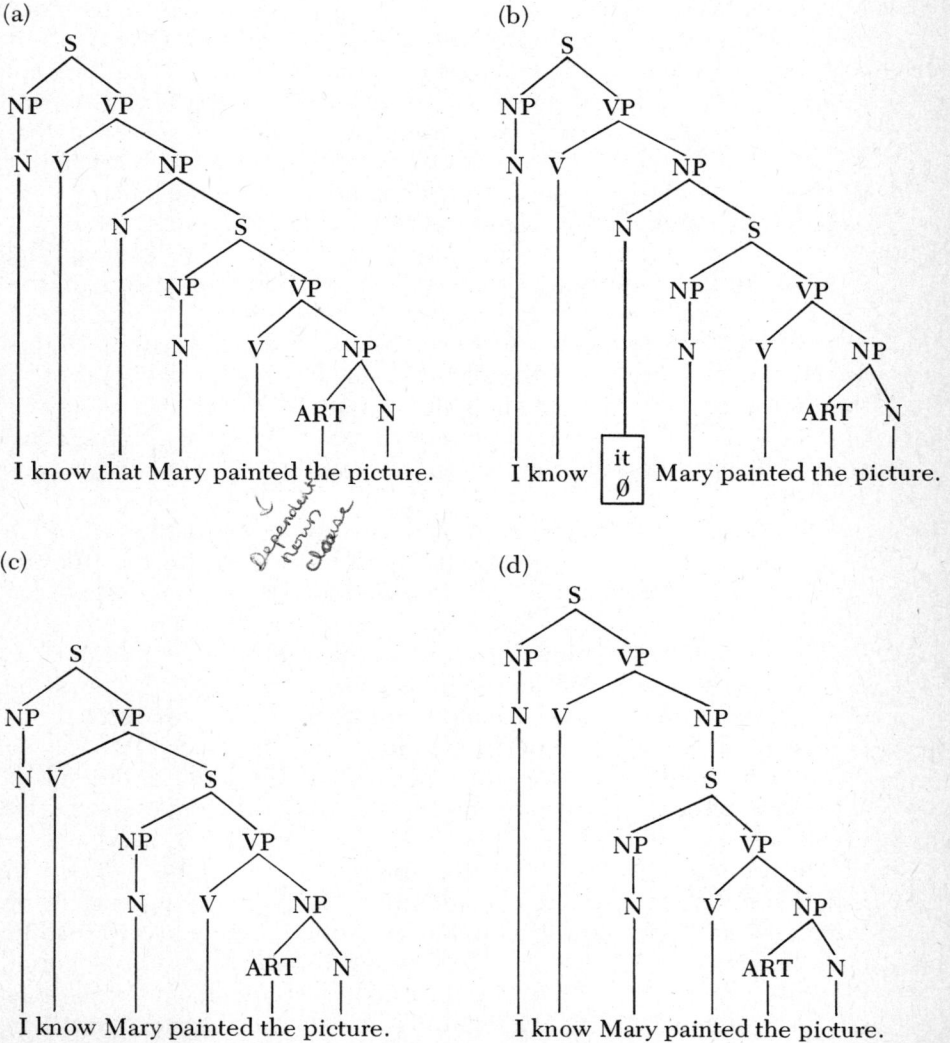

(a) I know that Mary painted the picture.

(b) I know it/∅ Mary painted the picture.

(c) I know Mary painted the picture.

(d) I know Mary painted the picture.

The phrase structure rules we have been using thus far require that every noun phrase contain at least a noun, with a following sentence optional. We might therefore assume that the underlying structure of both sentences is as in (a). Sentence 2 is then treated as a direct representation of the underlying structure, while sentence 1 has undergone *that* deletion. This analysis is supported by an understanding of the historical development of this construction: *I know that: Mary painted the picture* > *I know that Mary painted the picture*. (Of course it can be argued in rebuttal that diachronic evidence is irrelevant in a synchronic description.)

The *that* of (a) is inserted by phrase structure rules under the label N and should therefore be a content word. But it is not altogether clear whether it is a content word or a function word. Ostensibly it is a pronoun—that is, a member of a subclass of nouns that represent other nouns mentioned previously or else understood from the context. Seemingly *that* pronominalizes the embedded sentence that follows. But it does not replace this sentence; the two might better be viewed as elements in apposition. And at the same time *that* is as much a conjunction as a pronoun. We might therefore argue that (b) is more appropriate as the underlying structure. We can say that *it* occurs in the underlying structure as a pronominalized copy of the embedded sentence that follows; *it* is then deleted in sentence 1 and *that* is inserted in its place in sentence 2. A variation of this analysis would hold that the object noun has no lexical content in the underlying structure at all. This zero quality is seen as triggering *that* insertion, as either an optional transformation or an obligatory step with later deletion an optional possibility to account for sentence 1.

Compared with this analysis, (c) seems quite straightforward. The only possible objection is that we would have to revise the rule for elaborating the VP to allow the introduction of S. The analysis of (d) would avoid this necessity but would require modification of the rule for elaborating NP to allow for S instead of N as one possible option. Any one of these approaches seems as good as another. In some cases it may even seem difficult to find significant differences in the proposals. Arguments can be developed for and against each. Whichever solution is finally adopted, some new apparatus must be added to either the phrase structure or the transformational component of the grammar—or to both.

The proper analysis of *that* complements cannot be decided in isolation but must take into consideration the overall requirements of the grammar. A simplification in one part of the grammar will lead to complications elsewhere. A complication in one place will be offset by simplification in another. There is always a tradeoff, and numerous alternatives must be weighed until linguists are satisfied that they have devised the optimal system.

5.15 INFINITIVES AND PRONOMINALIZATION

As an example of the kind of problems that must be considered together, we can observe that infinitive complements are similar in many ways to *that* complements. If the two are similar, we would expect the grammar to account for them in similar ways; and if a particular analysis is clearly required for one, this may be enough to tip the balance in favor of applying the same analysis to the other. Consider possible underlying structures for the sentences *I want to paint a picture* and *I want Mary to paint a picture,* given in Figure 5–7.

FIGURE 5–7   Infinitives

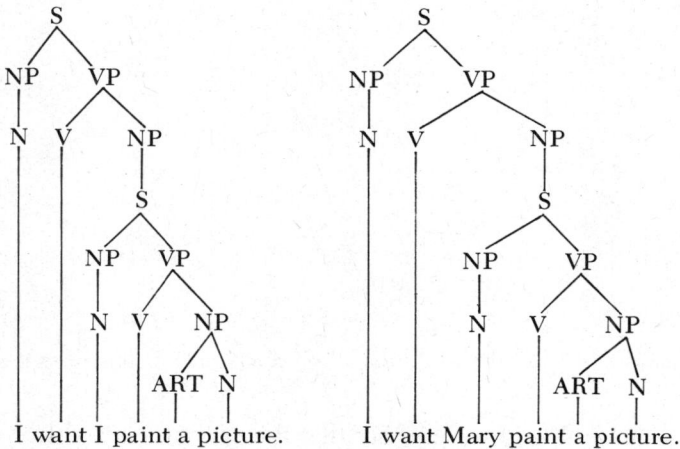

I want I paint a picture.   I want Mary paint a picture.

It appears that we have essentially the same kind of indeterminacy here that we had with *that* complements. The underlying structures have been represented after the fashion of Figure 5–6 (d), but we could just as easily have used one of the other schemes. However, it appears in this case that we must posit a transformation to insert the infinitive marker *to,* for to assume that *to* is always present in underlying structures would require its deletion in most instances. We therefore have some basis for concluding that in the earlier example we should also think of *that* as absent from underlying structures and inserted transformationally.

If this reasoning is correct, we can eliminate Figure 5–6 (a) and (b) from contention. This narrows the choice to (c) and (d), and we can concentrate on looking for evidence that would favor one of these over the other. We need not pursue the matter further at this point since the intention is not to present a complete grammar of English but simply to illustrate the reasoning process required in constructing such a grammar.

Notice that in the foregoing example the subject NP of the embedded sentence is deleted if it is identical with the subject NP of the matrix sentence. This process, termed **identical NP deletion,** can best be understood in connection with another transformational process known as **pronominalization.** Consider possible underlying structures for the sentences *I said I painted the picture* and *John said he painted the picture,* given in Figure 5–8.

FIGURE 5–8   Pronominalization

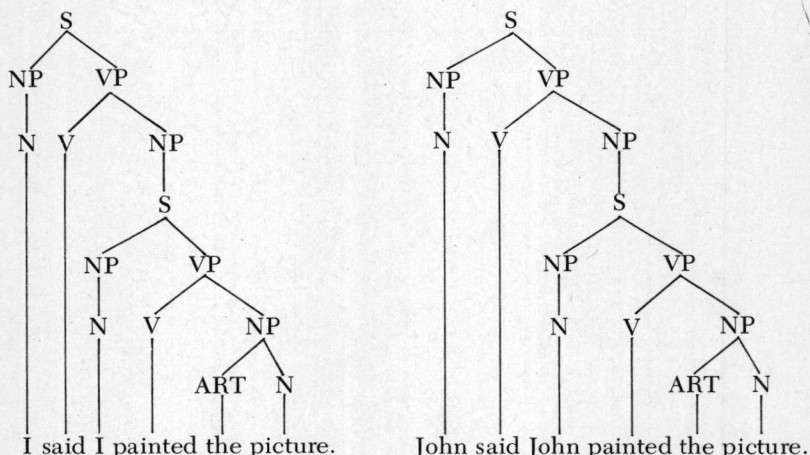

I said I painted the picture.   John said John painted the picture.

As a general rule we can say that the second occurrence of a noun is pronominalized as, for example, when *John* is replaced by *he.* This is true not only of embedded sentences but also of conjoined sentences: *John painted the picture, and he sold it for fifty dollars,* where *he* replaces *John* and *it* replaces *the picture.* Pronominalization also applies across sentence boundaries within a discourse, as any speaker of English can readily confirm.

But notice that these statements are valid only for third person animate and inanimate nouns, such as *John* and *picture.* First and second person pronouns, since they are automatically a part of every speech situation, apparently are handled differently. *I* and *you* are variable pronouns. They have no fixed referent, such as 'John' or 'picture,' but symbolize 'speaker' and 'listener' respectively, regardless of who the speaker and listener are. Since *I* is already a pronoun, it can hardly be replaced by another pronoun in the above example. It is simply retained. One conclusion that we are forced to reach is that pronouns are sometimes part of underlying structures and sometimes inserted transformationally as replacements for nouns.

5.16 THE LINK BETWEEN MEANING AND FORM

Not all transformationalists would agree with the preceding statement about pronominalization. Much has been written on the subject in transformational grammar, and most published discussions have retained the notion from traditional grammar that pronouns in some sense replace nouns. This notion in traditional grammar was never formalized in a precise way, but in transformational grammar such notions are always stated very precisely. If one unit is said to replace another, both units must be treated as concrete entities, and the environment for each must be spelled out. This no doubt explains why transformational discussions of pronominalization have focused on nouns and pronouns symbolizing third persons. The nouns and pronouns in this category are the most concrete, and the environment for replacement can be stated with relative ease.

First and second person pronouns seemingly need to be described in terms of variable concepts such as 'speaker' and 'listener,' and it is therefore difficult to describe them as replacements for concrete nouns. The development of transformational grammar is such that it has tended to describe language in terms of concrete linguistic units and at the same time has avoided dealing with meaning.

The relationship between meaning (i.e., content) and form in language, first discussed by the Stoics (§2.2), was taken for granted in traditional grammar. It remained so in historical grammar, where the comparative method depended on identifying units in two or more languages that were similar in both meaning and form. Saussure's greatest impact on modern linguistics stemmed from his distinction between diachronic and synchronic studies. But he also incorporated the traditional distinction between meaning and form in his linguistic scheme, urging the study and classification of form as more amenable to scholarly examination than meaning.

Saussure's urging fell on willing ears. Countless exotic languages never previously studied by Europeans were accessible in the early twentieth century, and an energetic handful of linguists, confident in the newly perfected science of phonetics, set out to survey these languages. An awareness that many of these languages were spoken by small communities nearing extinction contributed to a sense of urgency. The task at hand was to record and describe the material while it was still available. The emphasis, naturally enough, was on phonetic and morphological structures. It was of course necessary to note the meaning of forms recorded, but the investigators, focusing their attention on the target languages as self-contained structural systems, could, like Joos (1958:96), say that "languages could differ from each other without limit and in unpredictable ways." This seemed true enough against a background of the familiar Indo-European languages, but it is a statement that can be understood only with reference to the phonetic and morphological structures to which it was applied. Boas and his students did not discuss meaning except in terms of the glosses provided for individual morphemes. And linguists had not yet collected enough samples of varied structural systems to begin asking what the actual limits on variation were.

Structuralists dedicated themselves to collecting and describing data with as much precision as possible. By the beginning of the 1950s, much data had been assembled and the techniques for describing it had grown increasingly sophisticated. But the question of meaning remained unsettled. Whorf, following a suggestion of Sapir, under whom he had studied, sought to relate meaning to form by arguing that speakers of languages with different structural categories are compelled to view the world in totally different ways. Linguists found Whorf's notions provocative but were unable to find any way of either confirming or refuting the Whorfian hypothesis.

Harris was undoubtedly closer to the mainstream of American linguistics when he carried structuralism to its logical conclusion by arguing that linguistic analysis could proceed on the basis of structure alone, with no reference whatever to meaning. All that would be required, Harris said, would be knowledge of whether any two forms were "same" or "different." Given this knowledge, it would be possible to work out a statement of the distribution of forms—that is, a grammatical statement. To be sure, "same" or "different" implies 'semantically same' or 'semantically different,' but the approach could work in principle without knowing the actual meaning of forms in question. An analysis using numerical or algebraic codes would be just as valid as one using conventional glosses since it would show just as effectively which forms were the same and which were different.

Noam Chomsky arrived on the scene at precisely the right moment and brought with him exactly the required background to instigate a major advance in linguistics in the mid-1950s. Chomsky had a background in mathematics and had studied philosophy before taking up linguistics as a student of Harris. His mathematical background included automata theory and string rewriting systems. His master's thesis was a study of the morphophonemics of Hebrew. The study of morphophonemics, as we have already seen, requires positing abstract units that underlie the actually occurring phonemic units. Chomsky's doctoral dissertation, also written under Harris, proposed that grammatical transformations constitute a fourth major level of linguistic analysis coordinate with the levels of phonemics, morphemics, and syntax.

Chomsky's view of transformational grammar, as stated in *Syntactic Structures* (1957), was essentially that presented in this chapter. The goal was to account for all possible grammatical structures by positing two basic components. The first was a set of phrase structure rules to provide for rewriting the abstract category S into a grammatical string of constituents and inserting lexical units under the appropriate constituent headings. The process of lexical insertion was the only point at which meaning entered the system—a continuation of the antimeaning bias prevalent in structuralism. The units thus plugged into the constituent structure were viewed as wholly concrete—that is, every unit was an actually occurring morpheme in the language, although many of these morphemes, such as 'PLURAL,' were set up as abstract morphophonemes.

The second component was a set of transformational rules that altered the elements of underlying structures in various ways. Since certain transformations, such as those applying to 'PLURAL' or to tense, were obligatory for every sentence, the result was that every underlying structure was more "abstract" than its resulting sentence in just the way that morphophonemes are more abstract than the phonemes they represent. But beyond this, some sentence pairs were additionally abstract in the sense that one member of the set was a direct representation and the other was a rearrangement of the elements of the first. This, for example, would be true of sentences resulting from the particle shift transformation.

Chomsky himself described the model (1957:107) as having three components: "A grammar has a sequence of rules from which phrase structure can be reconstructed and a sequence of morphophonemic rules that convert strings of morphemes into strings of phonemes. Connecting these sequences, there is a sequence of transformational rules that carry strings with phrase structure into new strings to which the morphophonemic rules can apply." Such a model of language might be represented as in Figure 5–9.

FIGURE 5–9   The 1957 Model of Transformational Grammar

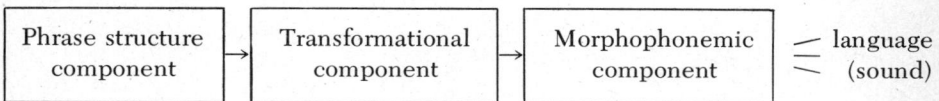

The model shown in Figure 5–9 is quite different from the model presented in Figure 1–3. As already noted, Chomsky's original proposal for transformational grammar continued the antimeaning bias of the structural era. In 1965 Chomsky proposed a major revision in the model to incorporate a semantic component. This proposal will be among the extensions and revisions of transformational grammar to be discussed in Chapter 6.

summary

In the 1950s reanalysis of two unresolved problems from structural grammar led to a new approach that has been called transformational grammar. In attempting to describe allomorphic, or morphophonemic, variation within morphemes, some linguists came to favor an approach that set up abstract underlying structures and derived the actually occurring forms from these by a series of process rules. Analysis of the seemingly endless variety of sentence patterns, compared with the more manageable patterns for word structure, was handled in a similar manner. Sentences were analyzed in terms of their constituent parts, and this analysis was restated as rules for the formation of abstract sentences that could be related to actually occurring sentences by process rules.

The grammar of a language like English can be viewed as based on phrase structure rules which specify that a sentence consists of a noun phrase and a verb phrase; that a verb phrase consists of a verb and optimal elements such as a particle, a noun phrase or adjective, and one or more prepositional phrases; and so forth. The output of these rules is an underlying structure that may be processed by transformational rules to convert it into an acceptable surface structure. In some cases transformational rules mediate between "allosentences": *He put on his cap; He put his cap on.* In other cases, such as those involving relative clauses, the rules apply to abstract structures that, although logically related to surface structures, are not themselves grammatical.

The approach adopted by transformational grammar is generative. That is, the rules are intended to produce, or generate, all the grammatical sentences of a language—and only grammatical sentences. The key words are *all* and *only.* The rule scheme is similar to that used by mathematicians to specify an infinite set of numbers. The difference, of course, is that the linguist is interested in specifying an infinite set not of numbers but of sentences.

further reading

General: Chomsky 1957, Jacobs and Rosenbaum 1968, Langacker 1973. **5.2** Harris 1951. **5.3** Hockett 1954b. **5.4** Chafe 1968b, Pearson 1972b. **5.7** Wells 1947b, Postal 1964. **5.9** Chomsky 1957. **5.10** Jacobs and Rosenbaum 1968. **5.11** Langacker 1973, G. Lakoff 1970. **5.12** Langacker 1973. **5.13** Chomsky 1957. **5.14** Rosenbaum 1967, Jacobs and Rosenbaum 1968, Langacker 1973. **5.15** Jacobs and Rosenbaum 1968. **5.16** Saussure 1959, Wells 1947a, Joos 1958, Whorf 1956, Harris 1951, Chomsky 1951, 1957, 1975.

6 the impact of transformational grammar

6.1 THE RISE OF TRANSFORMATIONAL GRAMMAR

The preceding chapter was intended to show the rationale for transformational grammar by tracing its development and examining problems typical of those taken up by transformationalists. We have made a point of emphasizing the continuity between structural grammar and transformational grammar. Chomsky owes much of his whole approach to grammar to his teacher, Harris, one of the leading structuralists. Chomsky and his followers, however, have emphasized the points of difference between themselves and their predecessors, asserting vociferously that the structuralists were careless and unscientific in their approach to linguistics. The situation in many respects is a modern version of the dispute a century earlier between the *Junggrammatiker* and their predecessors (§3.10).

Transformationalists, while setting themselves apart from structuralists, found much to admire in Sapir, who was not closely identified with the structural movement and who relied on process statements in his linguistic descriptions. Transformationalists admire Jespersen, a scholarly prestructuralist schooled originally in historical grammar. Transformationalists also profess to find their philosophical precursors among traditional grammarians, especially those of the seventeenth century. But the admiration has been selective. Most transformationalists have made only cursory studies of traditional grammar and have ignored historical grammar entirely. As a result, members of the school have sometimes proposed what they considered novel solutions without realizing that their solutions were already familiar to earlier linguists. A case in point is the process phonology of transformational grammar (§5.3), which is the synchronic application of internal reconstruction (§3.11).

Although transformationalists have built on the findings and methods of structural grammar, they are quite right in pointing out that they have gone far beyond the structuralists in systematizing their findings. Whether this should count as a continuation of structural grammar or a revolutionary break with the structural tradition is something that future historians will have to judge.

6.2   AUXILIARIES AND TENSE

One way in which transformational grammar has far exceeded structural grammar is in the analysis of tense, aspect, and modality. The subject was intentionally omitted from Chapter 5, but in actuality it was Chomsky's concise distributional analysis of English tense that most impressed linguists in 1957.

Corpus 6–1 contains a paradigm of certain English verbal constructions selected because their similarities and differences display the crucial facts of the language's complex auxiliary system. These facts were well known to structuralists; it was the novel interpretation of the facts that was Chomsky's contribution.

Every English verb phrase has a tense, either past, present, or future. But tense does not always appear in the main verb. It can appear in an auxiliary verb in sentences containing aspect. In addition, there are a number of modal auxiliaries that lack the usual third person inflection in present tense (e.g., *can, will, *can-s, *will-s*) and that have "irregular" past forms (*could, would*). The system has always impressed non-native speakers as one of the language's most frustrating complexities. But if we think of "tense" as something handled according to regular rules, its distribution (i.e., assignment) to either an auxiliary or the main verb is quite predictable.

Each of the sentences consists of a noun phrase followed by a verb phrase, in accordance with rule PS–1 presented in §5.8. We would expect from rule PS–2 that the verb phrase would contain a verb with one or more optional syntactic units following it. The verb phrase of sentence 1a contains a verb, but it consists of two morphemes: the main verb and the suffix *-s* agreeing with the third person singular subject. The verb phrases of sentences 1c and 1d also contain both a verb and suffix, in this case the past tense marker *-ed*. The verb of 1b has no overt suffix, but of course it is the very absence of a suffix that marks the verb as present tense; hence, the verb has the suffix *-∅*.

Each verb phrase, therefore, contains not only a verb but an **auxiliary**—that is, an element that specifies person, tense, modality, or aspect. In the sentences of 1, the auxiliary is basically a tense marker and systematically follows the verb. In 2 perfective aspect is expressed by a combination of some form of *have* followed by the past participle of the main verb. The tense marker emerges as part of *have*, and the past participle is marked by *-ed*. But this *-ed* is not the same as the suffix that denotes past tense; rather, it must be equated with the *-en* suffix of *driven* and *bitten*. We will therefore refer to it as *-en* to distinguish it from the past tense marker, bearing in mind that both units will vary morphophonemically.

CORPUS 6–1

(1) a. Noel protests.
 b. The radicals protest.
 c. Noel protested.
 d. The radicals protested.
(2) a. Noel has protested.
 b. The radicals have protested.
 c. Noel had protested.
 d. The radicals had protested.
(3) a. Noel is protesting.
 b. The radicals are protesting.
 c. Noel was protesting.
 d. The radicals were protesting.
(4) a. Noel has been protesting.
 b. The radicals have been protesting.
 c. Noel had been protesting.
 d. The radicals had been protesting.
(5) a. Noel will protest.
 b. The radicals will protest.
 c. Noel would protest.
 d. The radicals would protest.
(6) a. Noel will have been protesting.
 b. The radicals will have been protesting.
 c. Noel would have been protesting.
 d. The radicals would have been protesting.

In 3 progressive aspect is expressed by a combination of *be* followed by the present participle of the verb, marked by the *-ing* suffix. Again, tense emerges as part of the auxiliary rather than the main verb. In 4 we have both perfective and progressive. The general principles discussed thus far continue to apply. Perfective is expressed by *have* followed by a past participle. Progressive is expressed by *be* followed by a present participle. The auxiliary *have* comes first and carries tense; it is followed by *be* in its past participle form; the main verb comes last and is in the present participle form.

The sentences of 5 break the pattern slightly, but in so doing they point the way to the eventual solution. Sentences 5a and 5b contain only the modal *will*, which in this case precedes the main verb rather than following it, as does the tense suffix. The modal is actually *will* plus a zero variant of the present tense marker, a conclusion borne out by comparison with 5c and 5d containing the morphophonemic result of *will* plus past tense.

The sentences of 6 contain everything combined—a modal, perfective, progressive, and tense. As before, tense appears in the first auxiliary, *-en* is dependent on *have*, and *-ing* is dependent on *be*. The underlying relationship is fairly clear. The problem is that the units that logically belong together are discontinuous. We can solve the problem most effectively by positing an underlying structure in which related elements occur together. A simple transformational rule can then be posited to rearrange the elements as appropriate for surface structure.

To accommodate these facts we must include the auxiliary (AUX) in the verb phrase and provide rules for expanding AUX into its various constituents. We have already noted that AUX may contain a sequence consisting of modal (MOD), *have,* and *be,* all of which precede the verb. The tense marker, as previously noted, is attached to the first element in the sequence. The suffix *-en,* although dependent on *have,* is attached to the following verb; and the suffix *-ing,* dependent on *be,* appears in the following verb. We can therefore posit the following underlying sequence, in which optional elements are parenthesized:

C   (MOD)   (have-en)   (be-ing)   V

The element C (for "concord") stands for the set consisting of three elements: the third person singular present tense marker, the zero suffix that marks other present tense verbs, and the *-ed* past tense suffix (or its morphophonemic equivalent). The **affix transformation** (sometimes called affix hopping or "flip") applies to the affixes C, *-en,* and *-ing* by suffixing them to the following element, that is, to MOD, *have, be,* or V. The rule is designated T–6, continuing the numbering from Chapter 5.

(T–6)   affix   verb   ⇒   verb   affix

Thus, the underlying sequence

-ed will have-en be-ing protest

is converted by the affix transformation to the string

will-ed have be-en protest-ing

and by later morphophonemic rules to

would have been protesting.

6.3 REVISION OF PHRASE STRUCTURE RULES

To incorporate the rules for the auxiliary, we must elaborate the phrase structure rules adopted in §5.8. The revised rules will have the following form:

(PS–1)   S   →   NP   VP

(PS–2)   VP   →   AUX   V   (PART) $\left(\left\{ \begin{matrix} NP \\ ADJ \end{matrix} \right\} \right)$ (PP)

(PS–3)   AUX   →   C   (MOD)   (have-en)   (be-ing)

(PS–4)   C   → $\left\{ \begin{matrix} \text{-Z} \\ \text{-Ø} \\ \text{-ed} \end{matrix} \right\}$

(PS–5)   PP   →   PREP   NP

(PS–6)   NP   →   (ART)   N(-PL)   (S)

(PS–7)   lexical insertion

The rules, with slight modifications, are those presented by Chomsky (1957). We have added AUX to PS–2 of §5.8 and have added a rule to further specify the possible forms of AUX as well as a rule to specify the possible forms of C, which was introduced as part of AUX. The NP rule has been modified to allow PL (plural) as an optional element following N. Lexical insertion remains the final step, and we continue to assume the availability of a lexicon from which nouns can be selected for insertion under the label N, verbs for insertion under V, and so forth.

Using these rules we can now illustrate the complete derivation of a fairly complicated sentence such as 6c, *Noel would have been protesting*, shown in Figure 6–1.

FIGURE 6–1   **Sentence Derivation**

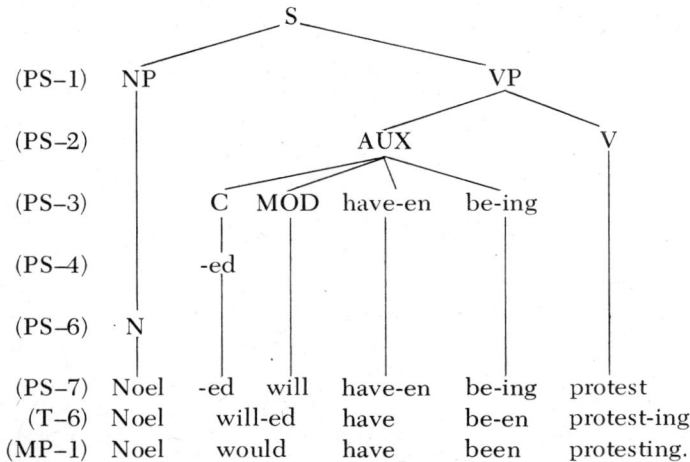

(PS–7)	Noel	-ed	will	have-en	be-ing	protest
(T–6)	Noel		will-ed	have	be-en	protest-ing
(MP–1)	Noel		would	have	been	protesting.

Application of rules PS–1 through PS–6 is quite straightforward. Under lexical insertion (PS–7) the noun *Noel* is inserted beneath N, the modal *will* is inserted under MOD, and the verb *protest* is inserted under V. The phonological elements *-ed, have-en,* and *be-ing* are provided by PS rules, and their repetition in PS–7 is a matter of carrying forward rather than supplying something new.

The application of T–6, the affix transformation, should be self-explanatory in light of the previous discussion. The rule listed as MP–1 is a morphophonemic rule that converts the sequence *will-ed* to *would.* A number of similar morphophonemic rules would convert sequences such as *take-ed* to *took, teach-ed* to *taught,* and so forth. A second type of morphophonemic rule will apply to the /-Z/ that marks the third person singular verbs, converting it to /-əz/, /-s/, or /-z/ as appropriate (§5.2). (When we return to phonology in Chapter 7, we will use different terms for the two types of morphophonemic rules described here. The first, which applies to specific roots, will be called morpholexical rules [§7.20]; and the second, which applies in a general phonological environment without regard to the morphemes involved, will be called phonological rules [§7.20].) Figure 6–1 clearly illustrates the three components posited in Figure 5–9: the phrase structure, transformational, and morphophonemic components.

6.4   DISTRIBUTIONAL ANALYSIS

The analysis of auxiliaries presented thus far is a purely distributional analysis. It does not rely on a semantic notion such as 'tense' but is based entirely on (1) the occurrence or nonoccurrence of identifiable morphemes and (2) the distribution of **bound morphemes** (which are always attached to other morphemes) with respect to **free morphemes** (which may occur independently). The categories are determined by the structure itself rather than any external criteria. As such it is an analysis in the best tradition of structural grammar.

The morphemes posited in the analysis are themselves reasonably concrete, certainly no more abstract than the typical morphophoneme with respect to its member phonemes. Categories such as noun, verb, and modal are treated in effect as content morphemes, while C, *have-en,* and *be-ing* are treated as function (i.e., grammatical) morphemes. This continues a useful distinction already familiar from structural grammar (§4.13). The grammatical unit C occurs as one of three elements: /-Z/ the third person present tense verb marker, /-Ø/ the present tense marker for other persons, and /-əd/ the past tense marker. The three occur in the same environment and therefore contrast in meaning. But within the category 'PRESENT' /-Z/ and /-Ø/ are complementary; and of course /-əd/, representing 'PAST,' is complementary with 'PRESENT.' Although these affixes are traditionally called tense markers, it is enough to group them together on the basis of their distributional properties alone. Since future tense is expressed by the modal *will*, it is analyzed as belonging to a different structural system and to a content unit MOD having nothing in common with C.

It may seem awkward to assign past and present tense markers to one category (C) and future to another (MOD), but the analysis is justified by the structural asymmetry between past and present on the one hand and future on the other. (See further discussion in §7.15.) The analysis is not intended to account for concepts such as 'tense,' but rather to provide a scheme for generating all the occurring syntactic structures of English without generating any nonoccurring structures. The rules succeed at this remarkably well. The structure defined in Figure 6–1 will serve not only for *Noel would have been protesting* but for an indefinite number of other sentences. In some of these only the components of the auxiliary would be different; in others the noun and/or verb could be different; and each change of noun or verb could of course be accompanied by any of the varied possibilities for the auxiliary. When we consider the possibilities for choosing different options within the rules to define different structures and add to that the possibilities for combining sentences, the ability of the grammar to generate grammatical structures seems virtually unlimited.

6.5 REVISIONS OF THE MODEL

Work undertaken in the early 1960s convinced Chomsky and others that certain refinements in the 1957 model were required. The original model, described in Chomsky's book *Syntactic Structures*, is depicted in Figure 5–9. The model was envisioned as having three components—a phrase structure component, a transformational component, and a morphophonemic component. This was adequate to account for the distribution of syntactic elements, but it made no statements about the meaning of the elements.

In structural grammar, meaning was associated with the morpheme. Although Bloomfield (1933) recognized the importance of meaning, he felt that its analysis involved a great many more variables than did phonemics or morphology. As a result, structuralists tended to adopt the attitude that meaning was highly subjective and not really capable of being analyzed. This avoidance of semantics was continued insofar as possible by transformational grammar.

6.6 SUBCATEGORIZATION AND SELECTION

It is not possible to ignore meaning entirely, however. The phrase structure rules of §6.3 are an improvement over those of §5.8, but they still fail to prevent all ungrammatical sentences. If we can select any noun or any verb from the lexicon, what is to prevent ungrammatical sentences like the following?

(7)   a.   *Everybody liked.
      b.   *The guide arrived the tourists.
      c.   *The book elapsed.
      d.   *The sandwich ate Dagwood.

Falling back on notions from traditional grammar, we can make certain relevant observations. *Like* in 7a is a transitive verb and requires an object. *Arrive* in 7b is an intransitive verb and cannot take an object. The two remaining sentences may seem more perplexing. We are forced to say that *elapse* in 7c is a very special verb that occurs only with subjects having to do with time. To deal with 7d we must say that sandwiches simply do not eat people in the world as we know it. Does that mean that 7d is ungrammatical for our world but grammatical for other worlds that we can only imagine? Can we construct a grammar that does not depend on extralinguistic information for its statements of grammaticality?

In the case of verb subcategorization, it is fairly simple to posit phrase structure rules of the following type:

$$(8) \quad V \rightarrow \begin{Bmatrix} V_{intrans} \\ \\ V_{trans} \end{Bmatrix}$$

Such a rule would have to be incorporated into PS–2, along with the differing possibilities for prepositional phrases, NP objects, and so forth, which would follow the verb. In the case of nouns, the basic approach has been to subclassify the noun as either animate or inanimate, then to subclassify these categories as human or nonhuman (if animate), as abstract or concrete (if inanimate), and so on. Rules have usually been stated as shown in 9 and have been regarded as part of the phrase structure "base" on which the grammar is built.

(9)   a.   N → [±animate]
      b.   [+animate] → [±human]
      c.   [−animate] → [±abstract]

Strictly speaking, the arrow used in this part of the grammar does not mean 'is replaced by' but signifies 'is further specified as.' In Chapter 7 we will introduce a double-headed arrow (→ ›) to express this notion, but transformationalists have preferred to let the standard arrow do double duty. The use of a feature with a positive value to represent a property (e.g., animate) and a negative value to represent its opposite (e.g., inanimate) had already become established in phonology by the mid-1960s, and its extension to syntax seemed quite natural. Such features have often been called **syntactic selectional features** since they function to select certain items for particular syntactic slots, while ruling out other items. Although selectional features have a syntactic function, it can hardly be denied that they identify properties that are essentially semantic.

Rules of the type presented in 9 produce what have been called **complex symbols.** These are commonly represented in the following manner:

(10)
$$
\begin{bmatrix} N \\ +\text{animate} \\ +\text{human} \end{bmatrix}
\begin{bmatrix} N \\ +\text{animate} \\ -\text{human} \end{bmatrix}
\begin{bmatrix} N \\ -\text{animate} \\ +\text{abstract} \end{bmatrix}
\begin{bmatrix} N \\ -\text{animate} \\ -\text{abstract} \end{bmatrix}
$$

Since each feature is added to the original noun, the resulting complex is a noun specified as having certain properties. The entire complex is then inserted at the appropriate node of a tree structure, and once inserted it imposes restrictions on the verb types that may accompany it. These restrictions are stated as part of the lexical entry for each verb. For the four verbs in 7, a simplified version of the lexical entry might appear as follows:

(11) like (+V, +[+N, +animate]____, +____NP)
      arrive (+V, [+NP]____)
      elapse (+V, [+N, +time]____)
      eat (+V, [+N, +animate]____, (+____NP))

Each entry is a verb (+V). The entry for *like* denotes that it must follow a [+animate] noun (its subject) and precede another noun phrase (its object). The entry for *arrive* indicates that it follows a noun phrase of any kind and does not occur with a following noun phrase. *Elapse* follows a noun specified as [+time]. *Eat* requires a [+animate] subject; the presence of an object is optional.

The emphasis is on distributional properties that are basically syntactic. Brackets, used in phonetics to enclose a phonetic transcription, are now used to enclose individual features as well as feature complexes. The features serve to specify co-occurrence restrictions— that is, restrictions on the kinds of items that can occur in the same sentence. Among these are the type of noun that a verb must have as its subject and the occurrence or nonoccurrence of an object noun phrase. Since this latter is the syntactic property that distinguishes transitive and intransitive verbs, rules such as 8 are actually specified by the co-occurrence restrictions contained in lexical entries and are not required as separate statements.

We are now in a position to see why sentence 7d will not be allowed by the grammar: *eat* must follow an animate noun, and *sandwich* does not satisfy this requirement. On the other hand, we can easily imagine the derivation of the grammatical sentence *Dagwood ate the sandwich*, given in 12. Each terminal node of the tree is narrowly restricted, and these restrictions must be matched with the specifications that appear in the lexical entries of individual words.

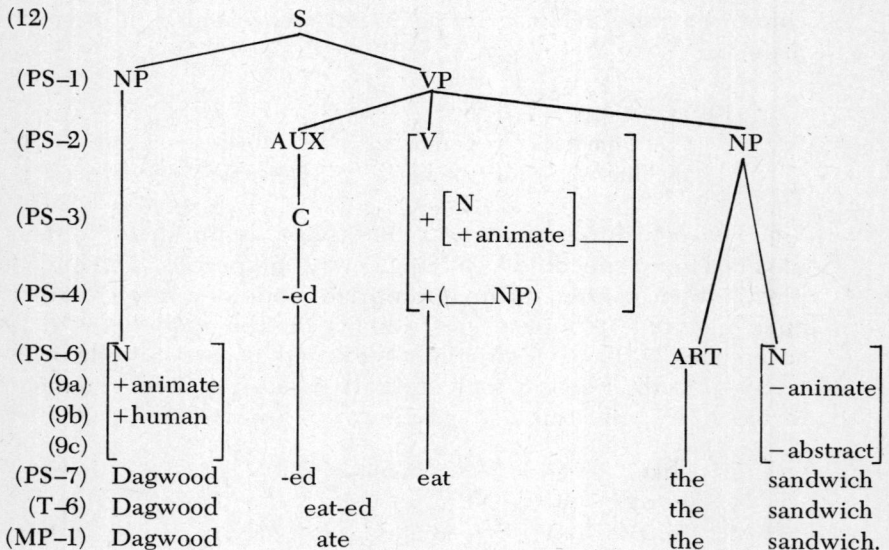

(12)

	S			
(PS–1)	NP		VP	
(PS–2)		AUX	$\begin{bmatrix} V \\ \end{bmatrix}$	NP
(PS–3)		C	$+\begin{bmatrix} N \\ +animate \end{bmatrix}\_\_\_$	
(PS–4)		-ed	$+(\_\_NP)$	
(PS–6)	$\begin{bmatrix} N \\ +animate \\ +human \end{bmatrix}$			ART $\begin{bmatrix} N \\ -animate \\ -abstract \end{bmatrix}$
(9a)	+animate			
(9b)	+human			
(9c)				
(PS–7)	Dagwood	-ed	eat	the sandwich
(T–6)	Dagwood	eat-ed		the sandwich
(MP–1)	Dagwood	ate		the sandwich.

6.7 UNDERLYING STRUCTURE

Semantics of course had been implicitly recognized in the 1957 model as the common bond between certain transformationally related sentences. For example, the particle shift transformation (§5.9) by its application or nonapplication converts a single underlying structure into two different surface forms:

> (13) a. The ushers *turned away* the gate-crashers.
> b. The ushers *turned* the gate-crashers *away*.

The underlying form in this case is directly represented by 13a and modified transformationally in 13b, but the fact remains that both sentences are surface manifestations of the same underlying form and have the same meaning.

The 1957 model also proposed a negative transformation and a question transformation. These operated with other transformations to convert declarative sentences into negative statements and questions:

(14) a. The mayor voted.   (basic sentence)
     b. The mayor did vote.   (*do* transformation)
     c. The mayor did not vote.   (*do*, negative [=NEG])
     d. The mayor didn't vote.   (*do*, NEG, contraction)
     e. Did the mayor vote?   (*do*, question [=Q])
     f. Did not the mayor vote?   (*do*, NEG, Q)
     g. Didn't the mayor vote?   (*do*, NEG, Q, contraction)

[handwritten annotations: "PS Rules" pointing to (14a); "changed by Trans. Rules" bracketing items b–e]

It is awkward to say that some transformations (e.g., particle shift) function to preserve the meaning of underlying forms and others (e.g., negative and question) function to alter the original meaning. While there is nothing in principle to prevent language from utilizing transformations with two very different properties, there is a certain elegance in being able to claim that all transformations perform essentially the same function. This requirement can be satisfied easily enough by restating PS–1 so that question (Q) and negative (NEG) become optional elements of the base structure:

(15) (PS–1′) S → (Q) (NEG) NP VP

The presence of Q or NEG in the underlying structure can then serve to trigger the appropriate transformations. Sentences such as 14a and 14c are seen as differing only in the presence or absence of NEG in the underlying structure. The presence of NEG or Q is seen as triggering a *do* transformation, which is not itself viewed as altering the underlying meaning of the sentence. Contraction of course remains an optional transformation without a meaning-changing effect.

The discussion has still neglected a number of fine points, but we have at least established a framework within which unresolved questions can be attacked. Most important, we have developed a model that is now capable of handling meaning. We have devised a formal system with base rules for generating underlying structures. The underlying structures tell us everything we need to know about the sentences of a language. Transformational rules act on the underlying structures to produce surface structures, which in turn are modified morphophonemically by a phonological component to produce a phonetic interpretation of the sentence. And at the same time interpretive rules of a similar type can act on the underlying structures to provide a semantic interpretation of the sequence. The underlying structure therefore becomes the all-important link between form and meaning. As such, its status has been recognized by terming it **deep structure.**

6.8 IDIOMS

Among the syntactic phenomena most resistant to analysis are **idioms**
—constructions whose meaning cannot be inferred from the component parts. The expression *to hit the ceiling*, for example, is not to be
interpreted in the same way as the similar syntactic construction in *the
archer hit the target*. The idiom does not literally mean 'to strike the
overhead portion of an enclosed room.' Its meaning is more accurately
expressed by the predicate *to become angry*. If we expect deep structure to provide a semantic interpretation of idioms, the semantic content must somehow be more than the sum of the parts.

But the component parts must also be present in deep structure
because they are often subject to transformational processes.

> (16) a. Alice made up her mind before the meeting.
> b. Alice's mind was made up before the meeting.

In this case the idiom *make up one's mind*, which might be glossed
'decide,' can clearly undergo passivization. The same is not true of the
idiom *hit the ceiling*.

> (17) a. The President hit the ceiling when the news leaked.
> b. *The ceiling was hit by the President when the news leaked.

It appears then that idioms must be represented in deep structure as
complex symbols containing at least three elements: (1) information as
to semantic content; (2) a full representation of syntactic structure;
and (3) information as to transformational idiosyncracies.

We might therefore imagine that a sentence like *the President hit
the ceiling* with the idiomatic meaning 'the President became angry'
would have the deep structure representation given in Figure 6–2.
The verb *hit the ceiling* is represented as an idiom meaning 'become
angry,' which is incapable of undergoing passivization. The past
tense marker *-ed* will be associated with *hit* in surface structure,
just as though *hit* were the main verb rather than part of an idiom.
Semantic interpretation will be based on the meaning associated
with the higher level verb, while phonetic interpretation will be based
on the lexical units inserted at the terminal node of each branch.

To suggest that 'become angry' can be represented at one level of
analysis as a verb may seem strange since the construction is traditionally analyzed as a linking verb followed by a predicate adjective.
However, the internal composition of the verb phrase is a peculiarity
of English that should not obscure the verbal nature of the expression.
In many languages 'become angry' is expressed as a unitary verb. The
Japanese counterpart of *the President became angry* is:

(18) daitōryō - wa okori - mašita
'President-SUBJ become angry-PAST'

A number of uncertainties continue to surround idioms. The fore-going discussion, which generally follows Fraser (1970), serves at least to suggest an approach for describing idioms within the frame-work of transformational grammar. Clearly the analysis of idioms calls for the inclusion of a semantic component somewhere in the grammar.

FIGURE 6–2   Deep Structure of an Idiom

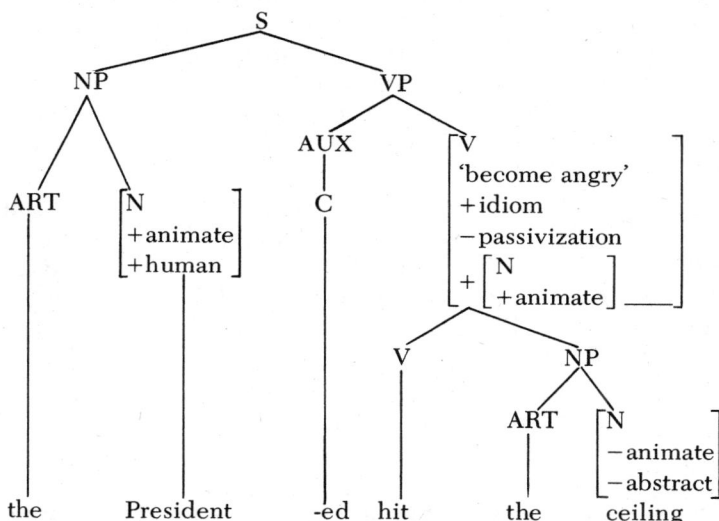

6.9 LEXICAL INSERTION

In the revised rules presented in §6.3, lexical insertion was included among the base rules of the phrase structure component. In reality it is better to think of lexical insertion as something quite separate. The phrase structure component creates a tree structure in which each terminal node is defined in such a way that, if matched with a suitable item from the lexicon, the result will be a grammatical sentence. More accurately the result will be an underlying structure capable of being transformed into a grammatical sentence.

Given the rules that have been posited thus far, lexical insertion most likely is not a single step but a series of steps. The introduction of verbs depends crucially on the accompanying nouns, which quite literally constitute a frame designed to accept certain verbs and reject others. We can think of the introduction of nouns, verbs, and certain related categories, such as adjectives, as taking place in a series of ordered steps in a **first lexical lookup,** or reference to the lexicon to select items for lexicon insertion. Formatives given phonological shape at this stage join the various grammatical formatives denoting tense, modality, and aspect, which are supplied by the phrase structure component.

The operation of transformational rules will in some cases lead to surface structures containing elements not present in deep structure. This is true, for example, of pronominalization, which deletes the lexical item associated with the original noun, leaving only its semantic features and the added feature [+pronoun] and in certain contexts [+relative]. In such cases it appears necessary to posit a **second lexical lookup** following application of the transformational rules. At this stage the feature [+pronoun] in combination with features for animate, masculine, feminine, and so forth, will trigger insertion of the pronouns *he, she, it, which,* and so forth. In addition to pronouns a number of transformationalists have argued that other categories including prepositions and certain adverbs are inserted in the second lexical lookup.

Numerous details remain in dispute. Some linguists have argued that the insertion of verbs should precede nouns. In essence the argument holds that random selection of nouns will lead to numerous sentences that are impossible because they constitute a frame into which no verb will fit.

> (19) a. *The table _____ the chair.
>   b. *The salad _____ the hostess.
>   c. *The dish _____ the spoon.

Perhaps by various stretches of the imagination it is possible to supply the missing verbs. A table might hit a chair during an earthquake. A salad might conceivably worry a hostess. We all remember the dish who (which?) ran away with the spoon. But most speakers of English will regard these sentences as abnormal in some way. Some linguists have argued that it is immaterial whether nouns or verbs are inserted first; the two approaches may be considered notational variants of each other. In principle questions like this should have an answer. In practice it is possible to find as many arguments on one side as on the other.

6.10 INTEGRATION OF THE COMPONENTS

The revisions in the 1957 model point toward a definition of language quite different from the one proposed in §1.2. **Language is a formal system for specifying the relationship between phonological sequences and their semantic interpretations.** The device (= grammar) that specifies the relationship relies heavily on syntactic analysis and posits rule components of several types, all centering around syntax. A set of phrase structure rules constitutes the base component. A pass through the lexicon provides a deep structure, which serves two important functions. On one hand it serves as the basis for a semantic interpretation. On the other it is processed by a set of transformational rules to yield a surface structure, which in turn is processed by a phonological component to provide a phonetic interpretation. The model, represented schematically in Figure 6–3, is noticeably different from the original model of Figure 5–9.

FIGURE 6–3   The 1965 Model of Transformational Grammar

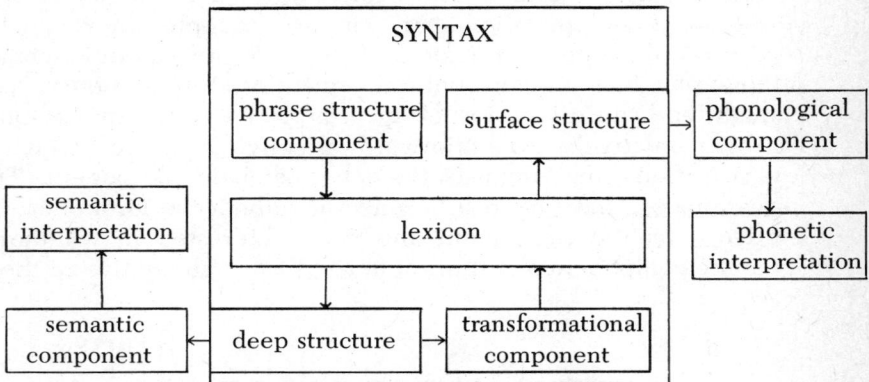

The 1965 model, set forth in Chomsky's *Aspects of the Theory of Syntax,* is often described as the *Aspects* model to distinguish it from the earlier *Syntactic Structures* model. The primacy of syntax is apparent from the arrangement of the components and the direction of the arrows. Critics of Chomsky, both within the transformational camp and on the outside, have argued that the model imposes a directionality on language that is not there. The model, critics claim, makes semantics dependent on syntax when in fact syntax should be dependent on semantics. Chomsky has replied that the appearance of directionality in the model is merely an artifact of the rule system. It is descriptively convenient to begin with syntax, but the system itself merely specifies the relationships without actually implying any kind of directionality. The arrows in diagrams such as Figure 6–3 could just as well point in both directions—or neither direction. Although many other issues have arisen in the post-*Aspects* discussions of transformational grammar, the fundamental issue has been whether semantics is interpretive or generative.

6.11 INTERPRETIVE SEMANTICS

The orthodox position (Chomsky has called it the "standard" theory) espoused by Chomsky and his closest followers is that the optimally efficient grammar follows the *Aspects* model—that is, it contains a semantic component that provides an interpretive reading of deep structure. As outlined by Katz and Fodor (1963), the process is accomplished through formal **projection rules** that act on the semantic features (called **semantic markers**) associated with each morpheme in deep structure. The semantic markers are elements such as animate, human, masculine, and so on, that occur in varying combinations in nearly all lexical items and that have well-known grammatical functions. A second type of element called a **distinguisher** serves to differentiate grammatically similar lexical items. Distinguishers are enclosed in single quotation marks in the examples in 20, and the phonological content of lexical items is represented in standard orthography. The concept behind semantic interpretation is simple enough, and the discussion of an interpretive semantic component has been relatively straightforward, although it has received much less attention from linguists than the syntactic component. Transformationalists have been less concerned about the form of an interpretive semantic component and more interested in whether the semantic component should be interpretive or generative in the first place.

(20)

N	N	N	N
+animate	+animate	+animate	+animate
+human	+human	+human	−human
'holder of	+male	+male	+male
college or	'an unmarried	'a young	'young male
university	individual'	knight in	fur seal
degree	*bachelor*	service of	kept from
signifying		another	breeding
completion		knight'	territory
of under-		*bachelor*	by older
graduate			males'
curriculum'			*bachelor*
bachelor			

6.12 GENERATIVE SEMANTICS

The concept of a generative grammar, proposed originally by Chomsky, is now accepted by virtually all linguists. The idea that the pen-and-paper grammar of linguists should duplicate as nearly as possible the internalized grammar of the speaker is also widely held. However, the orientation of transformational grammar toward syntax has led to several problems. For one, it has tended to reify the syntactic component as the creative element in language. It has created the impression that speakers are able to produce novel sentences because of syntactic rules rather than because of the semantic properties of language. To answer critics on this point, and for other reasons as well, Chomsky has sought to draw a distinction between competence and performance (§5.10). Competence is what speakers know about their language, and the model of Figure 6–3 can be construed as a formal system for representing this knowledge. Performance has to do with what a speaker does in the process of actually forming sentences and includes whatever strategies a speaker may use to string words together in a meaningful way. Performance involves numerous hesitations and false starts, which children learning their native language must systematically disregard in the process of constructing an internalized grammar. Chomsky has therefore argued that the proper concern of linguistics is competence rather than performance.

But if the pen-and-paper grammar is to duplicate the internalized grammar as nearly as possible, one can certainly raise legitimate questions about the primacy of syntax—particularly if one concedes that language is a system for expressing meanings in the form of speech. If the speaker starts with semantics and eventually converts this into speech, one might reasonably expect the pen-and-paper grammar of the linguist to reflect this in some way. Moreover, there is the purely formal argument that the rules of an interpretive semantic component inevitably duplicate many transformational rules and therefore make the grammar more complicated than one that progresses in a single direction from semantics to syntax and from there to actual speech.

Once we admit categories such as *animate, human,* and the like into descriptions of syntax, it becomes increasingly difficult to draw a sharp line between syntax and semantics. The logical next step is to posit additional abstractions, either in branching tree diagrams or as parts of complex symbols, until we have produced a kind of abstract syntax that can be equated with semantics. This is precisely the approach that has been adopted under the name **generative semantics.** Those who figure most prominently in the movement—Ross, Lakoff, and McCawley—are young scholars whose training in transformational grammar came, directly or indirectly, as students of Chomsky. Their approach, like Chomsky's work, shows the influence of mathematics in its formalizations and at the same time goes considerably beyond Chomsky in positing a grammar that resembles the propositional logic developed in philosophy.

Some idea of the approach adopted in generative semantics can be gained by examining the following sentences:

(21) Noel would have been protesting. (= 6c)

(22) a. I think John will not succeed.
      b. I don't think John will succeed.

(23) a. John is alive.
      b. John is dead.
      c. John died.
      d. Walter killed John.

The "orthodox" analysis of 21 in transformational grammar was presented in Figure 6–1, where tense, modality, perfective, and progressive were analyzed as constituents of the auxiliary. The generative
semantics approach has been to analyze each auxiliary verb as a
separate semantic-syntactic unit within the verb phrase. Several different analyses have been proposed, but all have the general form
shown in Figure 6–4. The affix transformation operates to produce the
intermediate structure:

Noel do will-past have be-en protest-ing.

FIGURE 6–4   **Abstract Representation of a Sentence**

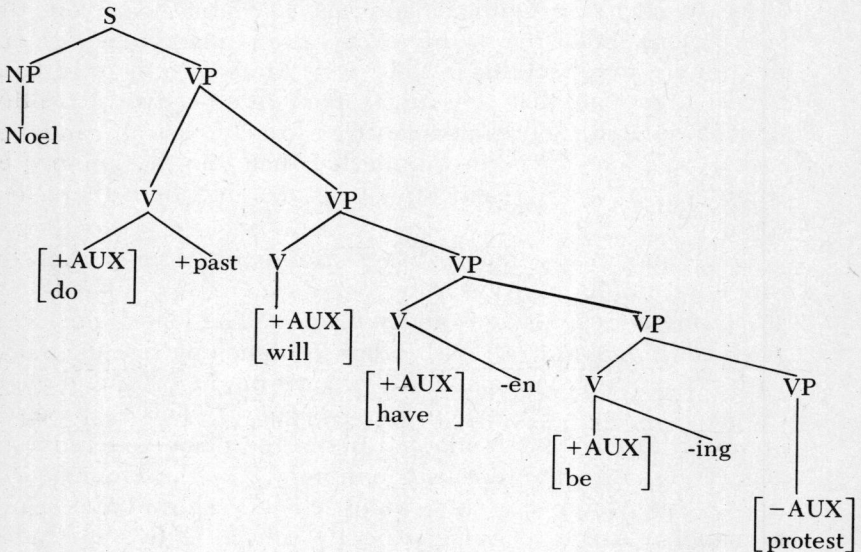

The presence of *do* in underlying structure obviates the need for a
do transformation and makes *do* automatically available for questions
and negative sentences. But now a transformation is required to
delete it when it is not followed by a tense affix:

Noel will-past have be-en protest-ing.

This is converted to *Noel would have been protesting* as in Figure 6–1. The two analyses differ more in the status they accord individual constituents than in any claims they make about overall sentence structure.

For the sentences of 22, it is possible to argue that both derive from the logical structure that underlies 22a. That is, a statement like 22b makes sense only if it is assigned the structure appropriate to 22a: to say *I don't think John will succeed* can only mean *I think John will not succeed*. The two forms of the sentence are complementary to each other and of course overlap in meaning. Specifically, the distribution of NEG is complementary in the two structures given in 22'a and b.

(22') a.

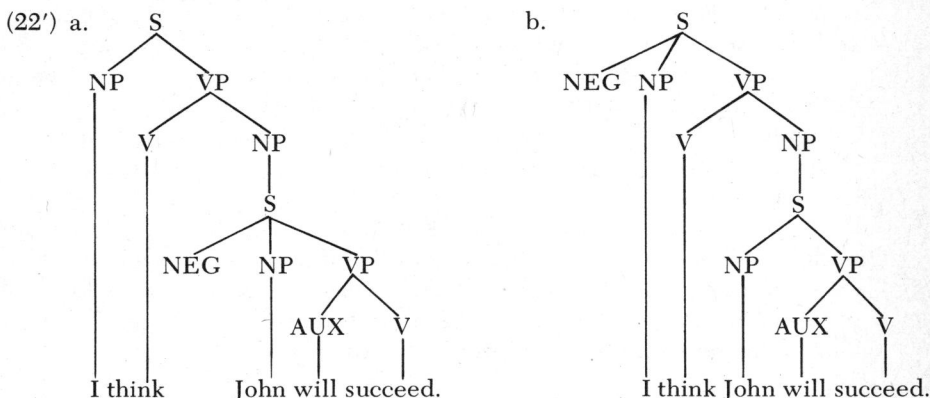

I think   John will succeed.

b.

I think John will succeed.

Only one occurrence of NEG is possible. If it occurs in the lower sentence, it cannot occur in the higher sentence and vice versa. If we take 22'a as the underlying structure of both sentences, we can derive 22'b from it by positing a transformation that we can call **negative raising.** This is an optional transformation that applies to embedded sentences following verbs such as *think, believe, want,* and so on. The transformation deletes the negative from the embedded sentence and assigns it to the next higher sentence, that is, the matrix sentence.

A similar analysis is possible for the sentences of 23 once we recognize that the content of 23a is repeated in each of the subsequent sentences, along with additional material:

(23') a. John is alive.
      b. John is dead.   (= John is not alive.)
      c. John died.   (= John became not alive.)
      d. Walter killed John.   (= Walter caused John to become not alive.)

Tree structure diagrams, slightly simplified, can be represented as shown in Figure 6–5. To account for 23c–d we must posit a **predicate raising** transformation. This operation takes the lowest predicate and consolidates it with the next higher predicate in a cycle that continues until no further consolidation is possible. At each stage of the cycle, the repeated noun phrase that is identical with the noun phrase of the next higher sentence is deleted, an operation for which there is well-established precedent (§5.10, §5.15). Since the consolidation of separate predicates precedes insertion of the lexical item that encompasses the more complex structure, the operation is sometimes described as a **prelexical transformation.** The claim is that a knowledge of the syntactic-semantic primitives is part of an individual's innate linguistic ability, whereas mastering the possible prelexical transformations is part of the process of learning a particular language. In the case of English, which allows both *John is not alive* and *John is dead,* the transformation of the abstract elements is apparently optional. In other languages such a transformation might never occur, might always be obligatory, or, as in English, might be optional.

Another novel feature of the analysis of these sentences is the treatment of *alive* as a verb. Such words have been classed as adjectives in traditional grammar, and this analysis has been the basis for both the *Syntactic Structures* model and *Aspects* model of transformational grammar. But it is clear that adjectives are a kind of predication and therefore have much in common with verbs. This is easy to see in the case of predicate adjectives.

(24) The book is expensive.

But this is also true of attributive adjectives, which are transformationally derived from predicate adjectives.

(25) The expensive book. . . .

Therefore, it has seemed reasonable to many linguists to think of verbs as a class comprising two subcategories: verbs proper and adjectives. This approach has been particularly appealing to those who have felt that semantic evidence should be admissible in syntactic analysis. It is an analysis that can be supported also by cross-linguistic evidence from languages in which adjectives and verbs form a single structural class. Japanese is such a language and so are a number of American Indian languages. One can always argue that the analysis of one language should not be influenced by evidence from another language, but this argument loses some of its force if one accepts the notion that linguistics should take an interest in the universal properties of language rather than concentrating narrowly on individual languages as isolated entities. The treatment of adjectives as verbs opens interesting possibilities in generative semantics and has been influential in the development of case grammar and meaning-structure grammar.

FIGURE 6–5   Abstract Representation of Syntactic-Semantic Primitives

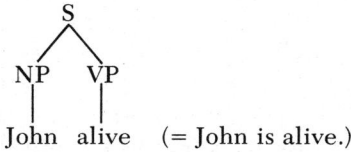

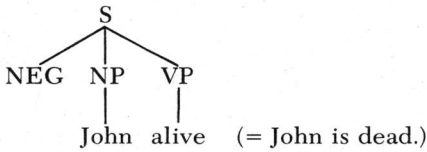

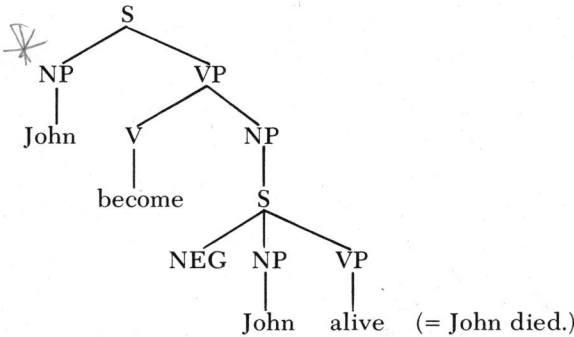

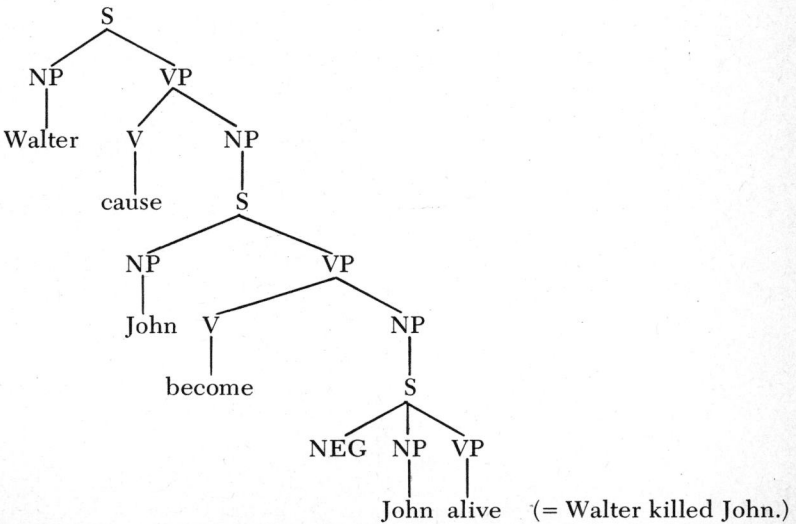

```
        S
       / \
     NP   VP
     |    |
   John  alive   (= John is alive.)
```

```
         S
        /|\
     NEG NP  VP
         |   |
       John alive   (= John is dead.)
```

```
           S
          / \
        NP   VP
        |   /  \
      John V    NP
           |    |
        become  S
               /|\
            NEG NP  VP
                |   |
              John alive   (= John died.)
```

```
           S
          / \
        NP   VP
        |   /  \
     Walter V   NP
            |   |
          cause S
               / \
             NP   VP
             |   /  \
           John V    NP
                |    |
              become S
                    /|\
                 NEG NP  VP
                     |   |
                   John alive   (= Walter killed John.)
```

In the last few years, generative semantics has become the dominant influence in linguistics. Chomsky continues to defend an approach that is only a slight modification of the 1965 *Aspects* model. A number of linguists continue to practice structuralism, and several scholars have proposed alternative models quite different from either the *Aspects* or generative-semantics versions of transformational grammar. The attraction of generative semantics has been its rigorous formalism, inherited from Chomsky, combined with its promise of atomizing syntax into semantic primitives. As one might suspect, the issues that have been debated in journal articles and in the mimeographed papers circulated from one university to another are much more complex than the discussion in the preceding paragraphs would suggest. There has been no shortage of competing proposals, of arguments to support them, and of rhetoric to rally the faithful to their respective camps. The abbreviated discussion presented here serves merely to illustrate the kind of data examined in generative semantics and the type of analysis favored. A firsthand examination of the relevant literature will serve the advanced student much better at this point than a prolonged secondhand account.

6.13 CASE GRAMMAR

Still another approach that has developed within the framework of transformational grammar is the case grammar of Charles Fillmore (1968). Fillmore's proposal attracted considerable support when it first appeared and was adopted by Stockwell, Schachter, and Partee (1973) in the UCLA grammar that appeared originally in 1968. More recently, however, enthusiasm has waned, and most of the syntacticians who originally supported case grammar have been won over to generative semantics. Since the defactors have from time to time included Fillmore himself, case grammar is of interest primarily for two reasons. First, its unorthodoxy compared to the *Aspects* model makes generative semantics seem quite orthodox in comparison. And second, Fillmore's model exercised an important influence on Wallace L. Chafe, whose views will be taken up in the next chapter.

The basic data used by Fillmore in his development of case grammar involved sentences in which the function of subject and object seemed to bear no relationship to semantics:

(26) a. *The door* opened.
      b. *Chuck* opened the door.
      c. *The key* opened the door.
      d. *The door* was opened by Chuck.
      e. *The door* was opened with the key.
      f. *Chuck* opened the door with the key.
      g. *The door* was opened with the key by Chuck.
      h. *The door* was opened by Chuck with the key.

These sentences represent varied statements that might be made about a single event. In each case the subject has been italicized. Since the concepts of subject and object figure prominently in both traditional and transformational grammar, one might expect these grammatical categories to be related systematically to meaning. But this is not the case. Three different nouns occur as subject, but the role each plays in the sentence is quite different. On the other hand, each noun, whether it occurs as subject, object, or object of a preposition, is related in an unchanging way to the action described by the verb. *Chuck* is always the **agent** (the doer of the action), *door* is always the **object** (the recipient of the action), and *key* is always the **instrument** used in connection with the action. The constant, therefore, is the semantic relationship rather than the syntactic role.

By adding additional sentences to the paradigm, it is possible to identify other semantic relationships:

(27) a. Chuck gave Wally the crown.
   b. Chuck gave the crown to Wally.
   c. Wally was given the crown by Chuck.
   d. The crown was given Wally by Chuck.

Again, each noun stands in the same semantic relationship regardless of its syntactic position. *Crown* is the semantic object in each sentence, just as *door* was the semantic object in the sentences of 26. Similarly *Wally* benefits from the action in the same way in all three sentences even though it is grammatically an indirect object in 27a and 27d, the object of a preposition in 27b, and the subject in 27c. In an inflectional language like Latin, the dative case of nouns customarily marks this semantic relationship, although dative has other uses as well. Fillmore adopted the term **dative** from traditional grammar to describe this relationship, but he was careful to define it as a semantic relationship rather than a grammatical function.

Given this approach, the sentences of a language can be described as consisting of a varying number of nouns, each specified as having a semantically defined case relationship to the verb associated with it. Each case configuration provides a sentence frame into which certain verbs can be inserted and others will not fit. A semantic case may appear in surface structure in various ways. Dative, as we have seen, may appear in English as subject, indirect object, or the object of a preposition, while in Latin the dative relationship is always expressed inflectionally—as are the other case relationships.

The notion of case as a semantic constant opens the way for an analysis of the transformational relationship between sentences containing a prepositional phrase and sentences that express the same meaning but lack a prepositional phrase. The usual pattern in English is for only one noun, the subject, to precede the verb. The subject is never part of a prepositional phrase, but some "subject" nouns are associated with prepositions when they follow the verb. This is true of agents (*by Chuck*), instruments (*with the key*), and datives (*to Wally*). The semantic object never occurs with a preposition, and the dative loses its preposition when it occurs immediately after the verb, as in 27a.

To the four cases identified thus far, Fillmore added two others on the basis of sentences like the following:

(28) a. The carpenters built the barn.
       b. The barn is red.
       c. The wreckers demolished the barn.

(29) The jurors elected Ted foreman.

(30) a. Eric went to Chicago.
       b. Chicago is windy.
       c. It is windy in Chicago.
       d. Eric is in Chicago.
       e. Eric went into Chicago.
       f. Eric entered Chicago.

FIGURE 6–6   Semantic Categories of Case Grammar

Case		Semantic function	Preposition
Agentive	(AGT)	instigator (typically animate) of the action identified by the verb	*by*
Instrumental	(INST)	inanimate force or object causally involved in the action or state identified by the verb	*with*
Dative	(DAT)	animate being affected by the state or action identified by the verb	*to*
Objective	(OBJ)	object or being affected by the action or state identified by the verb	Ø
Factitive	(FACT)	object or being resulting from the action or state identified by the verb or understood as part of the meaning of the verb	Ø
Locative	(LOC)	the case that identifies the location or spatial orientation of the state or action identified by the verb	variable

Barn in 28a–b is not exactly the same as *barn* in 28c. The latter is clearly the semantic object—sometimes affected by the action of the verb. But in 28a *barn* is not affected in the same way. It is brought into existence by the verb, and this is quite different from the tangible effects that can be discerned and described in an object already in existence. Nor is there any basis for claiming that *barn* in 28b is affected by an action. The verb in this sentence describes a state, a fact that produces no tangible effects on the noun associated with the state. In this respect *barn* of 28a–b is like the predicate complement *foreman* of 29. Fillmore termed this relationship **factitive** to distinguish it from the affective relationships associated with other cases.

In the sentences of 30, *Chicago* designates a **location** even though it is used in various ways. Even though all such sentences might be classed together, Fillmore suggested that the choice of a particular preposition such as *in* or *into* could be semantically significant. The six case relationships of case grammar are summarized in tabular form in Figure 6–6 (p. 176).

6.14 CASE FORMALISMS

The rule formalisms of case grammar are much like those of the *Aspects* model, despite crucial differences in concept. Although a complete case grammar would presumably be as complex as any other generative grammar, the basic rules can be reduced to the three rule formalisms of 31:

$$(31) \quad (CG\text{-}1) \quad S \rightarrow MOD \ PROP$$

$$(CG\text{-}2) \quad PROP \rightarrow V \begin{pmatrix} AGT \\ DAT \\ OBJ \\ INST \\ LOC \\ FACT \end{pmatrix}$$

$$(CG\text{-}3) \quad \begin{bmatrix} AGT \\ DAT \\ OBJ \\ INST \\ LOC \\ FACT \end{bmatrix} \rightarrow PREP \ NP$$

The rules have been labeled CG (for case grammar) and numbered in the order of application. Rule CG–1 states that a sentence consists of modality and a proposition (PROP). The proposition, according to CG–2, consists of a verb and from one to six of the possible case relationships. The use of parentheses to indicate **inclusive disjunc-**

tion anticipates a convention that will be used in Chapter 7. The convention is that any one or all of the items linked together by parentheses may be selected. Rule CG–3 says that each case consists of a preposition and a noun phrase. The familiar brace convention to denote **exclusive disjunction** requires CG–3 to apply separately to each case relationship selected from CG–2.

The rules create a tree structure similar to those of transformational grammar. However, Fillmore stipulates that the left-to-right arrangement of elements in the rules need not imply a linear orientation in the constituents themselves. This is an important point because, if case grammar represents universal semantic relationships, the relationships should be stated in a way that is independent of any particular language. (In general, all languages seem capable of expressing substantially the same semantic relations in spite of considerable diversity in surface structures.) We might therefore expect that once the constituents and their relationships are defined, the linear arrangement appropriate for the surface structure of any particular language could be prescribed by transformational rules.

The rules presented as CG–1 and CG–2 appear to be universal rules in the sense just described. Rule CG–3 is quite obviously a language-specific rule needed for English and other prepositional languages. We can easily imagine rules that would specify the appropriate prepositions from Figure 6–6 for English or an alternative rule to specify an inflectional affix or other signaling device for other languages. Similarly, it is not difficult to imagine the rules required to develop modality into the appropriate categories of tense, mode, and aspect appropriate for English or whatever other language is under investigation.

To illustrate the application of the rules, let us consider sentences 26f–h as diagramed in 32. Rule CG–1 will of course have the same outcome for every sentence to which it applies. CG–2 as applied here involves the selection of agentive, objective, and instrumental cases, all of which appear in 26f–h.

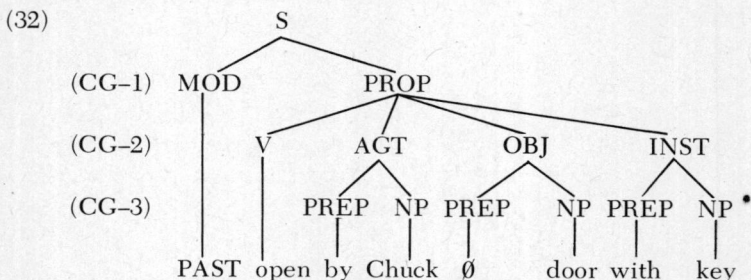

(32)

```
(CG-1)  MOD              PROP
                      _____|_____
(CG-2)    |    V     AGT      OBJ      INST
          |    |    /  \     /  \     /  \
(CG-3)    |    |  PREP NP  PREP  NP  PREP NP
          |    |    |   |    |    |    |   |
        PAST open  by Chuck  Ø  door with key
```

The sentences of 26 are repeated below as 33, with the case frames of each sentence indicated.

(33) a. The door opened.   OBJ
      b. Chuck opened the door.   AGT, OBJ
      c. The key opened the door.   OBJ, INST
      d. The door was opened by Chuck.   AGT, OBJ
      e. The door was opened with the key.   OBJ, INST
      f. Chuck opened the door with the key.   AGT, OBJ, INST
      g. The door was opened with the key by   AGT, OBJ, INST
          Chuck.
      h. The door was opened by Chuck with the   AGT, OBJ, INST
          key.

Once the case frame has been established, CG–3 develops a preposition and noun phrase for each case. Additional rules for developing modality, selecting the appropriate prepositions, and inserting noun(s) and verb are little different from the rules in other versions of transformational grammar. For the verb *open* the lexical entry must be specified in the following manner:

(34) open [____ OBJ (AGT) (INST)]

The notation says that *open* occurs in a case frame in which OBJ is always present and AGT and INST are optionally present. In 33a the only case selected is OBJ; in 33c and 33e OBJ is accompanied by INST, while in 33b and 33d the accompanying case is AGT. The remaining sentences, those diagramed as 32, have all three cases. Sentences containing the same case frames but differing in surface structure are different because the verbs in sentences 33d, 33e, 33g, 33h have been specified as [+passive], triggering the passive transformation. If the verb in a sentence containing both AGT and INST is [+passive], it is apparently optional in surface structure whether the agent or instrument comes immediately after the verb (33g, 33h).

In English only one noun, the subject, can precede the verb. If a verb is specified as [+passive], OBJ is normally assigned the subject position (as in 33d). But if both DAT and OBJ are present, DAT may optionally be transformed into the subject (as in 27c). For verbs not specified as [+passive], the transformational process is as follows: If there is an AGT, it becomes the subject; otherwise, if there is an INST, it becomes the subject; otherwise, the subject is the OBJ. The treatment of FACT seems to parallel OBJ, and LOC is selected as subject only when it is accompanied by no other case (as in 30b).

6.15 TRANSFORMATIONAL RULES

As one might expect in an approach called transformational grammar, transformational rules occupy a position of central importance. The energies of transformationalists have been directed toward identifying the principles of syntactic behavior in English and other languages, stating these principles in the form of transformational rules, and abstracting from these rules a set of generalizations about the nature and structure of human language. In practice this has meant compiling evidence for or against particular transformations that have been posited on the basis of observable syntactic patterns. Much attention has been given to determining the allowable properties of transformational rules since these rules tend to be equated with the properties of language itself.

In §5.9 we considered a transformation that had been posited to account for the relationship between sentences like the following:

(35) a. The student put away the book.
      b. The student put the book away.

The approach was to adopt 35a as embodying the underlying form for both sentences and derive 35b from it by means of a particle shift transformation, stated as follows:

(T–1) V PART NP $\Rightarrow$ V NP PART

Rule T–1 is an abbreviated version of the following statement:

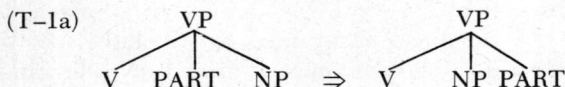

(T–1a)

$$\text{VP} \qquad\qquad \text{VP}$$
$$\text{V} \quad \text{PART} \quad \text{NP} \Rightarrow \text{V} \quad \text{NP} \quad \text{PART}$$

As presented in T–1 the rule described the constituents and gave the particular sequential arrangement required for the rule to operate. The notation of T–1a provides the additional information that these constituents are parts of a verb phrase. This information can be incorporated in T–1 by using labeled brackets to enclose the appropriate constituents:

(T–1b) $_{VP}$[V PART NP] $\Rightarrow$ $_{VP}$[V NP PART]

The labeled brackets identify the constituents as dominated by a verb phrase. Structures of any degree of complexity can be represented by following the bracketing procedures outlined in §5.7.

Rule T–1b follows the basic format developed in *Syntactic Structures*. In recent years slightly different notational devices have been used:

(T–1c) $_{VP}$[V PART NP] $\Rightarrow$ 1 3 2
             1   2   3

In T–1c the index numbers given to the left of the arrow are used to the right of the arrow to stand for the original constituents. The compactness of such notation is a distinct advantage in rules requiring complex structural descriptions. The notation of T–1c sets the stage for still another scheme in which the double-shafted arrow is eliminated in favor of a two-part statement containing a structural description (SD) and a structural change (SC):

(T–1d) SD: $_{VP}$[V PART NP]
                       1   2   3

          SC: 1   3   2

We can see from the sentences of 35 that T–1 is an optional transformation. A further condition on this transformation can be inferred from the following sentences:

(36) a. *The student put away it.
      b.   The student put it away.

It appears that the transformation is optional only if the noun phrase contains a noun. If the noun phrase contains a pronoun, the transformation is obligatory. This state of affairs can perhaps be explained by the fact that the last word in the sentence ordinarily receives full stress. A noun can accept full stress, but pronouns normally cannot. The differential treatment of nouns and pronouns is reflected syntactically in a condition (COND) attached to the transformational rule, which can now be given in its complete form:

(T–1e) SD: $_{VP}$[V PART NP]
                       1   2   3

          SC: 1   3   2

      COND: (1) optional if 3 is noun
             (2) obligatory if 3 is pronoun

Still another characteristic of transformational rule notation can be illustrated by the following sentences:

(37) a. (Then) the boy (quickly) pulled the wagon (with all his might).
      b. (Then) the wagon (quickly) was pulled by the boy (with all his might).

The sentences contain **variables**—that is, constituents that might assume various forms, including a null form, but that have no bearing on the transformation itself. These can be represented in the structural description by the cover symbols X, Y, Z. (Some linguists prefer to repeat the same symbol, usually X, to mark the location of each different variable.) If we take the active sentence (37a) as the underlying form, the structural change must specify several distinct steps:

$$\text{SD:} \quad _S[\ \begin{matrix} X & NP \\ 1 & 2 \end{matrix} \ _{VP}[\ \begin{matrix} Y & AUX & V & NP & Z \\ 3 & 4 & 5 & 6 & 7 \end{matrix} \ ] \ ]$$

$$\text{SC:} \quad (1) \quad \begin{matrix} 1 & 6 & & 3 & 4 & 5 & 2 & 7 \end{matrix}$$

(2) insert *by* before 2

(3) change 5 to *be* 5 *-en*

COND: optional

The structural description is an abstract characterization of the structure of 37a. Because of its abstract nature, it describes not only 37a but any number of other sentences having the same structural properties. Variables X, Y, Z remain in their original positions and are not affected by the structural change. The transformational steps, as applied to 37, include exchanging 2 (*the boy*) and 6 (*the wagon*), inserting *by* before 2 (*by the boy*), and modifying 5 by placing *be* before it and suffixing *-en* to it. The tense component of the auxiliary will be associated with *be* by the affix transformation (§6.3), and subsequent morphophonemic rules will eventually produce the appropriate form of the verb. The suffix *-en* is the past participle marker, which must also be adjusted morphophonemically, in this case to *-ed*. Although the description of the rule's application has been in terms of the examples in 37, it should be emphasized again that the rule is stated in general terms and will apply to any sentence meeting the same structural description.

6.16 DERIVATION

what you get from rules

In transformational grammar the term "derivation" has ordinarily referred to the derivation of one tree diagram from another—that is, a process of deriving surface forms from underlying forms through a series of intermediate forms. In traditional usage the term has referred to the conversion of a form belonging to one part of speech into a form belonging to a different class. The need for an explicit description of such derivational processes (in the traditional sense) is just as important in transformational grammar as it is in traditional and structural approaches. If anything, the need is more compelling because transformational grammar, unlike earlier models, professes to be generative—to provide an explicit account of all grammatical forms without positing rules that would lead to ungrammatical forms in the process.

Early transformational treatments (Chomsky 1957, Lees 1960) sought to use transformational rules to account for derivation. The approach was to treat derivation like all other general processes of the language. The difficulty is that derivation is not a general process. A transformational approach requires a great many nouns to be derived from nonoccurring verbs:

(38)   a.   *the enemy aggressed in 1939 ⇒ the enemy's aggression in 1939
       b.   *the enemy offended in 1939 ⇒ the enemy's offensive in 1939

A similar situation is found with attributive adjectives, which in transformational grammar are supposedly derived from relative clauses in which the adjective occurs predicatively:

(39)   a.   *the reason is main ⇒ the main reason
       b.   *a stranger is total ⇒ a total stranger
       c.   *the system is nervous ⇒ the nervous system
       d.   *a horse is runaway ⇒ a runaway horse

In other cases a predicate adjective has no attributive counterpart:

(40)   a.   the man is asleep ⇒ *the asleep man
       b.   the patient is alive ⇒ *the alive patient

Cases of idiosyncratic behavior like the above call for special statements somewhere in the grammar. We could list, as part of each transformation, the fictive words to which it applies and the words exempt from it. Or we could list, as part of the lexical entry for each word, the morphological and syntactic properties of that word. The first approach would complicate the transformational component while maintaining maximal simplicity in the lexicon. The second approach, by complicating the lexicon while streamlining the transformational apparatus, would have the opposite effect. The first approach has been called the **transformationalist position**, while the second has been called the **lexicalist position**.

To determine which approach or what combination of approaches will strike the optimal balance, we must examine varied data until we are satisfied that we have uncovered the operational patterns of the language and can make a decision on a principled basis. We find that many words exhibit regular patterns that could be described by transformational rules of general applicability, for example, *refuse* in the following paradigm:

(41)   a.   John refused the offer.
      b.   John's refusing the offer caused problems.
      c.   John's refusal of the offer caused problems.
      d.   John's refusing of the offer caused problems.
      e.   They expected John to refuse the offer.
      f.   They knew that John would refuse the offer.

All of these sentences (specifically the various forms of *refuse*) could be derived transformationally from the underlying structure of 41a—with the possible exception of the derived nominal in 41c. Derived nominals assume idiosyncratic forms: *refuse/refusal, continue/continuation/continuity, delay/delay,* and so on. Since the suffix itself is not predictable on the basis of the transformation, the appropriate suffix for each form must be listed in the lexicon. And since some verbs form more than a single derived nominal, each with a slightly different meaning, it appears that each nominal form (and its meaning) must be given separately in the lexicon.

Additional examples would lead to a number of related problems, but the general conclusion is already clear. Derivational patterns are sufficiently limited in productivity that we must rely, in part at least, on the lexicon rather than transformational rules to account for them.

6.17 CONCLUSION

It is as important to recognize the continuity between structural grammar and transformational grammar as it is to see the differences. Although transformational grammar has gone beyond structural grammar in demanding an explicit description of the total language, it is also true that transformational grammar has simply remained true to the standards of methodological rigor that were esteemed by structuralists. We can hardly blame linguists of the 1930s for not living a generation later and being able to build on the foundation of their own earlier work.

Transformationalists seek to develop generative rules for predicting linguistic forms, whereas structuralists sought to describe an existing corpus without necessarily projecting beyond it. This is a fundamental difference. The acceptance of process rules in transformational grammar and their avoidance in structuralism is another difference that has already been mentioned. The question of meaning in language was something that was generally avoided by structuralists. Transformational grammar adopted the same antimeaning stance in its earliest stages, but by 1965 it had recognized the importance of including an explicit account of semantics as part of any grammatical system. An increasing emphasis on grammar as a model of mental processes has made an interest in meaning virtually the hallmark of transformational theory in recent years. In this respect transformationalists differ profoundly from the earlier structuralists. But while transformationalists agree on the importance of meaning, the various proposals that have been advanced within transformational grammar to account for meaning are quite different and mutually incompatible.

In spite of their disagreements, transformationalists are united in their commitment to a theoretical approach built around a formal rule system in which rules performing syntactic transformations are of central importance. Transformationalists agree that an empirical understanding of semantics is most likely to come from a thorough-going study of the syntactic properties of language, and this study remains their primary objective.

summary

The distribution of tense, aspect, and modality in the main verb and auxiliary verb(s) of English sentences is accounted for with precision and elegance by positing an abstract underlying structure in which logically related elements occur together and are then rearranged by transformational rules. Inclusion of these and other morphological units leads to an elaboration of the phrase structure rules presented in the previous chapter.

A need to block the generation of ungrammatical sentences leads to the establishment of subcategorization and selectional rules. These rules have the effect of (1) subcategorizing syntactic units in terms of the units with which they can co-occur and (2) further specifying units as animate, inanimate, or the like to prevent the insertion of inanimate nouns in slots calling for animate nouns, and so forth.

The resulting model of language is significantly more complex than the 1957 view of a grammar, which posited a phrase structure component, a transformational component, and a morphophonemic component. The syntactic component is now seen as consisting of a phrase structure component and lexicon, which jointly lead to the generation of underlying, or "deep," structures. These structures are subject to transformational modification and further lexical insertion, leading to a surface structure. The deep structure is processed by a semantic component to yield a semantic interpretation, while the surface structure is processed by a phonological component to yield a phonetic interpretation. Language itself is viewed as a formal device for relating sound and meaning.

Some linguists, dissatisfied with the orthodox transformational model, have proposed systems in which the underlying structure is viewed as an abstract syntactic arrangement of elements whose properties are as much semantic as syntactic. One approach, called case grammar, has posited semantic categories such as agentive, objective, and instrumental for underlying structure on the assumption that underlying structure is a network of semantic relationships that give rise to surface syntactic structures.

further reading

General: Chomsky 1957, 1965; Jacobs and Rosenbaum 1968, Stockwell, Schachter, and Partee 1973, Grinder and Elgin 1973, Liles 1972, 1975, Lyons 1970a, 1970b, 1971, Bach and Harms 1968, Reibel and Schane 1969, Jacobs and Rosenbaum 1970, Fillmore and Langendoen 1971. **6.2–6.4** Chomsky 1957. **6.5–6.6** Chomsky 1965, Katz and Postal 1964. **6.7** Chomsky 1965. **6.8** Fraser 1970. **6.9** Jacobs and Rosenbaum 1968. **6.11** Katz and Fodor 1963, Jackendoff 1972, Chomsky 1972b. **6.12** McCawley 1970, G. Lakoff 1971, R. Lakoff 1968, Ross 1969, Keenan 1972, Peterson 1973, Shibatani 1972b, 1973a, 1973b. **6.13–6.14** Fillmore 1968, Stockwell, Schachter, and Partee 1973, Cook 1971a, 1971b, 1972, 1973, Starosta 1973, Sasaki 1971. **6.15** Stockwell, Schachter, and Partee 1973. **6.16** Chomsky 1957, Lees 1960b, Winter 1965, Bolinger 1967, Stockwell, Schachter, and Partee 1973.

7

meaning-structure grammar

7.1 LANGUAGE AS SYMBOLIZATION

In §1.3 it was emphasized that language is a means of communication. This is an abbreviated way of saying that language is a highly complex system for encoding a message from the universe of meaning and converting it into a sequence of sounds standing for the original meaning. The process of allowing one thing to stand for another is known as **symbolization.**

Because the most significant advances in linguistics since the nineteenth century have depended on analysis of the formal structure of language, the communicative aspect of language has frequently been neglected. This was not entirely the case in historical grammar, where similarities in both form and meaning are important. But it was increasingly the case in structural grammar. Meaning, it was felt, could not be observed directly. Therefore it was subjective and intuitive. Discussions of meaning were rejected as "mentalistic."

This view was carried to its logical conclusion by Harris (1951), who took the position that linguistic analysis could focus solely on formal structure and proceed without reference to meaning at all. It was merely necessary to know if two linguistic forms were "same" or "different." This requires knowledge of whether the forms in question belong to the same or different meaning category, but it would not be necessary to know the actual content of the meaning category.

Chomsky, a student of Harris and a product of the structural era, adopted the antimeaning bias of the period, observing: "Grammar [i.e., syntax] is best formulated as a self-contained study independent of semantics" (1957:106). Chomsky and his followers were later to criticize the "autonomous" phonology of structuralism for its refusal to allow grammatical statements in phonological descriptions. But in

Chomsky's revised version of transformational grammar (1965) and in his more recent work (1972), syntax is treated as a largely autonomous component. The dependence of phonology on grammar is recognized, but semantics is treated as an appendage that can be described, for the most part, in terms of syntax.

The generative semanticists have seen this as a shortcoming of conventional transformational grammar and have sought to state syntax in terms of semantics. But as students trained originally in syntax, they tend to see semantics as a complex kind of syntax.

The concept of symbolization—which is to say language as communication—was introduced not by a linguist trained in transformational grammar but by one trained in anthropology. The term was introduced by Chafe in 1967 and given a central place in his later book *Meaning and the Structure of Language* (1970b).

7.2   THE ORIGIN OF LANGUAGE

The notion of biological evolution as applied to human beings has long been accepted by most educated persons. Humankind is now thought to have emerged as a species distinct from other primates at least 3 million years ago in central Africa. The primates in turn diverged from other mammals at a still earlier period. The chain of evolution can be represented in a tree diagram similar to that used for the Indo-European languages in Figure 3–4. In such a diagram, humans and chimpanzees would appear as sister species, humans and dogs as distant cousins, and so on.

Behavior patterns exhibited by modern humans have parallels in the behavior of all other species. As might be expected the similarities between humans and chimpanzees are much more striking than the similarities between humans and dogs. But animal behaviorists are able to recognize precedents for human behavior even in simple organisms such as protozoa. It should not be surprising then to suggest that human communication, like other patterns of human behavior, represents a development and possibly a refinement of behavioral patterns found in other species.

Speculation about the origin of language was a popular activity in the nineteenth century. Theories discussed at this time were uninformed by the infant science of anthropology and of course antedated modern studies of animal behavior. As a result the discussion tended to be simplistic and superficial. The more fanciful proposals had the effect of bringing the whole subject into disrepute for many years.

Interest in studying the formal structure of language, dating from the beginning of historical linguistics, was another factor in diverting attention from questions about the origin of language. It has been fashionable during the era of transformational grammar to emphasize the formal complexities of language, particularly the transformational rules that play such an important role in this model. Human language and animal communication systems have accordingly been represented as totally different in kind rather than different only in degree. Many have adopted the position expressed by Langacker that "there is no reason to posit any significant relation between the communication systems of humans and other animals" (1967:21).

Animal behaviorists and anthropologists would disagree. Certainly there must be a relationship. The problem is simply to explain how human language could have developed from some prehuman communication system. Recognizing this, Langacker drops his earlier statement and says simply: "We learn nothing conclusive about the origin of language by examining the various ways in which animals communicate. Some animal communication takes place via fixed systems of signals, but this similarity to human language is such a vague and general one that it can hardly be taken as indicating any special relationship to language" (1973:18). This viewpoint, although not ruling out totally a link between animal communication and human language, still has the effect of discouraging inquiry into the nature of the relationship. If we wish to examine the design features of animal communication systems in comparison with human language, or if we wish to determine the conditions under which language might have developed from a nonlinguistic communication system, we must at least be willing to assume that such an inquiry can be fruitful. We must assume, at the very least, that both systems can be described, that comparison of the systems is possible, and that comparison will lead to useful insights.

The communication systems of chimpanzees, dogs, and our other mammal relatives consist of a finite number of discrete messages that can be described as barks, howls, squeals, growls, and the like. The number of messages may be as high as thirty-six in the case of vervet monkeys. Most dog owners can easily recognize a number of signals used by their pets. These could be described by citing the presumed meaning in single quotation marks and using an arrow to link it with a description of the resulting signal, as in Figure 7–1.

FIGURE 7–1   Animal Communication

'I'm glad to see you'	→	series of short, sharp barks accompanied by excited jumping and wagging of tail
'unfamiliar person or animal in the vicinity'	→	persistent barking
'keep away'	→	growl, teeth bared
'pain'	→	sharp, high-pitched yelp
'restlessness'	→	low, soft whine

To be sure, the exact meaning is often much less certain than indicated in the figure, but clearly we are dealing with a communication system.

The system differs from human language in several significant respects. The message inventory is limited to a finite set of unitary signals, and each signal must be described holistically in terms of its characteristic sounds and posturing. Human language, on the other hand, has a potentially unlimited message inventory, and each message must be described in terms of certain components that recur in varying combinations. Posturing or gesturing continues to accompany most messages, although the message is normally intelligible without it.

The careful observer of a pet dog can doubtless observe various signals beyond the few given in Figure 7–1. Certainly any dog owner knows that a dog can understand numerous audible signals that it is not able to transmit in return. Recent studies with chimpanzees indicate that these near relatives of humans are capable of understanding and transmitting fairly complex messages using the sign language of deaf persons. Apparently the crucial difference is not in the inability of chimpanzees to conceptualize, but in their slightly different vocal tract and slightly less efficient control of the vocal tract musculature.

At some time in the remote past, our direct ancestors must have had a message system roughly comparable to that of modern chimpanzees living in the wild. At that stage our own ancestors and those of the chimpanzees must have been quite similar. But for some reason chimpanzees never advanced beyond a system containing a fixed number of calls while the human line did.

The prehumans who lived between 2 and 3 million years ago were competing for a niche in an unfamiliar setting. They had left the forest and had moved to the grasslands of east-central Africa. Unlike the baboons, who reverted to all fours in the same environment, our ancestors tried an upright posture. Those who survived in this setting were the individuals who differed from their parents in the direction of modern humans. Their posture was more upright; their legs and feet were better suited to walking and running; and their hands were better suited for grasping. Since every day they were required to figure out solutions to novel problems, only the cleverest survived. But the survivors possessed a remarkably enlarged brain. Cranial enlargement was accomplished at the expense of a reduced mandible, but a large jaw became expendable as early humans came to rely more on manual dexterity and the use of simple tools. These factors led to slight, but nonetheless significant, changes in the vocal tract configuration.

Upright posture led to a sharp curve in the vocal tract, creating three distinct resonance chambers: the oral cavity, the nasal cavity, and the pharyngeal cavity (Figure 4–1). The reduced protrusion of the snout led to a small mouth with lips flat—no longer curved around with the extremities in parallel planes and the front portion in a third plane. All of this made possible the production of calls that could be described increasingly in terms of the phonetic units found in modern languages rather than the more apelike barks, howls, and squeals.

We can assume that the ability to make close acoustic discriminations accompanied—and contributed to—the development of an enlarged phonetic inventory. Careful attention to the ever-present sounds of nature must countless times have meant the difference between death and survival. Knowing whether the snap of a twig was produced by a predator or by an animal that could itself be hunted must often have meant the difference between a full stomach and an end to the human experiment. This kind of acoustic discrimination paved the way for mastery of subtle phonetic distinctions as intraspecies calls became increasingly important.

As an increased inventory of sounds became available to emerging humans, it became possible to expand the message inventory with a greatly decreased risk of confusing similar messages. Two different varieties of growls might not be readily distinguished, but two growls having markedly different phonetic properties would remain distinct. As messages acquired increasing phonetic properties, the signals themselves became increasingly arbitrary.

We still cannot say that the sounds produced by emerging humans were phones in the technical sense because they were not part of a sound system incorporated into a language. Indeed, language in the technical sense did not yet exist. Emerging humans had an elaborate call system, but this call system did not become a language until it developed **duality of patterning.** This development converted a closed call system into an open-ended system in which the message consisted of two parts: (1) a fixed inventory of components and (2) patterns for arranging these components into novel messages of increasing complexity.

7.3 DEVELOPMENT OF DUALITY

The whole concept of duality and its development can best be illustrated by imagining the call system of a humanlike community that might have existed between 2 and 3 million years ago. We can assume a call system at least as complex as that of modern vervet monkeys, probably more so. Among the fifty or more calls in the message inventory, there must certainly have been a danger signal:

Stage 1. 'danger' → gr

We call the starting point Stage 1 for convenience and symbolize the message 'danger' as *gr*. The hypothesized symbolization has obvious mnemonic value but should not be taken seriously as a reconstruction of prelanguage phonetics. The symbols *g* and *r* can be thought of as convenient cover terms for consonant and vowel or, better still, merely as algebraic symbols.

Since there are different degrees of danger in any culture, we can imagine that the normal danger signal might have been repeated a second time to indicate more than normal danger. This leads to a second stage, which at first seems hardly different from the starting point:

> Stage 2.   'danger'   →   gr
> 'great danger'   →   grgr

Notice, however, that Stage 2 contains a single component *gr* and a pattern of arrangement—reduplication—that leads to the creation of a new message. As an isolated development this is of little consequence. Reduplication of every signal in the inventory at this stage would double the possible output, but the system itself would remain closed. Still, an important principle is established: it is possible for signals to differ not only as holistic units but also as components of some larger unit.

Let us imagine that the two principal sources of danger at this stage were saber-toothed cats and cave bears. The danger may not have been equal, however. The saber-toothed cats may have learned that they were better off chasing a horse or deer than attacking bands of incipient humans. And the cave bear might still have been competing with early humans for places of shelter. Under these circumstances the signal for 'danger' would normally occur in the context of saber-toothed cat and the signal for 'great danger' in the context of cave bear. Complementary distribution in terms of semantic environments, as we saw in §3.5, leads the units in question to be classed as different. Stage 2 is therefore reanalyzed as follows:

> Stage 3.   'saber-toothed cat'   →   gr
> 'cave bear'   →   grgr

The components *g* and *r* remain in complementary distribution since *g* always begins a syllable (or word) and *r* always ends a syllable (or word)—assuming of course that these words are typical of the phonetic patterns found elsewhere in the call system. But at this stage the message for 'cave bear' is more detailed than necessary to distinguish it from 'saber-toothed cat.' If all speakers in the band drop the initial *g* in this word, the messages will remain distinct:

Stage 4.   'saber-toothed cat'   →   gr
            'cave bear'   →   rgr

But now the contrast can no longer be stated in terms of overall acoustic impressions. The two words consist of exactly the same components; it is the arrangement of components that is significant. At this stage r can occur initially and finally; g can occur medially and initially, where it contrasts with r. The pattern of distribution must be stated in the same terms used for stating the distribution of phonemes in modern languages.

At this stage there is no distinct word for 'danger' apart from its manifestation in cave bears and saber-toothed cats. The gap could be filled by a new coinage using the same phonemic inventory:

Stage 5.   'danger'   →   grg
            'saber-toothed cat'   →   gr
            'cave bear'   →   rgr

The first item is associated with a verblike property, while the last two denote nounlike objects. We can easily imagine possible combinations of these two types to create new messages:

gr grg   'danger from saber-toothed cat'
rgr grg   'danger from cave bear'

Or, used in a different pattern, we can imagine that the word for 'danger' could take on the meaning 'endanger' or 'create danger for' or simply 'hunt':

grg gr   'let's hunt saber-toothed cat'
grg rgr   'let's hunt cave bear'

And what began as a closed call system is no different at this stage from languages spoken in the world today.

We have focused on the development of a single call in a system that already must have been fairly complex. Similar changes may have taken place simultaneously with other calls in the original system, but this is beside the point. A small change limited to one part of the system can have far-reaching consequences for the entire system.

It is important to emphasize again that we have no way of knowing the exact sequence of steps leading from a call system to a language with duality of patterning. The five stages posited here are intended as a model of what might have occurred rather than as actual history. We know that some such steps did indeed take place because modern man has language and our prehuman ancestors did not.

7.4   SEMANTIC SPACE WITHIN THE VERB

It is useful to think of semantic space as though it is capable of being subdivided into like and unlike areas, with the latter bounded from each other. Philosophers since Plato have continued in one way or another to ask whether words are related to objects in a natural or arbitrary way. In modern times the question emerges in relationship to natural segmentations in the real world. Do humans use language to impose order on a universe inherently lacking in order, or do language categories merely reflect the natural organization of the universe?

The mistake of course is to suppose that it is entirely one way or the other. In this chapter we shall assume that there is a high degree of natural order in the universe and that this order is reflected systematically in language. At the same time we must acknowledge the existence of fuzzy areas where "natural" order is uncertain and where languages differ in their treatment of external phenomena. We intentionally avoid a philosophical examination of reality. Speakers of a language deal with the nonlinguistic world as though it is indeed real and our perceptions of it are reliable. It will be fruitful for purposes of analyzing language to work on the same assumption.

In terms of semantic space, we can speak of a fundamental dichotomy between nouns and verbs. While all languages seemingly provide for the conversion of one type into the other on occasion, it is generally the case that a structure can be classed as one or the other in any given utterance. We may therefore think of the typical sentence as consisting of a proposition symbolized by a verb. The proposition is typically accompanied by one or more arguments symbolized by nouns. Note that the verb is taken as the central unit and the nouns as satellites. In this respect meaning-structure grammar differs from both transformational grammar and case grammar, even though the overall formulation is similar in many ways to case grammar.

When we consider the types of verbs and the various categories of nouns that must be posited, it is clear that nouns must be described in terms of verbs rather than the other way around. Consider the following sentences:

    (1)   The water is cold.
    (2)   The pond froze.
    (3)   The children skated.
    (4)   The angler caught a fish.

In sentence 1 a **state** is described. In sentence 2 we are dealing not with a state but with a change from one state to another—from the unfrozen to the frozen state. Such a change can be termed a **process.**

Sentence 3 describes an **action** performed by the children. Sentence 4 involves an action from the standpoint of the angler and a process from the standpoint of the fish. Accordingly, as in Figure 7–2, we can classify verbs into four types: (1) states; (2) processes; (3) actions; and (4) those falling into the intersection of processes and actions.

FIGURE 7–2   The Division of Semantic Space Within the Verb

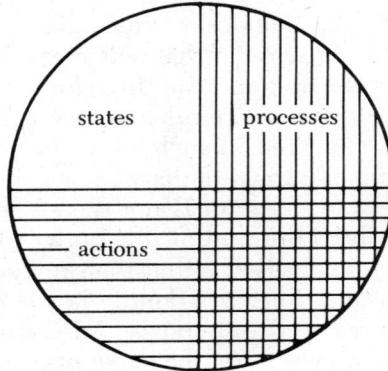

We notice that the noun associated with an action verb is always an **agent**—that is, an instigator of the action. Although there are a few specialized exceptions to be discussed below, an agent is typically an animate being acting on its own volition. This is not the case with nouns involved in states or processes. These nouns are **patients** in the sense that they are involved in the state or process through no conscious effort on their own part. Given the verbal category STATE or PROCESS, we can predict the occurrence of a patient noun; given a patient noun, we have no way of knowing which type of verb is associated with it. This asymmetry between nouns and verbs is one of a number of reasons for stating the occurrence of nouns in terms of verbs rather than the other way around.

In English and in many other languages, it is possible for a verb to have no noun associated with it in a sentence:

(5) It's hot.
(6) It's raining.

The examples of course appear to have nouns—or at least the pronoun *it*. But in actual fact these are not the usual anaphoric pronouns referring to some identifiable antecedent. The pronouns in these examples have no real semantic content at all. The verb in 5 seemingly describes a state, but it is an all-encompassing state that is not localized in any clearly identifiable noun. Similarly, the verb in 6 describes an action, but the action is part of a natural phenomenon that lacks an identifiable agent. In both cases we are forced to say that the verb describes an **ambient** state or action—something that is part of the total environment. The pronoun is semantically empty.

7.5 STATES, PROCESSES, AND ACTIONS

Having made the foregoing observations, we can now devise a formal system for building a grammar that will incorporate these categories. Unlike transformational grammar, in which the basic structure is determined by phrase structure rules, we must posit a system in which semantic space is specified in such a way that it is successively narrowed until it matches a concept that can be expressed by an available lexical item. The starting point is not the sentence itself, but rather the verb around which the sentence is built. And the rules entail the notion of **further specification** rather than replacement. We therefore adopt the convention of using a double-headed arrow instead of the single-headed arrow used previously. To distinguish optional rules from obligatory rules, we adopt the convention of using an arrow with a broken shaft to denote optionality. Taking V (denoting verb) as the initial symbol, we can posit the following three rules to account for the verbal specification of sentences 1 through 6:

$$(S\text{--}1) \quad V \quad \dashrightarrow \quad \text{state}$$

$$(S\text{--}2) \quad \underset{-\text{state}}{V} \quad \longrightarrow\!\!> \quad \left(\begin{array}{c} \text{process} \\ \text{action} \end{array}\right)$$

$$(S\text{--}3) \quad \underset{-\text{process}}{V} \quad \dashrightarrow \quad \text{ambient}$$

The rules may appear forbidding, but their interpretation is relatively straightforward. Rule S–1 says that a verb may optionally be further specified as a STATE. (The prefix S is intended to identify the rule as a semantic structure rule.) Rule S–2 says that if a verb is not specified as a STATE, it must be specified as either a PROCESS, an ACTION, or both a PROCESS and ACTION. Rule S–3 says that if a verb is not specified as a process it may optionally be specified as AMBIENT. The three rules therefore constitute a shorthand way of specifying precisely the semantic structures that were described in §7.4.

Some combination of rules S–1 through S–3 is responsible for generating the following semantic structures, which correspond to sentences 1 through 6. In the following diagrams the numbers without parentheses refer to the semantic rule responsible for adding the specification in question.

(1) V   (2) V   (3) V
    state 1   process 2   action 2

(4) V   (5) V   (6) V
    process 2   state 1   action 2
    action 2   ambient 3   ambient 3

Subsequent rules, to be discussed in detail in §7.8, have the effect of attaching an agent noun to verbs specified as actions and attaching a patient noun to verbs specified as either a state or process, provided the verb is not specified as ambient. Since ambient verbs lack a satellite noun with genuine semantic content, they remain without an attached noun in semantic structure. The pronoun *it*, which appears in surface structure, is a postsemantic addition required to make the resulting sentence conform to the prevailing subject + verb pattern of English. After the attachment of nouns, sentences 1–6 have the following semantic structure:

(1)   ┌──────────┐
    │   patient
    V   N   *e.g.*, The water is cold.
    state

(2)   ┌──────────┐
    │   patient
    V   N   *e.g.*, The pond froze.
    process

(3)   ┌──────────┐
    │   agent
    V   N   *e.g.*, The children skated.
    action

(4)   ┌──────┬──────────┐
    │   patient agent
    V   N   N   *e.g.*, The angler caught a fish.
    process
    action

(5)   V   *e.g.*, It's hot.
    state
    ambient

(6)   V   *e.g.*, It's raining.
    action
    ambient

7.6 COMPLETABLE, EXPERIENTIAL, AND BENEFACTIVE

There are numerous sentences in English that have a surface structure similar to sentence 4:

    (7)   The soprano sang a song.
    (8)   The package weighs a pound.
    (9)   The carpenter built a cabinet.

However, we cannot really say that *song* is a patient in 7 in the same sense that *fish* is a patient in 4. The verb *sing* is certainly an action, and *soprano* is the agent. But *song* itself adds no semantic content to the verb; there is really nothing besides a song that can be sung anyway. In Delaware, an American Indian language, verbs of this type are simple action verbs:

    /atēhwamwi-w/ → atehómu   'she sang a ceremonial song'

In Delaware there is actually no distinction between masculine and feminine, but this particular verb stem refers only to a type of ceremonial song sung by women. A Delaware speaker describes the ceremony with a simple action verb; an English speaker describing the same ceremony uses a verb followed by an object.

    Similarly, even though *pound* in 8 is the object of a verb, it is not a patient. The Japanese equivalent of 8 is:

    kotacu no omosa wa iči kiro desu   'the weight of the package is one kilogram'

The verb in both languages describes a state, and the unit of weight is a necessary part of describing the state.

    Finally, *cabinet* in 9 cannot be a patient because it is not even in existence until it is completed by the carpenter.

    The best way to analyze the forms in 7, 8, and 9 is to say that the verb is a state or action that has been further specified as **completable.** That is, the semantic content of the verb is somehow incomplete without the presence of a complement noun. Notice that there are differences from one language to another on this point and that within a single language different verbs allow different alternatives. In English, for example, we can say *She sang* but not **The package weighs.*

    We can allow for completable verbs by positing the following rule:

    (S–4) V
            $\begin{cases} \text{state} \\ \text{action} \end{cases}$ →» completable

That is, a verb specified as either STATE or ACTION may optionally be specified as COMPLETABLE. The rule as stated is intended to describe the English sentences under consideration, but some version of the rule could be expected in all languages.

Another group of sentences which in English fits into the same subject-verb-object pattern must be distinguished from the process-action type of sentence 4:

(10)   John saw the painting.
(11)   Alice heard the symphony.

While it appears that *painting* and *symphony* are both patients, *John* and *Alice* are certainly not involved in the activity of the verb in the same way as in the following:

(12)   John looked at the painting.
(13)   Alice listened to the symphony.

Clearly the apparent prepositional phrases in 12 and 13 are merely disguised adverbial particles similar to those identified in §5.9. The difference is that the particles in 12 and 13 are so tightly bound to the verbs that application of the particle shift transformation is impossible. We cannot say **John looked the painting at* or **Alice listened the symphony to*. In these cases *look at* and *listen to* must be regarded as inseparable units. Sentences 12 and 13 describe an action. The agents *John* and *Alice* participate consciously and voluntarily. Sentences 10 and 11, however, describe an **experience.** This is not something one "does"; it involves mental activity that may be wholly conscious, minimally conscious, or quite involuntary. Such a distinction is reflected in Delaware by the use of distinct verb stems:

/n-məlāw-ā-w/ → nəməlá·o   'I (involuntarily) smell him'
/n-kwəsəyāl-ā-w/ → ŋgwəsiyá·la   'I (voluntarily) smell him'

The first is an **experiential** process, while the second is an action process. As suggested by the English glosses, both meanings also occur in English semantic structure, although they are not systematically distinguished in surface structure. A similar semantic distinction can be posited for 'taste' and 'feel,' but in this case neither English nor Delaware distinguishes the meanings in surface structure.

The following sentence must also be analyzed as EXPERIENTIAL:

(14)   Noel wants an aspirin.
(15)   Robin knows the solution.
(16)   George likes salami.

In these examples, however, it appears that the experience involves a state rather than a process. Thus, it appears that EXPERIENTIAL as a category may co-occur with either states or processes, but not with actions. The situation can be expressed by the following rule:

(S–5)   V
     −action   -→ >   experiential
     −ambient

That is, a verb that is not specified as ACTION or AMBIENT may optionally be further specified as EXPERIENTIAL.

Still another verbal category is required on the basis of the following sentences:

(17)   Henry has the answers.
(18)   Richard lost the key.
(19)   Gerald found a job.

The subject noun in these sentences is neither an agent nor an experiencer. It seems instead to be the **beneficiary** of the situation described by the verb. We may therefore say that verbs are specified as **benefactive** in addition to whatever other specifications are present—STATE in 17 and PROCESS in 18 and 19. Use of the term BENEFACTIVE is not intended to imply that the benefits conveyed are always favorable; they may indeed be negative, as in 18.

It appears that *have* is always BENEFACTIVE. In the case of *lose* and *find,* this specification is optional since it is possible to say *The key was lost* or *A job was found* without direct reference to the beneficiary. In the case of action verbs, we find a similar situation:

(20)   John gave Mary a rose.
(21)   Richard bought Jerry a convertible.
(22)   Nick sold Alexi a used car.

It appears that *give* (in the sense of 'transmit') is always BENEFACTIVE. In the case of *buy* and *sell,* this specification is optional since it is possible to say *Richard bought a convertible* or *Nick sold a used car* without specifying the beneficiary. The simplest and most general rule for introducing BENEFACTIVE therefore seems to be the following:

(S–6)   V
     −ambient   -→ >   benefactive

That is, any verb not specified as AMBIENT may optionally be further specified as BENEFACTIVE.

7.7 LOCATIVE AND INSTRUMENT

Location is expressed in various ways, among them the following:

(23) a. The pencil is in the drawer.
      b. The book is on the table.
      c. The receiver is off the hook.

All three examples involve both a state and a location. We might there-fore propose the following rule for introducing **locative:**

(S–7) V
              state $\rightarrow\rightarrow$ locative

That is, any verb specified as STATE may be further specified as LOCATIVE. In previous examples of state verbs, we have analyzed the surface adjective as an underlying verb. In this case it is the surface preposition that appears to be the "verb"—semantically at least.

The examples of 23 can be explained by S–7, which applies to state verbs. But we find locatives with actions and processes as well:

(24) a. Cecil sat in the chair. (i.e., 'sat down in,' not 'was sitting in')
      b. The cat jumped on(to) the table.
      c. Walter fell off the wagon.

In these examples the basic verbs are *sit, jump,* and *fall*. The first two are actions and the last is a process. But with the addition of the appropriate surface preposition, these verbs acquire a locative noun that might be described as the goal of the action or process. In this context "goal" is broadly understood to include motion from (e.g., 24c) as well as toward (e.g., 24a and b). Sentences 23 and 24 differ in one important detail: if a pause occurs in the sentence, it comes before the surface preposition in 23 and after the preposition in 24. Structures of the latter type can be considered derived locatives (see Chafe 1970b:160–162).

There is still another type of locative construction involving actions and processes:

(25) a. The children played in the park.
      b. The fish flopped on the table.
      c. Walter fell on the wagon. (i.e., 'while on the wagon, Walter fell')

In these sentences the locative element is not the "goal" of the verb as in 24; instead, the locative noun conveys information about the location of the process or action denoted by the verb. In this respect the sentences more closely resemble those of 23, where the element associated with the location was a single noun rather than a verb and its noun satellite together.

The one remaining relationship of noun to verb can be identified by examining sentences like the following:

(26) a. John opened the door with a key.
      b. The key opened the door.
(27) a. John opened the door.
      b. The door opened.

If we considered 26b in isolation, it might appear that *key* is the agent of the action. But it is clear from 26a that *John* is really the agent and that *key* is merely an **instrument** used by the agent. The presence of an instrument does not seem to be dictated by any semantic specification of the verb because it is clear from 27 that the instrument need not be mentioned. In this respect the instrumental relationship is unique among the noun-verb relations. It is therefore appropriate to present the rule for introducing instrument nouns in the next section, along with the other rules for attaching nouns to verbs.

7.8   ATTACHMENT OF NOUNS TO VERBS

We have considered seven possible relations of nouns to verbs: agent, experiencer, beneficiary, locative, instrument, patient, and complement. The rules for attaching these nouns to the appropriate verbs can be stated by the following rules:

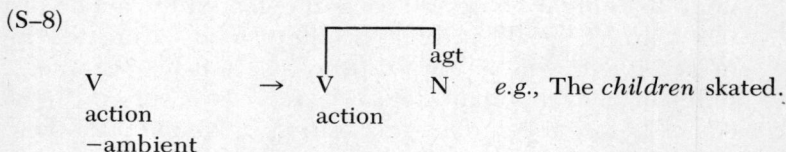

(S–8)

$$
\begin{array}{ccc}
\text{V} & \rightarrow & \overbrace{\text{V} \qquad \text{N}}^{\text{agt}} \\
\text{action} & & \text{action} \\
-\text{ambient} & &
\end{array}
$$

e.g., The *children* skated.

The rule says that a verb specified as ACTION but not AMBIENT is replaced by a construction consisting of the original verb with an agent noun (agt) attached to it. Because the semantic unit AMBIENT was introduced at a point where it could apply only to certain verbs, it must be specified negatively in this rule and in S–13, although not in other noun attachment rules.

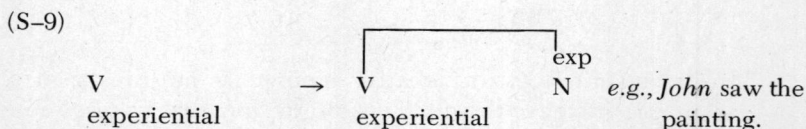

(S–9)

$$
\begin{array}{ccc}
\text{V} & \rightarrow & \overbrace{\text{V} \qquad \text{N}}^{\text{exp}} \\
\text{experiential} & & \text{experiential}
\end{array}
$$

e.g., John saw the painting.

A verb specified as EXPERIENTIAL is replaced by a construction in which the original verb has an experiencer noun (exp) attached to it. Rules S–8 and S–9 are presented separately, but they could just as easily be combined into a single rule. The specifications ACTION and EXPERIENTIAL are mutually exclusive (see rule S–5), and consequently agent and experiencer nouns always occur in complementary environments—agent nouns with ACTION verbs and experiencer nouns with EXPERIENTIAL verbs. This fact has important consequences that will be apparent when we consider the semantic relationships that are possible within a simple sentence and the symbolization of these relationships in surface structure.

Rules similar to S–8 and S–9 account for the attachment of beneficiary nouns (ben) to benefactive verbs and of locative nouns (loc) to locative verbs:

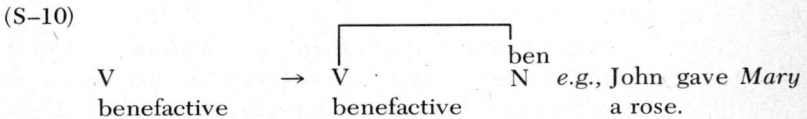

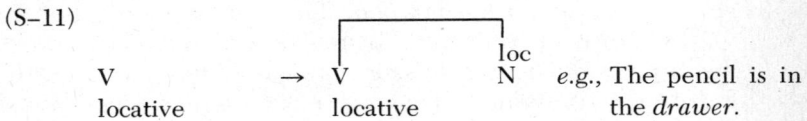

(S–10)

$$V \atop \text{benefactive} \quad \rightarrow \quad \underset{\text{benefactive}}{V} \quad \overset{\text{ben}}{N}$$

e.g., John gave *Mary* a rose.

(S–11)

$$V \atop \text{locative} \quad \rightarrow \quad \underset{\text{locative}}{V} \quad \overset{\text{loc}}{N}$$

e.g., The pencil is in the *drawer.*

As noted in §7.7, the attachment of an instrument noun (inst) is not dependent on the presence of any semantic unit within the verb. The only restriction seems to be that instrument nouns must be attached to verbs that are inherently of the process-action type:

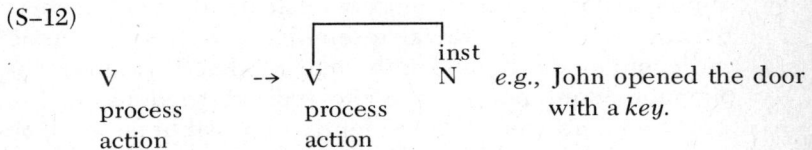

(S–12)

$$\underset{\substack{\text{process}\\\text{action}}}{V} \quad \rightarrow \quad \underset{\substack{\text{process}\\\text{action}}}{V} \quad \overset{\text{inst}}{N}$$

e.g., John opened the door with a *key.*

The rule says that a process-action verb may optionally have an instrument noun attached to it. Note that in certain cases an inherent process-action verb may have either the process or action omitted: *He ate with a fork; It was drawn with a crayon.*

Rules for the attachment of a patient noun (pat) and complement noun (comp) are similar to those presented earlier:

(S–13)

$$
\begin{array}{l}
V \\
\left\{\begin{array}{l}\text{state}\\\text{process}\end{array}\right\} \\
-\text{ambient}
\end{array}
\quad \rightarrow \quad
\begin{array}{ll}
\overbrace{\qquad\qquad}^{\text{pat}} \\
V & N \\
\left\{\begin{array}{l}\text{state}\\\text{process}\end{array}\right\}
\end{array}
\qquad
\begin{array}{l}
e.g.,\ \text{The } water \text{ is cold.}\\
\text{The } pond \text{ froze.}
\end{array}
$$

(S–14)

$$
\begin{array}{l}
V \\
\text{completable}
\end{array}
\quad \rightarrow \quad
\begin{array}{ll}
\overbrace{\qquad\qquad}^{\text{comp}} \\
V & N \\
\text{completable}
\end{array}
\qquad
\begin{array}{l}
e.g.,\ \text{The\quad soprano}\\
\text{sang a } song.
\end{array}
$$

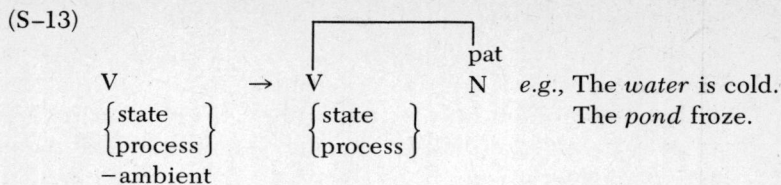

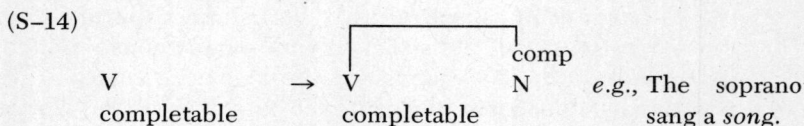

In each case the attachment of the noun is obligatory. Since STATE was introduced at a point where it could be further specified as AMBIENT, it is necessary to restrict rule S–13 from applying to verbs so specified. The semantic categories STATE and PROCESS themselves are mutually exclusive; whichever appears to the left of the arrow must also appear to the right.

Patient nouns and complement nouns often occur in complementary environments—patients with action-process verbs, and complements with action-completable verbs. However, patients and complements occasionally occur in the same sentence: *The hairdresser gave the customer a shampoo.* The sentence does not involve *give* in the sense of 'transmit.' Instead, the sentence is no different in meaning from *The hairdresser shampooed the customer.* In both cases *hairdresser* is agent and *customer* is patient. In one case *shampoo* is an action-process verb, and in the other we have an action-process verb *give* with a complement *shampoo.*

Agent and experiencer, as already noted, are mutually exclusive categories. Hence, only one can occur in a simple sentence. Either may be accompanied by a patient noun and in some cases by a complement noun as well. The patient always is more closely related to the verb than is the agent, and if a complement occurs in the same sentence, it is even more closely related to the verb than is the patient. Because of the superficial resemblance between beneficiary nouns and complement nouns on the one hand and patient nouns and complement nouns on the other, certain restrictions on co-occurrence must be mentioned. It is evidently impossible for agent, beneficiary, patient, and complement to fit into a simple sentence. (A possible exception would be dialects that permit sentences like the following: *We elected us Eisenhower President.* In this case, however, *President* could perhaps be analyzed as a reduction of *as President* or *to be President.*) In any event an agent noun can certainly be accompanied by any two of the set consisting of beneficiary, complement, and patient. Instruments, as previously noted, can occur in any sentence, provided the sentence contains an action-process verb. Locatives involve some special problems, but in general a locative of one type or another can be accommodated in most sentences along with other noun-verb relationships.

As suggested above, some nouns are much more closely related to the verb than others. Agent and experiencer nouns, for example, often occur in contexts where their semantic content is already known from previous statements. Since the nouns contribute nothing new to the discourse, they can be pronominalized or (in some languages) omitted entirely. Complement nouns, on the other hand, constitute an essential—and indispensable—part of the verb. Patient nouns, although less intimately connected to the verb than complements, are closer to verbs in the hierarchy than either agents or experiencers are. Instruments and locatives also seem closely related to the verb, at least in the sense of providing new information. Beneficiary nouns are somewhat more remote from verbs in the hierarchy, although they are more likely to provide new information than agents or experiencers.

If all seven types of noun-verb relationships occurred in a single sentence, the hierarchical relationship would be something like that shown in Figure 7–3. It should be repeated, however, that no simple sentence will accommodate all seven relationships. Moreover, the exact status of each noun within the hierarchy is by no means firmly resolved. Even more pertinent, the entire question of hierarchical noun-verb relationships seems quite irrelevant to linguists who remain committed to transformational grammar, where language continues to be analyzed in terms of syntactic rather than semantic patterns.

FIGURE 7–3   Hierarchy of Noun-Verb Relations Within a Simple Sentence

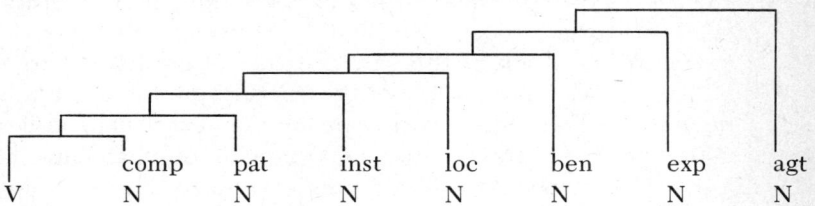

	comp	pat	inst	loc	ben	exp	agt
V	N	N	N	N	N	N	N

The use of ordered rules leads quite naturally to a hierarchical structure like that of Figure 7–3 because each rule applies to the output of previous rules. Thus, given a verb specified as PROCESS and ACTION, rule S–8 will create the following structure:

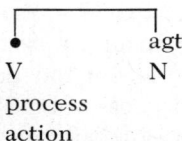

	agt
V	N

process
action

Rule S–13 will subsequently apply to the verb, replacing it with a structure that will occupy the position formerly occupied by the verb in the overall structure. This is the spot marked as a node in the preceding and following diagrams.

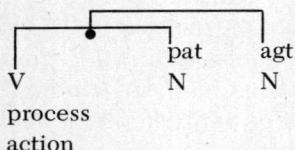

```
              ┌─────┐
    ┌─────────●     │
    │         pat   agt
    V         N     N
  process
  action
```

The structure at this stage is regarded as consisting of elements having formally defined relationships but lacking linear order. The diagrams are drawn in an arbitrary linear order since there is no other way to represent them on a two-dimensional surface, but they are better thought of as a mobile whose parts have no fixed order. The assignment of linear order corresponding to the order of elements in the surface structure is a function of the linearization rules to be discussed in §7.19.

7.9　SEMANTIC SPACE WITHIN THE NOUN

It is useful to think of semantic space within the noun as capable of being partitioned in much the same way as in the verb. Specifically, it seems reasonable to suggest that a noun is a unit occurring under a relationship label such as AGENT or PATIENT or the like. Nouns, like verbs, may be further specified in various ways—for example, as ANIMATE. This specification partitions nouns into two mutually exclusive categories, those specified as ANIMATE and those lacking this specification. Lack of this specification is equivalent to a specification INANIMATE. But in meaning-structure grammar the approach has been to treat features as either present or absent. This differs from the usual practice in transformational grammar of regarding all features as present and specified either plus or minus. The meaning-structure approach is based on the concept of **marking,** or **markedness,** mentioned in §4.11. The feature ANIMATE is taken as the marked member of the opposition; a noun not so marked (the **unmarked** noun) is automatically construed as inanimate.

Features such as ANIMATE are termed **selectional units** since they serve to narrow semantic space within the noun until this space can be identified with the domain of an individual lexical unit. Selectional units appear to exist in a hierarchy, with various possibilities for cross-classification. The result is that a diagram of the possibilities for partitioning semantic space within the noun cannot easily be constructed on a two-dimensional surface. We will therefore proceed immediately to a discussion of the selectional units within the noun and only later (in §7.14) attempt to represent these in a diagram.

7.10 SELECTIONAL UNITS WITHIN THE NOUN

A thoughtful glance at Figure 7–3 suggests definite restrictions on the kind of noun that is capable of occurring in any particular noun-verb relationship. For example, agents, experiencers, and beneficiaries can be animate, whereas locatives and instruments are never animate. Patients and complements may be either animate or inanimate. The grammar should contain formal rules to specify this. However, the noun cannot be specified merely in terms of the unit ANIMATE because this feature, in turn, is dependent on other selectional units:

$$(S–15) \quad \begin{Bmatrix} exp \\ agt \\ ben \end{Bmatrix}_N \quad \rightarrow> \quad \begin{pmatrix} count \\ potent \end{pmatrix}$$

Rule S–15 says that an experiencer, agent, or beneficiary noun must be further specified as either COUNT or POTENT or both. The unit COUNT is found in all countable nouns, that is, those having plurals such as *girls, squirrels, books,* and *ideas.* Nouns lacking the selectional unit COUNT are often termed mass nouns since they lack plural forms, for example, *water, rice, flour.* The unit POTENT seems to be required in the case of certain agents that are not actually animate, for example, *sun* in *The sun dried the clothes.* Thus, a distinction is possible between natural forces that are POTENT but not ANIMATE and living creatures that are both POTENT and ANIMATE.

$$(S–16) \quad \begin{bmatrix} loc \\ inst \\ comp \\ pat \end{bmatrix}_N \quad -\!\rightarrow> \quad count$$

Rule S–16 provides that a locative, instrument, complement, or patient noun may optionally be further specified as COUNT. Nouns lacking this specification, as noted above, are mass nouns. Within the group of nouns covered by S–16, three may contain the unit POTENT:

$$(S–17) \quad \begin{Bmatrix} inst \\ pat \\ comp \end{Bmatrix}_N \quad -\!\rightarrow> \quad potent$$

Rule S–17 says that instrument, patient, and complement nouns may optionally be further specified as POTENT.

(S–18) $\begin{bmatrix} \text{count} \\ \text{potent} \end{bmatrix}$ -→ >   animate

We now see the complicated relationship between the units ANIMATE, COUNT, and POTENT. Rule S–18 says that a noun containing both COUNT and POTENT may optionally be further specified as ANIMATE. The overall effect of rules S–15 through S–18 is to require the unit ANIMATE with agents, experiencers, and beneficiaries; to prevent it with locatives and instruments; and to make it optional with patients and complements. This is precisely the distributional pattern described at the beginning of this section. The potent but inanimate nouns such as *heat* or *the sun,* which are partial exceptions to the pattern, are covered by the optional nature of the rules and the alternatives within S–15.

7.11 HUMAN AND ASSOCIATED UNITS

A great many additional selectional units within the noun can be identified. However, we will limit the discussion that follows to those units occurring in English that figure most prominently in grammatical processes. The intention of this chapter, as elsewhere, is to acquaint students with the issues so they will be in a position to understand studies now in progress and eventually contribute to these studies. The answers to vexing problems in linguistics are not always to be found in the back of a book; they remain to be worked out, and they are equally accessible to all investigators.

(S–19)   animate   -→ >   human

Rule S–19 says that an animate noun may be further specified as HUMAN. Notice that the rule itself says nothing about the category NOUN. But ANIMATE was earlier introduced in such a way that it can occur only as part of the hierarchy of semantic units found within the noun.

(S–20)   human   -→ >   feminine

Rule S–20 says that a noun specified as HUMAN may be further specified as FEMININE. This amounts to saying that FEMININE is a marked unit; a noun not specified as FEMININE will automatically be treated as unmarked, that is, masculine. This seems to be a correct statement in terms of traditional usage.

This usage, which admittedly denies equal status to women, has recently come under attack along with various social institutions in the wake of the women's liberation movement. Thus, *chairman,* historically a neutral form, is now self-consciously replaced by *chairperson* or paired with *chairwoman*—a usage that actually reinforces gender distinctions rather than neutralizing them. At the same time a term like *guy/guys,* originally restricted to masculine usage, is being extended to feminine referents. This is a sign of instability; the unit FEMININE is undergoing changes in distribution. As characteristic in such cases, the changes are often contradictory, making it difficult to predict the eventual outcome.

There was a time in our own culture when nouns such as *doctor* and *lawyer* were never specified as FEMININE. Even today many speakers probably regard the FEMININE specification of these nouns as exceptional. In the Soviet Union, however, the normal situation, in terms of the average person's experience, is for *doctor* to be specified FEMININE. In the United States, *nurse* has traditionally carried the specification FEMININE, but as an increasing number of men enter this profession, speakers will no doubt reanalyze the occurrence of FEMININE in this noun as optional rather than obligatory.

$$(S-21) \quad \text{human} \quad \rightarrow > \quad \begin{pmatrix} \text{first} \\ \text{second} \end{pmatrix}$$

Rule S–21 says that a noun specified as HUMAN may be further specified as either FIRST PERSON or SECOND PERSON or both simultaneously. Specification of first person and second person is reasonable enough (inflection for PLURAL will be discussed in §7.16), but does English ever require the simultaneous presence of both units? The answer to this can be found by considering everyday conversations involving two persons, A and B:

    A: "What are you going to do this evening?"
    B: "We're going to a movie."

B's statement can mean either (1) that B plans for B and A to go to a movie together or (2) that B plans to go to a movie with some third person and that A is not included. Since the two meanings are not systematically distinguished in English, people sometimes find themselves in difficulty when their listener makes the wrong interpretation.

Many languages automatically make this distinction. Delaware has separate pronouns [ni·lú·na] 'we (excluding second person)' and [ki·lú·na] 'we (including second person)' and indexes this information in all verb forms: /n-pā-hm-nā/→ [mbá·həna] 'we (excluding second person) go'; /k-pā-hm-nā/→ [kəpá·həna] 'we (including second person) go.' Since the distinction is conceptually present in English, we can regard it as present in semantic structure. The fact that it is not symbolized in surface structure can be attributed to an accidental lacuna in the lexicon. The lack of a lexical item can thus be viewed as having a filtering effect on the symbolization of otherwise viable semantic structures.

A noun not specified as either FIRST or SECOND remains unmarked —that is, not specified as anything more narrow than HUMAN (unless also specified FEMININE). As such, these nouns are treated as third persons and are pronominalized by either *he* or *she*. Nonhuman animate nouns are pronominalized in the same way if the gender distinction is perceived as relevant. In animate nouns where the gender distinction is not viewed as relevant (and in all nouns not specified as animate in the first place), the pronominalized form is *it*.

7.12 UNIQUE NOUNS

Proper nouns exhibit certain properties that require a special rule:

(S–22) N
        count   –→ >   unique

That is, any noun specified as COUNT may optionally be further specified as UNIQUE. This is a unit that characterizes the proper names of persons, domestic animals, geographical places, and sometimes objects. Each of these items belongs to a category that is countable but, when specified as UNIQUE, is recognized as belonging to a set containing one member. This has two consequences. First, since it defines a set containing only one member, it effectively deletes the unit COUNT. (In diagrams we can represent unique nouns as lacking COUNT.) And second, it requires that a proper name be assigned to any noun carrying this specification. The following are examples of unique nouns:

N	N	N	N	N
unique	unique	animate	animate	animate
Excalibur	*London*	unique	human	human
		Fido	unique	feminine
			George	unique
				Harriet

7.13 LEXICAL SPECIFICATION

The selectional units discussed up to this point are important not only because they specify the division of semantic space within the noun and verb but also because they have widely recognized grammatical consequences. The presence of ANIMATE as a unit within the noun, for example, is crucial in allowing 28 while blocking 29.

(28)   The dog drank the milk.
(29)   *The table drank the milk.

It is possible to identify a great many other selectional units whose relevance is considerably more limited. The semantic paradigm in Figure 7–4 points toward one such unit that might be labeled YOUNG (or IMMATURE), the absence of which implies ADULT (or MATURE).

FIGURE 7–4   A Semantic Paradigm

					−YOUNG	YOUNG
COUNT	POTENT	ANIMATE	HUMAN	−FEMININE	*man*	*boy*
				FEMININE	*woman*	*girl*

In Figure 7–4 *man* appears as the least marked term, that is, not specifically FEMININE and not specifically YOUNG. *Woman* is marked as FEMININE, *boy* is marked as YOUNG, and *girl* is marked for both categories. We thus have strong grounds for positing YOUNG as a unit covering the distinction between the mature and immature of the species. But this unit, unlike ANIMATE, HUMAN, or FEMININE, has no significant implications for the overall grammar. It functions solely to distinguish individual lexical items such as those discussed above. For convenience we may call units of this type **subgrammatical selectional units.** (The selectional units of meaning-structure grammar correspond roughly to the **semantic markers** of Katz and Fodor 1963, while subgrammatical selectional units are analogous to their **distinguishers**—see §6.11.)

The identification of subgrammatical selectional units is of some interest to linguists, although they have traditionally been more concerned with units having broader grammatical implications. Subgrammatical selectional units are one of the chief concerns of lexicographers and occasionally occupy the attention of psychologists, anthropologists, and philosophers as well.

In principle it should be possible to specify additional subgrammatical selectional units until the semantic space within the noun or verb is narrowed in such a way that it can be matched with a single item stored in the lexicon. In actual practice it is convenient to abbreviate this process by using the following rule:

$$(\text{S--23}) \quad \begin{bmatrix} V \\ \\ N \end{bmatrix} \rightarrow \begin{bmatrix} V \\ root \\ N \\ root \end{bmatrix}$$

The rule says that a verb or noun is replaced by a unit containing the features of a verb root or a noun root. The root so specified is viewed as a semantic entity lacking phonetic properties. But as a semantic entity it can be matched with a word stored in the lexicon, and this word will of course have phonological properties.

Roots specified by S–23 will be labeled with the word that symbolizes the meaning involved, and these will be set in italics. This is the practice already adopted for the examples given at the end of §7.12. But it is important to remember that the italicized lexical unit refers to a **meaning** rather than to a **word**. The actual symbolization of the meaning takes place when the lexical specification is matched with a linguistic form stored in the lexicon. (Although lexical units will be printed in italics in this book, students will find it necessary to use underlining for class assignments or typed manuscripts.)

In a simple communication system such as that described in §7.2, the symbolization process is quite direct, taking the form:

$$\begin{aligned} A &\rightarrow x \\ B &\rightarrow y \\ C &\rightarrow z \quad \text{etc.} \end{aligned}$$

where capital letters represent meanings and small letters represent holistic messages. In a communication system as complex as language, symbolization is more complicated and much less direct. The build-up of semantic structure alone has required twenty-three rules so far, and the present chapter is far from exhaustive in its treatment of semantics. A number of semantic rules remain to be presented before we can claim to have completed even a cursory discussion of the semantic component.

We noted in Chapter 1 that meaning lacks linearity—although linearity is a necessary property of spoken language. Once we have completed our survey of the semantic component, we must therefore turn to the syntactic component, where semantic relations are replaced with arbitrary linear arrangements. Only after this step is completed is the resulting linear string symbolized, as each morpheme is replaced with a form stored in the lexicon. Following symbolization we can still expect that many morphemes (e.g., 'PLURAL') will be modified in accord with rules stored in the phonological component. The process of symbolization in language is indeed indirect.

7.14 FURTHER EXAMINATION OF THE NOUN

Following lexical specification both nouns and verbs are inflected in various ways. But before taking up inflection it will be helpful to consider in greater detail the categories of semantic space within the noun. These are sketched in Figure 7–5. The pie diagram is built in layers working outward from the center. Thus, ANIMATE occurs within the intersection of COUNT and POTENT; HUMAN occurs within ANIMATE; FEMININE occurs within HUMAN; and so on. Points labeled within the diagram represent lexical units occurring within the designated semantic space. These are exemplified below:

(a) N
rice

(b) N
potent
heat

(c) N
count
tree

(d) N
unique
Excalibur

(e) N
count
place
river

(f) N
place
unique
Mississippi

(g) N
count
potent
gamma ray

(h) N
potent
unique
the sun

(i) N
count
potent
animate
zebra

(j) N
count
potent
animate
anthro
big bad wolf

(k) N
potent
animate
anthro
unique
Fido

(l) N
count
potent
animate
anthro
feminine
little red hen

(m) N
potent
animate
anthro
feminine
unique
Lassie

(n) N
count
potent
animate
feminine
mare

(o) N
count
potent
animate
human
person

(p) N
potent
animate
human
unique
John

(q) N
count
potent
animate
human
feminine
woman

(r) N
potent
animate
human
feminine
unique
Jane

The units ANTHROPOMORPHIC (ANTHRO) and PLACE are included in Figure 7–5 even though they were not introduced in the text. Strong arguments can be advanced in favor of these units, but there are also certain problems that should be noted. A noun such as (n) *mare*, for example, is clearly ANIMATE and FEMININE. It is a further specification

FIGURE 7–5   **Some Divisions of Semantic Space Within the Noun**

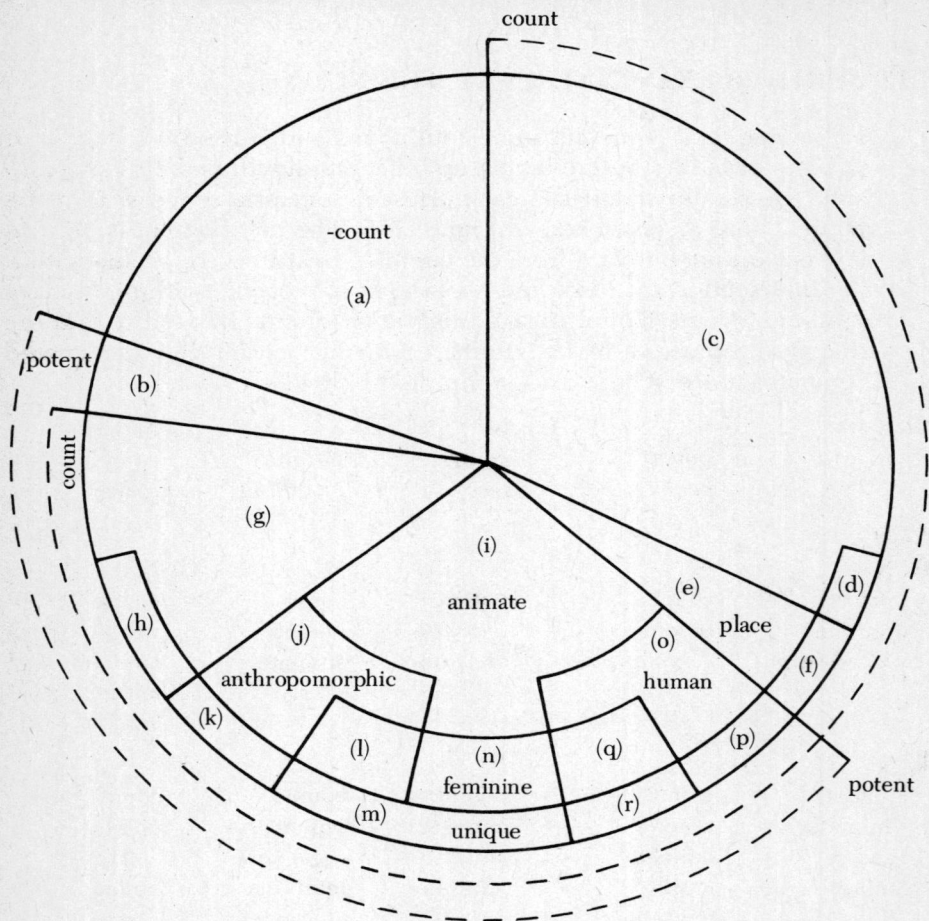

of *horse*, which is specified as ANIMATE but lacks the unit FEMININE. However, *stallion* is also a further specification of *horse* and contrasts with *mare* by being explicitly MASCULINE. The situation is further complicated by the presence of a term such as *gelding*. In cases of this type, we may wish to say that the lexical unit *horse* may function also as a selectional unit (see Chafe 1970b:116–118) and that the contrast between MASCULINE and FEMININE within this unit involves subgrammatical selectional units. The alternative would be a complete restatement of the distribution of FEMININE as a selectional unit.

Note also that a noun such as (m) *Lassie* could conceivably be analyzed as lacking the feature ANTHROPOMORPHIC, that is, simply as ANIMATE. The unit ANTHRO is included in the analysis presented here on the grounds that any animal specified as UNIQUE must be viewed anthropomorphically. Hence, the potential contrast based on the occurrence or nonoccurrence of ANTHRO in nouns of this type apparently is not realized.

7.15 INFLECTION OF THE VERB

Once semantic space has been narrowed to the domain of a single nominal or verbal concept, it is fairly easy to symbolize that concept. But these concepts are still modified in various ways. Verbs, for example, are ordinarily associated with tense, and nouns regularly are associated with singular or plural. These categories may be regarded as **inflections.** Consider the following sentences in which the parenthesized elements are intended to suggest the probable linguistic environment but will not be included in the analysis.

(30) Bob goes to work (every day).
(31) Bob starts work (tomorrow).
(32) Bob started work (yesterday).
(33) Bob is working (now).
(34) Bob has worked (forty years).

Sentence 30 describes an ongoing **generic** condition, a general truth, something not bound by time. Such verbs are traditionally described as present tense, but they are present only in the sense that they are not specifically inflected as past. It would be more accurate to say that verbs of this type are unmarked for tense.

The verb in sentence 31 is also unmarked for tense, a fact that makes it clear that in English the unmarked tense can encompass both present and future. Historically there were only two tenses in English, past and nonpast (i.e., unmarked). Modern English uses several devices to specify future tense, including *will, is going to,* and the unmarked tense as in 31.

In 32 we see the past tense inflection. In 33 we have an example of progressive aspect, and in 34 we have perfective aspect. Note that the category of aspect is distinct from tense and occurs as an optional further specification in conjunction with either past or unmarked tense. Structures like 30 through 34 can be generated by the following rules:

(S–24) V $\rightarrow$ generic

(S–25) V $\rightarrow$ past

(S–26) V $\left\{\begin{array}{l}\text{action}\\ \begin{bmatrix}\text{state}\\ -\text{generic}\end{bmatrix}\\ \begin{bmatrix}\text{process}\\ -\text{generic}\end{bmatrix}\end{array}\right\}$ $\rightarrow$ perfective

(S–27) V
$$\left\{\begin{array}{l} \text{action} \\ \left[\begin{array}{l} \text{process} \\ -\text{generic} \end{array}\right] \end{array}\right\} \quad \text{-→>} \quad \text{progressive}$$

Rule S–24 says that any verb may be further specified as GENERIC. This rule will serve our purposes, although a more precise formulation would include certain restrictions on the types of verbs that can be specified as GENERIC (see Chafe 1970b:168–170). Rule S–25 says that any verb may optionally be further specified as PAST. Verbs not specified in this way will of course remain unmarked for tense. Rule S–26 says that a verb may be specified as PERFECTIVE if it is (1) an action; (2) a nongeneric state; or (3) a nongeneric process. Finally rule S–27 says that a verb may be specified as progressive if it is either an action or a nongeneric process.

We will omit specific discussion of future tense as well as the various categories of modality that give rise to auxiliaries such as *may, might, ought to, must,* and *should.* While numerous questions could be raised over details, it should not be too difficult to imagine in broad outline how these categories could be accounted for within the meaning-structure model.

The remaining inflectional categories within the verb can be handled by the following two rules:

(S–28) V -→> $\left(\begin{array}{l} \text{negative} \\ \text{interrogative} \end{array}\right)$

(S–29) V
$$\begin{array}{l} -\text{past} \\ -\text{interrogative} \end{array} \quad \text{-→>} \quad \text{imperative}$$

Rule S–28 allows any verb to be specified as either NEGATIVE or INTERROGATIVE or both. Rule S–29 allows any verb not specified as PAST or INTERROGATIVE to be further specified as IMPERATIVE. The consequences of these two rules should be self-evident.

7.16 INFLECTION OF THE NOUN

Most of the inflectional categories discussed in connection with the verb had temporal implications. This seemingly is related to the intrinsically temporal nature of states, processes, and actions. Nouns lack this temporal quality but contain other intrinsic qualities that lead to certain characteristic inflections.

The fundamental dichotomy within the noun is between those nouns specified as COUNT and those lacking this specification—that is, between countable and noncountable nouns. In the case of countable nouns, it is necessary to distinguish between (1) a single member of the class denoted by the noun; (2) a group consisting of more than one; or (3) the entire class as an aggregate. In the case of noncountable nouns, it is necessary to distinguish between the general substance and specific units of the substance in question. And when specific members of units are mentioned, it is convenient for speakers to have a way of indicating whether they assume listeners are already familiar with the member or unit referred to. These requirements intersect in a fairly complex way, as may be seen from the following sentences:

(35) Wally saw an elephant.
(36) The elephant drank (some) water.
(37) Elephants like peanuts.
(38) The elephant is a strong beast.
(39) Pink elephants drink ambrosia.

In sentence 35 the only noun (apart from the UNIQUE noun *Wally*) is an individual member of the class symbolized by the label *elephant*. In 36 an individual member of this class, one already known to the listener, is mentioned. The sentence also refers to a measurable unit of the noncountable substance *water*. In this sentence an unstressed form of *some* occurs as an optional element; the meaning would be unchanged if it were omitted. Phonetically the word is [sm], and linguists sometimes write it *sm* to distinguish it from the stressed form found in *sometimes* and in contexts like *They drank some but not all*.

Sentence 37 is generic; the entire class of elephants and peanuts are referred to. Sentence 38 is also generic, but the elephant in this case is viewed as an aggregate rather than as a collection of countable individuals. The entire predicate in this sentence is analyzed as a single verb (see Chafe 1970b:201–203). Sentence 39 is another generic sentence, with *pink elephants* viewed as a countable collection and *ambrosia* viewed as a general substance rather than as a measurable unit of the substance. These rather intricate specifications are obtained with the following rules:

(S–30) N $\rightarrow$ >   definite

(S–31) N
$\quad$ −definite $\rightarrow$ >   generic / V
$\qquad\qquad\qquad\qquad\qquad$ generic

(S–32) N
$\quad$ generic $\rightarrow$ >   aggregate / count

(S–33) N
$\quad$ count
$\quad$ −unique $\rightarrow$ >   plural
$\quad$ −aggregate

Still another rule could conceivably be proposed to add DEFINITE as an automatic further specification of unique nouns since any unique noun is by definition DEFINITE. For most unique nouns in English, however, there is no surface reflex of the unit DEFINITE—although it is possible to speak of *the Smiths* or *the Joneses*. It appears that DEFINITE is part of the semantic structure of all unique nouns but is marked in surface structure only in certain cases. Explicit rules accounting for this would be required in a complete grammar but will be omitted here. Unique nouns in the diagrams that follow will be represented as though lacking the unit DEFINITE.

Rule S–30 says that any noun may optionally be inflected as DEFINITE. Rule S–31 says that any noun not specified as DEFINITE must be specified as GENERIC if it occurs in a sentence with a verb carrying this specification. Rule S–32 says that a noun specified as GENERIC may optionally be further specified as AGGREGATE if it is a countable noun. Finally Rule S–33 says that a noun specified as COUNT, but not UNIQUE or AGGREGATE, may be specified as PLURAL. To illustrate the interaction of these rules, semantic structure diagrams of sentences 35 through 39 are presented below as 35a through 39a:

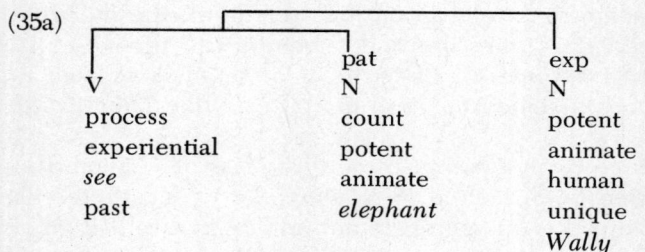

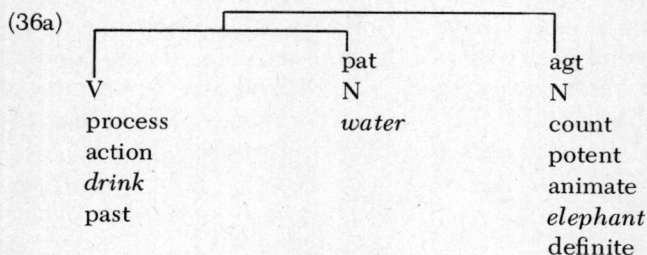

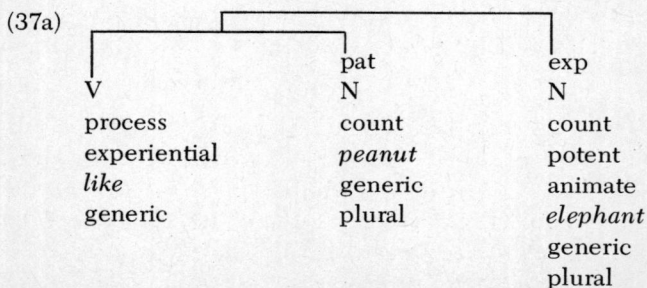

(35a)

V	pat N	exp N
process	count	potent
experiential	potent	animate
see	animate	human
past	*elephant*	unique
		Wally

(36a)

V	pat N	agt N
process	*water*	count
action		potent
drink		animate
past		*elephant*
		definite

(37a)

V	pat N	exp N
process	count	count
experiential	*peanut*	potent
like	generic	animate
generic	plural	*elephant*
		generic
		plural

(38a)

```
        ┌───────────────────┐
        V                   pat
        V                   N
        state               count
        a strong beast      potent
        generic             animate
                            elephant
                            generic
                            aggregate
```

(39a)

```
        ┌──────────┬────────────┐
        V          pat          agt
        V          N            N
        process    ambrosia     count
        action     generic      potent
        drink                   animate
        generic                 elephant
                                modified
                                pink
                                generic
                                plural
```

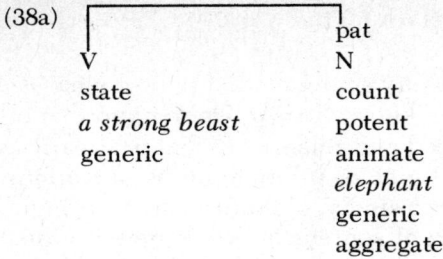

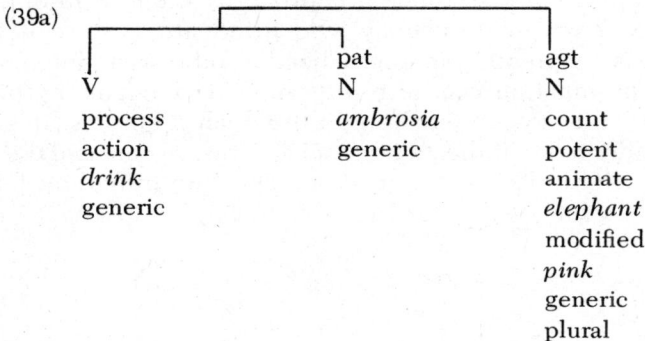

Given the above semantic structures, the surface structures presented as 35 through 39 can be explained in a very mechanical way:

> The semantic units DEFINITE and AGGREGATE fall together postsemantically to become the surface *definite article*. The surface item known as the *indefinite article* actually can be regarded as a reflection of the selectional unit COUNT; that is, it appears in the surface structure whenever there is semantically a count noun which is neither definite, aggregate, nor plural—precisely in those situations where there is no other surface article or suffix. The optional surface item (sm) identifies a noun which is neither generic nor definite in those cases where the indefinite article is not present. Finally, the semantic unit PLURAL is represented in surface structure by the well-known sibilant suffix, or in less regular ways with certain noun roots. GENERIC has no direct surface reflection. (Chafe 1970b:194)

Moreover, it should not be difficult to see how different semantic specifications in the above sentences would lead to slightly different surface structures. For example, if *elephant* in 37 were GENERIC but not PLURAL, we could expect the surface structure *An elephant likes peanuts*. Or if *elephant* were GENERIC and AGGREGATE, we could expect *The elephant likes peanuts*.

7.17 OLD AND NEW INFORMATION

It is typically the case in any sentence that part of what is said refers to objects that are already known to the listener and that one or more new objects are introduced and related to what is already known. We can speak of these two types of information as **old information** and **new information.** Not surprisingly, old information in English tends to come near the beginning of sentences, while new information tends to come near the end and to carry higher pitch and greater amplitude. This is understandable since it is primarily the new information that the speaker wishes to convey. Old information, since it is already familiar, is frequently pronominalized or otherwise deleted.

New information can be represented in diagrams by placing the semantic unit NEW under the unit to which it applies. In such cases NEW is indented to indicate its special status. Absence of the specification NEW indicates old information. The rule providing for this can be stated as follows:

(S–34) *root* -→ *root*
new

The rule is stated as an option available to all lexical units. In actuality, the option is exercised in a very predictable way based on the fact that a particular lexical item has occurred previously in the discourse or denotes an object visible to both speaker and listener. Moreover, it is usually the case that agent and experiencer nouns convey old information while beneficiaries, patients, and complements convey new information. Typically the verb conveys new information. Exceptions to these norms lead to special marking in surface structure in either the linearization of elements or distribution of stress or both.

7.18 POSTSEMANTIC PROCESSES

Semantic structures are not symbolized directly. We have already noted that a nonlinear semantic structure must be converted into a linear surface structure before it can be symbolized. Even before this can happen, certain semantic units must be segmented from the noun or verb in which they occur and made available for eventual symbolization as independent words or, in some cases, as bound morphemes. Such is the case with the definite and indefinite articles of surface structure, both of which originate as semantic specifications within the noun (§7.16). The development of PLURAL as a bound suffix is a similar process. Within the verb, PAST becomes a bound suffix, while the various specifications of aspect and modality are realized as auxiliary verbs. The surface arrangement of these elements was examined in Chapter 6 in transformational terms. The analysis of meaning-structure grammar differs only in assuming that the elements originate as semantic, rather than syntactic, units.

7.19 LINEARIZATION

It was emphasized in §7.8 and §7.13 that semantic structure is inherently nonlinear. A semantic structure consists essentially of a verb and one or more nouns associated with it. The noun and verb are tied together by a precisely defined semantic relationship rather than by linear order. In the diagrams of semantic structure, we have adopted a convention of placing the verb on the left and attaching nouns in a hierarchical arrangement to the right of the verb. This was motivated partly by the semantic priority of the verb and partly by the need to adopt an arbitrary arrangement to fit a two-dimensional surface. It does not imply that verbs occur before nouns in thought; it is simply a conventionalized way of representing the well-formedness conditions within semantic structure. The ideal arrangement, as already noted, would be to represent semantic-structure diagrams as freely swinging mobiles.

In transformational grammar, deep structure is viewed as inherently linear from the application of the first phrase structure rule until the last transformation produces the final surface structure. The assumption has been that if syntactic structures can be described, semantic relationships can be stated in terms of syntax. The assumption of meaning-structure grammar is quite the opposite: if semantic relationships can be described, the syntax of surface structure can be explained in terms of the underlying semantics.

There are certain advantages in starting with a nonlinear semantic structure. Chief among them is the fact that a single semantic structure will generally serve to account for very diverse surface structures expressing the same meaning in two or more languages. Similarly a given semantic structure is valid for all historical stages of a single language even though the surface structures of the language may undergo drastic changes through time. Finally a system in which semantic structures give rise to surface structures seems to bear a direct relationship to the way in which thought gives rise to actual speech. The model can therefore be applied not only to competence but to performance as well.

Linearization actually involves two slightly different phenomena. **Primary linearization** involves the arrangement of major sentence elements such as nouns and verbs in the appropriate linear order. **Secondary linearization** involves the linear arrangement of bound morphemes occurring within major elements such as the noun and verb. These morphemes include plural suffixes, tense suffixes, and the like. We will concentrate for the present on primary linearization.

The various steps can be stated as formal rules, but it will be adequate for present purposes to describe the processes informally.

If only one noun occurs with a verb, its relationship to the verb (denoted by the label AGT, PAT, INST, or the like) is replaced by the designation SUBJECT. This is a natural step since labels such as AGT and PAT are appropriate to semantic structure, while the term SUBJECT traditionally refers to a surface category.

If more than one noun occurs with a verb, it is often the case that only one noun conveys old information—that is, lacks the specification NEW. This is the noun whose label is replaced by SUBJECT. (Cases involving two nouns, both specified as NEW, are examined below.)

Once a noun has been labeled SUBJECT, it is assigned a linear position preceding the verb. This is apparently what has happened in the following sentences. In each case the italicized noun, regardless of its original semantic label, has somehow been designated SUBJECT and placed before the verb. Words bearing an acute accent convey new information.

(40) a. The *food* is cóld.
      b. The *ship* sánk.
      c. The *clown* smíled.
(41) a. *Richard* saw Jóhn.
      b. *Richard* cheated Jóhn.
(42) *Vincent* painted a pícture.
(43) a. The *gambler* opened the door with a kéy.
      b. The *gambler* set the cards on the táble.
(44) a. *John* gave Mary the bóok.
      b. *John* gave the book to Máry.

The sentences of 40 represent the simplest case, where a single noun is associated with the verb. The sentences of 41 are naturally understood as answering the respective questions *Who did Richard see?* and *Who did Richard cheat?* In a similar way, 42 appears to answer the question *What did Vincent do?* In both 41 and 42, it appears that the noun not designated SUBJECT is automatically designated OBJECT and assigned a linear position following the verb.

But the situation in 43 and 44 is more complicated because we must distinguish between an **inner object,** which occurs closer to the verb, and an **outer object,** which occurs farther from it. Both of these convey new information, although only one carries primary stress. In 43 it appears that a noun labeled PAT is automatically INNER OBJECT if it occurs in the environment of a noun labeled INST or LOC. This leaves the instrument or locative to be designated OUTER OBJECT. It is significant that the outer object is accompanied in surface structure by a preposition that reflects the semantic origin of the noun.

The two sentences of 44 have traditionally been analyzed as having exactly the same semantic content. In transformational grammar they are ordinarily assigned the same deep structure and said to differ only because they have been subjected to different transformational options. When considered in a context, however, it is fairly clear that the two sentences answer different questions. The unmarked sentence 44a answers the question *What did John do?* while 44b is a response to *Who did John give the book to?* Thus, in 44a both *Mary* and *book* are NEW, but in 44b only *Mary* is NEW. Given a choice between two nouns both specified as NEW, the beneficiary noun is ordinarily chosen as the inner object (as in 44a). If only the beneficiary is NEW (as in 44b), it cannot be chosen as the inner object. That designation falls to the only remaining noun, the patient; the beneficiary is then selected as outer object and is marked with the preposition *to*. We must therefore conclude that the two sentences differ slightly in semantic content. The difference is expressed in terms of the distribution of old and new information, a subtlety that has not as yet been incorporated in transformational grammar.

Still, since the difference between 44a and 44b is so slight, it remains true that we have two surface patterns available to convey essentially the same information. What if a speaker, for some reason, chooses the syntactic pattern of 44a to convey the information of 44b? In this case a third surface structure emerges:

(44) c. *John* gave Máry the book.

The difference remains subtle, but it is one that has been familiar to linguists since the era of structural grammar. Primary stress, normally assigned to the last word of the sentence (since that is the word ordinarily conveying new information), is shifted to *Mary* while *book* receives a reduced degree of stress. Whether the choice between 44b and 44c is purely optional or depends on a semantic distinction that might be described in terms of contrastive emphasis is a question we will not attempt to answer here.

It is possible of course that sentences 41 and 42 could also have a different distribution of old and new information. Let us imagine that the semantic content of these sentences occurs in response to a different set of questions and consider the different surface structures that will result.

(41)   Who saw John?
    a'. Ríchard saw *John*.
    a". *John* was seen by Ríchard.
         Who cheated John?
    b'. Ríchard cheated *John*.
    b". *John* was cheated by Ríchard.
(42)   Who painted the picture?
    '.   Víncent painted the *picture*.
    ".   The *picture* was painted by Víncent.

Again two surface patterns are available to convey essentially the same information. If the agent or experiencer is chosen as subject, it must be marked by high pitch since it now conveys new information, contrary to the usual expectation. The only way to introduce new information at the end of the sentence is to adopt a passive construction. This involves special syntactic devices to mark the surface subject as a semantic patient rather than agent, an arrangement that is also contrary to the usual expectation.

The notion put forth by transformational grammar of the passive transformation as a purely optional choice is basically false. Passive and active sentences cannot be freely interchanged in the same contextual setting. The passive construction is possible only if the usual distribution of old and new information has been disturbed. In such a case either a passive construction or an adjustment of stress patterns is necessary. This is the only choice that appears to be optional, and this choice exists only in spoken discourse. In writing, which lacks a systematic way of representing stress, passives are often the only way to mark an unusual distribution of old and new information.

Pronominalization (§5.15) has not been reexamined in connection with meaning-structure grammar, and its omission has led to a certain degree of artificiality in the sentences that have just been discussed. But the reader can easily see how the process of linearization and the distribution of old and new information determine the basic conditions for pronominalization. At the same time, pronominalization is constrained by the need to maintain maximal clarity. The important point is that the interplay of these conditions and constraints must be stated in terms that are basically semantic and only in part syntactic.

The effort to state linearization and the assignment of stress in terms of the distribution of old and new information holds a great deal of promise. This is not to claim that all points have been covered in this brief discussion. Indeed, much remains to be said. Exceptions to the principles discussed here can always be found, and these must eventually be explained. It will be enough if the principles described here can be taken as a basis for the description of the inevitable exceptions.

7.20 THE RESULTING PICTURE

The foregoing presentation of meaning-structure grammar, although necessarily abbreviated, is sufficient to illustrate the four components of language that were presented originally in Figure 1–3. The emphasis in this chapter has been on describing the semantic component in as much detail as possible. The assumption has been that an understanding of the semantic component will automatically lead to an understanding of the syntactic component.

The semantic component, as conceived in meaning-structure grammar, is composed of various semantic units and rules for their arrangement. The units themselves are determined on the basis of semantic paradigms. In some cases these paradigms are whole sentences that are structurally parallel but different in meaning:

> The man came.
> The leaf fell.

In terms of semantic content, the different function of *man* and *leaf* is explained by saying that one is an agent and the other a patient. This difference, in turn, is related to semantic categories ACTION and PROCESS that are attributed to the verb. In other cases the semantic paradigm may consist of individual words that are partially alike and partially different in meaning. Such was the case with the set consisting of *man/woman/boy/girl* examined in Figure 7–4. Rules governing the arrangement of semantic units are inferred on the basis of apparent combinations of these units in semantic paradigms.

The syntactic component is seen as a set of rules for assigning linear order to the inherently nonlinear semantic arrangements produced by the semantic component. These linearization rules, although similar in function to the transformational rules of transformational grammar, are viewed in meaning-structure grammar as having no special status. The application or nonapplication of a particular linearization rule has nothing to do with determining the supposed alternate surface forms a given underlying structure may assume. Variations in surface structure are seen as governed by differences in the semantic structure associated with each variant, and the linearization rules that apply to a given semantic structure are regarded as wholly determined by the content of the semantic structure itself.

In meaning-structure grammar the process of symbolization stands as a watershed at which units having semantic content are converted into units having phonological content. Since this conversion is accomplished in a single step, there is no need for two lexical lookups as commonly required in transformational grammar (§6.9–6.10). Since the process of symbolization requires the matching of meanings with phonological forms, the organization of the lexicon must be more like a thesaurus than a standard dictionary. In other respects, however, the lexicon is very much like an ordinary dictionary. A rough idea of the kind of data entered in the lexicon can be gained by considering the items needed to symbolize the meanings expressed by the sentence *A dog bit the postman*. Lexical entries are enclosed by vertical bars:

$$\begin{bmatrix} \text{count} \\ -\text{definite} \\ -\text{plural} \end{bmatrix} \rightarrow \left\{ \begin{array}{l} |\,\text{ən}\,|\ /\ \underline{\quad}\text{V} \\ \\ |\,\text{ə}\,| \end{array} \right\}$$

'dog'   → | dog |

'bite'   → $\left\{ \begin{array}{l} |\,\text{bit}\,|\ /\ \text{PAST} \\ \\ |\,\text{bayt}\,| \end{array} \right\}$

'definite'   → $\left\{ \begin{array}{l} |\,\text{ðiy}\,|\ /\underline{\quad}\text{V} \\ \\ |\,\text{ðə}\,| \end{array} \right\}$

'postman'   → | powstmən | (unchanged plural)

'plural'   → | -z |

'past'   → | -d |

The indefinite article, a semantic complex (i.e., morpheme) consisting of COUNT but not containing DEFINITE or PLURAL, is symbolized in one of two ways: /ən/ before words beginning with a vowel, /ə/ otherwise. Variation of this sort, which can be specified within the lexicon, is termed **morpholexical variation.** Other examples of morpholexical variation are found in the forms symbolizing 'bite' and 'definite.' The fact that 'postman' has the same form for both singular and plural is also noted. (The written form *postmen* contrasts with *postman* in spelling, but not in pronunciation.) Other forms given in the above example symbolize 'dog,' 'plural,' and 'past.' The replacement of semantic complexes by phonological units drawn from the lexicon can be termed an **initial symbolization.**

An initial symbolization is of course modified extensively by the phonological component before it becomes a **final symbolization** (i.e., phonetic representation). This modification is accomplished in several steps. In English, for example, a number of morpheme sequences are contracted in informal speech. *Cannot* becomes *can't, is not* becomes *isn't,* and so forth. Variation of this type, which must be specified partly in terms of a phonological environment and partly in terms of a grammatical environment (e.g., the occurrence of a specific morpheme), can be termed **morphophonemic variation.** This type of variation has been handled by transformational rules in some versions of transformational grammar. Although morphophonemic processes are quite limited in English, they are extremely common in languages having greater morphological complexity than English. A second, and by far more common, process is ordinary **phonological variation,** which involves the replacement of one phoneme by another in environments that can be described in purely phonological terms. In English this is most apparent in the modification of the plural suffix and past tense marker: | kæt-z | → /kæts/, | stap-d | → /stapt/.

The last step in the phonological component is the specification of **allophonic variation.** One such process in English aspirates initial voiceless stops while leaving other voiceless stops unaffected:

/kæts/ → [kʰæts], /stapt/ → [stapt]

7.21 THE WORLD OF EXPERIENCE

In §7.1 we observed that language is a complex system for encoding a message from the universe of meaning and converting it into a sequence of sounds standing for the original meaning. Linguistics therefore cannot be entirely divorced from the nonlinguistic world or from our perceptions of this world.

No two events or objects in the world around us are ever identical. We apply the word *chair* to a variety of objects made of wood, plastic, or metal. Some chairs are upholstered; some are not. Some have arms; some do not. Each time speakers of English encounter a new piece of furniture, they must decide anew whether or not the term *chair* can be extended to it. Similar decisions are required each time a verb is used. A verb like *sit* describes a very different posture when it applies to a human and when it applies to a dog, but most English speakers have no difficulty seeing something in common in the two usages. If speakers were unable to see similarities in these perceptibly different phenomena, we would be forced to devise a new term for each item of furniture, each physical action, and so on. Communication would be impossible because no two people would have any experience in common. Indeed, every event in every individual's life would be a unique experience having nothing in common with previous experience. The individual would have no basis for organizing perceptions. Thought would be impossible.

Every extension of a familiar word to a new situation is, in effect, a **metaphor.** However, the term is normally reserved for those extensions of striking novelty involving the juxtaposition of a single point of likeness against a backdrop of overall dissimilarity. Thus, the term *fox*, describing a clever person, is a metaphor of long standing in English, and one whose meaning is virtually self-evident since foxes and humans are perceived as having few other traits in common. **Idioms** can be viewed as metaphors of a special kind. Characteristically they involve complex syntactic structures expressing a unitary meaning. But the meaning is not the literal sum of the component parts. Chafe has described the syntactic structure of idioms as a **literalization** of the underlying meaning. Thus, a meaning 'to procrastinate,' which might be symbolized *to drag one's feet*, is treated in surface structure as though the literal action of dragging one's feet is under discussion. The analysis of idioms in transformational grammar (§6.8) and in meaning-structure grammar is much the same—largely because no serious effort was made to deal with idioms in transformational grammar until after Chafe began to write on the subject.

The experiential world, as viewed by the human observer-participant, is a collage of objects and events that are partially distinct and partially blurred. The evolution of plant and animal life has been such that we have cats and dogs as distinct genera, with no intermediate genus. A language system that recognizes cats and dogs as distinct entities by assigning them different terms therefore reflects the natural organization of the world. Not all facts are so distinct, however. To speakers of English it seems natural to distinguish *hand* and *arm,* but to speakers of Greek it seems natural to use a single term *xeri* for the entire appendage. Since the human body is much the same in the experience of both language communities, the difference in terminology may seem arbitrary. But it is certainly much less arbitrary than, say, a term that designated 'right arm and left arm' or some other ad hoc combination of body parts.

In short the events of the experiential world do not come already segmented for the convenience of speakers. Each community must tacitly work out its own segmentation of reality according to whatever heuristic principles seem applicable. The remarkable fact is the striking degree of similarity achieved by the diverse languages of the world in their adaptation to perceived realities. The differences among languages, far from being unpredictable and without limit, are on the whole superficial and fall within narrow, describable limits.

The segmentation of reality is important because it is this process that provides the manipulable units that are symbolized in language. These units, which can be arranged according to conventional patterns and symbolized phonologically, have the effect of converting thought into a form that can be encoded by language. To the extent that both thought and language can be described as consisting of units and patterns for arranging these units, both exhibit duality of patterning and are isomorphic systems.

For people who share a number of common experiences, the discourse setting ordinarily provides enough information that verbal messages themselves contribute little that is not already in the consciousness of both speaker and listener. It is this very factor that enables children to learn their native language. When a mother gives her child a cup of white fluid and says *Drink your milk* or a cup of orange fluid and says *Drink your juice,* she creates simultaneously a linguistic and an **experiential-behavioral paradigm** that the child can hardly fail to grasp. The more complex situations of later life are always encountered against a background of accumulated experience that makes novel elements intelligible. This is true whether the novel elements are linguistic or situational. But it is not simply the case that experience makes language intelligible, for language itself can be a surrogate for direct experience and, as such, may serve to interpret other experiences, both linguistic and situational.

Language in its present form has developed such flexibility that there is no situation, however novel or abstract, completely lacking an experiential analog that makes it capable of symbolization. This of course is really a commentary on human adaptability because language is, after all, a human construct. The categories we have been describing—agent, patient, experiencer, or whatever—all represent compartments of human experience.

summary

Consideration of the role of meaning in language leads to a view of language as a system of symbolization. Comparison of human language with animal communication suggests that language is best described as a system of animal communication that has developed duality of patterning. This means simply that the system, instead of containing a fixed number of unanalyzable units, consists of two parts: (1) a limited inventory of components and (2) patterns for arranging these components into novel messages of increasing complexity.

Semantic units seldom occur in such a way that they can be matched with morphemes in a direct way, but their existence can nonetheless be inferred by examining paradigms consisting of words (or larger units) that are related in meaning but slightly different. Thus, verbs can be categorized as containing units such as STATE, PROCESS, ACTION, and the like; nouns can be classified as related to verbs as AGENTS, PATIENTS, BENE-FICIARIES, and the like. Selectional units are semantic units that narrow the semantic scope of a verb or noun so that it can be matched with a particular symbolization, or sequence of phonemes, stored in the lexicon. Inflectional units are semantic units that are added to the lexical specification of a verb or noun without affecting the basic meaning of the lexical unit—for example, tense in the case of verbs or plurality in the case of nouns.

Linearization of semantic structures in meaning-structure grammar is a process that is "transformational" in nature. But since the starting point is a nonlinear semantic structure rather than a linear syntactic structure, the postsemantic rules of meaning-structure grammar function in a way that makes them quite different from transformational rules in transformational grammar. And since the application of postsemantic rules is governed entirely by the information present in semantic structure, the possibilities for optional application of postsemantic rules are quite different from those assumed for transformational rules in transformational grammar. For example, the distribution of old and new information within a sentence, rather than any supposed optional syntactic transformation, is seen as governing the occurrence of passive constructions.

In a semantic model of language, the semantic component is regarded as central. Semantic structures give rise to the linear syntactic arrangements that underlie surface structure. These arrangements are symbolized as the semantic elements are replaced by symbolizations drawn from the lexicon. The initial symbolization is modified by the phonological component to produce a phonetic output that can be interpreted by other language users in terms of the nonlinguistic elements being symbolized. Language is thus seen as a human device for representing experience and exchanging messages about the world of experience.

further reading

General: Chafe 1970a, 1970b, Pearson 1972a, 1976, Langacker 1972b, Heny 1972, Cosmos et al. 1973. **7.1** Harris 1951, Chomsky 1957, Chafe 1967a, 1970b. **7.2** Jespersen 1922, Révész 1956, Hocket 1960, Hockett and Ascher 1964, Lancaster 1968, Gardner and Gardner 1969, Premack 1970, Chafe 1970b, Hill 1972, 1974, Swadesh 1971; for a different viewpoint Hewes 1972, Langacker 1973 (Chaps. 2, 7), Lenneberg 1967, Lieberman and Crelin 1971, Lieberman 1975. **7.3** Hockett 1960, Hockett and Ascher 1964, Chafe 1967a, 1970b. **7.4** Bolinger 1973. **7.4** through **7.19** Chafe 1970b, Seropian 1971. **7.19** Gunter 1966, Chafe 1974. **7.20** Chafe 1970b, Pearson 1972a, 1976, A. Makkai 1974. **Morpholexical variation:** Bloomfield 1939, 1957, 1962, Goddard 1969, Pearson 1972a, 1976. **Morphophonemic variation:** Chomsky 1957, Goddard 1969, Pearson 1972a, 1976. **Phonological variation:** Schane 1973, Harms 1968. **Allophonic variation:** Pike 1947b, B. Bloch 1948. **7.21** Chafe 1967a, 1968a, 1970a, Fraser 1970, A. Makkai 1972, 1974.

8 structural variation in language

8.1 LANGUAGES OF THE WORLD

Current estimates place the number of languages being spoken in the world in the neighborhood of 3,000. Nobody knows the exact number because many languages, especially those spoken by small communities in remote areas, have never been adequately described. Even where descriptions are available, it is not clear whether two languages are to be classed as related dialects or as distinct languages. This question cannot even be asked when data is lacking entirely.

As a general rule, languages that are mutually intelligible are classed as dialects of the same language. Dialects that are not mutually intelligible are different languages. But it is often the case that two dialects spoken at opposite borders of a country are classed as dialects of the same language even though speakers from these two areas might not be able to understand each other. The two dialects might be linked together by a chain of intervening dialects, each mutually intelligible with the next, even though speakers at each end of the chain cannot communicate. Or the two dialects may both be mutually intelligible with a national "standard" language spoken in the nation's capital or some other political, social, or economic center. Classification therefore hinges as much on social and political factors as it does on purely linguistic considerations.

Many languages now being spoken in small communities face imminent extinction in the face of competition with dominant communities. Linguistic data is available for a number of languages already extinct, and one can only guess at the number of extinct languages that have disappeared with no written records at all. If we can assume that human languages much like those in existence today were being spoken 1 million years ago, the number of languages spoken since the rise of humankind must be quite large. Even if we suppose that language did not evolve to its present state until the last 50,000 years, the number of languages spoken since that time must be in the tens of thousands. If language goes back 1 million years or more, the number could be in the hundreds of thousands.

When we consider that human populations were still moving into uninhabited areas until just the last few thousand years, therefore diverging from whatever parent community remained behind, the possibilities of a single language giving rise to daughter languages and language families is truly staggering. The number of variables makes it impossible to calculate the exact number even if we knew the precise starting date, the number of languages at the outset, and the rate of divergence. Many population movements must have involved an entire community, so that no split into divergent communities occurred. When splits did occur, the number of resulting communities could vary from two to three or even more. Each of the resulting communities in turn would be subject to further divisions depending on factors such as the birth rate, mortality rate, and optimal size of groups for hunting, foraging, and other economic activities. Occasionally two undersized groups might have joined forces, with a consequent reduction in the number of separate languages. In the early stages the trend must have involved expansion into uninhabited territory, accompanied by language divergence. Once the available area was inhabited, further expansion of prosperous communities would be possible only to the extent that these groups were able to displace other groups. This is known to have happened in historic times, for example, as Indo-European speakers moved into Europe and either absorbed the indigenous populations or pushed some of them, like the Basques, into outlying areas.

The English of just over 500 years ago, although a direct ancestor of our own speech, was different enough that the two could be classed as mutually unintelligible. This suggests that, even without divergence into two or more separate communities, the changes that accumulate in a language through time alone are enough to produce a "new" language every half millennium or so. When we consider all these factors, even if we allow a time depth of only 50,000 years, it is not difficult to imagine a single parent language for all of today's languages. The comparative method can show relationships at a time depth in excess of 5,000 years, but the fact that the method is unable to confirm more remote relationships does not necessarily prove a lack of relationship. It is always possible that the accumulated changes are so great that inherited resemblances between two remotely related languages are obscured beyond recovery.

We will probably never know whether all the world's languages spring from a single ancestor or from several ancestral languages that developed simultaneously. Nor are we likely to know for sure just when our ancestors developed duality of patterning and the other features that transformed their communication system into a full–fledged language. Probably the threshold from call system to language was crossed quite without conscious awareness—no more consciously, say, than the watershed from one valley to the next was crossed as humankind gradually spread into all parts of the earth.

8.2 LANGUAGE CLASSIFICATION

A survey of world languages requires some method of classification. The methods that linguists have used over the years have been typological, areal, and genetic. A typological classification could in principle be based on any arbitrarily selected linguistic feature. Thus, we could imagine a class of all languages containing a contrast between vowels and consonants. Since all known languages have this distinction, a classification based on it is of limited usefulness except insofar as it identifies a universal attribute of language. The class of all languages containing tones would include a number of languages spoken in Asia, the Americas, and Africa, but these languages would be connected in no other way. Similarly languages could be classed into those having contrasts between three vowels, four vowels, five vowels, and so on. Again the resulting classes would most likely be unrelated in other respects, but the classification serves to clarify the structural features that are universal among languages. The topic of language universals, once approached on a priori grounds, has received renewed attention in recent years from linguists who have made the subject a matter of empirical investigation.

Efforts to devise a typological classification of languages were popular in the nineteenth century and, although not widely used today, have contributed terms that remain in occasional use. Various proposals have centered around four types of languages: isolating, agglutinating, inflectional, and polysynthetic. An **isolating** language is one in which each morpheme comprises a separate word. Chinese has often been cited as an isolating language even though in reality many Chinese words are compounds of two or more morphemes. **Agglutinating** languages are those in which words consist of a stem with one or more additional morphemes affixed to it without phonological modification. Turkish and Japanese are often cited as examples of such a language. **Inflectional,** as originally used, referred to the process of stem-internal modification found in Indo-European and Semitic languages—for example, English *man/men*. In a broader sense the term can apply to languages in which words consist of stems to which are added complex morphemes as in Latin *laud-ō* 'I praise,' where the unanalyzable suffix symbolizes person, tense, and mood. **Polysynthetic,** or incorporating, languages are those in which the word consists of numerous morphemes. Often the word includes free morphemes that are incorporated as bound parts of a larger word. Morphemes are commonly subject to phonological modification that makes identification of individual morphemes difficult. Eskimo is frequently cited as the classical example of such a language because of its morphological complexity. The Iroquoian languages, which practice incorporation of noun roots as part of a polymorphemic verb, can also be included in this class.

The shortcoming of the scheme is that no language is a perfect representative of any of the four types. A more useful approach is to think of morphological types as ranging along a continuous scale whose extreme categories are analytic and synthetic. A fully **analytic** language would have a ratio of exactly one morpheme per word, while a **synthetic** language would have a much higher morpheme-to-word ratio. The nineteenth-century terms can then refer to points along this scale, as suggested by Figure 8–1:

FIGURE 8–1   Language Typology

← Analytic   Synthetic →

|——|

isolating   agglutinating   inflectional   polysynthetic

Greenberg (1960a) has carried the approach of Figure 8–1 to its logical conclusion by quantifying points on the scale in terms of the average number of morphemes per word, based on a sample text from eight different languages—Sanskrit, Anglo-Saxon (Old English), Persian, English, Yakut (a Turkic language), Swahili, Annamite (Vietnamese), and Eskimo. In the Greenberg study, Annamite at 1.06 was the most analytic and Eskimo at 3.72 was the most synthetic. English at 1.68 came near the analytic end of the scale, exceeded only by Persian and Annamite.

Even this approach has certain problems. A form like Latin *laud-ō* contains only two morphemes even though it symbolizes at least four units of meaning: (1) action verb 'praise'; (2) present tense; (3) indicative mood; and (4) first person singular as agent. Greenberg's approach was to count each meaning of a complex morpheme separately. Once matters of this sort are settled, the procedure is quite mechanical, and the outcome is a figure that can be used to define morphological types. Greenberg proposed three categories. Analytic languages would be those having a morpheme-to-word index of 1.00 to 1.99, synthetic languages from 2.00 to 2.99, and polysynthetic languages over 3.00.

The second type of classification—areal classification—depends solely on geographical distribution. The languages of Asia would therefore be a legitimate class but would consist of many diverse families and types. A smaller area such as India has greater legitimacy. The languages of India represent two major families, but over the years they have so influenced each other in grammar and phonology that the area is more homogeneous than one might expect at first. Similarly the northwest coast languages extending from northern California into British Columbia, although representing several different families, have developed a number of common phonological and grammatical features.

The most useful classification, however, is on the basis of genetic relationship—with *genetic* used metaphorically to denote the development of daughter languages from a common protolanguage. Genetic relationships can be established by the comparative method. Since a genetic relationship implies historical continuity of transmission, the relationship has nothing arbitrary about it. Typological and areal classifications are always arbitrary to some extent. In cases where genetically related languages also form a typological or areal group, the grouping can quite naturally be attributed to preservation of inherited features, settlement of related tribes in adjacent areas, and similar factors.

Our survey of world languages will therefore be based on current knowledge of genetic relationships. The discussion will begin with Indo-European and proceed to other families in roughly the order that Europeans became aware of these languages. In general, we will refer to the languages in geographic terms appropriate to their location at the time of first contact with Europeans. Emphasis will be on calling attention to structural characteristics of the various languages and introducing the student to resources for further study.

It will be useful to keep in mind that a **family** is a group of languages having a demonstrable genetic relationship on the basis of extensive similarities of both form and meaning. It is sometimes convenient to speak of **branches** within a family—that is, groups of individual languages that constitute a subgroup within the family. A language having no known genetic connection with any other language is described as a **language isolate.** In the case of separate families that have similarities suggesting a genetic connection, it is customary to speak of a **phylum** or **superfamily** to make a distinction between groupings at this level and groupings at the family level. However, the term "family" is sometimes loosely applied both to groupings that are technically phyla and those that are actually branches within a diverse family. The inconsistent usage is indicative of the uncertainties that still surround genetic classification.

8.3 INDO-EUROPEAN

The Indo-European family, the first to be identified by linguists, is represented by subfamilies spread geographically from India to Europe. In modern times several of the European representatives have been established in other parts of the world where they have tended to displace the indigenous languages. As a family the group is inflectional. Nouns are marked for gender, number, and case, while verbs are inflected for person and number, tense, mode, aspect, and voice. English is exceptional, having lost most of the inflectional system and replaced it with more analytical structures involving prepositions and other markers. But even those languages that preserve inflections as the primary signaling device have simplified the original system.

A family tree diagram of the principal Indo-European languages was given in Figure 3–3. Such diagrams are useful for showing subgrouping, the relative chronology of separations, and absolute chronology insofar as it is known. But no diagram can be more detailed or more accurate than the information on which it is based. In the absence of positive evidence for subgrouping at the earliest stages of Indo-European, Figure 3–3 has treated the various branches as coordinate rather than positing subgroupings. The earliest reconstructible stage of Proto-Indo-European contains a certain amount of dialect variation, suggesting that the language was actually a group of closely related dialects. The sharp breaks implied by the family tree diagram fail to convey this subtlety. As long as mutually intelligible dialects are spoken in adjacent areas, features that gain currency in one area can spread to another and continue to influence the development of other branches even after a supposed separation. This view of language development is called the **wave theory** to distinguish it from the family tree model. The two models are not necessarily in conflict; they represent different parts of the total picture. Figure 8–2 represents the Indo-European family in a manner compatible with the wave theory. The diagram suggests the geographical relationships but does not represent time perspective in any useful way. To make the diagram a true representation of the wave model, it would be necessary to add lines enclosing the languages that exhibit common features. Since a large number of features could be identified, the diagram would soon be quite complex. As in the case of dialect maps (§10.3), the various boundary lines would seldom coincide exactly. In addition certain features of the protolanguage that might be preserved independently in geographically separate languages, could not easily be represented by a connected line.

The protolanguage had eight noun cases. In addition to nominative, genitive, dative, and accusative (§2.9), there were instrumental, locative, ablative (indicating separation or direction away from), and vocative (used for direct address). Pronouns distinguished first, second, and third person. First and second occurred as singular, dual, and plural but without gender distinctions. Third person distinguished masculine, feminine, and inanimate in both singular and plural. (The system apparently developed from an earlier two-way contrast between animate and inanimate.) Adjectives exhibited the same morphology as nouns. (This fact does not argue against the predicative nature of adjectives but can be explained as the indexing of nominal information in the predicative forms accompanying nouns.)

A notable feature of verb formations was the process of vowel change known as ablaut. The process is prominent in Germanic (§8.4) and is described more fully in connection with that language.

FIGURE 8–2   **Major Extant Branches of the Indo-European Language Family**

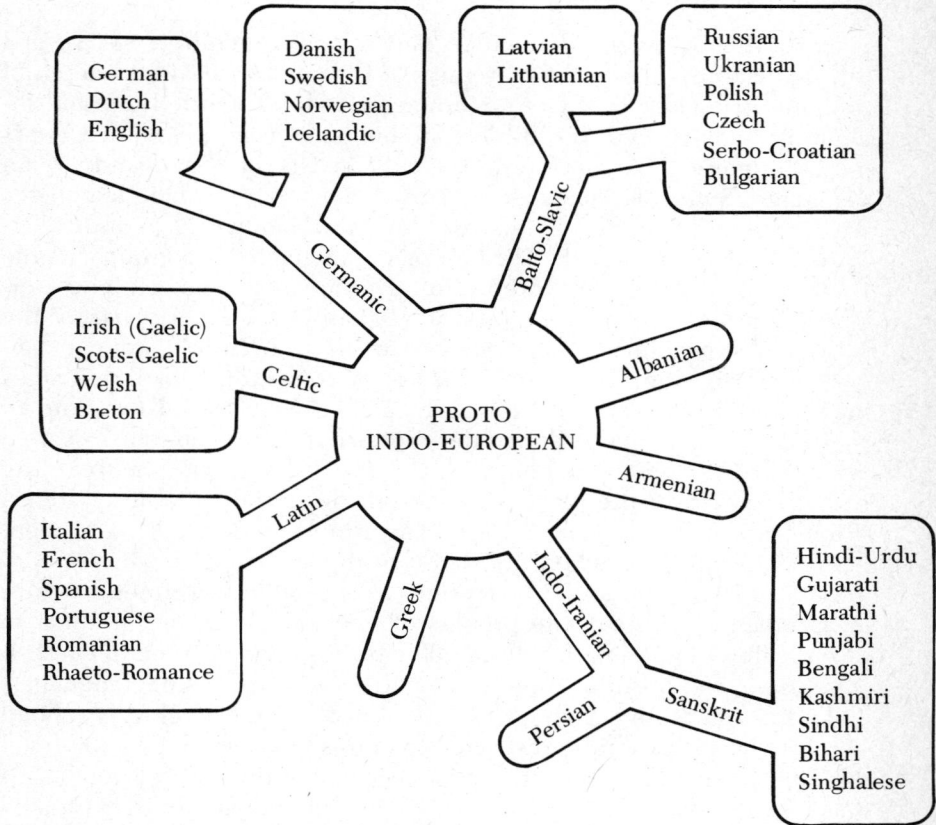

The sections that follow give brief descriptions of the principal language groups: Germanic, Romance, Balto-Slavic, Greek, Iranian, and Indic. Several other groups that will not be described in detail should be mentioned here. (1) Celtic is represented today by Irish, Scots-Gaelic, Welsh, and Breton. Extinct languages include Cornish and Gaulish. Of these languages Irish is of special interest for its preservation of archaic features. (2) Albanian is an Indo-European isolate surrounded by Slavic languages and Greek but having no close affinity with these languages. (3) Armenian, the official language of the Armenian Republic of the Soviet Union, is related to Thracian and Phrygian, both now extinct. (4) Tocharian is known in two dialects (Tocharian A and B) from manuscripts found in Chinese Turkestan dating from the seventh and eighth centuries A.D. (5) The Anatolian branch includes Hittite, Lycian, and Lydian—all extinct. Hittite, the language of an empire that flourished from 1900 to 1200 B.C., is the oldest recorded Indo-European language. It is represented on cuneiform tablets unearthed in the Anatolian Plateau of Turkey.

8.4 GERMANIC

The Germanic branch, of which English is a member, has spread through the northwestern extremity of Europe. An eastern branch of the family consisted of Gothic, now extinct but recorded in a fourth-century translation of the Bible. The language was spoken in what is now Bulgaria. The northern branch consists of the Scandinavian languages Swedish, Danish, and Norwegian, and the island languages Icelandic and Faroese. The west Germanic languages include German, Dutch, and English. The Germanic languages as a group diverge in several respects from other Indo-European languages. The Germanic sound shift was described in §3.3 and §3.4. A large part of the Germanic vocabulary is not cognate with other Indo-European languages, suggesting extensive borrowing from indigenous languages now extinct. Other features of Germanic can be traced to a known source. Germanic has reduced the Proto-Indo-European tense system to two forms: past and nonpast; and the languages have fixed the variable stress of the protolanguage on the initial syllable of stems. Both features are characteristic of the Finno-Ugric family and were apparently imitated when the two speech communities were in contact between 2,000 and 3,000 years ago. Another prominent feature of Germanic is **ablaut**, the process of root vowel change in verbs to mark different grammatical forms. The process is preserved in English *sing, sang, sung*. But in English as well as other Germanic languages, ablaut is now losing ground to regular formations. The closely related term **umlaut** is generally restricted to nouns where a process of vowel harmony is evident from the presence of a conditioning suffix (German *Ball/Bälle* 'ball/balls') or can be reconstructed (English *mouse/mice* < **mūs/mȳs-i*). The origin of ablaut can be traced to the phonetic consequences of variable pitch (in the protolanguage) and stress (in the various successor languages).

8.5 ROMANCE

By the time of the Roman Empire, Latin had completely displaced its sister languages Oscan and Umbrian. Latin reduced the number of Proto-Indo-European noun cases to six, dropping instrumental and locative as separate categories. The principal verbal inflections of the protolanguage were retained, although phonological reshaping was extensive. To cite just one example, we can note that the original first person singular suffix **-mi* is preserved only in *sum < *sumi* 'I am' (Figure 3–1). Elsewhere in verbal paradigms it is replaced by *-ō* (Corpus 2–1 and Corpus 2–2). By the fifth century A.D., spoken Latin, which was now established in the Roman provinces, was quite different from classical Latin of the first century B.C. The classical language had a five-vowel system, with contrasts between long and short vowels. Length was later lost as a contrastive feature. In some cases the contrast of length was continued by differences of vowel quality (i.e., earlier allophonic differences that became phonemic); but *ā* and *a* merged as *a* with the result that certain case distinctions were obscured. Thus, nominative *capra* 'goat' and ablative *caprā* were not distinguished in Late Latin. By the fifth century only two cases remained: nominative and accusative. Other case distinctions were now signaled by prepositions, which had earlier been a redundant part of the message. Verbs also underwent considerable reshaping. Typical was the future suffix of classical Latin, which was replaced in Late Latin by a reshaped stem followed by an auxiliary. This construction in turn was replaced in the successor languages by a new suffix as the auxiliary became bound to the verb. Modern Italian, Spanish, Portuguese, French, Romanian (or Rumanian), and Rhaeto-Romance are the more prominent descendants of Late Latin. Each of the successor languages has made its own characteristic innovations, but the morphological patterns of Latin have undergone similar changes in all. In general, Spanish and Italian have been conservative in preserving Latin phonology and verb paradigms; French has been more innovative in both areas.

8.6   BALTO-SLAVIC

Balto-Slavic is a group with two branches of unequal size. The Baltic group includes Old Prussian, extinct since about 1700, and the still vigorous Latvian and Lithuanian. The last of these is of special importance because of its archaic character.

The Slavic languages, which have spread throughout eastern Europe and all of Siberia, can be divided into three groups. The western group includes Polish, Czech, and Slovak. The southern group includes Slovene, Serbo-Croatian, Macedonian, and Bulgarian. The eastern group, which has spread over the greatest territory, includes Ukrainian, Byelorussian, and Russian.

The Slavic family has been marked by extensive phonological innovations. At an early stage Common Slavic adopted a surface constraint making open syllables obligatory. To achieve a consistent CVCV pattern, all syllable-final consonants were dropped, a sound change that had far-reaching consequences for the inflectional endings. Weak vowels were later lost, creating new consonant clusters that abound in the modern languages.

The most pervasive feature of the Slavic languages has been the palatalization of consonants before certain vowels and the subsequent development of these consonants into affricates and, if voiced, into spirants. The process has taken a slightly different course in different languages, but the development of the back consonants has been quite uniform:

$$\begin{Bmatrix} k > k' > č \\ \\ g > g' > ǰ > z \end{Bmatrix} \quad /\underline{\quad} \quad \begin{bmatrix} +vocalic \\ +front \end{bmatrix}$$

Once this sound change had been accomplished, the stage was set for other developments. New front vowels developed from earlier diphthongs and became the conditioning segments for another palatalization that ran a similar course:

$$\begin{Bmatrix} k > k' > c \\ \\ g > g' > ʒ > z \end{Bmatrix} \quad /\underline{\quad} \quad \begin{bmatrix} +vocalic \\ +front \end{bmatrix}$$

Thus, Russian *cena* 'prince' is cognate with Lithuanian *kaina,* which preserves the original form common to both languages.

Russian retains seven nominal cases, having lost only ablative. The verb paradigm has developed in such a way that aspect has become more prominent than tense. Verbs are either perfective or imperfective, with each basic aspect subcategorized in various ways. Some verbs have developed paired stems, for example, Russian *dat'/davat'.* Both mean 'give,' the former as perfective action, the latter as imperfective action.

The phonology of modern Russian presents what has become a classic example of the difficulty in identifying a phonemic level. Russian has a contrast between voiced and voiceless occlusives (i.e., stops, affricates, and fricatives) /p b, t d, k g, f v, s z, š ž/ with the exception of /x, c, č/, which have no voiced counterparts but have voiced allophones [ɣ, ʒ, ǰ] when followed by another voiced obstruent. However, Russian has a general rule that voices all obstruents in final position if the next word begins with a voiced obstruent; otherwise obstruents in final position are voiceless. These facts lead to the following inconsistency:

mok l'i	→	/mok l'i/	→	[mok l'i]	'was (he) getting wet?'
mok bi	→	/mog bi/	→	[mog bi]	'were (he) getting wet'
žeč l'i	→	/žeč l'i/	→	[žeč l'i]	'should one burn'
žeč bi	→	/žeč bi/	→	[žeǰ bi]	'were one to burn'

That is, voicing leads to phonemic contrast in one situation but not another, even though the phonetic facts are the same in all forms. Halle (1959:21–24) cites the above data as an argument for eliminating the phonemic level from linguistic description. The position of this book has been to accept the general validity of a phonemic level while recognizing that language systems develop in such a way that they merely approach, but seldom achieve, perfect symmetry.

8.7 GREEK

The Greek Peninsula, the islands of the Aegean Sea, and the western coast of what is now Turkey were settled by Greek-speaking tribes migrating in successive waves from the north during the second millennium B.C. Considerable dialect variation is evident even in the earliest recorded forms, but the Attic dialect spoken around Athens became the most important literary dialect in classical times. The *Iliad* and the *Odyssey*, first written down in Athens in the sixth century B.C., were composed in a conventionalized literary dialect that included Attic features. From the fourth century B.C. onward, a fairly uniform variety of Greek known as *he kōinē dialektos* 'the common language,' or simply *kōinē*, came into use. This is the Greek of the Christian New Testament. The literary style that came into use after the sixth century A.D. is commonly called Byzantine Greek. Written forms at this time—and up to the present—have been influenced by classical models, while the spoken language has undergone steady change.

Modern Greek has simplified many features of the classical language, particularly in the inflectional system. Dative case, dual number, and the optative mood have been lost, and the inflectional perfective has been replaced by an analytical construction. Phonological changes have included simplification of the vowel system and spirantization of voiced and aspirated stops: $b > v$, $dh > ð$, $gh > ɣ$, $ph > f$, $th > θ$, $kh > x$. In classical Greek the infinitive marker was *-ein*. Loss of *n* in final position led to homophony between the infinitive and third person singular forms. This anomaly led eventually to a restructured system in which embedded complements are marked for person:

Stage 1	Stage 2	Stage 3	
thél-ō gráph-ein >	thél-ō gráph-ei >	thél-ō gráph-ō	'I want to write'
thél-ei gráph-ein >	thél-ei gráph-ei >	thél-ei gráph-ei	'he wants to write'

8.8 IRANIAN

Iranian is regarded as forming a subgroup with the Indic languages (§8.9). Avestan and Old Persian literary texts date from the sixth century B.C. The modern languages are Persian, spoken in most of Iran; Kurdish, spoken in western Iran, Iraq, and parts of eastern Turkey; Pashto, the national language of Afghanistan; Tadzik and Ossetic, spoken in parts of the Soviet Union; and Baluchi, spoken in eastern Iran, Pakistan, Afghanistan, and the Soviet Union. The Iranian languages have drastically simplified the inflectional system in both the noun and verb so that fixed word order has now become the primary signaling device. Modern Persian vocabulary has borrowed extensively from Arabic and to a lesser extent from Turkish.

8.9 INDIC

Sanskrit, the classical language of India, flourished from about 1500 to 500 B.C. Its replacement by divergent local dialects led to the grammatical study culminating in the work of Pāṇini (300s B.C.), a study inspired by the belief that a "correct" pronunciation of sacred texts was necessary to insure their efficacy. Although Sanskrit by this time was no longer spoken as a native language, it remained the language of literature, religion, and government for another thousand years in India and was carried to other countries of Southeast Asia as well. Its influence continues to the present day, particularly in learned vocabulary. In all respects the use of Sanskrit in India parallels the use of Latin in Europe.

Sanskrit preserved the eight nominal cases posited for the protolanguage as well as the elaborate verbal conjugations. The modern Indic languages for the most part have reduced noun inflections to two cases: direct and oblique. The latter is augmented by postpositions that have taken over the earlier case functions. (A postposition is a grammatical marker that follows a noun.) Punjabi has been more conservative but has nonetheless made drastic reductions in the system. Gujarati and Marathi have preserved the three-gender system of the protolanguage; Hindi has developed a two-gender system. The original system of three numbers (singular, dual, plural) has been reduced to two with the elimination of dual in the modern languages. The numerous verbal conjugations have been reduced in all the languages.

Hindi is spoken by about half the population of India. A variety of Hindi used by Muslims and written in Arabic script is called Urdu. Other major Indic languages are Gujarati, Marathi, and Punjabi (all mentioned above), and Bengali, Kashmiri, Sindhi, Bihari, Singhalese, Rajasthani, Oriya, and Assamese. Romany, the language of the Gypsies, is an Indic language that has been preserved by many wandering groups, with local dialects showing the influence of surrounding languages.

8.10 AFROASIATIC

The Afroasiatic grouping of language families includes Semitic, Egyptian, Berber, Cushitic, and Chadic. Of these, Semitic was known to European scholars at an early period because of the Hebrew scriptures. Contact with some of the other families has been quite recent. Languages in the group are spoken over a vast territory extending from West Africa, through the Sahara, into East Africa and the Arabian Peninsula, and in surrounding parts of southwestern Asia. The group was formerly divided into two subdivisions: the Semitic languages forming one group, with the other four families classed as Hamitic languages. Since these four families are no closer to each other than any of them is to Semitic, the Hamitic grouping is no longer considered valid.

The Semitic languages are divided into a northern and southern branch. Within the northern branch there is an eastern division, represented by Assyro-Babylonian, and a western division, represented by Hebrew, Phoenician, and Aramaic. Assyro-Babylonian, or Akkadian, became extinct during the first century A.D. Hebrew and Phoenician were spoken in Biblical times in Palestine but had been displaced by Aramaic by the time of the Roman occupation. Aramaic is still spoken in rural parts of Syria, and the closely related Syriac is spoken by small groups in Iran and Iraq. Although technically extinct, Hebrew survived as the liturgical language of the Jews and has been revived as an official language of modern Israel—a unique development in the history of language.

The southern branch consists of two divisions, a northern and a southern. The former is represented by Arabic, spoken in several dialects by about 120 million persons spread through North Africa and extending eastward to Iran. The southern division includes South Arabic, which is quite different from the other Arabic dialects, and several languages spoken in Ethiopia, the most prominent of which is Amharic.

The complex verbal morphology of the Semitic languages is based for the most part on roots containing three consonants that are inflected by processes of ablaut (§8.4) and affixation. Derivation and inflection comprise a single interlocking system that can be illustrated by the following examples, drawn from Hebrew:

šəmartíihuu	'I guarded him'	zəkartíihuu	'I remembered him'
šəmartíihaa	'I guarded her'	zəkartíihaa	'I remembered her'
šooméer	'watchman'	zookéer	'one who remembers'

To describe this rather simple corpus, we must posit two verb roots /s__m__r-/ 'guard' and /z__k__r-/ 'remember' having a three-consonant (i.e., triliteral) framework into which various vowels are inserted. For derived agent nouns the vowels are /oo__ée/; for the type of action-process verb shown here, the vowels are /ə__a/. We must also posit a first person agent suffix /-tíi/ that follows the verb root as well as two third person patient suffixes that follow the first suffix. The masculine patient is /-huu/ and the feminine patient is /-haa/. The ablaut system is highly elaborated in Arabic, less so in the other languages. Whether it was a feature of Proto-Semitic that subsequently weakened in some of the languages or was merely incipient in the protolanguage and developed most fully in Arabic is a matter of uncertainty. Either way it would appear to be an archaic feature. Indo-European ablaut is known to have arisen in the protolanguage as a secondary development conditioned by variable pitch and stress. Ablaut as a signaling device in Semitic (or any other language) must have a similar history (see §8.26).

The second member of the Afroasiatic phylum is Egyptian, now extinct, and its descendant Coptic, which remains in use only as a liturgical language among the Coptic Christians of Egypt.

The Berber languages are spoken by groups scattered through North Africa and the Sahara. Included in this group are Kabyle, Shilh, Zenaga, and Tuareg.

The Cushitic languages comprise a large family spoken in several countries of East Africa. Four branches are recognized: a northern, central, eastern, and western. Two eastern languages, Somali and Galla, are spoken by large populations, as is Beja, the northern language. In Beja a plural involving vowel change occurs: *or/ar* 'son/ sons.' This type of plural is also found in Semitic languages.

The Chadic family, located to the south and west of Lake Chad in west-central Africa, contains nine branches and some fifty languages altogether. Most are spoken by fairly small populations, but Hausa is one of the principal languages of Nigeria and is an important trade language in other parts of West Africa.

Hausa has developed phonemic tone, an areal feature found throughout West Africa and reported by some investigators for Cushitic as well. The Hausa verb root is a CVC or CV matrix that is inflected by a combination of suffixation and variation of tone in both suffix and root. The system does not include ablaut.

8.11 URALIC

The Uralic languages, together with the Altaic languages (§8.12), comprise the Ural-Altaic stock, which stretches from Europe through central Asia to the Pacific. Korean and Japanese are thought to be outlying members of the family.

The Uralic family is represented in Europe by the Finno-Ugric languages and in Siberia by the Samoyedic languages. In the Finnish group are Finnish, Estonian, Karelian, Livonian, Lapp, and a number of other languages. Several Finnish languages, including Mordvin and Zyryan, are spoken in the Soviet Union in areas scattered from the middle Volga to the upper Divina. The Samoyedic languages include Enets and Nenets, both spoken along the Yenisey River. The Ugric group is represented chiefly by Hungarian.

Proto-Uralic was probably spoken in a region between the Ural Mountains and the middle reaches of the Volga River some 6,000 years ago. Thus, the Finns, Hungarians, and Samoyeds represent an expansive movement from the original homeland; and at the same time the expansion of Slavic languages has broken up what would otherwise be a continuous Uralic area. Loan words from Iranian, Lithuanian, Germanic, Russian, and Turkish indicate successive periods of contact with other language groups of the region. The history of contact is of course different for each language.

Finnish and Hungarian have an elaborate case system. Grammatical categories are marked by suffixation, and most of the languages exhibit vowel harmony—a form of reverse umlaut (§8.4) in which lag assimilation modifies the vowel of a suffix so that it is partially or wholly assimilated to a vowel of the stem. Lapp and the Finnish languages of the Baltic region have consonant gradation as well. This is a process comparable to ablaut in which consonant alternations occur either morphophonemically or as a grammatical signaling device. The possibility of a remote relationship to Indo-European has been suggested but remains an unconfirmed hypothesis.

8.12 ALTAIC

The grouping of Altaic with Uralic is based more on structural similarities than on a demonstrated core of common vocabulary with sound correspondences. The status of Ural-Altaic as a genetic group is therefore less certain than it is for a group such as Indo-European.

The Altaic family consists of three groups: Turkic, Mongolian, and Manchu-Tungus. The closely related Turkish languages include Turkish, Uzbek, Uighur, Turkmen, Tatar, Bashkir, Kazakh, Altai, Yakut, and a number of others. The Mongolian languages, also quite closely related, include Mongol, Buryat, Daghur, Kalmyk, and a few others. The Manchu-Tungus group consists of a southern group with Manchu and Nanai and a northern group with Evenki and Lamut.

The languages contain few consonant clusters, and most have vowel harmony. Prefixing is absent, but the system of suffixation is fairly complex. Grammatical gender is absent, as is a distinction between singular and plural. (A specific number can be used with an unmarked noun if an exact number is important and is not already clear from context.) Altaic languages are usually described as having only three formally distinct parts of speech: nouns, verbs, and particles. Nouns and verbs are frequently built from the same stems. In the Turkic and Mongolian languages, nouns and adjectives are described as belonging to the same form class.

8.13 KOREAN

Korean is spoken on the Korean Peninsula and coastal islands, where it has been established for at least 2,000 years. No closely related languages are known, although a distant relationship to Altaic is posited on the basis of similar grammatical features and the presence of a few purported cognates. The Korean phonological system is noted for its three-way consonant contrast: lenis (nontense) /p t k/, fortis (tense) /pp tt kk/, and fortis aspirated /ph th kh/. Nouns do not express gender or number but are marked by a postposed particle or postposition as subject, object, or the like. Verbs and adjectives form a single class and take the same inflectional endings. Verbal inflections include tense and mode and can indicate whether the speaker is repeating hearsay or relating something known from personal experience. The usual sentence order is subject, object, and verb. The language has been influenced by lexical borrowings from Chinese, and the writing system (§9.10) also developed under Chinese influence. A relationship to Japanese at a time depth exceeding 2,000 years has been posited on the basis of cognate sets and regular sound correspondences.

8.14 JAPANESE

Japanese is spoken on the four Japanese islands and several smaller islands adjoining them. The earliest centers of Japanese culture were in the extreme south and west of the islands, the area nearest Korea and the Asian mainland. The Japanese expanded to the north and east, eventually occupying the major islands and displacing the indigenous Ainu, who now live only in the northernmost island. (The Ainu language is unrelated to Japanese and has no known affinity with any other language. Racially the Ainu are Caucasian, although there has been recent intermarriage between Ainu and Japanese.)

Modern Japanese has five vowels and fifteen consonants. Proto-Japanese had a larger vowel inventory that was reduced through mergers. The number of consonants has probably increased in the same time and, indeed, exceeds fifteen in the analysis of some investigators. As in Korean, nouns do not express gender or number but are marked by a postposed particle that denotes their grammatical role in the sentence. Adjectives fall into several classes with different structural properties, but in general they pattern with verbs. Verbal inflections constitute a rich system for indicating tense, mode, aspect, voice, and degree of formality. The usual sentence order is subject, object, and verb. Japanese has borrowed freely from Chinese, and the writing system (§9.9) is based on Chinese. During the feudal period Japanese contacts with the outside world were limited, but a few Portuguese loan words were added to the language. Since 1867 the language has been receptive to borrowings from other European languages, including a large number of industrial and technical terms from English.

8.15 CAUCASIAN

Some forty languages known collectively as the Caucasian languages are spoken by about 5 million persons on either side of the Caucasus Mountains between the Black Sea and the Caspian Sea. Although the languages form an areal and typological group, there is no demonstrated genetic relation between the northern and southern groups. The best known of the southern, or Kartvelian, languages is Georgian. Like its neighboring languages Georgian has a rich inventory of consonants and allows consonant clusters of up to six segments, for example, *prckvna* 'peeling.' In Georgian the nominative case marks the subject of intransitive verbs and the object of transitive verbs, while a special ergative case (erg) marks the subject (i.e., agent) of transitive verbs. The ergative construction occurs only in the aorist (i.e., past) tense; elsewhere nominative marks the subject of transitive verbs, and dative case marks the object:

k̇ac-i	(nom)	midis			'the/a man goes'
k̇ac-ma	(erg)	mok̇la	datv-i	(nom)	'the/a man killed the/a bear'
k̇ac-i	(nom)	k̇lavs	datv-s	(dat)	'the/a man kills the/a bear'

Verbal structures include a process of vowel ablaut similar in function to the ablaut of Indo-European.

The northern languages fall into two genetically related groups, a western and eastern, although the relationship is by no means close. Languages in the north include Abkhaz, Abaza, Adyghian, Kabardian, and Ubykh. An inventory of seventy consonants is reported for Abkhaz and eighty for Ubykh. The languages are characterized by relatively simple noun forms and complex verbal structures. The vowel system of the western group is reported to consist of only two vowels *a* and *ə*. The former has a variety of allophones determined by consonantal environments, and the latter is said to be a juncture feature. If this is correct, the system could be analyzed as having a single vowel. Other northern languages have at least five vowels and sometimes as many as twenty or more. Features of contrast include length, nasalization, and pharyngealization in addition to tongue position.

8.16 BASQUE

Basque is now spoken by about half a million persons in southwestern France and northern Spain. The language once occupied a larger area, as indicated by place names, but was gradually displaced by other languages. Basque, called Euskara by the Euskaldunak who speak it, has no demonstrable relationship with any other language. The sound system of Basque is similar to that of Spanish. The language has five vowels, few permissible consonant clusters, two series of stops (voiceless *p, t, k* and voiced *b, d, g,* the latter not completely stopped in certain environments); nasals *m, n, ñ* (palatal); *l, ll* (palatal); *r* (flap), *rr* (trill); and voiceless sibilants and affricates with three articulations: *s, ts* (apical, or tongue tip); *z, tz* (predorsal, or tongue blade); and *x, tx* (palatal). Basque is an ergative language, a factor that has led to speculation concerning a possible relationship with Caucasian languages. Such a relationship, like others that have been proposed, remains unconfirmed, however. Noun phrases are marked by suffixes that denote number and case: *etxe-a* 'the house,' *etxe berri-a* 'the new house,' *etxe berri-a-ri* 'to the new house.' Verbs are indexed for the noun phrases that accompany them and may have as many as three personal references—subject, direct object, and indirect object.

8.17 CHINESE

Measured by the number of speakers alone, the Chinese languages must be taken as one of the world's principal language families. But in addition the languages have been the vehicle of an important culture that has dominated East Asia for the past 3,500 years. Travelers' accounts of China and the Chinese languages have been available to Europeans since the time of Marco Polo, but only since the nineteenth century has anything approaching an adequate linguistic description of any of the languages been available.

The development of Chinese can be broken into five historical periods: Proto-Chinese prior to 500 B.C., Archaic Chinese from 500 B.c. to A.D. 600, Ancient Chinese from 600 to 1200, Medieval Chinese from 1200 to 1650, and Modern Chinese since 1650. Although the region was earlier inhabited by non-Chinese-speaking people, little is known of them; and if words from these languages were borrowed into Chinese, they have been so thoroughly assimilated to Chinese phonological patterns that they now escape detection. One of the few foreign borrowings attested prior to the modern period is the word for 'glass' (Pekingese *pōlí*), a known borrowing from Sanskrit *spahtika* 'rock crystal' in the fifth century A.D., when glass manufacture was introduced to China.

On the basis of both internal and comparative evidence, it appears that Chinese developed from a polysyllabic language having morphological processes that included prefixing and suffixing. Morphemes in the modern language, however, are invariable monosyllables, and the language is usually described as monosyllabic in structure, although morphemes are frequently combined to form compound words of more than one syllable. This monosyllabic tendency was apparent even in the earliest recorded forms of the language. The affixing stage of the language antedated written records, but pitch contours associated with affixes were left behind in the form of tones that became a distinctive part of the monosyllabic morphemes. Ancient Chinese is thought to have had six tones. These have merged to four in Pekingese, but a six-tone system is still found in Cantonese. Ancient Chinese had a number of initial consonant clusters and permitted a variety of final consonants; but initial clusters have been simplified over the years, and the number of permitted final consonants is greatly restricted in the modern languages.

The end result of these sound changes is an abundance of homonyms in the modern languages. This is partly offset by the development of new compounds in which two words of similar meaning, each of which might be misconstrued by itself, are combined to create a new form having a less ambiguous meaning. In the absence of inflections, syntactic arrangement has become the primary signaling device. Each root, within the confines of its basic meaning, can be used as a noun, verb, or modifying word depending on its syntactic collocation.

Although the languages of China are often described as dialects, they are in fact mutually unintelligible as spoken languages. Since the different languages are written in the same logographic writing system (see Chapter 9), it is possible for Cantonese speakers to "read" a Pekingese document by giving the logographs their Cantonese pronunciation, but this does not mean they would be able to understand the spoken forms the author had in mind when the document was written. Cultural and political unity, as well as a shared writing system, have tended to minimize the actual differences as far as the Chinese themselves are concerned.

The principal languages of China are Pekingese (also called Mandarin) in the north, central, and west; Wu in the Shanghai area; the Min languages, including Fuchow, Amoy, and Taiwanese along the south-central coastal area; Kan and Hakka in the south-central inland region; Hsiang farther to the south; and Cantonese in the extreme southern coastal area.

8.18 TIBETO-BURMAN

The Tibeto-Burman languages are related to the Chinese family even though the time depth is considerable. Languages in this family are spoken in Tibet, Burma, the Himalayas (including Nepal, Sikkim, and Bhutan), Assam, Bangladesh, and by scattered tribal groups in Southeast Asia and western China. The whole of Southeast Asia is an area of extreme linguistic diversity, and many details of language classification in the region remain uncertain.

Tibetan is spoken in Tibet itself and in neighboring parts of China. In overall structure the language is similar to Chinese, but to a limited extent Tibetan has retained syllabic prefixes and suffixes.

Burmese includes Burmese-Lolo, Kachin, Kuki-Chin, Bodo-Garo, Karen, and numerous related languages spoken in Burma and parts of the Malayan Peninsula. Indications are that the Burmese speakers are relatively recent arrivals in the area.

8.19 TAI

The Tai languages are spoken in parts of Southeast Asia including Thailand, Laos, Burma, North Vietnam, parts of southern China, part of the island of Hainan, and as far west as Assam in northeastern India. The best-known languages are Thai (Siamese), spoken in Thailand, and Lao, spoken in Laos. The Miao-Yao languages are spoken in China, Yuan in Thailand, Shan in Burma, and Kadai on Hainan. The distribution of Tai-speaking tribes in China was once more extensive than at present, and similarities between Tai and Chinese are now thought to represent ancient borrowings of Tai forms into Chinese rather than a demonstrable genetic relationship between the two families or borrowings from Chinese into Tai. Modern Thai has five tones:

maa	'to come'	(level tone)
màak	'areca nut'	(low tone)
mâak	'much'	(falling tone)
máa	'horse'	(high tone)
mǎa	'dog'	(rising tone)

These and other structural similarities between the Tai and Chinese families can be interpreted as examples of parallel development rather than evidence of a genetic relationship.

8.20 AUSTROASIATIC

The Austroasiatic languages consist of the Munda languages spoken by hill tribes in east-central India, the Nicobar languages spoken on the Nicobar Islands in the Indian Ocean, and the Mon-Khmer languages of Southeast Asia. The distribution of the languages suggests early settlement throughout the area, with the settlements now made discontinuous by the more recent arrival of other language groups. Principal languages of the Mon-Khmer group are the Mon languages spoken in Burma, Khmer in Cambodia, and Vietnamese in Vietnam. In structure the languages range from the complex morphology of Munda with prefixes, suffixes, and infixes (i.e., grammatical elements inserted into a root) to a language like Vietnamese, which has developed monosyllabic structures similar to Chinese and Tai.

8.21 AUSTRONESIAN

In terms of geographic expanse, the Austronesian family is unrivaled by any group except possibly the Indo-European family. From a center of dispersion, probably in Indonesia, the Austronesian languages spread from Madagascar, off the coast of Africa, to Easter

Island in the eastern Pacific, and from New Zealand northward to Taiwan and Hawaii. The settlement was accomplished in prehistoric times across uncharted oceans, whereas the spread of the Indo-Europeans took place on a connected landmass and did not extend beyond the continental limits until modern times. Since the Austronesian migration involved settlement of islands isolated from one another by considerable distances, the situation favored dialect differentiation and development of distinct languages. Some 500 different languages are now recognized, a number far exceeding the modest diversity of the Indo-European family.

The Austronesian family, sometimes termed Malayo-Polynesian, is divided into a western and eastern group. The western languages include Malagasy, spoken in Madagascar; Malay, spoken on the Malay Peninsula; Indonesian, Javanese, Sundanese, Madurese, and Balinese, spoken in Indonesia; Brunei, Ngaju, and a number of lesser-known languages spoken on Borneo; Tagalog (Pilipino) and Ilocano, spoken in the Philippines; tribal languages spoken on Taiwan; the Chamic languages spoken by hill tribes (Montagnards) in Vietnam and Cambodia; Chamorro in the Marianas; Palau in the western Carolines; and other languages of the Celebes, eastern Indonesia, and western New Guinea. Most of the languages are spoken in several different dialects.

The eastern group is geographically more widespread and consequently more diversified. The Melanesian division alone contains some 250 different languages. The best known of this group, located on the islands east of New Guinea, is Fijian. Islands in the area have been inhabited for at least 3,000 years; the languages therefore are not closely related. The Polynesian division fills a large triangle, with New Zealand, Easter Island, and Hawaii at the three corners. The languages within this strikingly homogeneous group include Maori (New Zealand), Hawaiian, Tahitian, Tongan, Samoan, and Easter Island. The Micronesian division—on the small islands north of New Guinea and east of the Philippines—consists of Marshallese, Gilbertese, Trukese, Ponapean, Kusaiean, Carolinean, and Ulithian. The area also includes two western languages (Chamorro and Palau) mentioned above, two Polynesian languages (Nukuoro and Kapingamarangi), and two languages of uncertain affinity within the family (Yapese and Nauruan).

The protolanguage had a phonemic inventory that included four vowels (*i, *e, *u, *a), six voiceless stops (*p, *t, *T, *c, *k, *2), five voiced stops (*b, *d, *D, *j, *g), seven continuants, or continuous sounds (*l, *r, *R, *h, *s, *z, *Z), and two semivowels (*w, *y). Most of the modern languages have expanded the vowel inventory while reducing the consonant inventory. The protolanguage favored a CV syllable canon that has generally been preserved in the modern languages. This is particularly true of the eastern languages. The Polynesian languages have reduced the consonant inventory, developed extended vowel sequences, and allowed word canons of considerable length. Hawaiian for example has reduced the inventory to five vowels /i, e, a, o, u/ and eight consonants /p, t, k, ʔ, m, n, w, l/. The eastern languages tend toward analytical structures, while the western languages, which tolerate greater phonological complexity, have more compact words and greater morphological complexity. Tagalog, for example, is noted for its infixes. Complexity of voice and case systems is reported for other Philippine languages. Because of the great time depth involved, vocabulary differences among languages in the family are extensive. The process of vocabulary replacement was accelerated in many cases by a tabu on certain words, for example, the name of a deceased person and other words related to that person's name. The English word *tabu* itself is from Fijian *tabu* (*tapu* in most of the Polynesian languages, *kapu* in Hawaiian).

It is difficult to generalize about a language family having the geographic range and diversity of the Austronesian languages. The difficulty is heightened by the fact that many of the numerous languages still have not been studied in detail. Further study of these languages can therefore be expected to produce a wealth of information about prehistoric migration patterns, language change, and possibilities for structural variation within a family.

8.22 PAPUAN

The Papuan languages are centered in New Guinea but also found on islands to the east and west. The term applies to some 400 languages known to be genetically related, but it is also used as the designation for several hundred other languages of uncertain affinity spoken in the same area. Enga, spoken on New Guinea by 130,000 persons, is the language with the largest group of speakers. Many are spoken by small populations. The languages are characterized by extreme grammatical complexity, with verb structures containing ten or more morphemes not at all uncommon. The limited geographical distribution and considerable diversity within this limited area suggest a long period of settlement.

8.23 AUSTRALIAN

The aboriginal languages of Australia belong to a single family. Although more than 200 separate languages have been identified, many are spoken by small populations. Among the better-known languages are Tiwi and Walbiri. Considerable diversity is found among the languages in the north as compared with those of the south, suggesting that the first settlements were in the north, and migration into the south came much later. However, no link to Papuan or any other language family has yet been established. The languages are characterized by considerable structural complexity, including prefixing, suffixing, and infixing. Men of the Walbiri tribe have a "secret" language that involves the use of semantic opposites. The language is used much like children in English-speaking countries use pig latin or other code forms of language.

8.24 DRAVIDIAN

Among the non-Indo-European languages still spoken in India, the most prominent are the Dravidian languages. The languages are located in the south of India, with a few outposts in the hills of central India, where they are surrounded by Indo-European languages and remnant tribes speaking Austroasiatic languages. The northern area now occupied by Indo-European was formerly a Dravidian region. The principal Dravidian languages are Telegu, Tamil, Kannada, and Malayalam, all spoken in the south, and Brahui in Pakistan, the only language to have survived in the north. Tamil is spoken in Sri Lanka (Ceylon) alongside Singhalese, the Indic language of the majority. Over the years the influence of Dravidian and Indic on each other has led to numerous structural similarities in phonology and morphology as well as vocabulary. Dravidian verbs are inflected for tense, mood, and aspect, while nouns are inflected for six cases. The typical sentence order is subject-object-verb. Phonology is relatively complex, with up to six articulatory positions distinguished for stops and nasals:

p, m	(bilabial)
ṭ, ṇ	(dental)
t, n	(alveolar)
T, N	(retroflex)
c, ñ	(palatal)
k, ŋ	(velar)

8.25 CONGO-KORDOFANIAN

By far the largest phylum of languages on the African continent is the Congo-Kordofanian, a stock that stretches from West Africa through the equatorial region to the east coast and south to the cape. Most of the languages in this group belong to the Niger-Congo family; the Kordofanian division consists of a single group of related languages spoken in the Sudan.

The Niger-Congo division contains six subgroups: (1) West Atlantic languages centered in Senegal, Gambia, and Guinea. The languages include Wolof, Fulani, and about twenty others. (2) Mande centered in the Ivory Coast. Languages include Malinke, Bambara, Susu, Mande, Loma, Kpelle, and others totaling about thirty. (3) Gur centered in Ghana, Togo, Dahomey, and Nigeria. Languages in this group number about fifty. (4) Kwa stretched along the coast from Liberia eastward into Nigeria. Languages in this group include Kru, Ewe, Akan, Yoruba, Nupe, and Ibo. (5) Adamawa-Eastern from south of Lake Chad stretching eastward through the Central African Republic. This group includes more than eighty languages. (6) Benue-Congo covering the larger part of central and southwestern Africa. The group includes more than seventy-five languages ranging from Efik and Tiv in Nigeria to the Bantu languages that have spread south and eastward in fairly recent times. Although the Bantu languages cover an extensive area, they are merely one subfamily within the Benue-Congo branch of Niger-Congo. By far the most important of the Bantu languages is Swahili, a trade language spoken throughout East Africa. Other prominent languages are Kongo, Luba, and Ngala in Zaire; Shona in Rhodesia; Ganda in Uganda; Kikuyu in Kenya; Rwanda in Rwanda; Rundi in Burundi; Bemba in Zambia; and Zulu, Xhosa, Swazi, and Tswana in South Africa.

A characteristic feature of the Niger-Congo languages is an elaborate system of classificatory affixes used with nouns. Thus, the Bantu languages have *mu-/ba-* 'singular/plural' for humans, *le-/ma-* 'singular/plural' for objects that come in pairs, and so on. This morphological trait provides important material for comparison and genetic grouping of the languages.

8.26 NILO-SAHARAN

Extending from Kenya through Uganda, Sudan, and Chad in an area made discontinuous by the intrusion of Afroasiatic languages is the Nilo-Saharan family. The family has six branches. Songhai is located far to the west of the main body of languages. Its speakers are situated along the Niger River in Mali. The Saharan languages are spoken in Chad. The Maban languages are spoken in enclaves surrounded by Afroasiatic languages in Ethiopia and Sudan. Fur is situated in similar enclaves in Sudan and the Central African Republic. The Koman languages are also spoken in enclaves in Ethiopia and Sudan. The sixth member of the family, Chari-Nile, has a number of subdivisions. Most of the languages are spoken in the region north of Lake Victoria, but several are spoken in outlying enclaves. Members of the Chari-Nile group include the Nubian languages, the Nilotic languages (among which are Nuer and Masai), Bongo, Gamba, Makere, and Efe.

An indication of the inflectional complexity of Chari-Nile can be seen from the following Nuer noun paradigm:

lêp	'tongue'	θók	'mouth'	nominative singular
léab		θwɔ'h		genitive singular
lèb		θóɣ		locative singular
lïf		θúuh		nominative plural
lɪɪfnä'		θúuhnä		genitive/locative plural

Greenberg observes that the "intricate internal variations of languages like Nuer must be the result of changes induced by former affixes which have been dropped after influencing the root" since "this is the manner in which internal changes are normally known to develop where historical evidence is available" (1966:92).

8.27 KHOISAN

Situated in South Africa, Botswana, South West Africa, and Angola are the Khoisan languages. These include the languages of the Bushmen and Hottentots in the south of Africa and two language isolates, Sandawe and Hatsa, spoken in Tanzania. The most notable feature of the languages is the frequent occurrence of phonetic clicks produced by placing an articulating organ—the tongue—against the palate and withdrawing the organ to create a vacuum. The resulting sound, which occurs only in initial position, is integrated into the stream of speech and is normally represented by a special symbol /!, //, /, #/ representing the specific type of click and a consonant symbol representing the type of release. The two constitute a single unit. As a result of vocabulary borrowing, clicks are also found in the neighboring Bantu languages.

The cattle-raising Hottentots follow a way of life quite different from the hunting-and-gathering Bushmen, who now live in the Kalahari Desert, having been displaced from more desirable areas by Bantu and European populations. Hottentot languages include Nama and Korana. Bushman languages include !Kung, Auen, Hiechware, /Xam, Naron, and /Auni. Structural similarities between Hottentot and Bushman can be seen in the following noun paradigms:

Nama:		*Naron:*		
	kxoe-b		kwe-ba	'man'
	kxoe-s		kwe-sa	'woman'
	kxoe-i		——	'person'
	kxoe-kxa		kwe-čəra	'men (dual)'
	kxoe-ra		kwe-šəra	'women (dual)'
	kxoe-ku		kwe-či *or* kwe-//kwa	'men'
	kxoe-ti		kwe-si	'women'
	kxoe-n		——	'persons'

8.28 PALEOSIBERIAN

The only remaining languages in the Old World are known as Paleo-siberian. The term refers to four separate families having no estab-lished connection with one another or with other language families. Two of the families, Yukaghir and Gilyak, consist of single languages. The Yeniseian family is currently represented only by Ket (Yenisey-Ostyak); related languages became extinct in modern times. The fourth family, Luorawetlan, is represented by Chukchi spoken near the Bering Sea; Kamchadal spoken on the Kamchatka Peninsula; and Koryak, Aliutor, and Kerek, all spoken by small populations in the Kamchatka area. Chukchi, with 12,000 speakers, is spoken by the largest group. The languages represent different structural types but as a group exhibit considerable morphological complexity. An exam-ple is the discontinuous *ga . . . ima* 'in' of Chukchi:

ga- tor-orw -ima	'in (the) new sleigh'
ga- morik-orw -ima	'in our sleigh'
ga- morik-tor-orw -ima	'in our new sleigh'

Borrowings from Turkic and Altaic as well as from Ainu (see §8.14), Eskimo, and more recently from Russian attest to contact with neigh-boring languages. Contact in this case has also involved competition, and the Paleosiberian languages have been hemmed in by their more expansive neighbors and confined to a small portion of their former territory.

8.29 ALGONKIAN

Many languages in the New World were encountered by Europeans at almost the same time. Spanish explorers became acquainted with the languages of Central and South America in the early 1500s, and in many cases these languages were described by the priests who accompanied the conquistadors. Rather than attempting to follow an exact chronology of contact with individual languages in different parts of the New World, it will be simpler to begin with North America and proceed from there to the languages of Central and South America.

The Algonkian (Algonquian) family at the time of European con-tact was spread along the east coast from the Carolinas to the mouth of the St. Lawrence, from the Great Lakes to Hudson Bay, and west-ward across the plains to the Rockies. (Strictly speaking the move-ment onto the plains came after the Indians acquired the horse, but the simplest procedure is to describe each language group in terms of its location at the time of first contact—even though contact on the coast and on the plains came at different times.) Eastern Algonkian languages (from north to south) include Micmac, Malecite-Passama-quoddy, Penobscott-Abnaki, several extinct New England tribal languages, Delaware, and Powhatan (now extinct). The other languages include Cree and Ojibwa (still spoken by sizable populations in Canada), Shawnee, Menomini, Sauk-Fox-Kickapoo, and the languages of the groups that moved onto the plains: Arapaho, Blackfoot, and Cheyenne.

In addition, two languages of northern California, Wiyot and Yurok, are distantly related to the Algonkian family. The Algonkian languages are strikingly similar both in phonology and morphology. Nouns mark animate and inanimate gender, and there is a complex system for indexing the person, gender, and number of nouns associated with each verb.

8.30 MUSKOGEAN

The Muskogean languages of the Southeast are now known to be related to the Algonkian languages, forming between them a large family that spread through much of the eastern part of the continent. Languages in this family are Choctaw-Chickasaw (originally spoken in Mississippi), Alabama-Koasati (Alabama), Mikasuki-Hichiti (Florida panhandle), and Muskogee (Georgia). Muskogee is also known as Creek. The Muskogee who fled to Spanish Florida became known as the Seminole. Four languages spoken along the lower Mississippi and Gulf of Mexico—Natchez, Tunica, Chitimacha, and Atakapa—are considered distant relatives of the Muskogean languages.

Muskogean verb structures are fairly complex. Creek, for example, has a present tense, four past tenses distinguishing degrees of remoteness in time, and two future tenses distinguishing degrees of certainty. These categories are in addition to prefixes and suffixes for indexing persons associated with the verb. Tunica pronouns distinguish singular, dual, and plural for all three persons. In addition a distinction between masculine and feminine is maintained in both third and second person.

8.31 IROQUOIAN

The best-known Iroquoian languages are associated with the Five Nations of central New York State: Seneca, Cayuga, Onondaga, Oneida, and Mohawk. The Tuscarora, originally situated in North Carolina, later joined this confederation. The Cherokee, also of North Carolina, are also classed as Iroquoian. The Wyandot (Huron), located in Canada, spoke an Iroquoian language even though they were never part of the Five Nations. At the time of contact, the Iroquoian languages formed two enclaves (New York and North Carolina) surrounded by speakers of Algonkian and other languages, but it appears that the Iroquoians were the original inhabitants and their neighbors the recent arrivals.

Iroquoian languages have a relatively simple phonological structure. The modern languages are unusual in having no labials except *w*. Underlying forms are nonetheless subject to phonological processes that create extensive allomorphic variation. Verbal morphology includes the incorporation of inanimate patient or complement nouns into the verb. Thus, the sentence 'We two made a snowsnake for Bill' is symbolized as follows in Onondaga:

<pre>
  1   2   3   4   5 6 7
/wa?-shak-ni-hwęht-ǫni-ę-? bil/→[wa?shagnihwęhtǫnyé? bil]
</pre>

Units within the verb are (1) semantically empty prefix; (2) first person agent acting on masculine beneficiary; (3) dual specification for agent; (4) 'snowsnake'; (5) 'make'; (6) benefactive marker; (7) punctual aspect.

8.32 SIOUAN

Although the Siouan Indians eventually came to typify the Indians of the plains, their original location appears to have been east of the Mississippi. Siouan is considered a distant relative of Iroquoian, and the extinct languages Biloxi, Ofo, and Tutelo were still situated in the southeast at the time of first contact. Catawba, spoken in South Carolina into the present century, was a Siouan language. Other Carolina languages now extinct may also have been Siouan. Yuchi, spoken in the southern Appalachians, is classed as a language isolate within the Siouan family. Probably Iroquoian, Siouan, Catawba, Yuchi, and Caddoan (see §8.33) should be regarded as coordinate families within a Siouan phylum.

The closely related Siouan languages of the northern plains include Dakota, Winnebago, Assiniboin, Omaha, Ponca, Osage, Crow-Hidatsa, Iowa, Mandan, Missouri, Quapaw, and Kaw. Languages in the family are characterized by phonological and morphological complexity. The Lakota dialect of Dakota, taken as a representative example, distinguishes between plain stops, aspirated stops, and glottalized stops. Winnebago, along with other Siouan languages, uses instrumental prefixes with verbs, for example, *gi-* 'by striking':

<pre>
    gi-sák   'to kill, knock unconscious'
    gi-kúnuk   'to chop, hammer off'
    gi-pére   'to hammer thin'
</pre>

8.33 CADDOAN

Located on the southern plains are the Caddoan languages: Caddo, Wichita, Pawnee, Kitsai (now extinct), and Arikara (now spoken in North Dakota). The languages have complex phonology and morphology. Many Caddo verbs have a semantically opaque prefix that has been cited as evidence for a relationship with Siouan languages:

ki-náh?y	'to cut'
ki-paáhnu?	'to scratch oneself'
ki-saki	'to pound, mash, crack'

Comparison of the Caddo and Seneca pronominal prefixes suggests a possible relationship with Iroquoian languages:

	Caddo		*Seneca*		*Protosystem*	
	subject	*object*	*subject*	*object*	*subject*	*object*
'first person'	ci-	ku-	k(e)-	wak(e)-	*ke-	*ko-
'second person'	yah?-	si-	s(e)-	sa-	*se-	*so-
'indefinite person'	yi-	yu-	ye-	(ya)ko-	*ye-	*yo-

The possibility of a connection between a Siouan phylum and other language families has been suggested but remains unconfirmed.

8.34 ATHAPASKAN

The Athapaskan languages are strikingly similar in phonology and morphology. The area of greatest diversity, in northern Canada and Alaska, is generally considered their original homeland. Languages in this area include Dogrib, Hare, Chipewyan, Slave, Yellowknife, Kutchin, Beaver, Sarsi, and Carrier. A smaller group including Hupa and Mattole was located on the northern California coast at the time of first contact. A group of closely related languages is still spoken in Arizona and New Mexico. Of these, Navaho, with over 130,000 speakers, is the most vigorous. Several dialects of Apache are spoken in the same area, and Jicarilla, Lipan, and Kiowa-Apache are actually dialects of Apache. The last-named group had moved eastward and was living among the Kiowa at the time of first contact. The Athapaskan family is related to Eyak, spoken in southern Alaska, and probably to Tlingit and Haida, spoken on islands off the coast of Alaska and British Columbia. The larger grouping is known as the Na-Dene phylum.

Proto-Athapaskan had five vowels /*i, *e, *ə, *u, *a/, six voiceless stops /*t, *ƛ (= tl), *c (= ts), *č, *ḳ, *k/, a corresponding glottalized and voiced series /*t', *ƛ', *c', *č', *ḳ', *k'; *d, *ƛ, *z, *ž, *g̣, *g/,

voiceless and voiced fricatives, three nasals, and possibly a set of
labialized velars. The basic structure of the system is preserved in
the modern languages even though the phonetic details are different.
Verbal morphology is complex. Every verb has at least three prefixes
and may have as many as nine. Suffixation is not used. Aspectual and
modal categories are represented in the verb rather than tense as such.

8.35 ESKIMO-ALEUT

Eskimo-Aleut is the northernmost language family in North America.
The Aleut branch, in Alaska, now faces extinction. Eskimo is still
spoken in Alaska and Canada, but only in Greenland is the number
of speakers actually increasing. A small group of Eskimo speakers in
eastern Siberia represents a fairly recent migration from North
America. Eskimo is remarkably uniform throughout a vast area, suggesting relatively recent settlement. Greenlandic Eskimo has three
vowels /i, a, u/, four stops /p, t, k, q/, three spirants /β, ɣ, ɣ̌/, and
four nasals /m, n, ñ, ŋ/ as well as /l/ and two sibilants /s, ṣ/. Other
Eskimo dialects have a greater number of consonants—for example,
back velars, labialized velars and back velars, voiceless spirants, and
the like. Morphological processes, which are exclusively suffixing, are
extremely complex, involving derivational processes as well as
number (dual and plural), and various categories of case and mode.
Suffixation gives rise to extensive phonological alternations.

8.36 HOKAN

From the Rocky Mountains west, the linguistic picture in North
America is extremely complicated. The Hokan phylum consists of
several related families that must have settled in California and
Mexico at an early period. They were pushed into the California
hills by later Penutian arrivals (§8.37), and the languages of the
California and Arizona deserts and Baja California were separated
from the others by the intrusion of Uto-Aztecan tribes. The languages
in Mexico form small enclaves surrounded by other families.

Pomo is spoken in the coastal mountains north of San Francisco.
Karok, Chimariko, Yanan (Yana and Yahi), Shasta, and Achumawi-
Atsugewi were spoken in the northern California mountains. Washo
is spoken in the area of Lake Tahoe. Esselen, Salinan, and Chumashan
were spoken in the coastal mountains south of San Francisco. The
Yuman languages (Diegeño, Mohave, Yuma, and Havasupai-Walapai-
Yavapai) are still spoken in the California and Arizona deserts.
Another Yuman language, Kiliwa, was spoken in Baja California.
Mexican languages still spoken are Seri (in Sonora), Tlapanecan and
Tequistlatecan (in scattered coastal enclaves south of Mexico City),

and Jicaque (in Honduras). Coahuiltecan, now extinct, was spoken in northern Mexico and Texas.

Phonological structures in the different languages are varied, often showing similarities with neighboring languages. Morphology is generally complex. Karok verbs, for example, specify location or direction of action by an affix included in the verb stem: *paθ* 'throw,' *páaθ-roov* 'throw upriver,' *páaθ-raa* 'throw uphill,' *páaθ-rípaa* 'throw across stream.' A single prefix may indicate both subject and object, as in Karok *ni-mmah* 'I see him' and *ná-mmah* 'he sees me.'

8.37 PENUTIAN

The Penutian phylum consists of several diverse families including the Tsimshian languages of British Columbia; a group of families in Oregon including Chinookan, Yakonan, Kalapuya, Coos, Sahaptan-Nez Perce, Molale, Cayuse, Takelma, and Klamath-Modoc; and language families that occupied the central valley of California, including the Maidu family in the eastern Sacramento Valley, the Wintun family in the western Sacramento Valley, Miwok in the central valley and the area immediately north of San Francisco, Costanoan in the Bay area and immediately south, and Yokuts in the San Joaquin Valley. Zuñi, a pueblo language, belongs in the California Penutian group. The Mayan languages of the Yucatan Peninsula are generally classed as Penutian, as are the Mixe-Zoque and Totonacan languages of Mexico's Gulf coast. Chipaya-Uru, spoken in Bolivia, is also thought to be a Penutian language.

As with the Hokan phylum, the time depth for Penutian is considerable, making generalizations difficult. Morphology is complex, with suffixation more common than prefixing. The languages have a rich inventory of consonants, including glottalized consonants, and exhibit complex phonological alternations. In Sierra Miwok, for example, the stem meaning 'to ask' occurs in four allomorphic shapes: /hasu·l-, hasul-, has·ul-, haslu-/.

8.38 UTO-AZTECAN

The Uto-Aztecan languages are associated primarily with the Great Basin, where hunting-and-gathering techniques were barely able to sustain life. But by the time of first contact, groups from this body had expanded outward in all directions. The Kiowa-Tanoan group had moved eastward, where the Kiowa adopted a plains life and the Tanoan speakers became pueblo dwellers. Of the Shoshonean group, the Paiute, Ute, and Mono-Bannock remained in the Basin, while the Shoshone and Comanche moved to the plains. Another Shoshonean branch consisting of Luiseño, Gabrieliño, Serrano, and Tübatulabal moved into Southern California, while the Hopi became pueblo dwellers. A third branch, the Sonoran group consisting of Cora, Huichol, Cahita, Yaqui, Mayo, Tarahumara, Pima, Papago, and Tepehuan settled in southern Arizona and northern Mexico. The most prominent group, however, are the Nahuatl (Aztecs), who had established themselves in Mexico City and built a sizable empire by the time of Spanish contact. Nahuatl, in various dialects, is still spoken by more than 1 million persons in the states of Mexico, Michoacan, Puebla, Hidalgo, and Vera Cruz and in outposts in El Salvador and other parts of Central America.

Uto-Aztecan languages are mildly synthetic, with a few prefixes and many suffixes. Aspect is well developed, although tense as a formal category is little developed or absent. Hopi, for example, distinguishes *wari* 'he ran, runs, is running' (as a reported event), *wariknwe* 'he runs' (as a generic statement), and *warikni* 'he will run' (as an anticipated event). Facts such as this led Whorf to his controversial hypothesis that Hopi perception of time differs significantly from that of persons who speak English or other European languages (see §10.2).

8.39 PACIFIC NORTHWEST

The languages of the Pacific Northwest (Washington, parts of Idaho and Montana, most of British Columbia, and part of Alberta) include several distinct language families. These families, although not demonstrably related, have developed a number of similarities, particularly in phonological structures. Large consonant and small vowel inventories, glottalized consonants, and extended consonant clusters are commonplace. The Salish family, consisting of some thirty languages, is the most widespread in the area. Located on Vancouver Island and the coast north of the island are the Wakashan languages. These include Nootka, Nitinat, and Makah (forming the Nootkan subgroup) and Kwakiutl, Bella Bella, and Kitamat. Chimakuan, consisting of Quileute and Chimakum, is located on the Olympic Peninsula of Washington. Kutenai, a language isolate spoken in the Rockies near the Canadian-U.S. border, was thought by Sapir to be related to Algonkian, but the hypothesis remains undemonstrated.

8.40 LANGUAGE ISOLATES

Several other North American languages of uncertain affinity should be mentioned. Timucua, now extinct, was spoken in Florida. Beothuk, also extinct, was spoken in Newfoundland. Yuki, spoken in two enclaves north of San Francisco, has no known relatives. Tonkawa, spoken in Texas, may be related to Muskogean and Algonkian. Karankawa, also spoken in Texas, has no known relatives. Keres, a pueblo language isolate still being spoken, has no apparent connection with neighboring pueblo languages. Tarascan, of Michoacan State in Mexico, is another language isolate.

8.41 OTO-MANGUEAN

The Oto-Manguean phylum consists of several language families situated in central and southern Mexico and in Honduras, Nicaragua, and Costa Rica. The languages seemingly were early arrivals in the area and have since lost some of their former territory to the expanding Aztecs and Mayans. Families in the group include Tlapanec, Otomi-Mazahua, Popoloc-Mazatec, Mixtec, Zapotec, Chinantec, Mangue, and Huave.

8.42 CHIBCHAN

The Chibchan phylum is represented by the various Chibchan languages of Honduras, Nicaragua, Costa Rica, Panama, and Colombia. The languages were probably spoken more extensively in South America before the expansion of the Incas. Related to Chibchan are the Misumalpan languages of Nicaragua. Several language isolates —Paya and Lenca of Honduras and Xinca of El Salvador—are sometimes classed with this phylum. Chibchan languages spoken in South America include Tunebo and Yanomamö.

8.43 ARAWAKAN

As with the languages of North America, many questions remain unanswered concerning the classification of languages in South America. The problem in South America is intensified by lack of information, creating the impression of greater diversity than may eventually prove to be the case. For the present it is necessary to be content with a brief statement of established relationships and confess to a great deal of uncertainty beyond the known facts.

Arawakan languages were widely distributed in Brazil and adjoining countries, from the Andes to the Atlantic and from the Argentine border into the Caribbean—and most likely the southern tip of Florida. Taino, an Arawakan language, was the first New World language to be encountered by Europeans. Island Carib was an Arawakan language spoken originally by the women survivors of a tribe whose men were killed by Caribs (see §8.44) and who were then taken as wives by the victors. Both languages were preserved by later generations, one as men's speech and the other as women's speech. Many Arawakan languages are now extinct, but a number of the languages are still spoken in Brazil, Peru, Colombia, Venezuela, and neighboring countries. The best-known languages include Goajiro (Colombia), Campa and Machiguenga (Peru), and Mojo and Bauré (Bolivia).

8.44 CARIB

The Carib languages, whose speakers gave their name to the Caribbean Sea, have declined drastically since first contact. Carib is still spoken in Surinam, Trio in Surinam and Brazil, Chocó in western Colombia, and several other languages are spoken in Brazil. A relationship with Tupian (§8.45) seems likely.

8.45 TUPI-GUARANÍ

Tupi, Guaraní, and related languages numbering about fifty are widely distributed in Brazil south of the Amazon. These languages were expanding their territory at the time of first contact, and although some are now extinct, Gauraní ranks alongside Spanish as a national (but not official) language of Paraguay, where it is spoken by 1 million persons of Indian ancestry who have adopted Hispanic culture.

8.46 GE

The Ge [že] family is a small group of inland languages in eastern Brazil. The family may possibly be related to the Tupian languages.

8.47 QUECHUA-AYMARA

The Quechua and Aymara families, sometimes called Quechumaran, are situated in the Andes from southern Colombia to northern Argentina. Both languages were used by the Inca Empire. Aymaran languages are spoken in Bolivia and Peru; Quechuan languages are spoken in Colombia, Ecuador, Peru, and Argentina. Both seem to be growing rather than declining in numbers. Whether the two families are genetically related or have developed extensive similarities as a result of prolonged contact is a matter that is still disputed.

8.48 TUCANOAN

The Tucanoan family, numbering about thirty languages, is located in the western Amazon region of Brazil and in Colombia and Peru.

8.49 PANO-TACANAN

The principal languages of the Panoan and Tacanan families are spoken near the headwaters of the Amazon in Peru and in Bolivia and Brazil. A related group of languages, now mostly extinct, were spoken in Tierra del Fuego and adjoining parts of southern Argentina.

8.50 UNCLASSIFIED LANGUAGES

We have mentioned only the best known of the estimated 1,500 languages spoken in South America. Remaining languages are either spoken in limited areas, or by few speakers, or simply have not been described adequately. Many appear to be language isolates, but in the absence of adequate data, it is often impossible to identify possible genetic relationships. Other languages that should be mentioned are Araucanian, spoken in roughly the central third of Chile and in Argentina; Guaycuruan, spoken in the Chaco region of Argentina, Paraguay, and neighboring countries; and Mataco-Maccá, a family spoken in the same general area.

Morphologically the languages of South America range from moderately to extremely complex. Suffixation rather than prefixing is preferred. Quechua and Aymara use only suffixation; Arawakan languages favor suffixes but use a few prefixes; languages like Ge, Carib, and Tupian tend toward analytical structure. Tupian languages distinguish between noun and verb roots, but in languages like Quechua and Araucanian, a single root can be inflected as either a noun or verb. Guaycuruan verb stems provide detailed information about the location and direction of the action specified by the verb root.

8.51 LANGUAGE UNIVERSALS

A brief survey can hardly do justice to the structural diversity of the world's languages or serve as more than the barest introduction to the subject. Nonetheless, several facts should be apparent from the discussion of the preceding pages. Most of the more than 3,000 languages still spoken in the world can be grouped into some fifty phyla containing a somewhat larger number of families. Within each family, structural similarities are common, but profound typological differences can arise rather quickly. Thus, in little more than 1,000 years, two related languages can become so divergent in their overall structure that a genetic relation may all but escape detection. Conversely two totally unrelated languages, either by chance or through borrowings, may develop structural similarities that give every appearance of being genetic.

It should also be clear that structural diversity has limits. Languages differ in their phonemic inventories—from the thirteen pho-

nemes of Hawaiian to the more than eighty reported for Ubykh, a
Caucasian language—but all languages have a fixed inventory of structurally significant sounds. All languages have consonants and vowels,
usually a limited number of vowels, and a somewhat larger number of
consonants. Certain sounds are found in almost every language, while
other sounds are found only in certain families or geographic areas.

The greatest diversity seems to occur in morphology. Languages
range from the extremely analytical structure of Chinese and Vietnamese to the highly synthetic structure of languages like Eskimo
and the Papuan or Iroquoian languages, in which a single word composed of five to ten morphemes is quite common. In general, verbal
structures are more complex than nouns. Nouns may have no inflection at all, but inflections for gender, number, and case are common.
Some languages mark nouns as present or absent, visible or invisible,
or the like. Categories associated with the verb vary extensively from
one language to another. Languages range from total lack of verbal
inflection to varied combinations of tense, mode, aspect, and voice.
Verbal inflections often include an index of agent, patient, and sometimes of beneficiary. In some languages the verb stem includes
morphemes relating to the location and manner of the action or to an
instrument associated with the action.

Syntax offers fewer possibilities for diversity inasmuch as major
sentence elements are subject to the same linear constraints in all
languages. Thus, the verb may either introduce the sentence, occur
in the middle of the sentence, or come at the end. Adjectives associated with a noun may either precede the noun or follow it. Two or
more nouns associated with the same verb may be differentiated
either by case markings or by a conventionalized syntactic arrangement. Thus, the typical pattern is for subject to precede object in
one of the following patterns: VSO, SVO, or SOV (§1.7). The relationships that can be expressed as subject and object must of course be
stated in semantic terms. We therefore find that all languages provide
for the familiar relationships of agent, patient, beneficiary, and so
forth, and that all languages have much the same hierarchy for selecting certain relationships as subject, object, and the like. Since the
fundamental purpose of language is to communicate meaning, it is
only natural that the universal properties of language must be stated
ultimately in semantic terms.

summary

Languages can be classified according to structural type, geographical area,
or genetic relationship to other languages. Of these, the last provides the
least arbitrary and most useful classification. The more than 3,000 languages currently spoken in the world can be grouped into about fifty
distinct families. The Indo-European family extends from the Indian sub-

continent to northern Europe and eastward through the Soviet Union to the Pacific Ocean. Representatives of the family have also been established in North and South America in the last few hundred years. Only a few non-Indo-European languages are still spoken in Europe, but a number of diverse families are found in Asia. Chinese is spoken by the largest population, but Austronesian is geographically most widespread. The whole of Africa contains only four language families.

The greatest linguistic diversity, however, is found in the New World. More than a dozen family groupings are recognized in North America. Many of the languages are already extinct or nearing extinction, although a number of them are still spoken by sizable groups in Canada and in the United States west of the Mississippi. The Indian languages of Mexico and Central America are, if anything, more widely spoken than Spanish. In South America some 1,500 languages are still spoken. The number of language families is probably as great as in North America, but precise details of genetic relations remain to be worked out.

Possibilities for phonetic variation among languages are limited by the sound-producing capacities of the human voice. The greatest diversity among languages seems to occur in the area of morphology. Syntax offers fewer possibilities for variation since all languages are subject to essentially the same linear constraints. The kind of semantic information encoded in language, although differing in minor details from one language to another, is remarkably uniform among all languages.

---

further reading

General: Encyclopaedia Britannica 15th edition; Meillet and Cohen 1952; Ruhlen 1976; Voegelin and Voegelin 1964–66, 1976; Sebeok 1963–75, of which the following volumes are relevant: (1) Russia and East Europe; (2) East Asia and Southeast Asia; (4) Ibero-America and the Caribbean; (5) South Asia; (6) Southwest Asia, North Africa; (7) Sub-Saharan Africa; (8) Oceania; (9) Western Europe; (10) North America. **8.1** Greenberg 1957, 1968, 1971. **8.2** Greenberg 1960a, Jesperson 1922, Sapir 1921, Emeneau 1956. **8.3** W. Lockwood 1969. **8.4** Baugh 1957, Pyles 1964. **8.5** Palmer 1954, R. Hall 1974. **8.6** Entwistle and Morrison 1964, Halle 1959. **8.7** Buck 1955. **8.8** Boyle 1966. **8.9** Burrow 1965, J. Bloch 1965. **8.10** Greenberg 1966. **8.11** Collinder 1965. **8.12** Poppe 1965. **8.13** Martin 1966, Martin et al. 1967. **8.14** R. Miller 1967. **8.15** Kuipers 1963. **8.16** Lafon 1972. **8.17** Forrest 1948, DeFrancis 1950. **8.18** Chang and Shefts 1964, Cornyn 1944. **8.19** Li 1974. **8.20** Diffloth 1974. **8.21** Dyen 1971. **8.22** Laycock and Voorhoeve 1971. **8.23** Wurm 1971, Hale 1971. **8.24** J. Bloch 1954, Zvelebil 1970. **8.25** through **8.27** Greenberg 1966. **8.28** Worth 1963. **8.29** through **8.40** Sherzer 1975, Sapir 1929. **8.29** through **8.50** Sebeok 1976. **8.29** Bloomfield 1946, 1957, 1962, Haas 1958a, Goddard 1967, 1969, Teeter 1971, Pearson 1972a. **8.30** Haas 1941, 1958b. **8.31** Lounsbury 1953, Chafe 1967b, 1970a, 1973b. **8.32** Chafe 1973b. **8.33** Chafe 1973b. **8.34** Krauss 1973b. **8.35** Krauss 1973a. **8.36** Bright 1964. **8.37** Bright 1964. **8.38** Bright 1964. **8.39** Thompson 1973. **8.40** Haas 1965, 1969. **8.41** through **8.50** Hoijer 1946, Greenberg 1960b, Loukotka 1968, Zisa 1970. **8.51** Greenberg 1963.

9 writing and language

9.1 IMPORTANCE OF WRITING

We have emphasized repeatedly that language, as far as the linguist is concerned, is speech rather than writing. In the rise of *Homo sapiens* during the past several million years, it was the development of language as much as any single thing that set humans apart from the other animals. The emergence of an audible system of communication having duality of patterning dramatically extended the range of subject matter that could be communicated from one individual to another.

Animal communication systems typically are restricted to a finite number of signals relating to the emotional state of the sender. This is true of wild chimpanzees today. Even so it is possible for young chimpanzees to learn simple technology by direct observation—for example, the technology of using a twig to fish termites out of a hole. Probably our prehuman ancestors also developed a fairly elaborate food-gathering technology even before early call systems developed into anything that could be called language. But the development of language made possible a greatly elaborated technology and facilitated its transmission. Direct observation, while still important, could be replaced by a linguistic surrogate. The individual could learn manufacturing techniques, sources of food supply, and signs of potential danger even in the absence of opportunities for direct experience. The information could be stored in one's memory and utilized in time of need, even without the presence of the person whose experience was being applied. Accumulated knowledge of this type is what anthropologists term culture, and culture as we know it is almost entirely dependent on language for its elaboration and transmission.

Language, as suggested already, has existed in more or less its present form for upward of 1 million years. Language can therefore be considered roughly coextensive with *Homo erectus,* who emerged between 500,000 and 1 million years ago, replacing the earlier pre-human known as *Australopithecus.* By about 300,000 years ago, *Homo sapiens* had begun to replace *Homo erectus* in Africa and Europe (the replacement was as recent as 100,000 years ago in East Asia), but the Stone Age technology associated with *Homo erectus* underwent only gradual changes until about 10,000 years ago. At that time we begin finding archeological evidence of horticulture, domestication of animals, and development of village life. By about 5,000 years ago, human culture in the Middle East had developed the complexities of urbanization and centralized political-economic systems that we call civilization. It was at this point that writing developed.

The claim that human culture was dependent on language for its elaboration and transmission does not mean that language preceded the development of human culture. It means simply that the two evolved together and have been mutually dependent throughout their history. The rise of civilization and the development of writing exhibit the same kind of mutual interdependence. Farming nearly always requires records of landownership, and centralized government requires tax rolls and other records of commercial transactions. For people like ourselves, who are almost never without a notepad, it is easy to underestimate the ability of preliterate people to transmit important information orally and store large amounts of data in their memory. Many blind persons in our own society and illiterate persons everywhere rely entirely on memory, unaided by writing, to store the information needed for fairly complex lives. (Braille, a tactile version of the visual alphabet, partially replaces writing for many blind persons but is less versatile than writing.) In Muslim countries it is still common for the devout to commit the entire Koran to memory. Such feats of memory present no real difficulty for the person whose need or desire provides sufficient motivation. Even so, writing is a genuine aid to memory, particularly when the information to be stored is such that one item does not lead naturally to the next. Thus, writing is almost a necessity for the administrative records spawned by civilization. Its convenience in the modern world has induced us to use it even when it is not an absolute necessity. As a result, many literate persons have learned to distrust their memory and depend on writing. For such persons writing is not merely a convenience but has become, in effect, a necessity.

Because of our habitual dependence on writing, it often seems that writing is the usual form of language and speech a secondary form. Writing of course is a conscious form of language; for most people speech remains largely unconscious, except possibly under the most formal circumstances. Writing is still a way of representing speech; speech is not an alternate form of writing. Most of our time is spent in oral communication, only a fraction of our time in reading and writing. Everyone reading these words can remember something of the process of learning to read as a child—although we often forget, once the habit is well established, how difficult it was at first. Our recollections of speaking are quite different. Oral communication is so thoroughly integrated into our lives from such an early stage that probably no one can recall the process of learning to speak.

In terms of human history, writing is a very recent development, a mere scratch on the surface of time. All our ancestors who lived more than 5,000 years ago knew nothing of writing. Even in the years since its development, writing has spread slowly and has generally been the property of an elite few. Writing has still not been extended to all parts of the world, and it is only within the past hundred years that any language community has even begun to approach universal literacy. Yet, viewed against the perspective of more than 1 million years of human development, we are forced to say that the spread of writing has been rapid indeed. And writing is so pervasive in modern society that it is difficult to imagine life without it.

9.2 FORERUNNERS OF WRITING

During the Upper Paleolithic era (45,000 to 14,000 years ago), people living in France and Spain had adopted the practice of decorating cave walls with pictures of animals and human figures. The paintings, which probably served a ceremonial function, are the earliest records consciously created that have been preserved. No doubt other human groups at an even earlier period were in the habit of drawing pictures on animal skins, bark, or pieces of bone, but, if so, these perishable artifacts have not survived. Sculptured human figurines from the Upper Paleolithic have been discovered throughout Europe and southern Russia. But it is the medium of drawing rather than sculpture that sets the stage for writing.

A picture of an event is a report of the event, just as an oral account is also a report. The two kinds of reports differ in a significant way, however. Oral accounts are carefully edited reports in which speakers select the details to convey and arrange them in a particular way to achieve whatever effect they have in mind. A pictorial representation comes much closer to duplicating the original event. The artist, unlike the speaker, is not forced to take details one at a time but is able to present the entire picture as a single unit. To be sure, the artist may emphasize some details at the expense of others, but the finished product remains a configuration to which viewers respond much as they would to the event it depicts. A picture of three men throwing spears at an elephant does not require a unique linguistic interpretation. Any number of verbal reports might be appropriate:

"The men are hunting the elephant."

"The hunters will kill the elephant."

"My father and uncles killed the big elephant the year my sister was born."

"It is good when the hunters are successful."

"May the guardian of the chase be with our hunters always."

There is no definite limit to the number of possible interpretations. A picture may speak a universal language, but it remains raw data unless we have some clue to its cultural significance. The same can be said of events themselves. A man running is simply a man running; the significance of the event depends on knowing whether the man is exercising, trying to catch a bus, escaping a police officer, or running for some other reason.

Language has the advantage of directing the listener's attention to whatever details the speaker considers most significant. A picture may fail to convey these details or may be subject to misinterpretation. Egyptian drawings for example represent the face in profile but depict the eye in front perspective. A viewer unfamiliar with this convention might comment "What strange eyes these people have" and completely overlook whatever details the artist was intending to emphasize. An awareness of artistic conventions is therefore quite important in interpreting even fairly simple pictures. A picture of a goat upright and a horse and rider upside down has no inherent meaning apart from a cultural system in which it denotes "This path can be traveled by goats but is not safe for horseback riding."

To avoid ambiguity, artists who wanted their pictures to convey specific messages found it increasingly necessary to conventionalize their drawings. We do not know the precise steps that led to the development of Sumerian writing, but we can make a number of inferences on the basis of conventions used by preliterate people in historic times. Thus, a North American Indian artist might draw a picture of men in a canoe alongside three suns under three arches to indicate that the men made a journey of three days. Unless such a convention is used, there is no way to represent the notion 'three days.' Conventionalization therefore serves to clarify the intended message even though it may give no clear indication of the exact phrasing to be used in reporting the message.

If pictures are to represent verbal messages without ambiguity, a further convention is required. Each picture must represent a single word, and the pictures must be arranged in a linear order corresponding to the sequence of words in speech. Such a system is called **logographic writing.** In a logographic system it is easy to represent concrete objects, but some ingenuity is required to represent abstractions. A picture of the sun in Sumerian writing can represent 'sun' and by extension 'bright, white' as well as 'day.' 'Woman' and 'mountain' are easily enough pictured, and the two together represent 'slave girl' since slave girls were brought into Babylonia from the surrounding mountains. Logographic writing has great difficulty in representing grammatical markers, and these often are simply omitted. Readers, in trying to convert the logography into speech, are on their own to supply whatever grammatical markers seem appropriate to the context.

9.3 SUMERIAN WRITING

Cuneiform writing (Latin *cuneus* 'wedge,' *forma* 'form') had its beginnings in Mesopotamia approximately 5,000 years ago. In its earliest form it consisted of pictures incised in clay tablets with a stylus. These **pictographs** were evidently used to record commercial transactions; one of the earliest tablets bears the message '54 cow(s) (and) ox(en).' The tablet contains five circles, each representing 'ten,' four bullet-shaped signs, each representing 'one,' a conventionalized picture of an ox head, and a similar picture of a cow's head. With the passage of time, the drawings became more and more conventionalized until they evolved into an arrangement of wedge-shaped marks bearing little resemblance to the original picture. In the case of the ox head, the earliest pictograph is already a conventionalized outline. The symbol is later turned on its side, and in time the drawn lines become five wedge-shaped impressions. Later forms of the symbol still have five strokes, although two are reduced in size, drastically altering the earlier proportions. The important feature at this stage is not a real or fancied resemblance to an ox but rather a configuration of strokes that is distinct from all other configurations in the system. The wedge-shaped strokes and their arrangement thus constitute a system with duality of patterning.

A true logographic system would have a different symbol for each word or morpheme. The development of cuneiform was such that it never became a true logographic system, however. Cuneiform made use of semantic extension to represent concepts such as 'bright' or 'slave girl,' but the principle of phonetic extension was also used almost from the beginning. Thus, the word *ti* 'arrow' could be expressed by a representational logograph, and by using the rebus principle, the same logograph could be used in writing 'life,' also pronounced *ti*. A rebus is a puzzle or riddle in which pictures are used to represent words. Thus, in English a picture of an eye could represent the pronoun *I*, pictures of a bee and a leaf might be used for *believe*, and so forth. (A rebus frequently ignores fine distinctions like *belief* as opposed to *believe*.) The Sumerian system, utilizing the rebus principle, came to rely increasingly on logographs for their phonetic rather than semantic value. Eventually logographs were used for writing a few hundred of the most commonly occurring words, and everything else was written with stock symbols having fixed phonetic values.

Any language has a strictly limited inventory of phonemes as well as restricted possibilities for combining consonants and vowels to form syllables. If a language has five vowels and twenty consonants and permits only syllables of the CV type, the language will allow exactly one hundred possible syllables. If a logograph originally representing an arrow is used to write a particular syllable in certain contexts (e.g., when it symbolizes 'arrow' or 'life'), the logical next step is to use the same graphic symbol to represent that syllable independently of meaning when that syllable occurs as part of longer words. Once a graphic symbol has become established for each possible syllable in the language, the symbols lose any possibility of reference to meaning and can have only a phonetic value. Such a writing system is called a **syllabary.** Each distinctive symbol in a syllabary (or any writing system, for that matter) can be called a **grapheme.** The term parallels the concepts of phoneme and morpheme and implies the availability of a term **allograph** to refer to nondistinctive differences among graphs comprising a single grapheme.

Sumerian cuneiform writing was essentially syllabic, but it embodies certain ad hoc features arising from the need to accommodate syllables other than the CV type. Thus, the Sumerian system had established graphemes for the syllables *ra* and *al* but none for *ral*, which was written (i.e., spelled) *ra-al* and read *ral*. Such irregular spelling practices are perhaps a natural continuation of the rebus beginnings of the system. Although cuneiform syllabaries were widely used in Mesopotamia for some 2,000 years, neither the original script nor any of its descendants ever developed separate symbols for all the contrasting sounds in these languages. Thus, it was common in most Mesopotamian scripts to use a single symbol to represent the syllables *ka, ga, qa.* The procedure was to specify the vowel precisely, but not the accompanying consonant.

The Sumerian writing system—or at least the idea behind it—was apparently diffused to neighboring peoples in the Middle East and to cultures as far away as India and possibly even to China. Of these early writing systems, the Sumerian itself along with the Proto-Indic, Proto-Elamite, Cretan, and Hittite have become extinct. The Chinese writing system, which remains in use, will be examined in §9.8. The Egyptian system is important because it is the lineal ancestor of the modern alphabet.

9.4 EGYPTIAN WRITING

The earliest Egyptian pictographs belong to the period just after 5,000 years ago, and because of known Mesopotamian influences in Egypt at that time, it seems likely that the idea was a borrowing even though the form was distinctly Egyptian. The earliest pictographs were quickly replaced by a fully developed system, much like the Sumerian, in which logographic symbols were used in combination with a hieroglyphic syllabary. The absence of a well-developed logo-graphic transition stage is taken by Gelb (1952) as evidence that the Egyptian system developed along the lines already worked out by the Sumerians as a result of direct influence. The Egyptians therefore did not have to discover independently the phonetic principle of the rebus.

The hieroglyphic symbols, which were used for public display purposes, first appeared about 2900 B.C. For everyday use a simplified version called hieratic was worked out about 1900 B.C. This in turn gave way to the demotic script in the years from 400 to 100 B.C. The three scripts, although different in appearance, represented a writing system that remained essentially unchanged throughout its history. The system contained some twenty-four symbols representing sim-plex syllables and some eighty symbols representing complex syl-lables. Simplex syllables had a CV structure, while complex syllables had a CVC structure. Thus, a CV sequence beginning with *m* could be represented by a falcon symbol; the phonetic value of the vowel was left unspecified but could be supplied from the context by anyone familiar with the language. A lion symbol represented the complex syllable having initial *r* and final *w*, with the intervening vowel un-specified. The practice of indicating consonants correctly, but not the accompanying vowel, was just the reverse of the most common Meso-potamian system. It was this feature of Egyptian writing that was incorporated in the Phoenician system.

9.5 PHOENICIAN WRITING

By about 1000 B.C. the Phoenicians living on the eastern shores of the Mediterranean developed a syllabic writing system that quickly served as a pattern for other Semitic peoples. The system contained twenty-two graphs, each representing a consonant followed by a vowel that was left unspecified. The Phoenicians were wide-ranging seafarers and traders who had extensive contacts with the Egyptians. But their development of writing shows little if anything that is a direct importation of Egyptian script. Rather, it appears that Phoeni-cian writing was a case of stimulus diffusion. That is, the Phoenicians became familiar with the idea behind the Egyptian system and bor-rowed the idea while devising their own symbols for transcribing the sounds of their own language.

Like the Egyptian system the Phoenician writing system and its immediate descendants represented each consonant without indicat-ing the accompanying vowels. The written record was therefore a de-fective representation of speech since a single form could represent different words depending on which vowels were intended. How-ever, this apparent ambiguity of representation was not a serious problem in the case of Semitic languages. Indeed, the structure of Semitic languages is such that the ambiguity of vowel representation posed no serious difficulties and may even have facilitated dissemination of the system.

The preponderance of triliteral roots in Semitic languages (§8.10) means that most words could be represented by an invariable sequence of three consonant graphemes. In effect the sequence of graphemes functioned as a logograph. Additional graphemes were added to the root as required to represent prefixes or suffixes. The phonological system contained enough built-in redundancy that in most cases the unwritten vowels could be inferred from the context. In modern times Semitic languages such as Hebrew and Arabic have indicated vowels by special diacritical marks accompanying the consonant graphemes, but the practice still remains optional.

Although it is convenient to speak of "consonant" graphemes in connection with Semitic writing systems, it is important to understand that in the system as it originally developed each grapheme was intended to represent an entire syllable. In words such as proper names, where the pronunciation of vowels might not be clear from context, two spelling systems were used in Old Hebrew—a "full" spelling and a "defective" spelling. In "full" spellings a syllabic sign beginning with a "weak" consonant (e.g., glottal stop or y) was used to show the vowel reading of the preceding syllable. Thus, the name 'David' could be written in a "defective" spelling $dV\text{-}wV\text{-}dV$, with readers on their own to supply the appropriate vowels: $d\bar{a}wid$. (The final grapheme in this case had to be read with a zero vowel.) When the name was written with an additional grapheme $dV\text{-}wV\text{-}yV\text{-}dV$, the yV grapheme did not represent a separate syllable but was intended to insure that the previous syllable would be read wi rather than wa, we, wu, or wo. Although the "full" spellings developed early in Semitic writing, they were used only as an adjunct to the preferred "defective" spellings. The "full" spelling contains the germ of a true alphabet, but it was not used systematically until the system passed into the hands of the Greeks.

In appearance the syllabaries used for Phoenician, Palestinian, and Aramaic were quite similar. A southern version of the syllabary gave rise eventually to the Ethiopic script. With the passage of time, the original Phoenician forms were modified as scribal traditions developed independently in separate language groups. The Hebrew script developed its familiar square form, and the much later Arabic script emerged in cursive form. Meanwhile the Aramaic script that was the prototype for both Hebrew and Arabic was diffused through the area that includes present-day Turkey, Iran, and India. In these places it was adapted to the needs of Georgian, Armenian, various stages of Persian, and the various languages of India. In modern times some of these writing systems have been replaced by the alphabets of dominant cultures—the Cyrillic alphabet of Russia, the Roman alphabet, or Arabic script. But modern descendants of the Devanāgari that was devised originally for Sanskrit are still in use in the non-Muslim parts of India. Devanāgari in turn has served as the basis for written Burmese, Thai, Lao, and Cambodian in Southeast Asia. The influence of Devanāgari has also extended into China and from there to Japan (see §9.8, §9.9).

9.6   GREEK ALPHABET

During the ninth century B.C. as a result of contact with Phoenician seafarers, the Greeks were exposed to the idea of writing. Early inscriptions dating from about 900 B.C. show wide variation in the form of symbols used in different parts of Greece, suggesting that the script was introduced independently in several different places at about the same time. In each case, however, the system is clearly traceable to a Phoenician prototype. But the Greeks made one important modification in the system they adopted: from the very beginning the script represented both consonants and vowels and was therefore a true alphabet. (An earlier form of Greek writing known as Linear B represented whole syllables, but this system had become extinct by the ninth century and is therefore not a direct ancestor of the alphabet.)

A number of syllabic signs in Phoenician script contained initial consonants that were not phonemic in Greek. These symbols therefore had to be either discarded or put to some new use, and the Greeks chose to use them to represent vowels. The adaptation was no doubt facilitated by the sporadic practice among Semitic peoples of using certain syllabic signs with "weak" initial consonants to indicate the vowel of the preceding syllable. Thus, a Greek observing two graphemes *dV-CV* and learning they were read *da* would logically conclude that the first represented *d* and the second *a*. This was the analysis incorporated into Greek writing from the beginning, and it was transmitted with the symbols themselves to all those who adopted the Greek system.

9.7   DIFFUSION OF THE ALPHABET

The Etruscans, who settled in the northern part of the Italian Peninsula probably during the eighth century B.C., brought with them a version of the Greek alphabet. This alphabet was taken over by the Romans, who by 300 B.C. became the dominant power in Italy. The alphabet of Rome used only twenty-one of the twenty-six letters that we now think of as the "Roman" alphabet (missing were *J, K, U, W, Y*). The letters *K* and *Y* were not needed for Latin and were used only for transcribing Greek words. The letter *C*, derived from Greek Γ [g], was used for [k]; and a new letter *G* was devised for [g]. The letter

Y, based on Greek Y [u], eventually gained the pronunciation [ü] and in Medieval times came to be interchangeable with *i*. The letter *J* developed in the late Middle Ages as a variant of *i*. Since *i* in Latin could be either a vowel or semivowel (i.e., consonant), the new grapheme *J* tended to be used as a consonant, while the older grapheme *I* was used as a vowel. Latin had a single letter V that, like *i*, could be either a vowel or semivocalic consonant—in this case [u] or [w]. Thus, the Latin word [wenio] 'I come' was spelled VENIO, and the name 'Julius' [yulius] was spelled IVLIVS. In later Roman times bilabial [w] became labiodental [v]. In modern times a cursive form of V that appeared in Medieval times became the vowel symbol U, while the original angular symbol came to represent the labiodental consonant V. Modern W was a scribal innovation following the Norman conquest of England. At that time a new symbol was needed to write English [w], a sound not represented by any letter of the Medieval alphabet.

Individual letters assumed much their present form in the second century A.D., although the only letters in use at that time were capitals. Small letters evolved during the Middle Ages. The spread of the Latin alphabet is clearly due to Roman domination of Europe, but it was more the influence of Christianity than the power of Roman civil or military authority that was directly responsible. Then as now missionaries found it necessary to teach their converts to read and write so they could study the scriptures. This policy of course was not limited to Christianity; it had its counterpart in the spread of Islam in the Arab world and of Buddhism in parts of the Orient. The Cyrillic alphabet, which was devised for Slavic languages in 861, was based directly on the Greek alphabet and was also inspired by the desire to spread the teachings of Christianity. The Poles and Czechs were converted by Roman missionaries, the other Slavic peoples by missionaries from Constantinople—hence the different alphabets in use for the related languages.

On the whole, differences in the various alphabets descended from the Roman alphabet are slight. Letters like *w* and *j*, which were added to the alphabet long after the fall of the Roman Empire, acquired different phonetic values in different parts of Europe. A few new letters were devised to accommodate sounds that had not occurred in Latin. In most cases this was accomplished by adding diacritics to existing letters—for example, ð in Old English, ø in Danish, and š in Czech. In other cases non-Latin sounds were expressed by arbitrary combinations of letters such as *th* in modern English and *ch* in both Spanish and English. In these cases it was of course necessary to choose letter combinations that would not otherwise occur as regular sequences. Finally as the process of sound change has operated during the past 1,000 years the phonetic value of letters associated with altered sounds has drifted away from the earlier values of Latin. The English vowel shift is a case in point. The result of this phonetic shift has been a change in the nature of cross-linguistic correspondences involving sound-letter pairs:

Old English / Old Spanish			Modern English / Modern Spanish	
i [i]	i [i]	>	i [ɪ, ay]	i [i]
e [e]	e [e]	>	e [ɛ, iy]	e [e]
.	.		.	.
.	.		.	.
.	.		.	.

Where these were once identity correspondences, the correspondences now exhibit the results of change.

The dominance of European nations in the modern world has extended the influence of the alphabet, especially the Latin alphabet. The Cyrillic alphabet has been used for writing previously unwritten languages in the Soviet Union but has not spread outside that country. Western European powers that established colonies in the New World, Africa, and Asia took with them not only their languages but their Latin-based writing system as well. Thus, languages as different as Navaho in North America, Quechua in South America, Swahili in East Africa, Turkish in western Asia, and Vietnamese in Southeast Asia are now written in systems based on the Roman alphabet. The Vietnamese system was developed by French missionaries in the 1600s to replace an earlier Chinese-based system. And Turkey in 1928 adopted the Roman alphabet as a replacement for Arabic script. While the change of policy in Turkey did not involve direct foreign influence, it was part of a broad modernization program that arose in response to world events.

9.8 CHINESE WRITING

The earliest Chinese pictographs date from about 1300 B.C., fully 1,700 years after the development of writing in Mesopotamia. While there is no direct evidence that Chinese script was influenced by Mesopotamia, both the timing and the certainty of sporadic trade contacts make this a strong possibility. Whatever the stimulus, Chinese writing quickly developed into a full logographic system in which the graphemes assumed stylized forms bearing little resemblance to the original pictographs. The pictographs themselves, which were inscribed on bones and tortoise shells, were already highly conventionalized. Since the writing system is still widely used, it is worth examining in detail. Forms cited in the following paragraphs are numbered consecutively and are found in Figures 9–1, 9–2, and 9–3.

In some cases—for example, the pictograph for 'horse' (1)—enough variant forms from early inscriptions are extant that the evolution of the modern logograph is hardly in doubt. In a number of other cases, the pictograph is so clearly representational that the only evolution in form occurred after graphemes began to assume their modern angular shape (2–4). In other cases where the earliest pictograph is presumably representational, the representation is, at best, highly conventionalized (5–12). The pictograph for 'woman' (12) is said to represent a seated figure holding a child or engaged in some other womanly pursuit. However, the transition from picture to arbitrary sign was quite rapid, and the pictorial interpretation of even simple logographs representing common objects is not always self-evident.

FIGURE 9–1   Evolution of Selected Logographs

	Representational form (Kadogawa)	Pictographic form (Karlgren)	Modern logograph	Meaning
1.				'horse'
2.				'eye'
3.				'sun'
4.				'moon'
5.				'water'
6.				'river'
7.				'child'
8.				'big'
9.				'hand'
10.				'tree'
11.				'bamboo'
12.				'woman'

FIGURE 9–2	Semantic Extension of Logographs	
	Logograph	*Formation*	*Meaning*

	Logograph	Formation	Meaning
13.	林	reduplication of 10	'woods'
14.	明	combination of 3, 4	'light'
15.	好	combination of 7, 12	'good'
16.	本	addition of bar to 10	'root'
17.	東	combination of 3, 10	'east'

FIGURE 9–3   Phonetic Extension of Logographs

	Logograph	Meaning
18.	枋	'board'
19.	坊	'district'
20.	紡	'spin'
21.	訪	'ask'

   The problem of symbolizing terms that did not lend themselves to easy pictorial representation was solved in two different ways, both of them having Mesopotamian parallels. In many instances it was possible by semantic extension to combine existing logographs so as to suggest a more abstract concept. Thus, the symbol for 'woods' (13) is simply two trees. The combination of 'sun' and 'moon' was used for 'light' (14). The combination of 'woman' and 'child' represents 'good' (15). A line added to 'tree' converts it to 'root' (16). And a combination of 'sun' and 'tree' represents 'east' (17), the latter-day explanation being that the sun rises through trees in the east. The other method for representing abstractions involved phonetic extension. By the time the writing system arose, Chinese was already a language of monosyllabic morphemes. Many of these involved identical phonemic sequences differentiated only by tone. Thus, several morphemes all pronounced [faŋ] but having different tones could be represented by selecting an existing logograph having this pronunciation and combining it with other logographs semantically related to the morphemes in need of symbols. The procedure was to indicate the semantic domain on the left and the pronunciation on the right. In this way the familiar symbol for 'tree' combines with a symbol chosen on phonetic grounds to represent 'board' (18). The same phonetic symbol in combination with 'earth' indicates 'district' (19), in combination with 'thread' indicates 'spin' (20), and combined with 'speak' indicates 'ask' (21).

By using a limited number of free logographs as bound components in the formation of new logographs, it was possible to provide symbols for every morpheme in the language. The most comprehensive Chinese dictionary lists about 45,000 logographs, some 80 percent of which are no longer in current use. A college graduate in modern China is expected to know only about 5,000 logographs. The writing system has been a unifying element in China because it has been uniform throughout the country even though its users speak mutually unintelligible languages. Its function is much like that of the Arabic numerals used throughout the world; the graphic symbols have a uniform semantic reference for all users, and it is a simple enough matter to supply the appropriate phonetic symbolization once the meaning is known. It is not necessary that the phonetic symbolization be the same for everyone.

The chief disadvantage of the system has been the difficulty of learning it. Even though the 5,000 logographs in common use consist of only a few hundred components that recur in varying arrangements, the burden of learning remains much greater than would be required to master an alphabet or syllabary having a phonemic base. Why then did the Chinese not develop a syllabary or alphabet for transcribing their language? The fact is that there have been a number of moves in this direction over the years, but for several reasons all of these have failed to displace the logographic system. First of all, the monosyllabic structure of Chinese makes for a nice fit between morpheme and logograph. Hence, there is no internal pressure for change. Second, despite occasional contact with the outside world, there was never a significant influx of foreign words that needed to be transcribed. Hence, there was no external pressure. And finally, as long as literacy was restricted to a few members of a leisure class, the burden of learning was no obstacle. If anything, it was a convenient means of excluding the unwashed masses from affairs that did not concern them.

The first real use of Chinese script for phonetic transcription came following the introduction of Buddhism in the first century A.D. In the course of translating Buddhist scriptures into Chinese, many Sanskrit names and philosophical terms had to be rendered using logographs chosen for their phonetic rather than semantic value. Since about the fifth century, logographs have been used as phonetic indicators on an occasional basis to aid in reading rare or difficult symbols in texts. By the twentieth century the system of phonetic indicators was fixed at fifty logographs used for syllable initials and twelve used for syllable finals. The need for such a system has increased markedly with the need to represent proper names from Western languages. Although many of the logographs used in the phonetic script were complex symbols, abbreviated forms in which each symbol was reduced to two or three strokes were also in use.

Reformation of the writing system has been perceived as an important issue in the political movements of the late nineteenth century and into the present century. In 1918 the government promulgated a phonetic system using forty symbols derived from logographs. The problem was seen as twofold—devising a simplified writing system and establishing a uniform spoken language. In the 1920s the speech of Peking was formally adopted as the national standard, and a program was launched to establish Pekingese as a second language for those speaking other languages. Little headway was made during the 1930s and 1940s, but the earlier goals have been reaffirmed and expanded by the Communist government. The adoption of spoken Pekingese as a national standard remains an important objective, although it is not clear that any real progress has been made toward this goal. The government has decreed drastic simplifications in the form of many complex logographs and has succeeded in implementing the changes. Finally in 1958 a romanized alphabet was adopted for such purposes as teaching the Pekingese pronunciation of logographs, transliteration of foreign words, compilation of indices and order filing, and eventually to replace the logographs entirely. No timetable for the changeover has been announced, and in all likelihood it will be a long process.

9.9 JAPANESE WRITING

The Japanese were aware of Chinese writing sometime before the fifth century A.D., when the first evidence of writing in Japan begins to appear. At first Japanese scholars were content to write in Chinese, much as Medieval scholars in Europe had written in Latin. By 760 Japanese was being written using Chinese logographs selected for their phonetic value—an approach possibly influenced by scribal practice already current in China. By the ninth century Japanese scholars had worked out forms of a *kana* syllabary derived from logographs that had been selected for their phonetic value. The *hiragana* were cursive forms of the logograph, and the *katakana* were based on two or three strokes selected from a complex logograph (see Figure 9–4).

It is possible to write Japanese using only one or the other syllabary, but the usual practice has been to use logographs for noun and verb roots and to use *kana* for verbal inflections, particles, and words for which no commonly used logograph is available. In recent years *katakana* have been used for foreign words, and *hiragana* have been reserved for native elements not written in logographs. As a general rule verb roots are written with a logograph that is given a reading corresponding to the native Japanese root. The same logograph is used in nominal compounds with a reading derived from the Chinese pronunciation at the time of borrowing. Many logographs have more than one Chinese reading, representing contact with different centers of learning in different periods.

FIGURE 9–4   **Derivation of Hiragana and Katakana [a]**

Logograph	*Modified form*	*Kana form*	
安	あ	あ	(hiragana)
阿		ア	(katakana)

Japanese grammarians have traditionally described the syllabaries as representing the *gojū on* ('fifty sounds') of Japanese since they form a matrix in which each of the five vowels is preceded by each of ten possible consonants (see Figure 9–5). The traditional order of syllables matches the general order used in Devanāgari, suggesting Sanskrit influence through Buddhism. Some of the syllables with initial *w* or *y* are nonoccurring in modern Japanese. (The form that was historically *wo* is used in writing the grammatical marker *o* and thus serves a logographic function.) The loss of a few syllables has been more than offset by additional syllable types that require special conventions. Syllabic *n* is written with a special grapheme. Voicing of the *k*, *s*, and *t* series is represented by two dots placed to the right of the grapheme. The *h* series is modified to *b* by the same diacritic and to *p* by the addition of a small circle. (The historical sound was *p*, which was voiced intervocalically and weakened to *h* initially.) Geminate stops are represented by a subscript *cu* grapheme preceding the geminate. Syllables in which the initial consonant is followed by *y* are written with a subscript symbol for the *y* syllable containing the appropriate vowel. The subscript follows the grapheme for the appropriate initial consonant with an *i* vowel. Thus, *kyo* is written *ki-yo*, a spelling reminiscent of Sumerian practices.

Following World War II the number of logographs in regular use was reduced and the writing of many remaining logographs simplified. Some technical publications have now adopted the practice of writing horizontally from left to right and citing foreign words in the original spelling. There has been little pressure, however, for complete replacement of the traditional system with an alphabetic system.

FIGURE 9–5   Hiragana Syllabary on Left and Katakana Syllabary on Right, with Phonetic Value of Each Grapheme. (Because of varying phonemic interpretations, Japanese is described by different scholars as having from fourteen to seventeen consonants.)

あ	い	う	え	お		ア	イ	ウ	エ	オ
a	i	u	e	o		a	i	u	e	o
か	き	く	け	こ		カ	キ	ク	ケ	コ
ka	ki	ku	ke	ko		ka	ki	ku	ke	ko
さ	し	す	せ	そ		サ	シ	ス	セ	ソ
sa	ši	su	se	so		sa	ši	su	se	so
た	ち	つ	て	と		タ	チ	ツ	テ	ト
ta	či	cu	te	to		ta	či	cu	te	to
な	に	ぬ	ね	の		ナ	ニ	ヌ	ネ	ノ
na	ni	nu	ne	no		na	ni	nu	ne	no
は	ひ	ふ	へ	ほ		ハ	ヒ	フ	ヘ	ホ
ha	hi	ɸu	he	ho		ha	hi	ɸu	he	ho
ま	み	む	め	も		マ	ミ	ム	メ	モ
ma	mi	mu	me	mo		ma	mi	mu	me	mo
や		ゆ		よ		ヤ		ユ		ヨ
ya		yu		yo		ya		yu		yo
ら	り	る	れ	ろ		ラ	リ	ル	レ	ロ
ɾa	ɾi	ɾu	ɾe	ɾo		ɾa	ɾi	ɾu	ɾe	ɾo

わ			を	ん	ワ				ヲ	ン
wa			o	ṇ	wa				o	ṇ

Japan is the only major country in the world with virtual 100 percent literacy, making the sheer weight of tradition a major obstacle to change. The phonetic fit between sound and symbol, for native words at least, is quite good; and the predominant CV syllable structure makes syllabic writing somewhat more compact than alphabetic writing. Logographs themselves are compact and, surprisingly enough, better suited to rapid recognition than a lengthy alphabetic sequence. Moreover, the logographs provide separate representations for the numerous homophones of Chinese origin that are found in literary style. The mixture of logographs and syllabic symbols serves nicely to mark word boundaries and other structural breaks. The Japanese writing system is alive and well and probably will remain so for some time to come.

9.10 KOREAN WRITING

The Koreans were in touch with Chinese culture much earlier than the Japanese. Chinese script was used in Korea as early as 500 B.C., at first to write Chinese and later in attempts to write Korean. This was eventually accomplished by using logographs in a sequence corresponding to Korean rather than Chinese syntax, with readers on their own to supply the Korean function morphemes that could not be accommodated by the system. The art of writing Korean in this manner, known as *itu*, was transmitted from one generation of scholars to the next and preserved as something of a trade secret. Certainly the complexity of the system would have prevented anyone from mastering it without special instruction.

The development of a phonemic writing system known as *hankul* came in the 1440s under the stimulus of Sejong, then king of Korea. Sejong is sometimes credited with the invention himself, although in reality it was worked out by scholars under his direction. The system is basically a syllabary, but it is considerably more sophisticated than the Japanese syllabary in that the grapheme for each syllable is composed of individual elements representing the initial consonant, the vowel, the final consonant, and so forth. The components are simple lines and geometric forms borrowed from logographs—Korean legend holds that Sejong was inspired by the decorative patterns on a palace door as he sat musing one evening. The scholars who devised the system were no doubt aware of the phonetic use of logographs in China and probably familiar with the Japanese syllabary as well, but the fact remains that their innovation went considerably beyond the practices of either neighboring country.

Although the favored syllable type in Korean is CVC, several variations of the basic pattern are possible. As a result, each syllabic grapheme has up to five possible components occurring in the relative positions shown below:

```
 ┌──────┬───┬───┐
 │  1   │   │   │
 │      │ 3 │ 4 │
 ├──────┤   │   │
 │  2   │   │   │
 ├──────┴───┴───┤
 │      5       │
 └──────────────┘
```

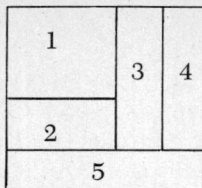

Fourteen consonants can occur initially (position 1) or finally (position 5).

k	n	t	l	m	p	s	ŋ	č	čh	kh	th	ph	h
ㄱ	ㄴ	ㄷ	ㄹ	ㅁ	ㅂ	ㅅ	ㅇ	ㅈ	ㅊ	ㅋ	ㅌ	ㅍ	ㅎ

The symbol for ŋ when written in position 1 represents a null element —that is, a syllable that actually begins with a vowel. Simple vowels occur in either position 2, 3, or 4. (Vowel transcription follows Martin et al. 1967 and differs from other transcriptions in use.)

Position 2: u	Position 3: a e	Position 4: i
─	ㅏ ㅓ	ㅣ

The addition of a short ascending perpendicular to the *u* grapheme represents *o*. Addition of a second short line to this grapheme or to the graphemes for *a* and *e* denotes a *y* onset. A pair of descending perpendiculars is added to the *u* grapheme to represent the *y* onset:

o	yo	ya	ye	yu
ㅗ	ㅛ	ㅑ	ㅕ	ㅠ

A short descending perpendicular is added to the *u* grapheme to represent a *w* onset. The resulting position 2 grapheme is used with the *e* or *i* grapheme of position 3 or 4 to denote *we* or *wi* and with the *a* grapheme of position 3 to denote *wa*:

wu	we	wi	wa
ㅜ	ㅝ	ㅟ	ㅘ

All simple vowels except *i* and all instances of *a* or *e* with either of the glide onsets can be modified by addition of the *i* grapheme of position 4, represented in the following transcriptions as *y*:

uy	ay	ey	oy	yay	yey	wey	way
ㅢ	ㅐ	ㅔ	ㅚ	ㅒ	ㅖ	ㅞ	ㅙ

Position 1 is always filled, although sometimes by a null symbol. Consonant clusters that occur initially or finally within a syllable are written in position 1 or 5, with individual symbols for the two consonants in a left-to-right sequence—for example, *kk* as a position 1 cluster in Figure 9–6. Fourteen such combinations occur. If a position is vacant in a particular syllable, the placement of occurring components is adjusted to fill the available space. Common syllable types are illustrated in Figure 9–6, with the positions in which graphic components occur listed following each gloss:

FIGURE 9–6   **Structure of Korean Graphemes**

susuŋ	스승	'teacher' 12, 125		kan	간	'room' 135
kwa	과	'department' 123		il	일	'work' 145
seyjoŋ	세종	'Sejong' 134, 124		kkway	꼬ᅢ	'much' 1234
ka	거	'edge' 13		hwaŋ	황	'yellow' 1235
i	이	'louse' 14		kayŋ	갱	'gang' 1345

wayŋwayŋ   왱 왱   'whistling sound' 12345, 12345

A sequence of words using only graphic elements of positions 1, 3, and 4 would, if written from left to right, have every appearance of an alphabetic transcription. Such sequences are not common of course, and in any case it is only in recent years that horizontal writing has begun to compete with the traditional vertical writing. Korean, like Japanese, could be written entirely in the phonetic script. Such a policy has in fact been adopted in North Korea, but in South Korea the standard practice is still to use Chinese logographs for most nouns and to write other sentence elements in *hankul*.

9.11 OTHER WRITING SYSTEMS

All writing systems now in use derive either from the Phoenician or Chinese systems. Of these, the Phoenician is known to stem from Sumerian writing via Egypt, and Chinese writing may also have been influenced by the Sumerians. The Aztec and Mayan writings in Central America appear to have arisen quite without Old World influence. The two systems were quite similar in appearance and structure, as might be expected due to geographic and temporal proximity. Both were limited as to the type of content that could be encoded, and neither developed systematic forms of phonetic representation. The Central American inscriptions were primarily calendars or historical accounts in which names and events are represented by pictorial means. Mictlantecutli, the Aztec prince of the underworld, is represented by a skull. An account of tribal migration contains a series of footprints drawn underneath the picture.

The beginnings of phonetic representation are found in occasional use of the rebus principle, as in the place name *Quauhnauac* 'near the forest.' The word was written with a logograph *quauh* 'tree, forest' for the first syllable and two signs for the second syllable. These were a repetition of *quauh* and an accompanying logograph *nauatl* 'speech,' evidently intended to suggest the initial consonant of the syllable. Other polysyllabic words were written syllable by syllable using dissyllabic logographs selected because the first syllable of each was a rebus. Thus, *teocaltitlan* 'temple personnel' was written with four logographs:

te-	te(ntli)	'lips'
-o-	o(tli)	'road'
-cal-	cal(li)	'house'
-ti-	Ø	[not represented]
-tlan-	tlan(tli)	'teeth'

Whether or not writing practices such as these would have developed into a full-fledged syllabary had it not been for the Spanish conquest is a matter of conjecture.

Another New World writing system of special interest is the Cherokee syllabary devised in the 1820s by Sequoyah. The achievement is a classic example of stimulus diffusion. Sequoyah could neither read nor write English, but he understood the principle of matching words with written symbols. Eventually he worked out an analysis of Cherokee syllabic structure and selected eighty-five symbols to represent the needed elements. Many symbols were drawn from the English alphabet and were assigned Cherokee phonetic values without reference to, or knowledge of, their English values. Others were freely invented or were derived variants of English letters. Almost overnight the Cherokee nation became a nation of literates; and newspapers, books, and magazines rapidly began to appear. Cherokee literacy suffered a severe setback in 1838 when most of the tribe was forcibly uprooted from North Carolina and relocated in Oklahoma, but the writing system remained in limited use into the present century.

9.12 WRITTEN EXPRESSION

Speakers have at their command a great many resources for converting thought into language. They have syntactic patterns and vocabulary, both of which emerge as a sequence of sounds, and they impose on the speech flow the suprasegmentals of pitch and stress. But in addition they utilize many subtleties of timing and intonation (which linguists have seldom attempted to describe) as well as nonlinguistic elements that have been called "body language." Above all, speakers know that if they are not understood, their listeners can stop them and ask for clarification. Writers must choose their words with much greater care. The written message must be conveyed almost entirely by vocabulary and syntactic patterns alone.

Modern writing systems have of course developed various punctuation marks to suggest intonation patterns and the like, but these rarely reflect the full range of devices available to spoken forms. Italic type (e.g., in English) or extra spacing between the letters of a word (e.g., in German) can be used to denote contrastive emphasis; but such devices are easily overworked and, even when used, may convey an informality that is inappropriate to the occasion. The contrast between capital and small letters is exploited in various ways. Capitals mark the beginning of a sentence, a redundancy because the first word in a text obviously begins a sentence—as does the first word following a period. But redundancy is useful in reducing the burden on the reader, just as it is in reducing the burden on the listener. Capitals may provide other structural clues. Proper nouns in English begin with capitals, as do all nouns in German.

Paragraphing is another important graphic device. It serves in part to break a mass of print into smaller, more psychologically manageable portions. It also marks a transition from one topic to another within the discourse. Headings of one kind or another can also be used to inform the reader of changes in subject matter. An oversized capital letter is sometimes used for decorative purposes at the beginning of each chapter in a book. During the Middle Ages, when all manuscripts were copied by hand, the elaborate decoration of initial letters with floral designs and figure drawings was a highly valued art. Illustrations included gold inlay as well as brilliant shades of red and blue. Medieval copyists took care to create letters of a uniform size, and even today the graceful design and uniform appearance of print is much admired. In countries using logographs of Chinese origin, a carefully drawn logograph is considered a work of art. Arabic script is similarly used for ornamental writing in which graphemes form intricate interlacing designs. In both Chinese and Arabic script, the content of the message and the artistic form are inextricable parts of an esthetic whole.

9.13 SPELLING

Languages written with an alphabet approach a one-to-one relationship between letter and phoneme but seldom achieve it perfectly. Letter combinations such as *ch* /č/ in Spanish and English may represent a single sound. Sometimes a single letter represents a sequence of two sounds, as in German *Zank* /tsaŋk/ 'quarrel.' Or the same letter may represent different sounds in different contexts. Thus, English *c* alternatively represents /s/ or /k/. In other cases a single sound is represented alternatively by different letters. English /ə/, for example, is represented at various times by each of the five vowel graphemes.

Occasionally alphabetic writing systems abandon a strict phonemic transcription in favor of morphophonemic representation. This is true of the English plural suffix, always written -*s* or -*es* but pronounced /s, z, əz/. Other examples of English morphophonemic spelling are worth mentioning. Vowel alternations in *history/historical, clean/ cleanliness, extreme/extremity, divine/divinity,* and so forth, are ignored in favor of a spelling that preserves the morphemic identity of the related words. But in cases like *able/ability, Spain/Spanish, pronounce/pronunciation,* the spelling is closer to phonemic than morphophonemic representation. We find similar inconsistencies in the representation of consonant alternation in English: *part/partial* alongside *democrat/democracy.* English vowel alternations are largely the result of historic sound shifts that occurred within the language. Consonant alternations (with some exceptions) stem from the pronunciation of Latin during the Middle Ages or Renaissance and came into English (sometimes via French) with the alternation already established. Under the circumstances it was natural that speakers of English would be conscious of borrowed alternations and represent them in the spelling system. They would be less aware of alternations in native words. The modern spelling system, with only occasional exceptions, continues to emphasize the "sameness" of native alternations and the "differentness" of borrowed alternations. Note that *part/partial,* although ultimately from Latin, was established in Middle English and treated as though a native form, while *democrat/democracy,* a post-Renaissance addition to the vocabulary, is treated as a borrowing.

The English spelling system affords a convenient means of distinguishing **homophones**: *night/knight, right/rite/write, to/too/two, way/weigh, sail/sale.* From a synchronic standpoint, the arbitrary spelling in such cases is a direct representation of meaning and is therefore purely logographic. Abbreviations such as *Mr., Mrs., Dr.* also function as logographs, as do the numerals and a variety of other widely used symbols: $ 'dollar(s),' & 'and,' and the like. One of the chief assets of the Chinese logographic writing system has always been its ability to distinguish homophones. The use of arbitrary spellings for English homophones serves the same purpose. But in other cases English spelling is quite tolerant of **homographs**: *tear* for /ter, tir/, *lead* for /liyd, led/, and *read* for /riyd, red/. Spelling systems, like other features of language, arise without conscious planning. The overall system may therefore contain numerous subsystems that conflict with the primary system and with other subsystems.

Despite the inconsistencies that have developed in many spelling systems, the fact remains that spelling is the one feature of language use that is most amenable to planned change. In extreme cases it is possible for a country such as Turkey to replace Arabic script with a Roman alphabet, but it is more common for less-sweeping changes to be instituted by legislative or administrative action. This has happened in recent years in Norway, the Soviet Union, and Portugal as well as in the simplifications adopted in China and Japan. Many of the American spellings that diverge from those of England (*honor* instead of *honour*, etc.) were introduced by Noah Webster, whose spelling book and dictionary became a standard reference work in nineteenth-century America. But English-speaking countries have generally lacked the centralized control of education that has made spelling reforms possible in other countries. Changes in English spelling have therefore tended to develop slowly as variant forms such as *catalogue/catalog, cigarette/cigaret* compete for acceptance.

To a limited extent written forms feed back to the oral language on which they are based and give rise to new spoken forms. This is true of spelling pronunciations such as [ɔftn̩] for *often,* which was pronounced without the *t* for hundreds of years. Japanese has homophones *širitsu* 'private support' and *širitsu* 'city support' that are written with different logographs for the first syllable. Many speakers use the readings these logographs would have as free forms to maintain a distinction: *watakuši-ritsu* 'private support' and *iči-ritsu* 'city support.' Letter abbreviations ranging from AAA 'American Automobile Association' to ZRH 'Zurich (Airport)' serve a logographic function and, if pronounceable, may become full-fledged words, as for example, *UNESCO.* In some cases Americans choose an acronym (e.g., *TV* /tiy viy/), while British speakers settle on a shortened form (*telly*). Acronyms may be based on syllables as well as initial letters: *Comintern* from Com(munist) Intern(ational), Japanese *kokuren,* the usual designation for 'United Nations,' from *kokusai rengō* 'international organization.' German *Nazi* shows a spelling based on Na(tional-so)zi(alist); the pronunciation would be the same if derived from Nati(onal-sozialist).

The need to facilitate international communication has led in recent years to the development of international road signs that are pictographic or logographic in nature. Thus, a diagonal red line drawn through an arrow curving to the right or left indicates that a turn in that direction is prohibited. A silhouette of a boy and girl carrying books means 'school zone' whether or not the picture is accompanied by the word SCHOOL. The geometric shape associated with individual signs provides useful redundancy.

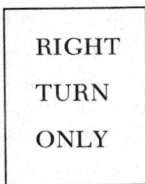

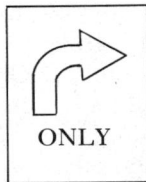

Experimentation with the two signs pictured above has shown that the sign using the logograph is more quickly recognized than the one

using only alphabetic words. This finding supports our earlier observation that logographs, by appealing directly to semantic content,
are more readily interpreted than symbols appealing to phonological
content that must subsequently be linked mentally with the intended
semantic content. The shortcomings of logographs, which have also
been noted—their inability to represent grammatical markers and the
difficulty of devising separate symbols for every possible meaning—
are enough to confine them to a small corner of a writing system dominated by phonetic symbols.

9.14 GENERAL CONSIDERATIONS

Writing, we have seen, is an outgrowth of drawing. Pictures are
holistic renditions of a message and do not require a unique linguistic
interpretation. But as drawings become more and more conventionalized, the range of possible linguistic interpretations is increasingly
narrowed. All efforts to convey a message through representational
pictures can be termed **prewriting.** Writing proper begins when the
system develops duality of patterning. In this case duality means a
fixed inventory of standardized units, pictographic or other, and patterns of sequential arrangement corresponding to the syntactic patterns of natural language. Typically, writing begins with a logographic
stage bearing traces of its pictorial origins and progresses to a syllabic
and eventually an alphabetic stage. All three stages exhibit duality of
patterning, but the unit of reference is progressively narrowed at each
stage. In its progression from holistic units to a system exhibiting
duality, writing parallels the presumed evolution of language itself
(§7.2–7.3).

Through the greater part of its history, writing has been the possession of a limited few. The Chinese had developed wood block printing
by the fifth century A.D. and used the technique for printing Buddhist
literature. The idea of printing was carried by Marco Polo (1254–
1324?) to Europe, where Johannes Gutenberg (1359?–1468?) developed a practical method for casting individual metallic letters from
molds of uniform size. The interest in learning kindled by the Renaissance contributed to the spread of printing, and the rise of a middle
class in European countries eventually led to policies of universal
education and a goal of universal literacy. The development is so recent that it is still difficult to assess its impact on language use and
language development. One possibility is that familiarity with the
written word will have a conservative effect, slowing or even stopping
changes that would otherwise occur in vocabulary, pronounciation,
and grammar. The other possibility is that change is so much a part of
language that writing will have no appreciable effect on the normal
rate of change. One might even argue that any technological development, writing included, that changes patterns of living will only ac-

celerate changes in language, which after all is a mirror of life.

Writing was a necessary development because it is both a permanent and a portable record of language. But in modern times the telegraph, telephone, and radio have become more effective than writing for rapid transmission over great distances. Television has had a special impact since it combines the normal visual component with the sound component that radio transmits as an isolated element. Modern sound-recording techniques, including videotape recordings, can give speech a permanence equal to writing. (Even so, people who handle tapes find it necessary to label them in writing.) In recent years the computer has revolutionized the recording, storage, analysis, and retrieval of linguistic (as well as numeric) data. Computer data can be recorded on magnetic tape or similar devices. The data is then fed into the computer, where it is stored in the computer's memory system. Computer memory commonly utilizes a network of cells, each of which can be charged negatively or positively. Patterns of plus or minus charges correspond to alphabetic or numeric data, and analysis of data is accomplished by retrieving bits of data from storage and reassigning them in different patterns to vacant storage space. The electronic codes of computers have sometimes been called **artificial languages** to distinguish them from the **natural languages** spoken by human beings.

Computers are human inventions, and we know exactly how they work; we have much to learn about the operation of the human nervous system, but it appears to work on the same principles as the computer. Human communication with computers has thus far relied on natural language or on modifications of natural language that the computer has been programmed to accept. But who knows what the future holds? Already computers are able to monitor and analyze the electrical impulses associated with the heartbeat and with brain activity. Perhaps the next step is a computer capable of being integrated directly into the human nervous system and accepting the language of its electrochemical impulses. If these impulses could be interpreted, the computer would presumably be able to exchange data with individuals and relay data between individuals using the language of the nervous system itself. Such a development, if really possible, would be more efficient than either writing or ordinary language.

The ability to use any language, real or artificial, depends on first cracking the code. In ordinary language the code consists of phonological and morphosyntactic units. In the language of both the computer and the nervous system, the code consists of patterns of electrical impulses. These patterns, in the case of the computer, are programmed to symbolize data, place the data in storage, keep track of where it is stored, and retrieve it when needed. These operations depend on the program and, if the human brain operates in a similar way, a knowledge of how its electrical impulses pattern would be requisite to decoding its program and understanding its language. We have not yet cracked this code. If it is ever cracked at all, the task will certainly require computer analysis because the vast amount of data and complex patterns are far beyond human sorting capacities. In the meantime both spoken and written forms of communication are likely to remain essential in the conduct of human affairs.

summary

Writing, although a secondary way of representing language, is extremely important in the modern world because of its permanence and portability. Modern writing systems are the outgrowth of pictographic representations of the Late Paleolithic age. The Sumerian writing system emerged about 5,000 years ago as a logographic system and quickly developed into a syllabary. The Egyptian system was also a syllabary, as were the Aramaic and Phoenician systems, which were inspired by trade contacts with Egypt. The Greeks took over the Phoenician system and began the practice of using separate symbols for consonants and vowels, thus creating a true alphabet. The Roman alphabet was borrowed from the Greeks and eventually diffused throughout Europe. The Cyrillic alphabet of Russia is a direct borrowing from Greek, while the modern writing systems of India and Southeast Asia derive from the Aramaic syllabary.

The Chinese writing system, which is logographic, is an independent development—although it may originally have been stimulated by trade contacts with Mesopotamia. Japanese writing combines Chinese logographs with a syllabary derived from logographs. The Korean script, which comes close to being a true alphabet, is also based on Chinese logographs. In the New World, Mayan and Aztec writing systems had advanced to a primitive logographic stage by the time of European contact. The Cherokee syllabary devised in the 1820s by Sequoyah was a case of stimulus diffusion based on contact with the English writing system.

A modern writing system like English is basically alphabetic, or phonemic. But the system uses a number of morphophonemic spellings as well as some arbitrary spellings that function as logographs. Certain kinds of traffic signs also hark back to earlier logographic, or even pictographic, forms. Modern devices such as the telephone, radio, television, audio and video tape, and the computer have greatly facilitated communication but have done so without presenting a genuine threat to the continuing usefulness of writing.

further reading

General: Gelb 1952, Chadwick 1958, Diringer 1948. **9.8** Karlgren 1962, Forrest 1948, Chu and Nishimoto 1969, Kadokawa 1956, DeFrancis 1950. **9.9** Sansom 1928, R. Miller 1967. **9.10** Martin et al. 1967.

10

applications of linguistics

10.1 AN INTERDISCIPLINARY SCIENCE

Linguistics can be pursued as an end in itself, to gain knowledge either of a particular language or of language in general. Of course, there is no way to understand "language in general" apart from a thoroughgoing knowledge of two or more individual languages. Ideally the languages chosen for study should represent diverse structural types. The more languages linguists are acquainted with and the more thorough their knowledge of each language is, the greater will be their ability to generalize. Knowledge of the general nature of language should contribute to the study of individual languages, and this in turn should add to the linguist's understanding at the general level. The relationship is an endless loop. The danger of generalizing on the basis of one's native language should be self-evident. But an intimate knowledge of one's native language, together with a superficial knowledge of a second language (particularly if it is structurally like one's own) and a commitment to a theoretical outlook that directs one's attention in a selective way, can still set traps for the unwary.

Because language permeates every aspect of human life, the study of language touches in some way or another on the interests of numerous widely varied academic fields. Linguistics is therefore as much an interdisciplinary science as an independent field of study. Indeed, it would be difficult to separate the study of language from the various settings in which the study takes place. Just as informed efforts to generalize about the nature of language require familiarity with a variety of languages, an enlightened theory of language must be informed by many disciplines. And in turn one can reasonably expect that other disciplines concerned either directly or peripherally with language will benefit from awareness of the conceptual tools used by linguists. Exchange of information, techniques, and insights between disciplines is stimulating in many ways. It opens new avenues of thinking, it provides new arenas for testing ideas, and above all it protects each discipline from the unchallenged perpetuation of whatever dogmas enjoy currency within the discipline.

The sections that follow give a brief survey of the principal disciplines that have contributed to modern linguistics. In most cases these same disciplines have also been influenced by developments in linguistics, but in some cases the influence remains limited. The need to assimilate present knowledge and explore the new frontiers opened by recent studies is clear. Linguists and workers in related fields are likely to find the need for interdisciplinary effort increasing rather than diminishing in the years ahead.

10.2 ANTHROPOLOGICAL LINGUISTICS

Although modern linguistics in Europe can trace its descent through traditional grammar and historical linguistics, American linguistics is largely a child of anthropology. Franz Boas (1858–1942), the founder of American anthropology, was also the founder of American linguistics. As a result of his influence (§4.10) and the work of his students, an interest in the study of non-Indo-European languages and the interplay between language and culture has remained strong in the United States. Bronislaw Malinowski (1884–1942), who stressed the need for fieldwork and the study of language in its social context, contributed to a similar emphasis in England. Linguistics is an essential tool for the anthropologist for several reasons. The anthropologist often studies people whose languages have not been part of the traditional curriculum. Interaction with these people requires a knowledge of their language. Dependence on an interpreter is an encumbrance and, no matter how skilled the interpreter may be, some filtering of the data is bound to occur. In extreme cases this can lead to distortions that completely invalidate one's observations. Since the knowledge and beliefs that constitute a people's culture are habitually encoded and transmitted in the language of the people, it is extremely difficult to separate the two. This of course is why Boas and Malinowski considered language so important.

Children born into a society learn both the language and culture of their society as they grow up. Anthropologists, if they wish to understand what it means to be a participant in a culture, must undergo something approximating the experience of the native-born participant. This means learning to make the correct behavioral responses—including the correct linguistic responses—to situations that arise in the society. Linguists approach this task by undertaking to write a grammar of the language. If it is a complete grammar, it will specify the grammatical sentences of the language, and it will function, in effect, as a model of how the language is organized in the minds of the speakers. In addition it will specify, within certain limits, the kind of response that is appropriate (i.e., grammatical) as new information in the context of various kinds of old information. Thus, if someone in our own society says *Richard lost his job yesterday*, we might expect something like *He did?* or *Tough luck* as responses. Because old information is normally pronominalized, we probably would not expect *Richard did?* And because we expect the response to deal with the same topic, we certainly would not expect something like *The state fair is expected to set a new attendance record.* In other cultures the rules may be different. In Japanese the comment *samui desu ne* 'cold, isn't it?' normally elicits the response *samui desu ne.* In many North American Indian languages, the appropriate response to the announcement of bad news is thoughtful silence.

In constructing a grammar of a language, the linguist attempts to state the patterns in which the linguistic units occur and, insofar as possible, to relate these to the situational contexts in which the patterns are appropriate. The cultural anthropologist is primarily interested in the patterns of social behavior—that is, the situational context itself. But since the knowledge, beliefs, and activities of a people are not random but are patterned, it is possible to approach the task of describing behavioral patterns in much the way that the linguist describes language patterns. The ideal in cultural anthropology would therefore be a behavioral grammar that would specify the acceptable (i.e., grammatical) forms of behavior within the culture. Such a "grammar" would function, in effect, as a model of how knowledge and beliefs are organized to make possible behavioral patterns that are consistent with them. In addition a behavioral grammar should specify the range of behaviors that are acceptable in given situations, just as the ideal grammar of a language would specify a range of acceptable linguistic variants.

Needless to say, neither linguists nor anthropologists have yet achieved the ideal. Anthropologists have approached the study of cognition by trying to develop complete descriptions of limited domains. Kinship structure, for example, is a semantic field that is universal to human experience. People in every society have kin and terms for naming these kin. The biological possibilities for kin relationships are everywhere the same. The possibilities are sufficiently well defined to make description manageable, although in principle there is no limit to the number of kin a person may have. However, the fact that the biological possibilities are universal does not guarantee that the cognitive organization of kinship will be the same in every culture. For example, the English word *uncle* desig-

nates 'father's brother' or 'mother's brother.' English speakers think
of these two rather different relationships as somehow the same. For
persons in other societies, the relationships might be quite different
in terms of behavioral expectations, and this difference is normally
matched by different terms for the two categories. Kinship structure
and terminology are thus a convenient microcosm of both a culture
and the language associated with it.

The basic perceptual and cognitive strategy of humans (and other
organisms) is the classification of same and different elements into
their appropriate pigeonholes. Cultural anthropologists therefore
have a great deal of interest in learning how people go about classifying the objects and events in their world of experience. Classification
is often done quite consciously. In the taxonomy of zoologists, the
rabbit is classed as a lagomorph. Members of this order are classed
as mammals, which in turn are classed as vertebrates, chordates,
metazoa, and animals. The criteria for classification at each level are
explicitly defined. For the nonzoologist the taxonomic principles
are often less explicit and may be based on different criteria. Thus,
for many speakers of English, the rabbit is intuitively classed as a
rodent in a system whose remaining levels might be mammal, quadru-
ped, and animal. In a hunting-and-gathering society, rabbits might be
classed as food animals, setting them apart from other classes such as
nonfood animals, spirit animals, and the like. Such classificatory
schemes are called folk taxonomies.

For people the world over, the colors of the rainbow are the same,
but this fact does not require people speaking different languages to
divide the color spectrum the same way or use terms that designate
the same range of hue. Some languages have only two color terms:
black and *white.* The semantic range of the terms is something like
'dark' and 'light.' If a language has three color terms, the third term
is invariably *red,* a term that may include yellow and orange but that
has a focal point very close to the 'red' of English. The other colors
most commonly entering into linguistic systems are *yellow, green,
blue,* and *brown,* making a total of seven. Languages ordinarily do
not have terms for *pink, green, orange,* or *purple* unless the seven
basic colors have previously been differentiated. Even though languages vary somewhat in their color terminology, the variation is
apparently not random. It appears to follow a pattern related to the
human capacity for perceiving colors. If this is true, we might expect
to find that variation in other semantic and cognitive domains is
limited in similar ways. A word of caution is necessary at this point:
in cross cultural studies there is always the possibility that real differences in meaning will be obscured by translating everything into
one's native language. It is important to guard against this by looking
for the real-world correlates of meaning (rather than translation correlates) and by thinking in terms of the internal structure of the
system (rather than the internal structure of a translation language).

The world in which we live is only in part physical; to a large extent our environment includes the cultural world that each group of people creates for itself. Insofar as part of the cultural world is created (or at least perpetuated) with words, people are sometimes at the mercy of the words they use. The man who describes his wife to his psychiatrist by saying "She makes me feel like a child" has adopted a world view in which he has lost control of his own autonomy. He does not speak as though he has fallen into a pattern of behavior he would like to change; he speaks as though he has been taken over by an outside force. Presumably a psychiatrist can help such a person gain a better perspective on reality—but is it possible that the habitual modes of expression in different languages force speakers into equally extreme world views without their realizing it? Whorf believed that the tense-aspect system of Hopi provided speakers of the language with a conception of time that was quite different from the time concept built into most European languages. (Curiously, the Russian aspect system is similar to that of Hopi, but no one has suggested that the world view of Russians and Hopis is therefore similar.) The Whorfian hypothesis has captivated the interest of anthropologists for a number of years, although no one has yet succeeded fully in proving or disproving it. All that can be said for sure is that there is a close fit between linguistic categories and culture categories.

In some cases linguistic categories seem to be directly motivated by cultural circumstances. Thus, it seems natural that Eskimos should have a number of terms for different kinds of snow, or Arabs a variety of terms for camels. It is much more difficult to show that categories of tense, aspect, number, gender, and the like are related to culture in any significant way. Linguistics has only recently begun to develop a precise scheme for semantic analysis, and it may be that linguists and anthropologists will now finally be in a position to give proper attention to the Whorfian hypothesis. It may be that a careful reexamination of Whorf's claims will simply confirm what Boas and Hockett have already suggested: languages differ not so much in what it is possible or impossible to say but rather in what it is relatively easy—or even obligatory—to say. Languages tend to encode only a portion of the thoughts that presumably are in a speaker's mind, and each language is quite arbitrary about the things that it selects for automatic inclusion in the message. What these automatic habits of expression imply about a speaker's world view—or if they imply anything at all—remains an open question.

Since anthropologists have a long-standing interest in the origins and prehistory of humankind, the techniques of historical linguistics are an important tool. If a relationship can be demonstrated between two or more languages, it follows that the speakers of these languages once constituted a single community. This information in turn implies population movements, sometimes extending thousands of years into the past. In the case of preliterate people, the evidence of language relationships may be the only documentation available for tracing migrations. A reconstructed word list, together with reconstructed meanings, makes possible a number of inferences about the culture of earlier periods (§3.8). Even a short list can be quite illuminating.

10.3 SOCIOLINGUISTICS

The interests of sociology have been quite similar to those of anthropology, although sociologists have tended to focus their attention on complex urbanized societies while anthropologists have more often studied smaller and less complex societies. Sociologists have also concentrated more on the statistical norms of mass behavior rather than describing in detail the behavior of individuals or small groups. But sociologists since the time of Emile Durkheim (1858–1917) have at least recognized the importance of language in expressing what Durkheim called the "collective consciousness" of the social group.

However, it was the nineteenth-century historical linguists who began the first investigations in the sociology of language. We have already seen (§3.3) how a familiarity with German dialect differences was a factor in Jakob Grimm's development of the comparative method. By the latter part of the century, an extensive dialect survey was undertaken in Germany to test the basic assumption of the comparative method—the regularity of sound change. The survey was intended to pinpoint the boundary between the northern (lowland) area, where one encounters *make(n), ik, pund* 'make,' 'I,' 'pound,' and the southern (highland) area, where the forms are *machen, ich,* and *pfund.* In general the survey confirmed the existence of clearly defined dialect areas, but with interesting exceptions. For no two words did the dialect boundaries coincide exactly. And in the Rhineland area, where the political boundaries had shifted over the years, the dialect boundaries showed the greatest diversity.

The study of dialect geography (sometimes called linguistic geography) thus antedates sociolinguistics, which came into vogue in the 1960s; but both are directed at the same subject—linguistic variation. Synchronic variation in language can be measured along three parameters: geographical, social, and situational. Of these, the geographical differences, whether phonological, lexical, or grammatical, are perhaps the most conspicuous and the easiest to record—although a good study of geographical dialects requires much more care than the uninitiated might suppose. Social dialects are those associated with identifiable social groups who have no distinct geographical base. Yiddish spoken in a German community would be a social dialect, as is the English of most American blacks living outside the South. Situational, or stylistic, variation has its locus in the individual. Everyone speaks with greater care and precision in formal situations and shifts to a freer style allowing contractions, slang, and more loosely structured sentences as the situation becomes more relaxed.

Although the three types of variation are in principle quite distinct, they are not always so clear-cut in practice. McDavid and O'Cain have pointed out that "most of the linguistic features that appear to characterize inner city Negroes are shared not only by many whites of comparable socioeconomic standing, but also by cultivated speakers in the South, especially in casual speech" (1973:148). The linguistic separation of blacks and whites is not so sharp as it might appear at first. The dialect boundary must be stated, in part at least, in terms of a socioeconomic class cutting across racial lines. At the same time we must recognize "black" English as having roots in a geographically based southern dialect that was transplanted to other parts of the country, where it became the mark of a social dialect. For the most part black English and other forms of "nonstandard" speech can be traced back to linguistic variation in England prior to the colonization of North America. There is also evidence of limited African influence, which in some cases tended to reinforce English usages that have since disappeared from the "standard" dialect.

The fact that individuals are able to shift styles at will has interesting implications, as McDavid and O'Cain note: "The Southerner signals to interlocutors that they are in a casual situation by stylistic shifts to non-literary speech forms, such as the use of *ain't* or multiple negatives. Thus he is justifiably apt to characterize one who does not show a similar pattern of grammatical and phonological shifts as withholding intimacy. It is little wonder that Southerners find Midwesterners cold, stiff, overly formal, or even hostile" (1973:149).

Following the German dialect survey mentioned above, similar projects were undertaken in France and Italy. In the 1930s a dialect survey of the United States and Canada was begun. The survey has thus far led to publication of a linguistic atlas for the New England states, the upper Midwest states, and several works describing the speech of the Eastern seaboard. The unpublished data remains available for the examination of scholars and forms a repository of information about vocabulary and pronunciation that is certain to increase in value as the passage of time brings about changes in speech forms. Data providing a link with the past will be of value whether the changes of time eliminate old forms or extend their usage. Either way, it will be important to know of their earlier existence.

Although the American dialect survey was directed primarily at geographical variation, the data included a record of the educational background, occupation, and social history of each informant. By the 1960s the problems of the urban poor, especially the southern-reared blacks and Spanish speakers from Puerto Rico and the American Southwest, had shifted the attention of linguists (and funding agencies) to social rather than geographical variation. Much of the study was mission-oriented. The public was aware of the problems of minorities and sensed that the school system had somehow failed to acculturate these groups. People were conscious of language differences, recognized that these differences tended to set minority groups apart, and even suspected that the differences themselves might be the cause of the problems. A thorough study was needed to describe the usage of minority groups, immigrant groups, different age groups, and in particular to record the statistical frequency of competing usages. The circumstances called for new types of research instruments, new ways of recording data (including the use of tape recorders), and suitable statistical procedures for analyzing the findings.

Labov (1963) in a meticulous study of pronunciation on Martha's Vineyard was able to relate phonetic variation in the low back diphthongs /ai, au/ to different age groups and, in the case of younger speakers, to their degree of identification with the island population as opposed to the mainland population. Labov's study of language variation in New York City (1966) correlated five phonological variables with a number of indices of social status to draw a picture of finely graded social stratification. Wolfram's study of Detroit (1969) followed the Labov pattern but included grammatical (i.e., morphological) variables as well.

When the varieties of speech used in a single community lack mutual intelligibility, we must speak in terms of language contact rather than language variation. Contact situations arise under a number of circumstances—when one population is forcibly enslaved by another, when a group arrives as voluntary immigrants in a new land, when people reside along a political boundary that is also a language boundary, or when individuals engage in commercial ventures that involve travel and contact with other language groups. The dynamics of contact situations are of special interest because the two (or more) languages seldom meet on equal footing. The language of the dominant group tends to displace the language having lower prestige, but the process may take several generations and include drastic changes in the dominant language as a result of phonological, lexical, and grammatical borrowings. A common first step is the development of a **pidgin,** a language using a simplified grammar and vocabulary drawn from one or more of the contact languages. A pidgin is an artificial language in the sense that it is not the native language of any population. If a pidgin is adopted out of necessity by a community that has no common language of its own, the language is known as a **creole.** Children born in the community grow up speaking the creole as their native language, and the subsequent history of the creole is no different from any other language.

The study of linguistic variation is in many respects a branch of historical linguistics. Competing forms may be either the residue of earlier, more widespread, differences or the incipient development of dialect cleavage that, in the normal course of events, would lead to mutually unintelligible languages. Certainly language change, and social change in general, follows the same mechanism as biological change: variant forms develop more or less by chance and exist side by side indefinitely unless circumstances for some reason favor the survival of one form and the loss of another. There is, of course, no way to predict which of two variants will ultimately displace the other. Indeed, variant forms may coexist for centuries. When this happens, the variants quite naturally become indices of the social situation as, for example, the use of multiple negation and *ain't*, mentioned above.

Variants of this type can be found in phonology, syntax, and lexicon. In a classic study of the distribution of the English present participle endings /-in/ and /-iŋ/, John L. Fischer notes that these supposed free variants are in fact related to the sex, class, personality (i.e., aggressive/cooperative), and mood (i.e., tense/relaxed) of the speaker; to the formality of the conversation; and to the specific verb to which the ending is attached. He speaks of the alternants as socially conditioned variants that "serve to symbolize things about the relative status of the conversants and their attitudes toward each other, rather than denoting any difference in the universe of primary discourse"— that is, the nonlinguistic world (1958:51). Fischer further suggests (1975) that "all ongoing speech communities, even the smallest and most isolated, have internal variation by sex, by degree of formality, and the like. Cleavages of this sort are likely to persist indefinitely, neither melting away nor leading to separate dialects. In fact they are not really cleavages in the sense of an imperfectly shared code but rather are an important part of the code needed to convey the complete message."

The view, often attributed to English teachers, that linguistic variants fall into one of two categories—"good" or "bad"—is a gross distortion of the true facts. In fact, the assumption of "good" and "bad" smacks of a program to change society by promoting one variant while eliminating the other. The extent to which change is subject to human engineering is not clear because we still lack a full understanding of the factors that lead to variation in the first place and then preserve some variants while eliminating others. If we knew how to control change, we would still have to deal with serious questions of social policy in deciding which variants to foster and which to suppress. Perhaps what we really need is a better understanding of the kinds of variations and change that can be controlled in whole or in part and what kinds are beyond our control and should be accepted gracefully. Even this well-meaning goal is a bit smug. The most fundamental of human rights is the right to be oneself. Linguistically, this means feeling comfortable about the way one naturally speaks, accepting the speech of others, and feeling free to vary one's speech as appropriate to the situation—in Fischer's words (1975) "using effectively and appropriately the full resources of the language for social expression, including variation in phonology, syntax, and lexicon." To gain the understanding requisite to such a liberated attitude will require the complementary efforts of linguistic geographers, sociolinguists, and sociologists as well as the insights of anthropologists and psychologists.

10.4 PSYCHOLINGUISTICS

Psychology, like linguistics, has been a subject of investigation since the classical period of Greece. Both were treated as branches of philosophy until they emerged as separate disciplines about a hundred years ago. Early structural psychologists relied heavily on introspection to analyze conscious experience. This was an approach that Sapir accepted, although it was never a major dogma for him. Behavioral psychology, which gained prominence in the second decade of the twentieth century, reacted against this approach and insisted on the empirical study of observable behavior. Bloomfield, who had earlier been influenced by structural psychology, adopted behaviorism as the appropriate psychological framework for the empirical study of language. Bloomfield, however, was much more eclectic in practice than one might expect from a literal reading of *Language* (1933). It was the followers of Bloomfield who took the extreme step of attempting to divorce linguistics from mental activity and from meaning altogether. This was the tradition that Chomsky (1957) inherited, although he was later (1965, 1966, 1972a) to complete the cycle by arguing that linguistic formulations provide reliable insight into the workings of the mind.

The interests of psychologists in language have centered around problems of learning and child development but have touched on broader questions of mental activity as well. The study of word frequency by Edward Thorndike (1874–1949) was an early expression of the interest educational psychologists took in language. The study of child development by Arnold Gesell (1880–1961) touched on language development, and the ongoing work of Jean Piaget in the thought processes of children has contributed significantly to the study of concept formation and language use. Word association tests used in personality studies make certain assumptions about the use of linguistic units, and efforts to measure intelligence are invariably complicated by the difficulty of separating intelligence from language use and cultural orientation.

The field known as psycholinguistics, which came to prominence after 1957, has been closely identified with transformational grammar.

Early psychological experiments based on transformational theory tended to draw on established techniques in psychological research, such as the measurement of response time. It was assumed that transformations were literal, time-consuming operations in the production of sentences, and experiments were conducted to measure the time required to produce sentences like the following:

> The knave did not steal the tarts.
> The knave didn't steal the tarts.

The sentences are identical except that the second includes a contraction which should entail an additional transformation and therefore require slightly longer to process. But in fact such sentences require less time, a finding that was unexpected in terms of the theory, although not surprising in terms of common sense. Considerations such as this were among the factors leading to the distinction between competence and performance. Transformations were regarded as belonging to a grammar representing linguistic competence but not necessarily having any direct or measurable counterpart in the strategies used by speakers in producing sentences.

The concept of deep structure—a level equatable with cognitive structure—has also been important in psycholinguistics. The fact that in deep structure the simplest constituent grouping is *have-en be-ing* (see §6.3), although in surface structure the affixes *-en* and *-ing* are associated with different constituents, appears to confirm the cognitive (= logical) reality of deep structure. (The circularity of this argument will be dealt with in §11.4.) Much discussion on the part of both linguists and psychologists has dealt with the kind of grammatical rules seemingly required in natural languages and the implications of these rule formulations for understanding the workings of the mind. Chomsky (1972a) has pointed out that certain kinds of rules are common in human languages whereas other rules are either nonexistent or extremely difficult for humans to master. An example of a "natural" rule might be the transposition of subject and verb to mark interrogation. An example of a nonoccurring (and apparently impossible) rule would be reversing the linear order of every word in a sentence so that the first word would occur last, the second word would be next-to-last, and so forth. Such a rule would be no problem for a computer and would serve just as well to mark interrogation as any other rule, but no natural language has this kind of rule, and humans find such word manipulation difficult if not impossible.

Chomsky has also argued that the formal rule structure of a grammar is so complex that any theory of learning that relies on behavioral notions of conditioning must be dismissed as inadequate. Learning theories based on conditioning maintain that learning results when a particular response to a stimulus is rewarded. The rewarded behavior is reinforced and tends to be repeated. Rewards can include social approval, as when parents encourage an infant's first efforts to say *mama* or *dada*. But Chomsky has argued that a theory of reinforcement fails to explain how language learners eventually are able to create sentences they have never before heard. It is therefore necessary, he says, to assume that a language-using ability of a very specific sort is innate in the human organism. The child approaches the task of learning his native language with prior, inborn knowledge of the general type of rules he will encounter, "his problem being to determine which of the (humanly) possible languages is that of the community in which he is placed" (Chomsky 1965:27).

The term **rationalism** has been applied to the view of humans as having inborn rational faculties of a highly precise nature, and **empiricism** has been applied to the view that language use and other abilities are learned behavior. The terms have stirred more argument among linguists, however, than among psychologists. Investigators from both disciplines who have studied child language acquisition have tended to put ideologies aside and use whatever conceptual approaches seem best suited to the task at hand. There has been agreement that language acquisition is a complex process and that a better understanding of the process will cast light on mental functions in general. But there is not yet any consensus on the exact nature of the acquisition process, the relationship between language development and cognitive development, or the linguistic constructs that should be posited to describe the process. Pretransformationalists approached child language through detailed journal accounts of the acquisition process (Leopold 1939–49) or through a series of self-contained structural descriptions (Weir 1962). The earliest studies influenced by transformational theory (e.g., Braine 1963) analyzed two-word utterances by positing a "pivot" class and an "open" class of words, categories that have since fallen into disuse. Subsequent work (e.g., McNeill 1966) professed to see elaborate syntactic structure and transformational apparatus implied by even simple utterances. More recent work (summarized by Brown 1973) has been increasingly eclectic and has shown concern for dealing with cognitive development through case grammar or meaning-structure grammar.

10.5 NEURAL LINGUISTICS

The fact that language and language use are deeply rooted in human physiology can easily be overlooked in the course of investigating and classifying abstract structural categories. Phoneticians, who have traditionally been concerned with the articulatory organs, have always been more conscious than other linguists of the physiological basis of language. Even so, the interest has often been confined to the operation of the vocal tract, and little attention has been given to the neurological mechanisms that control speech production. In part this may be related to the structuralist bias against meaning and distrust of any approach attempting to relate observable linguistic behavior to presumed mental activity. But it also is related to lack of knowledge about the operation of the brain.

The brain is certainly the most complex organ and probably the one about which least is known. But a growing body of information about neural function is becoming available, and linguists are now teaming with medical specialists to add to this knowledge. The picture that is emerging suggests that the brain is an intricate computer-like processing device in which certain bodily functions are controlled by specific areas, and other areas are left free to process data from other parts of the brain. Thus, sensory input is received by the thalamus, a switching center that transfers the input to an appropriate center for further processing. Visual processing takes place in the occipital lobe of the cerebrum, and auditory processing takes place in a section of the temporal lobe. Most of our memories relating to sight and sound are stored in the remainder of the temporal lobe. The frontal lobe of the cerebrum is apparently the processing center where memories are called from storage and analyzed, where choices are made between the various stimuli competing for conscious attention, and where nervous activity is integrated. Speech itself seems to be localized in no single area but involves interaction of parts of the frontal, temporal, and parietal lobes of the left hemisphere. (Dominance of one brain hemisphere over the other is related to right- or left-handedness, but why speech should be associated with only the left hemisphere is not clearly understood.) As thoughts take shape and are assigned linguistic structure, the motor control centers along the central fissure (which separates the frontal and parietal lobes) relay precisely coordinated signals to the diaphragm, intercostal muscles, vocal folds, lips, tongue, and other organs to produce the appropriate sequence of sounds.

Present knowledge of neural functions has come from laboratory studies of cats and other experimental animals and from clinical studies of humans who have suffered brain damage from illness or injury or who have undergone brain surgery. Knowledge gained from the study of pathology has already been of value in speech therapy, but we have still made only the barest beginnings in exchanging information among linguists, physiologists, and speech pathologists. In particular we have no detailed knowledge of how language is represented in the brain or of what the neural analogs of grammatical rules may be. It is known that neurons connect with one another to form complex interlacing pathways. If a neuron requires the simultaneous stimulation of two other neurons for its activation, the neuron is an "and" organ: it performs the logical operation of conjunction. If a neuron requires the stimulation of only one of two possible connecting cells, it is an "or" organ: it performs the logical operation of disjunction. As von Neumann points out: " 'And' and 'or' are the basic operations of logic. Together with 'no' (the logical operation of negation) they are a complete set of basic logical operations—all other logical operations, no matter how complex, can be obtained by suitable combinations of these" (1958:53).

In short we can say that the brain receives sensory impressions from the outside world, is able to store these impressions as memories, and is then able to select memories for logical processing. The encoding principle is the same as that of the digital computer, but it is important to make a sharp distinction between the encoding principle and the encoding language. In a digital computer a given arrangement of positively and negatively charged cells represents numeric data, which in turn may represent alphabetic data. In the brain a given arrangement of cells represents sensory experience related to perception of the outside world. The language of the computer is numeric both in the sense that cell arrangements themselves are countable and in the sense that a given cell arrangement encodes numbers that stand either for themselves or for letters of the alphabet. The language of the brain is numeric at the level of cell arrangement, but cell arrangements themselves appear to be directly relatable to the world of experience.

In the foregoing discussion it seemed expedient to speak of the "language" of the brain and the "language" of the computer. It goes without saying that these are artificial languages (see §9.14) and not natural language as defined in §1.2. All languages, natural and artificial, can be expected to have certain properties in common, most notably duality of patterning. Duality is a property also of the genetic code, blood chemistry codes, and such codes based on natural languages as pig latin or the complex codes of military organizations and spy operations. All such languages are of some interest to the linguist, and by all rights the insights of linguists should be relevant to specialists in these areas.

10.6 COMPUTATIONAL LINGUISTICS

The development of writing made possible the preservation and analysis of data on a scale that had not been possible before. The development of the computer has expanded still further our capacity for the rapid storage, analysis, and retrieval of information. The term computational linguistics is used to refer to a variety of activities involving computer analysis of language data or computer testing of grammars. These activities by their very nature overlap with a great many other interests of linguists.

The tremendous advantage that computers have over humans is their ability to carry out operations of vast complexity with great speed and unfailing accuracy. Much of linguistic analysis involves sorting and classifying data, a necessary step in determining structural categories but a time-consuming and often tedious process. This is a task that computers can do more quickly and thoroughly than humans. The linguist of course must determine which features of the data are to be examined and how data with different features is to be classified. These instructions constitute a program for the computer to follow. In most cases the linguist must review the initial computer analysis and subject the data to further sorting before the analysis is complete. The linguist must supply the intelligence for the operation; the computer has no intelligence of its own. But computer programs can be designed to identify extremely subtle features, including features that are contingent on other features. The computer can thus identify environments or other complex patterns of co-occurrence. And, since it can work so quickly, it can consider interdependent factors that would normally elude the human analyst. In this respect it possesses a kind of artificial intelligence, although its intelligence is wholly dependent on its human programmer (see further discussion in §11.9).

Machine "intelligence" includes the ability to perform alternative operations and determine which operation more closely satisfies previously specified conditions of acceptability. This ability can be an asset in analyzing data, but it can also be harnessed to generate new data and thereby test grammatical rules. Given a set of grammatical rules and a lexicon, a computer can apply the rules to produce any desired number of sentences. The computer can detect inconsistencies within the rules—as, for example, when the operation of one rule requires an element that has not been introduced by a previous rule. Incorrect rules that lack internal inconsistencies, however, will not be spotted by the computer and will lead to ungrammatical output that only the linguist can detect.

Computer programming is heavily indebted to set theory, Boolean algebra, and automata theory. These same influences, particularly the concept of string rewriting that developed in connection with automata theory, were important in the development of transformational grammar. The formal grammars of transformationalists, in turn, have been of interest to computer programmers since a formal grammar strives for the same kind of explicit processing instructions that are required for computer operation. In addition, transformational grammar arrived on the scene just as the United States was undertaking an expanded program of science and technical education in response to the Soviet launching of Sputnik I. The new approach, with its mathematical orientation, impressed many as more "scientific" than earlier schools. At the same time an interest in Russian technical literature and a shortage of Russian language specialists spurred efforts in the United States to develop a computerized translation machine. Transformational grammar provided an analysis of language structures in a form suited to encoding by computers and, hopefully, for conversion to the equivalent structures of another language.

The early hopes for machine translation faded, however, as it became apparent that linguists had not yet come up with the minimum requisites: complete grammars of two languages constructed in transmutable terms. Pilot projects in machine translation required so much human editing that little was actually saved in time or effort. While the idea of a translation machine has not been totally abandoned, many linguists have felt it wiser to use computers to develop complete grammars before attempting machine translation. Part of the problem up to now has been that translation efforts have sought to equate vocabulary and syntactic constructions in the source language with vocabulary and syntactic structures in the target language. These are seldom fully transmutable, even between two closely related languages. The range of meaning for a word in one language overlaps partially with several words in another language—but not fully with any one of them. A syntactic pattern in one language may map onto several different syntactic patterns in another language. If language is merely a device for manipulating syntax, these problems should not be serious obstacles. But if language is a device for converting semantic structures into phonological strings, it will be necessary to approach machine translation from the standpoint of converting the semantic structure of one language into the phonological sequences of another. Whether meaning-structure grammar will have a contribution to make here remains to be seen.

10.7 MATHEMATICS AND LINGUISTICS

Mathematics and linguistics originated in Western thought as branches of philosophy, but the two disciplines quickly separated and have developed independently through most of their history. The separation is so deeply ingrained in our present cultural tradition that the Scholastic Aptitude Test, the most widely used instrument in the United States for measuring scholastic aptitude, is divided into two scores—one for verbal ability and one for mathematical ability. The validity of this distinction is supported by evidence suggesting that boys tend to excel in tasks involving numerical and mechanical skills, while girls tend to be superior in verbal and social skills. There are individual exceptions of course, and in any event it is not clear whether these findings represent a basic dichotomy between verbal and mathematical modes of thinking or simply a difference in the way boys and girls are socialized in our culture.

An awareness of similarities between mathematics and ordinary language as symbolic systems is largely a twentieth-century development traceable to two influences. One is the symbolic logic that developed from the mathematical and philosophical writings of Russell and Whitehead. The other, and perhaps the more immediate influence, is the trend toward formalism and symbolic representation in the structural grammar of Harris. Chomsky, a student of Harris, continued this approach and combined it with his own background in philosophy to create a model of language having formal properties that could be described in much the way that the axioms of an algebraic system can be stated.

Among the topics that have attracted the attention of mathematicians since the nineteenth century are the abstract algebra of groups, rings, and fields—all of which are closed formal systems. In transformational grammar language is treated as a formal system. Grammatical rules are stated as formal operations, and an algebraic form of notation is used to state the rules. The format inescapably calls attention to the parallels between natural language and formal mathematical systems. The properties of a grammar therefore interest the mathematician as a formal system, just as the properties of a mathematical system interest the linguist as a grammar.

The concept of generative rules, finite in number but capable of producing an infinite set of forms, was borrowed by linguists from mathematics (§5.13). With it was borrowed the technique of formal proof, used by transformationalists to demonstrate a property of language or show whether or not a particular rule is required in a grammar. (Unfortunately the data in linguistics is variable and the axioms uncertain, whereas mathematics is not concerned with "data" at all, but rather with idealizations that by definition are invariable. As a result it is possible for two different linguists to "prove" contrary propositions—an unthinkable occurrence in mathematics.)

The formal proof that the corpus of any natural language is infinite runs something like this. There is no upper limit on the length of a sentence. For any sentence S_i of a given length, it is always possible to construct a longer sentence S_j consisting of S_i plus an additional clause S_x. The process is unending; therefore, the output must be an infinite corpus.

This proof has been questioned by Paul Ziff, whose argument runs as follows: although in principle there may be no upper limit on the length of a sentence, in actual fact no individual has ever uttered or written an infinitely long sentence. Nor would this be possible in a finite life span. Since individual sentences cannot be infinitely long, a natural language can have an infinite corpus only if it can be shown that a given language (or languages) contains an infinite number of different sentences, each having a finite length. This also is impossible. Even if we started with the origin of language and count every sentence in every language up to the present and continue into the indefinite future, we would still have only an indefinitely large number. The number would be denumerable, not infinite.

The argument appears to hinge on whether we are willing to admit theoretical possibilities or confine ourselves to demonstrable events. Either way we have what amounts to an unbounded set of sentences—or at least one bounded only by the indefinite limitations of time, population, and loquaciousness. Whether a set is unbounded, potentially infinite, or indefinitely large is as much a philosophical question as it is mathematical.

10.8 PHILOSOPHY AND LINGUISTICS

Linguistics had its beginnings in ancient Greece as a branch of philosophy, and throughout the Middle Ages the two disciplines remained closely united. To be a grammarian was to be a philosopher. The interest in universal grammar, a legacy of the Latin era, persisted in post-Renaissance Europe. The *Port-Royal Grammar* published in 1660 has been cited by Chomsky and his colleagues as a precedent for their own interest in linguistic and cognitive universals. Linguists of the nineteenth century while developing the comparative method were also interested in the philosophical implications of language as a vehicle for thought. The views of Wilhelm von Humboldt (1767–1835) are fairly typical of the period. He saw in language an expression of the human genius for mental activity and supposed that some languages were better suited than others for expressing complex thought. If so, he reasoned, it must follow that different languages were representative of the national character of those who spoke them. Humboldt's typological classification of languages as analytical, agglutinating, inflectional, and polysynthetic (§8.2) was related to his belief that languages could be graded according to their degree of perfection. Like others of the period, he was interested in questions concerning the origin of language and its course of evolution through various typological stages. The relevance of these topics more than a hundred years later is not the point; for Humboldt and his contemporaries, the philosophical investigation of language was a way of casting light on the nature of humankind and their place in the world.

As methods of linguistic analysis were refined in the late nineteenth and early twentieth centuries, linguists concentrated on the systematic description of individual languages and, in many cases, actively rejected the philosophical interests of the previous era. In part this resulted from a growing awareness of the structural complexity of the supposed "primitive" languages. But it also grew out of two conscious decisions: (1) the desire to reject a priori notions of language universals and describe each language in terms of its own structure and (2) the rejection of mentalistic assumptions about language in favor of a behavioristic approach (§10.4). For many structuralists (the conspicuous exceptions were Sapir and Whorf) this position amounted to a denial of any common interests between linguistics and philosophy. In reality it was simply the adoption of a different philosophical stance—one holding that language should be studied for its own sake and not for what it might reveal about human mental processes or about questions of metaphysics or epistemology. Meaning was regarded as a subject outside the scope of linguistics proper.

With the rise of transformational grammar and the development of the concept of deep structure, linguists were willing to turn once again to philosophical issues. Chomsky has argued that the formal properties of (transformational) grammar reveal the nature of human mental processes and that the complexity of grammar, together with the relatively short time children require to learn their native language, constitute evidence for inborn linguistic abilities of a very specific kind. Transformational grammar has been willing to consider questions of how words are related to meaning, how the individual acquires word-meaning pairs, and how these word-meaning pairs are arranged syntactically to represent thought. These questions in turn are related to broader questions that have traditionally interested philosophers: What is meaning? What is knowledge? Given a knowledge of one fact, how do we know that another fact is logically deducible from it?

Philosophers approach questions of this kind against a background of discussion that extends back to the Greeks. We have already mentioned the Medieval interest in universal grammar, which was thought to underlie the particular grammar of individual languages. Following the Renaissance, philosophers became increasingly concerned with scientific and mathematical systems. The rationalism of Descartes (1596–1650)—specifically his notion of innate ideas—has been cited by Chomsky as the antecedent of his own study of language and the mind. Locke (1632–1704), who viewed the mind as a blank slate incapable of forming ideas in the absence of experience, is often regarded as holding a position totally opposed to that of Descartes. In fact, both agreed on the innateness of the human faculty for reason; the disagreement was over the conditions necessary to activate this faculty. At any rate, the empiricism associated with Locke and others who emphasize the importance of experience is regarded by transformationalists as sharply opposed to their own rationalist view of language, which they attribute—rightly or wrongly—to Descartes.

The work of Condillac (1715–1780) in developing Locke's ideas led to a revival of interest in universal grammar and contributed to further philosophical treatments of language. These treatments, typified by the work of Humboldt discussed above, stressed speculation concerning the origin of language and the role of individual languages in expressing the supposed national character of their speakers. Kant (1724–1804) sought to clarify the relationship between sensory perception of objects and the mental organization that makes perceptions meaningful. His work has important implications for the study of language, particularly in the area of psychology and semantics, but his immediate impact was felt in the nineteenth-century movements of transcendentalism and idealism, rather than in the area of language study. Twentieth-century interest in the philosophy of science also owes a considerable debt to Kant, and this branch of philosophy has a natural interest in examining the assumptions, goals, and methods of linguistics along with those of other scientific disciplines.

Philosophers of language in the present century have generally fallen into two camps. On the one hand are those such as Wittgenstein who have turned their attention to the richness and complexity of ordinary language, seeking to understand the meaning of words in ordinary use, identify ambiguous usages, and clarify the relationship between words and thought. On the other hand are those like Russell who have seen language as an imperfect tool for logical thought and have felt that an understanding of natural language can best be achieved by first developing a pure mathematical language for symbolizing logical relationships and then examining the way these relationships are expressed in ordinary language. Although they emphasize different approaches, the two schools are by no means incompatible with each other. Transformational theory, which has been influenced by mathematical models, has also been aware of the possibility of using logical structures as the base component for a generative grammar. Even those transformationalists who have chosen to retain a phrase structure component as the base have devoted considerable attention to the logical presuppositions of individual sentences.

Because of its emphasis on precise formulation and explicitness, transformational grammar has had strong appeal to philosophers of language. It has seemed to them that transformational grammar offers a way of formalizing questions of meaning that were not handled adequately in earlier schools. The optimism on this point should be restrained, however, by an awareness that the methods of transformational grammar were developed originally for syntactic analysis. Transformationalists remain in disagreement as to how these methods can best be extended to semantic analysis. Certainly the best hope for advancement in the understanding of language lies in the simultaneous exploration of many different approaches—syntactic analysis (using both the *Aspects* model and the generative semantics model), symbolic logic, and cognitive studies, among others. One might also expect that meaning-structure grammar, with its technique for analyzing a sentence into its component proposition and argument(s), will be used as a tool along with other conceptual tools. The varied approaches will not only cast light on different features of language but, in the process, the extent to which they provide genuine illumination will serve to test the usefulness of each approach.

10.9 LITERATURE AND LINGUISTICS

Although every speaker of a language gains full mastery for utilitarian purposes, speakers differ widely in their ability to command an audience for what they have to say. Every speech community seems to recognize certain individuals as having special skill in using language, and this skill is often crucial in qualifying for certain high-status social roles. On the tribal level both the traditional storyteller and the village chief must have special linguistic skills. In a complex society the confidence man and elected official alike must have superior language ability. So must the actor, poet, sportscaster, journalist, and author. The writer of formula "true confession" stories and the Nobel laureate have much in common. Both have special skills in using language, and both produce something that can be called literature. The two forms involve different literary styles and appeal to different audiences, but each is highly structured and involves the mastery of a specialized grammar.

Literature is not easy to define. Recognition of literary qualities is therefore quite different from recognition of grammaticality. Despite occasional borderline cases, members of a speech community seldom have trouble agreeing that certain sentences are acceptable (i.e., grammatical) and others are not. The judgment of literature is much more subjective, especially in a large, heterogeneous society. In the broadest sense we can say that literature is the skilled use of language, recognized as such by an entire speech community or some group within the community. Specifically the attributes of literature seem to be the following: (1) excellence of speech; (2) elegance; and (3) durability.

Excellence of speech is largely a matter of suitability—that is, appropriateness in terms of the mood that is to be evoked. The standards for judging excellence vary according to the subject matter and also differ from one culture to another and, within a culture, from one time period to another and from one group to another. In a relatively homogeneous preliterate society, the only literature may be the traditional folk tales that are transmitted orally. In more complex societies the form and subject matter of literature are likely to be more varied, and it is not at all unusual to find two or more different standards in competition with one another. Thus, the standards of excellence for popular fiction are quite different from the standards espoused by college English departments and literary critics. But the linguist, in principle at least, is equally interested in identifying the linguistic attributes making for excellence of speech in both kinds of literature. Certainly the linguist's methodical approach to language analysis has a precision and objectivity about it that are needed if we are to make anything of an elusive concept such as "excellence of speech."

Elegance is perhaps less elusive—but not much. The concept is largely a matter of word choice, a subject whose adequate treatment by linguists is still awaiting a more complete notion of what the lexicon should contain. But we can say this: To qualify as "elegant," vocabulary choices intended to convey specified meanings must do one of two things. They must (1) fall just outside the range of the vocabulary normally used in everyday speech or they must (2) so typify the vocabulary of everyday usage that a single replacement would destroy the entire mood. Either way we have language *par excellence.* Shakespeare is perhaps the classic example of the first type and Hemingway the second. Literary works set in pluralistic societies must of course include more than one form of diction if they are to represent faithfully the dialect of their different personages. Dickens, Shaw, and Twain are among the masters of this rather specialized literary (and linguistic) skill.

Pattern repetition is a special component of elegance that deserves mention both for its intrinsic importance in literature and because, if linguistics has any contribution to make to the study of literature at all, it should be in the area of pattern recognition. Pattern repetition in poetry assumes the familiar features of rhythm and rhyme, although this is not universal. Hebrew poetry relied on the repetition of parallel ideas. Old English poetry depended on meter and alliteration. Japanese poetry involves special diction and depends on a rhythmic pattern involving lines containing fixed numbers of syllables, but no rhyme. Free verse in English, although classed as poetry, rejects pattern repetition and relies on other devices for elegance. Pattern repetition in prose is usually more subtle than in poetry, but here also rhythmic cadence can be a factor in elegance. Parallelism is a common and natural form of pattern repetition. And when special care is given to rhetorical effect, we find examples like the *Veni, vidi, vici* 'I came, I saw, I conquered' of Julius Caesar.

Durability is a criterion that overlaps the other two, for judgments of excellence and elegance are always subject to the changing whims of fashion. A work highly regarded by one generation may be forgotten by the next. Conversely a work that attracts little attention when it first appears may grow in stature with the passage of time. In comparable fashion a work may be well received in one social group but not another in pluralistic societies. Or a work may be successful in one language community but fail in translation—or never be translated at all. The work that endures does so because its subject matter continues to speak to the human condition and because its language continues to win favor as excellent and elegant. In general the judgment of time is reliable, but there is nonetheless a certain element of chance involved. The epic poem *Beowulf* presumably enjoyed literary status in the banquet halls of local kings in eighth-century England. Eventually as life styles changed and the heroic seafaring past faded from memory, people must have lost interest in hearing the poem. It was therefore quite by chance that the poem was transcribed, found its way to the British Museum, survived a fire, was rediscovered, and finally was recognized as having literary qualities that had transcended time.

10.10 LANGUAGE TEACHING AND LINGUISTICS

Probably more energy goes into the teaching of language than any other school subject—much of this the "teaching" of one's native language. Yet with rare exceptions native-language teaching has been carried on without awareness of even the most elementary findings of modern linguistics. Teachers often assume that their task is to teach children the language they will be using for the rest of their lives, forgetting that by the time children enter school they have already had five or six years' experience in using the language as listeners and speakers. By the age of six, children have already mastered the basic phonological patterns of their language, and they know the basic semantic patterns and the grammatical analogs to them. They have an extensive vocabulary that will continue to grow during the school years and throughout adult life as they encounter new experiences. By the age of six, children are well acculturated in the folkways of their social group. They have learned the dialect of this group, and they may have difficulty understanding other dialects. Children at this age have already learned to be selective listeners, picking up everything they find interesting and screening out whatever they find irrelevant. Children who can follow a dialect that is not native to them have made a conscious decision not to screen out the material, but their comprehension strategy is likely to involve an unconscious translation of everything they hear into their native dialect. It is in this form that it will be stored and repeated.

The child entering the first grade is not exactly a blank slate, but this does not guarantee that reading and writing will be easy to master. In principle all a child needs to do is learn to match written symbols with the spoken forms they represent. The process is complicated, however, in languages like English that have many irregular and arbitrary spellings (§9.13). The fact that school materials are written in a standard literary dialect works to the advantage of middle- and upper-class children who are most likely to speak the dialect natively. It handicaps children who are not native speakers of the literary dialect, who are suspicious of those who are, and whose acculturation has reinforced the notion that the cards are stacked against them anyway. These are difficult obstacles for even the most sympathetic and well-informed teacher to overcome.

In teaching reading, any approach that works should be considered acceptable. The learner must become familiar with all the regular patterns of sound-symbol relationships and learn the arbitrary relationships by rote. Of course the teacher and textbook publisher can do much to simplify the task by grouping the arbitrary relationships in terms of their subregularities(In general the completely regular patterns should be presented first, then the arbitrary patterns involving subregularities, and finally the completely irregular formations. This kind of sequencing has been worked out in detail by Bloomfield and Barnhart (1961) but has yet to receive general recognition. Phonics as an approach to reading has received much attention in recent years in the United States, but there is nothing magic about phonics in itself. If a child becomes familar with a set of key words and develops the ability to analyze the sound-symbol patterns of these words and use these patterns to synthesize the pronunciation of new words, the approach succeeds. The child who learns sound-symbol relationships in isolation, as rules to be applied in pronouncing new words, may have difficulties. Ideally, analysis and synthesis must be used to reinforce each other.

Linguists find many features of the usual phonics textbook perplexing. To speak of the "long" or "short" sound of a particular letter is quite meaningless to any linguist schooled in phonetics and phonemics. To describe a consonant cluster as a "blend" strikes the phonologist as a confusing reference to the process of coalescence. As in other areas, cross-disciplinary communication would be helpful.

The Initial Teaching Alphabet (ITA) developed in England uses forty-four letters in an effort to strike a compromise between conventional orthography and strict phonemic representation. The letter *c* is used only for /k/, thus duplicating *k* but setting the stage for a later switch to standard orthography using both *k* and *c*. The same principle is used for representing two-letter units like *sh*, which appears in ITA as a unit ʃh. Complex vocalic nuclei /iy, ey, ay/ and the like appear as unit graphemes ɛɛ, æ, *ie* respectively. The symbols are not necessarily the ones that would be chosen by those familiar with either the International Phonetic Alphabet or the Trager-Smith phonemic representation, but this is not an important consideration. The system was designed as a reasonably systematized introduction to the vagaries of English spelling, not as an introduction to formal linguistics. The Initial Teaching Alphabet is widely used in England. It has been used experimentally in the United States and Canada, with good results, but has not gained widespread acceptance.

Writing is a skill that logically presupposes the ability to read.

Reading is therefore a necessary but not a sufficient precondition for writing. The art of writing also involves the mastery of various punctuation conventions that require little conscious attention on the part of the reader. But perhaps most crucial for the writer is somehow coming to understand that writing is a way of converting the nonlinear semantic configurations that we call thought into a linear speech surrogate that the reader can use to create something approximating the original thought. Among other things the process involves knowing how much the reader already knows about the subject and taking care to structure the discourse so that the reader will have the easiest time possible in putting everything together and coming out with the intended semantic content. And the writer must do this using a system that represents only a portion of the signals normally present in speech (see §9.12). Several years of practice are necessary before the child can speak comfortably even in informal situations; small wonder that many more years of practice should be required to develop skill in writing.

The teaching of grammar, in spite of everything that linguists have managed to learn about language, remains in most classrooms a matter of rote learning intended to bolster the standards of correctness that the school system is sworn to uphold. We have emphasized (§2.6) that traditional grammar does not have to be prescriptive. The categories of traditional grammar can certainly be used in the objective study of language. And for that matter, there is nothing wrong with the desire to promote good written style in a standard literary dialect—the goal that most often motivates a prescriptive approach in the language classroom. But this goal should be recognized for what it is and not clouded by notions of correctness and incorrectness or by the belief that the study of grammar will produce students gifted with a good literary style. The study of grammar is legitimate because language is an interesting subject for study. Knowing something about the history and structure of language is an end in itself. The data for studying language is immediately available to any investigator. All that is required is knowledge of a few fundamental principles and a willingness to grapple with data until a pattern can be recognized.

Any intelligent approach to the study of language (i.e., grammar) should be informed by an understanding of (at least) the five representative models that have been presented in this book. Traditional grammar continues to dominate the presentation of most school textbooks in spite of lip service paid to other models. Awareness of language change calls for a knowledge of historical grammar. Structural grammar and transformational grammar are essential for an understanding of the phonological, morphological, and syntactic structures of language. And the meaning-structure model has much to say about the complex process of converting semantic units to linguistic units. If students, aided by an informed teacher, can use the tools of linguistics to study grammar descriptively, they will hopefully be in a position to turn to the study of style with an inner freedom to set their own prescriptive standards.

10.11 FOREIGN LANGUAGES AND LINGUISTICS

Compared with the attention given to native-language teaching, the teaching of foreign languages is woefully neglected. Nonetheless, foreign languages remain part of the curriculum in most places and continue to afflict students or, occasionally, inspire them. We know that language is a spoken phenomenon and that children are able to learn their native language with relative ease in only a few years. Language teachers have made increasing use of these insights, particularly since World War II, when the need to study many non-Western languages drew a number of linguists into war-related language programs.

The **traditional method** of language learning involves study of the grammar and translation of passages into the student's native language. Unfortunately this method of learning seldom produces students who are actually able to use the language in speech or writing. A quite different approach, called the **direct method,** is based on the fact that children learn their native language by figuring everything out for themselves with no grammatical explanations to help them. A teacher using the direct method speaks to the students using only the target language. The teacher may point out objects, naming them in the target language and requiring students to respond using the same words. This practice continues until students gain full mastery of the language. Students using the direct method are often able to gain a near-native control of the language, but this does not mean that learning a second language is or should be the same as learning one's native language. Children learning their native language are driven by the need to communicate with those around them, and there are few other activities making demands on their time. The adult learning a second language has already mastered one language and could profitably use it to take a few shortcuts. No matter how strongly motivated one may be to communicate with people in the target language, it is difficult not to feel frustrated on comparing the difficulties of the learning situation with the ease of communicating in the native language. (Children probably experience similar frustration learning their native language. The difference is that adults can chuck it all and go back home if they really want to.) For children every waking hour is spent practicing their native language. Adults have many interests to occupy their attention and relatively little time to practice a second language.

Modern methods combine something of both the traditional and direct approaches. The student memorizes conversational sentences and practices basic structural patterns until their production becomes automatic. The use of the language for communication rather than translation is emphasized. Some description of structural patterns is given in the native language to save time, and a language laboratory is used to provide supplementary practice.

The teaching of second languages requires an adequate linguistic description of the target language, along with a comparison of features that are similar to the student's native language as well as different from it. Students approach the language learning task with prior knowledge of how semantic structures are encoded in their native language. When the encoding of semantic structures follows an identical pattern in the target language, the learning task is simple:

> *English:*   I have money.   =   *German:*   Ich habe Geld.

If structural patterns are systematically different, they require learning, but the learning effort is minimal. Such is the situation confronting the English speaker who must learn that the familiar SVO arrangement is matched in Japanese by an SOV pattern; that the subject is marked by *wa,* the object by *o;* and that DEFINITE is not symbolized:

> *English:*   The child ate the candy.   =
> *Japanese:*   kodomo-wa ame-o tabemašita.

When structural patterns differ in unpredictable ways, the learner is likely to have the greatest difficulty:

> *English:*   I am cold. $\longrightarrow\neq$— *Spanish:*   *Soy frio.
>
> $=$
>
> *English:*   *I have cold.—$\neq$— *Spanish:*   Tengo frio.

In many countries situated along language boundaries, bilingualism is the rule rather than the exception. This is true of Switzerland (French, German, Rhaeto-Romance), the American Southwest (English, Spanish), eastern Canada (English, French), and many other places. Since the language one speaks is an integral part of one's personal and ethnic identity, it is not at all unusual for a minority group to preserve its ancestral language with fierce pride for an indefinite period—witness Hebrew. While it is certainly more efficient for everyone to speak a single language, the linguist can hardly object to the preservation of language diversity. Indeed, it is ironic that middle-class American children are encouraged to study foreign languages at the same time that children of immigrants, Indians, and Chicanos are subject to considerable pressure in school to abandon the language of their parents. It often happens that the first generation of immigrants remains monolingual in its native language. The second generation is bilingual but oriented toward English and even ashamed of its foreign background. The third generation grows up mono-lingual in English but chooses to study the ancestral language in school, where it experiences the same language-learning difficulties as everyone else.

A recurring proposal to simplify international communication has been the development and adoption of a single international language. A number of such artificially designed pidgins have been proposed, the most widely publicized being Esperanto. Artificial interlanguages differ from other pidgins (see §10.3) in having a full range of grammatical processes and having fewer irregular patterns than most natural languages. But no interlanguage is completely neutral. Most are based on European languages and therefore are strongly biased against the languages of Asia, Africa, and other parts of the world. Moreover, no interlanguage has a population base speaking the language as its native tongue. English is in a better position to serve as an interlanguage in this respect. English is spoken natively by a large population distributed around the globe and is a second language for large numbers of people. The political and economic influence of the English-speaking countries has contributed to the language's prominence. Speakers of other languages have tended to learn English, and native English speakers have often been unwilling to learn other languages. These factors, while promoting the use of English, work against its acceptance as a "neutral" inter-language.

There is nothing really to prevent one who is sufficiently motivated from gaining effective control of at least one language besides one's native tongue. Motivation must of course be coupled with a suitable learning strategy. For example, a dedicated student might work hard to memorize vocabulary, but this would be an unwise strategy, for vocabulary without mastery of the basic grammatical patterns is use-less. Given the right strategy and enough determination, everyone in the world could have the option of being a participant in two or more language and cultural communities.

10.12 HISTORY AND AREA STUDIES

The historian ordinarily works with documentary materials, while the linguist is oriented toward oral materials. But as soon as the linguist transcribes oral materials, these become documents, and whenever the historian works with foreign language documents he or she be-comes a linguist. The decipherment of ancient manuscripts or inscrip-tions is a process that requires the skills of both linguist and historian. Any question having to do with the meaning or intent of a passage is a linguistic question. But since meaning is a matter of the connection between linguistic forms and the world of experience, questions of meaning inevitably involve the skills of the historian, the anthro-pologist, or the area specialist. This is not to suggest that these are the only specialists whose work is related to linguistics. Lawyers and judges attempting to interpret a statute or a point of constitutional law must all be linguists. (Law can be viewed as a specialized kind of behavioral grammar, in the sense of §10.2.) Anyone who has to interpret a text becomes a linguist for the nonce.

Linguists who have dealt with language history have generally tried to reconstruct earlier stages of a language on the basis of patterns preserved in later periods. They recognize their work as reconstruction and represent it as such. Historians working with documentary evidence are also engaged in reconstruction. They must judge the reliability of their documents, reconcile conflicting evidence, and fill in the gaps by positing events and relationships that are consistent with the overall pattern. The result in both cases is a reconstruction having a high degree of reliability but lacking absolute certainty. Of course, this is true of anything reported as a fact, including eyewitness accounts of an event—as anyone can demonstrate by staging a classroom event and asking the eyewitnesses to describe it.

We have already noted (§3.8, §10.2) how the linguist can help reconstruct the broad outlines of cultural history. We have also seen (§3.9) how linguistic analysis can often lead to interferences about relative chronology. These matters are of interest to the ethnohistorian, who is primarily an anthropologist, but most historians are interested in the details of fairly recent history. Even here the insights of the linguist can sometimes be helpful. For example, documentary records from the eighteenth and nineteenth centuries link the Shawnee Indians, a widely scattered tribe in eastern North America, with a group called the Savannah. The references are quite specific in asserting that the name *Shawnee* is derived from the earlier word *Savannah*. Since the manuscripts are quite early, even though the first contact with these Indians was in the seventeenth century, historians have tended to accept the manuscript record at face value. However, the linguistic evidence suggests that *Shawnee* derives from the Shawnee name for themselves [šaawanwa ~ šaawano] 'southerners,' while the term *savannah* 'flat, treeless grassland' was borrowed from Spanish. The term was applied to coastal plains, to a river running through the area, and to various tribes living along the river. The fact that one of these tribes had a name vaguely resembling the geographic term is apparently the source of a mistaken inference that was later repeated as fact. The real "fact" is no longer observable, but, all considered, in this case the linguistic reconstruction of history seems more reliable than the manuscript reconstruction.

Area studies are devoted to the intensive, integrated study of the language, culture, history, and social institutions of individual countries or geographic areas. The growth of such programs was accelerated following World War II, as the United States and other Western countries became increasingly aware of the need for a trained body of specialists to support their worldwide efforts in diplomacy, commerce, and humanitarian service. (The same skills can of course be harnessed for purposes of espionage and military activity.) Linguists and language teachers have been deeply involved from the outset in the development of area studies and in service projects such as the Peace Corps. Area studies have drawn many of their students from the ranks of returning Peace Corps volunteers, and graduates of area studies programs have often been attracted into the work of the Peace Corps or private agencies such as the American Friends Service Committee.

10.13 CONCLUSION

It should be clear that the interests of linguistics are wide ranging and dovetail with a variety of disciplines. We have emphasized repeatedly that the study of language touches on all areas of human life. One naturally hopes that the future will bring increasing opportunities for the study of language, both as an end in itself and as a means of furthering other worthwhile academic and humanitarian projects. However, a realistic appraisal suggests that knowledge for the sake of knowledge is one of the first things to lose funding when times are hard and that support for applied studies becomes closely tied to nonacademic considerations. The immediate future of linguistics—and academic life in general—is therefore related to the health of the economy and to the development of national (and worldwide) priorities that provide a place for language study. Linguists should have a voice in the development of the priorities. Certainly they will have no difficulty building a case for the contribution that linguistics can make to numerous other disciplines. The temptation will be to sell linguistics as a chameleonlike tool ready to serve any master, instead of arguing for the proposition that free intellectual inquiry is good for its own sake and deserves support.

summary

Because language permeates every aspect of human life, the study of language touches in some way on the interests of numerous widely varied academic fields. Anthropology and sociology are interested in the social setting of language use. Anthropologists have tended to focus on the languages of tribal societies, while sociologists have focused on complex, urban societies. Both have been interested in language variation, the dynamics of communication, and cognitive structure. The interests of psychology have also centered on cognitive structure but have touched on broader problems of learning and language acquisition as well. Ongoing investigations into the workings of the brain can be expected to contribute to a better understanding of the neural organization of language.

Computers, with their capacity for rapid storage, analysis, and retrieval of information, can be utilized in analyzing language data, testing grammars, and—perhaps some day—translating from one language to another. Because the formal properties of grammar are similar to those of formal mathematical systems, linguists and mathematicians have found much in common in recent years. The precise formalisms of modern grammar, together with a renewed interest in questions of meaning and the logical structure of language, have been instrumental in strengthening the interest of philosophers and linguists in each other's work.

The study of literature, traditionally associated with rhetoric, involves a study of the specialized use of language. The application of linguistics to native- and foreign-language teaching is a field of growing importance. Although we are still adding to knowledge of how children learn to read and write and how they can be taught most effectively, much of the information already available has been poorly utilized. The insights of linguistics have been more widely used in foreign-language study, where teachers tend to be more conscious of language structure and linguistics. The interests of linguistics impinge also on area studies and the interpretation of historical data, legal documents, and the like. The opportunities for applications of linguistic knowledge to human undertakings seem to be limited only by the kinds of institutions people choose to create for themselves.

further reading

General: Bartsch and Venneman 1975. **10.2** Sapir 1916, Mandelbaum 1949, Boas 1911, Malinowski 1923, Whorf 1956, Hoijer 1954, Hockett 1954a, Percival 1966, Hymes 1964, E. Hall 1959, Conklin 1955, Berlin and Kay 1969, Hickerson 1971, Landar 1966, Burling 1970, Bauman and Sherzer 1974, Farb 1974. **10.3** Bloomfield 1933 (Chap. 19), McDavid 1948, McDavid and McDavid 1951, McDavid and O'Cain 1973, Kurath et al. 1939–43, 1972, Kurath and McDavid 1961, Kurath 1972, Mencken 1963, Allen 1973–76, Hertzler 1965, Labov 1963, 1966, 1972, Shuy et al. 1968, Wolfram 1969, Wolfram and Clarke 1971, Bright 1966, Fishman 1968, 1972, Kerr and Aderman 1971, Shores 1972, Burling 1973, R. Hall 1965, Fischer 1958, 1975. **10.4** Leopold 1939–49, Weir 1962, Braine 1963, McNeill 1966, Smith and Miller 1966, Brown 1973, Moore 1973, Slobin 1971, Dale 1972, G. Miller 1973, Skinner 1957, Chomsky 1959, 1965, 1966, 1972a. **10.5** Penfield and Roberts 1959, Denes and Pinson 1963, Lenneberg 1967, von Neumann 1958. **10.6** Garvin 1963, Hays 1967, Crowley 1967, Schank and Colby 1973. **10.7** Chomsky 1975, Wall 1972, Kimball 1973, Ziff 1973. **10.8** Alston 1964, Fodor and Katz 1964, Katz 1966, Chomsky 1966, 1972a, Aarsleff 1970, 1971, Brekle 1966, R. Lakoff 1969, Keenan 1972, Peterson 1973, Pears 1971. **10.9** Sapir 1921 (Chap. 11), Hockett 1958 (Chap. 63), Sledd 1959 (Chap. 8), Chatman and Levin 1967, Levin 1964, Sebeok 1960, Uitti 1969, Gunter 1975. **10.10** Allen 1964, Abrahams and Troike 1972, Bloomfield and Barnhart 1961, Fries 1962, Mazurkiewicz 1967, Downing 1967, Burling 1973, Arthur 1973. **10.11** Lado 1957, 1964, Politzer and Politzer 1972. **10.12** Sapir 1916, Pearson 1974.

perspective on the future

11.1 THE PAST AS A POINT OF DEPARTURE

The chief analytical technique of traditional grammar was paradigm analysis. This was, in principle at least, a mechanical procedure based on classifying recurring partials as either "same" or "different." The only thing keeping the method from being a wholly mechanical procedure was the inability of traditional grammarians to deal with phonological alternation in bound suffixes. Thus, the human editor was compelled to deal with the results of the "method" to produce an analysis that fit into the available conceptual framework. Unanalyzed paradigms were laid before students, and students were expected to produce their own analysis—that is, to understand whatever principle was involved in the formation of the paradigm.

The classification of words into parts of speech and the analysis of words as sentence constituents in traditional grammar proceeded from definition and therefore tended toward being a deductive rather than inductive science. The definitions themselves were arrived at inductively by those first proposing them, but, once proposed, they were accepted for the most part without question by later grammarians. The result was that traditional grammar focused on a synchronic description of individual languages, with the descriptive categories defined ultimately in terms of structural categories relevant to Latin and Greek.

Historical grammar operated within the confines of traditional morphological terminology but with drastically different objectives. Linguistics was now viewed as a wholly inductive science. The goal was the diachronic description of individual languages by showing their relationship to a reconstructed protolanguage and their development from it. The comparative method involved identifying sound correspondences. These were sets of sounds occurring in analogous positions in cognates—that is, words exhibiting similarity in both form and meaning in different languages. The method was essentially a matter of paradigm analysis, but the relevant paradigm was now as much phonological as morphological. And the methods for determining whether two sets counted as same or different became quite sophisticated, although the underlying principle remained fairly simple: sets with overlapping membership that occur in complementary environments count as same; such sets occurring in the same environments count as different.

Internal reconstruction involves the identification of alternating sets of sounds within a single language. Members of these sets normally count as different, but if the alternating set belongs to a single morphological unit, members of the set must be regarded as same. The problem in internal reconstruction is to imagine the historical developments that could have given rise to the pattern conflict. By its nature internal reconstruction has fewer ground rules than the comparative method, but both are aimed at inferring earlier stages of the language.

Historical linguistics gave rise to both the study of dialect geography and the study of phonetics. Both were regarded originally as tools for historical analysis, but both eventually became objects of study in their own right.

Structural grammar continued the basic analytical techniques of historical linguistics, but with a sharp shift of emphasis. Historical studies had called attention to language as system, and structuralists directed their efforts to formulating synchronic descriptions of individual languages as self-contained structural systems. Structural grammar thus represented a return to the interest in synchronic description of traditional grammar, but the description was now carried out with the methodology that had been developed in historical grammar. The approach of structural grammar utilized phonetics and classified phonetically similar sounds (i.e., sounds with overlapping phonetic features) occurring in complementary environments as members of the same structural unit: the phoneme. The procedure was a direct continuation of the procedure developed in historical linguistics for classifying sound correspondences with overlapping membership.

Paralleling the phoneme in structural grammar was the morpheme, a unit of meaning whose members occurred in complementary environments. These members, allomorphs, often contained units that at the phonemic level would contrast but that on the morphemic level had to be regarded as complementary, hence members of the same unit. Although this kind of pattern conflict would have been subjected to internal reconstruction in historical linguistics, structural grammar, with its emphasis on synchronic analysis, favored an approach to morphology in which the basic elements were static units. By defining the morpheme as a set of static units in complementary distribution, it was possible to focus on the static qualities of individual allomorphs and overlook the environmentally determined variation of component phonemes. Historical linguistics would have reconstructed an underlying historical form from which the actually occurring forms could be derived by the regular processes of sound change.

In the area of syntax, structural grammar made only limited advances over traditional grammar. The advances that were made came about largely from a rejection of traditional terminology and a return to an inductive search for ways of classifying the structural units within the sentence. This procedure, in effect, applied paradigm analysis to sentences in an effort to identify recurring partials that could be classified as same or different. The basis for the analysis was made explicit, although the resulting description was little different from traditional grammar, except in terminology.

Structural grammar did not really deal with the relationship of sentences that were partially the same and partially different. A precise formulation of the structural relationship between two different sentences calls for a statement of the differences, a statement that implies a procedure for converting one sentence into the other or vice versa. But this is a process statement, a type not sanctioned by the item-and-arrangement approach favored in structural grammar. Not until it was seen that the simplest statement of the distribution of the tense morpheme within the various auxiliaries of the verb (§6.2) required a process statement was the door finally open to process rules.

The philosophical shift from rejection of process rules to reliance on such rules was sufficient to mark a transition from structural to transformational grammar. But the shift was based chiefly on the different kind of rule allowed. The analysis was still distributional. Two syntactic structures sharing the same basic components and differing only in a few particulars were seen as complementary to each other and were assigned to the same underlying structure. The emphasis was still on structure, but the structural unit receiving the greatest attention was now the sentence rather than the phoneme or morpheme.

It became possible to integrate syntax and phonology, embracing process rules in both. The lexicon was seen initially as a list of static items introduced into syntactically defined slots by phrase structure rules. In time, though, the lexicon came to be viewed as a repository of crucial information about lexical items, including features of a syntactic-semantic character and listings of exceptions to general grammatical rules. Only the position of semantics remained uncertain.

Given the fact that transformational grammar had its genesis in the study of syntax, it was perhaps natural that the earliest efforts to incorporate semantics into an overall scheme would assume that semantics could be explained entirely in terms of syntax. This approach has been questioned in recent years both from within transformational grammar and by linguists lacking transformational credentials.

Both groups now agree that semantics should be viewed as central to linguistic description rather than an appendage to syntax. The centrality of semantics is adopted largely for philosophical reasons, although it is generally defended on the ground that it leads to an overall simplification of linguistic description. Those schooled originally in transformational theory tend to see semantics as a complicated, abstract kind of syntax, and their arguments emphasize the distribution of semantic units that sometimes surface as separate words (e.g., *become, not, alive*) and sometimes coalesce into a single word (e.g., *die*). These options continue to be handled by transformational rules. Those approaching the subject from outside transformational theory tend to think in terms of the distribution of noun-verb relationships and the hierarchical relationship of semantic units within nouns and verbs. They assert that transformational rules, as normally conceived, are largely irrelevant to language description, although they readily acknowledge that many of the processes involved in converting semantic units into a surface structure are "transformational" in nature.

Semanticists view a rule sequence that starts with syntax and produces sound-meaning pairs as misrepresenting the true nature of language. Syntacticists reply in one of two ways. The "standard-theory" argument is that rule formalisms are simply a device for describing the relationship between meaning and sound. These formalisms need not imply directionality in the usual sense of the word. The "generative-semantics" argument is that an analysis in which syntactic units are decomposed into irreducible components is in fact a semantic analysis.

Linguists have justly been likened to the fabled blind men who examined different portions of the elephant and came away with drastically different conceptions of the beast. Those who have devoted their professional lives to transformational grammar see semantics as something very much like syntax. Linguists who have not invested the same amount of time studying syntax see semantics as having little in common with syntax. Nearly all linguists agree that semantics will loom with increased importance in the future study of linguistics, but it is too early to tell what consensus linguists will reach in their conception of the semantic component.

11.2 THE ROLE OF THEORY

Anyone engaged in scientific inquiry proceeds from certain assumptions. These assumptions have to do with the nature and scope of the subject being investigated, the kinds of questions to be raised, the type of evidence to be collected, the methods of collecting evidence, and the general nature of the expected answers. These assumptions constitute a theory of the subject and serve to guide further investigation by providing a conceptual framework within which the investigation can take place. Kuhn (1970) has termed this conceptual framework a scientific paradigm. In the natural sciences a paradigm for scientific investigation arises from notable achievements that have two characteristics. The novelty of the achievement serves to define legitimate problems and methods in such a way as to attract other investigators to the paradigm. And the achievement must be sufficiently open-ended that it leaves a number of problems calling for further investigation.

A paradigm in this sense is of course different from the concept of a paradigm as used in linguistic analysis, where it refers to a display frame in which same and different elements can be identified. A scientific paradigm is an arrangement of concepts to provide a framework for the investigation of the subject matter represented by these concepts. But both paradigms constitute a kind of framework for channeling the efforts of investigators.

A scientific paradigm, in the sense of Kuhn, is a theory—that is, a set of assumptions about the nature of the subject and the function of those who investigate it. Researchers who investigate the problems identified by the theory and who practice the methodology prescribed by the theory are engaged in what Kuhn calls **normal science.** In general, the practice of normal science results in an accumulation of data that can be explained by the theory and integrated into it. Theories themselves cannot be either proved or disproved. Theories do, however, give rise to hypotheses that are capable of proof or disproof within the framework provided by the theory. But since hypotheses are always formulated within the conceptual framework of the theory, they tend to be self-validating. Thus, while normal science leads investigators to test hypotheses, the expectation always is that the findings will be compatible with the theory. New data investigated in connection with hypothesis testing is expected to be explainable in terms of the theory and capable of being integrated into it. To the extent that a theory is able to explain a wide variety of observed data, the theory continues to stand and indeed gains in credibility.

However, it invariably happens that certain facts remain anomalous. In the initial stages of inquiry, this is seldom a problem. The investigator cannot hope to deal with everything at once, and it is only natural to begin with the data most readily explained by the theory and postpone investigation of the more difficult problems in hopes that they can be explained later in the light of subsequent findings. Often this turns out to be the case. Even so there are some anomalies that remain unexplained. As these anomalies accumulate, normal science enters a crisis period. Eventually someone comes forward with a new way of looking at the facts, a new theory that not only provides a different way of looking at conventional facts but furnishes an explanation for the former anomalies as well. The new theory leads to a new paradigm that redirects the practice of normal science. The change amounts to a scientific revolution. Those who have invested their lives in the old paradigm may resist the change, but younger scientists who see the new paradigm as more promising turn to it and abandon the old paradigm. Textbooks are written from the vantage point of the new theory, and past achievements in the discipline are reinterpreted in the light of current theoretical beliefs. Younger scientists rising to positions of prominence within the field tend to disparage the work of their predecessors.

Kuhn's description of scientific revolutions was originally presented with reference to the natural sciences, but it should be evident that the same view of development through revolution can be applied, at least in broad outline, to the history of linguistic concepts. We have attempted to trace the development of linguistic concepts by examining five different theoretical approaches and surveying language data using the concepts and methodology employed by each theory. Each theoretical approach has adopted the conceptual tools of its predecessor but has redefined the subject matter to set up new problems and goals. Each approach has also refined the methodology inherited from its predecessors to make it more suitable to current needs. These developments were traced in Chapters 2 through 7. Chapters 8 through 10 focus on topics that are not directly concerned with theory but must be dealt with regardless of the theoretical approach adopted. The initial and concluding chapters attempt to provide a framework for the entire study. Although an effort has been made to present each theory in its own terms, it would be a mistake to suppose that any study is completely free of theoretical bias. The admitted bias of this book has been the semanticist approach of Chafe's meaning-structure grammar. Readers must judge for themselves whether this approach constitutes a new paradigm for the study of language or is merely an aberration that fails to offer anything that cannot be provided as well or better by other models.

Traditional grammar did not always state its theoretical position explicitly. Part of its theoretical position, in fact, was that language structures could often be understood without an explicit description.

Historical grammar was self-consciously explicit in declaring both its goals and methods. Structural grammar adopted these methods while redefining the goals to concentrate on synchronic description. Structuralists frequently denied the possibility that language data could be expected to fit into any fixed set of categories. This position, far from representing the absence of theory, was part of a theoretical orientation that sought to analyze each language in terms of its own structure and was determined to avoid imposing predetermined structural categories on a language. For structuralists this commitment was necessary if they were to be faithful to the data they were describing. Analysis and description of data were the ultimate goals of structuralism.

The anomaly of structural grammar, as far as transformationalists were concerned, was its failure to deal effectively with syntax. The remedy was a formal description couched in phrase structure and transformational rules. The paradigm that emerged was one in which language could be viewed as a formal system, and the properties of human language as well as human mental abilities in general could be equated with properties of the formal system used in describing language. Inevitably transformational grammar has been theory-oriented rather than data-oriented.

The present discontent with transformational theory stems from the anomalous position of semantics in the model. Transformationalists disagree as to whether semantics can be described adequately by an "extended standard theory" or whether a major revision of the model such as "generative semantics" is required. Meaning-structure grammar is not an attractive alternative to those who have been schooled in transformational theory and are committed to it professionally. But for those not already committed to transformational theory, there is no sentiment for clinging to the old model whether the revisions are major or minor. With no ego involvement in the immediate past, the preference of nontransformationalists is for a sharp break with the current syntacticist approach and a new model redefining the scope of linguistic inquiry and emphasizing the primacy of semantics. Such an approach, the argument goes, will enable linguists to deal with the anomalies of the syntacticist paradigm and to gain a better perspective on linguistics as a field of inquiry without sacrificing the precision and explicitness associated with transformational theory.

11.3 GOALS OF LINGUISTIC THEORY

The obvious goal of linguistic theory is to provide a framework for understanding and describing language. But this of course cannot be accomplished apart from the understanding and description of individual languages. And, to be realistic, we must recognize that understanding and description is a rather broad goal attainable only through the achievement of several more specific objectives. In the past the goals of linguistic theory have been stated—or tacitly assumed—in varying ways in different periods. Given the history of linguistics and the range of present interests, it seems reasonable to expect linguistic theory to provide a unified and coherent set of conceptual tools for accomplishing four diverse but interrelated tasks.

1. It must provide a framework for the comprehensive synchronic description of individual languages.
2. It must make possible cross-linguistic statements about two or more languages, even when the languages are quite different typologically.
3. It must be able to account for the diachronic development of individual languages and language families.
4. It must provide a framework for describing the stages through which children pass in the process of acquiring the full grammar of their native language.

A number of additional goals could possibly be mentioned. Linguistic theory should perhaps have something to say about the relationship between language and cognition, or language and culture, or language and thought processes. One might expect linguistic theory to deal with philosophical questions of language and reality or pedagogical questions relating to foreign-language learning or the problems of learning to read and write one's native language. Perhaps linguistic theory should be related to the neural representation of language or to computer languages, including problems of machine translation. Or one might desire a theory that relates language to broader issues in the study of symbolic behavior and communication systems—for example, to the relationship between animal communication and human language. Each of these topics is important and each clearly impinges on the legitimate interests of linguistics. But these need not be taken as primary goals of linguistic theory. Each topic is subsidiary to the four primary goals given above, and an increased understanding in each of these subsidiary areas is likely to come as a by-product of achievements in one of the primary areas.

Of the four goals enumerated above, the first has been an integral part of every theoretical approach to language study. Although synchronic description was deemphasized in historical grammar, it was nevertheless taken for granted as a prerequisite for diachronic analysis. Synchronic description was of course the primary goal of traditional grammar and has been the chief goal of structural grammar and its successors.

The second goal is one that has received little direct attention in any school of linguistics, although it has often been an implicit matter of concern. The interest of traditional grammar in language universals, which tended to be equated with the surface categories of Greco-Latin grammar, might be considered a form of cross-linguistic analysis. Historical grammar was interested in cross-linguistic statements only to the extent that such statements were evidence of genetic relations. Structural grammar emphasized the uniqueness of each language's structural system, but structuralists were actively involved in language teaching, a process that involves learning to map a semantic structure onto the surface structures of two or more different languages. Transformational grammar resurrected the quest for linguistic universals in terms of phrase structure rules and transformational rules. Implicit in meaning-structure grammar is the assumption that all languages can be described in terms of a universal set of semantic units and various rules for arranging these units.

The third goal, diachronic description, was the focus of historical grammar; but linguists since the time of Saussure have made a point of distinguishing between the practice of diachronic and synchronic description. The distinction is useful and necessary. But since numerous features that are synchronic anomalies can be explained quite reasonably as the result of diachronic processes, it seems self-defeating to omit such observations from synchronic descriptions. The comprehensive description of language including all relevant material —synchronic and diachronic as well—has sometimes been called **panchronic** description.

Finally the study of native language acquisition, a study that began in the structural period and has risen to prominence in the transformational era, is rightly seen by Chomsky and others as providing valuable insight into the mental processes that underlie language. This study has been handicapped thus far by the need to describe different stages of the acquisition process in very different formats. Thus, some scholars speak of a one-word stage, a two-word stage, a syntactic stage, and so forth—as though each stage is organized according to a different grammatical scheme. Surely the entire process is organized according to a single set of overall principles, and whatever these principles are, they must be describable in semantic terms and relatable to an experiential-behavioral paradigm that is part of the child's world.

11.4 THE NATURE OF EVIDENCE

For the linguist normal science consists of analyzing and describing language data. This is ordinarily done with a specific purpose in mind, such as constructing a synchronic grammar, and makes use of the concepts provided by a particular theory. But the construction of a grammar is also a way of testing the theory. If the concepts provided by the theory suffice to describe the data, the theory is strengthened. If the data is not amenable to analysis in terms of existing theory, the linguist may be led to propose revisions in the theory. Testing and revising the theory has in fact been the primary interest of transformationalists, rather than the analysis and description of data as such. (This is one reason we have spoken of transformational grammar as theory-oriented rather than data-oriented.) It is of course preferable to propose refinements in an otherwise workable theory and avoid discarding the basic theory if at all possible. Only when anomalies accumulate to such an extent that a new theory is needed to make sense of the data is replacement of the basic theory necessary.

Theory and data are equally essential to the practice of normal science. Theory guides the analysis and description of data, a process that in turn tests the theory and either confirms its usefulness, points the way to refinement, or leads to its abandonment and replacement by a different theory. Data analysis without regard to an overall theory would be as valueless as an analysis that forced all data into predetermined molds or one that used data only for the purpose of bolstering a particular theoretical position. These are extremes that the linguist, like scientists in other fields, must be careful to avoid.

What then is the proper interplay of theory and data? How does the linguist avoid circularity in relating data to theory? What counts as evidence for or against a given analysis? A theory invariably prescribes the kind of evidence to be used within the theory, and the prescribed evidence almost inevitably leads to an analysis of conformity with the theory. It is only when investigators begin to ask whether or not the theory is directed to the real issues that there is any genuine possibility of switching from one theoretical position to another.

Traditional grammarians were generally satisfied with the descriptive model based on Greco-Latin grammar that they attempted to apply to all languages. It was only when investigators began to ask questions about language similarities that could be answered in terms of genetic relationships and historical development that a new paradigm was possible. In the new paradigm investigators sought to establish genetic relations by looking for sound correspondences in cognate words drawn from languages presumed to be related. This is a circular approach. Linguists first hypothesize on the basis of informal inspection that the similarities they encounter indicate a genetic relationship. Then with this presumption in mind, they set out to collect sound correspondences to validate the hypothesis, taking care to confine the search to true cognates while excluding borrowings and chance resemblances. In the ideal situation all phonological data would eventually be assigned to a particular sound correspondence or else ruled out as noncognate—that is, either a borrowing or some other postseparation vocabulary innovation. In actual practice a substantial amount of data may remain indeterminate.

But even with a residue of unanalyzed data, linguists eventually reach a point where they are satisfied that the hypothesis of genetic relationship has been sustained. Evidence for particular language relationships naturally counts as evidence in support of the genetic theory of language in general.

The development of genetic linguistics led to an understanding of language as system, but it remained for Saussure to ask if the systematic description of language could not be applied synchronically as well as diachronically. Once the question was raised, a new paradigm was possible. As structural grammar was eventually codified by American linguists, the rules of evidence became quite rigidly established. Phonemic systems (i.e., allophones and their distribution) were to be described using only phonetic evidence. Morphological systems (i.e., morphemes and their allomorphs) were to be described using the previously defined phonemes. Syntactic patterns could then be described using the units provided by the morphological analysis. In part this approach was adopted to break away from the process statements of historical linguistics, but in part it was motivated by a desire to avoid contamination of one structural system by data from another, presumably unrelated, system. The description of several autonomous components was also suited to the emphasis on describing observable data without drawing inferences about mental processes.

The replacement of the structural paradigm by transformational grammar came about as virtually all of these assumptions were challenged. Pike (1947a, 1952) adduced evidence to suggest that phonemic analysis was often dependent on the prior availability of a grammatical analysis, rather than the other way around. Chomsky argued that process rules, rather than being rejected on principle, could simplify both phonological and grammatical descriptions. But the failure of structural grammar to deal systematically and exhaustively with syntax was Chomsky's special target. His insistence on explicit descriptions and his willingness to posit abstract underlying forms set the stage for a new paradigm and opened the way for a theory that was willing to relate observable linguistic behavior to presumed mental processes.

Because of its original focus on syntax, transformational theory has tended to emphasize syntactic evidence at all levels of description. Thus, the notion of grammatical description as a prerequisite to phonological analysis was readily accepted. Since the basic unit of description was the sentence, grammatical description itself was accomplished by noting syntactic variation in similar sentences, attributing these sentences to a single underlying structure, and positing formal transformational rules for realizing the surface variants. The process of course is circular. Surface variants are used as evidence for underlying forms, and the underlying forms thus posited are used to account for the surface variants. As an increasing number of these circular arguments are assembled, however, they begin to form a coherent system that gains in credibility as it approaches a total description of a language.

The fact that certain sentences are "similar" was taken as self-evident in the early stages of transformational theory. Later it was recognized that the similarity depended on common semantic content, but by this time transformationalists were in the position of attempting to describe semantics in terms of a previously completed syntactic description. This anomaly is at the heart of the questions that are now being raised both within the transformational paradigm and outside it. The proposed remedies range from minor refinements (Chomsky's "extended standard theory") to more drastic revision ("generative semantics") to replacement by a new paradigm.

The questions being raised by Chafe and others experimenting with meaning-structure grammar are essentially the same as those being raised within the transformational paradigm. The answers are vastly different, however. The questions as raised within meaning-structure grammar imply a new paradigm. The fundamental issue is whether language can best be described in terms of syntactic or semantic units. Must phonology and semantics alike be described in terms of their relation to syntax, or can syntax be described in terms of its underlying semantic structure and phonology described in terms of syntax and semantics? In large part this is a restatement of the question raised earlier by transformational grammar with respect to structural grammar: Are the components of language autonomous or is there a fixed directionality of mapping from one component to another? Is the sentence the basic unit for linguistic analysis or are there discourse-related semantic features that carry over from one sentence to the next and determine the structure of successive sentences? Is a syntacticist or semanticist approach more useful in describing such phenomena as the one-word stage of native-language acquisition, structural variation within a language through time, and structural differences between languages? Finally can a theory that deals only with linguistic competence be preferred to one that deals with both competence and performance?

The evidence treated as admissible in the meaning-structure paradigm is little different from other schools insofar as the identification of surface units is concerned. The analysis of these units, however, relies more heavily than other schools on the identification of semantic units. The assumption is that speakers of a language use their language to convey meaning and are aware of (or at least can become attuned to) subtle differences of meaning in surface structure. These differences in surface paradigms can be correlated with differences in experiential-behavioral paradigms that can be independently verified by other speakers of the same language. The resulting analysis provides a semantic base for describing the surface categories of syntax and phonology. The assumption is that such an analysis is not only optimal as a formal system but is a faithful representation of language as a system of communication.

11.5 NORMAL SCIENCE

Scientific inquiry cannot take place apart from a theory, whether or not the theory is stated explicitly. The theory determines one's assumptions about the nature of the subject, the kind of questions to be asked, the kind of evidence to be sought, and the use to be made of the evidence collected. Thus, for the traditional grammarian the study of language was closely identified with pedagogical interests, either the teaching of foreign languages or the mastery of rhetorical skills in one's native language. Scholarly activity, as often as not, resulted in the production of pedagogical grammars.

For the historical linguist normal science was an intellectual exercise involving the tracing of language relationships and, for some practitioners at least, considering questions of man's place in nature. Scholarly activity was expressed in articles discussing evidence for genetic relationships—for example, a particular sound change—or in compendious works such as comparative grammars.

For structuralists normal science was, above everything, dedication to the study of language data. Of special interest were "exotic" languages—those that had not traditionally been studied by Europeans and that had structures quite different from the familiar European languages. For some the attraction was the fact that these languages were seemingly a key to the study of human diversity. The attraction was made all the more urgent by the spread of European culture that was threatening many of these languages with extinction. For other linguists the motivating factor was one that has often been an influence in language study—the desire to spread a particular religious teaching. Scholarly activity was characterized by the production of grammatical sketches, complete grammars, the collection of texts in the language being studied, the compilation of dictionaries, and (for some) the translation of religious materials.

In transformational grammar, with its emphasis on theory, many linguists have shown a disinclination to deal with languages other than their native language, where they are already familiar with the surface categories. Those who have analyzed other languages have often done so to test a theoretical point rather than because of any interest in the language itself. Scholarly effort has tended toward papers and monographs dealing with theoretical problems. Many scholars have become specialized, dealing only with phonology or only with syntax. The result has been a number of monographs dealing with overall theory and a multitude of short papers dealing with narrow theoretical issues, but few efforts to construct complete grammars of any language. The outsider often has the feeling of looking at a string of railroad cars, each perfectly formed by itself but no two having the same kind of coupler.

It remains to be seen whether or not an alternative model such as meaning-structure grammar will restore a proper balance between theory and data, but the record thus far is promising. Chafe himself was schooled in the structuralist tradition of undertaking a thorough description of an unfamiliar language, and his students have so far shown an interest in working on complete grammars. The interests of meaning-structure grammar coincide with many of the theoretical issues debated by transformationalists; but at the same time meaning-structure grammar represents a return, at least in part, to the data orientation of structural grammar. Meaning-structure grammar, like transformational grammar, claims an interface with psychology and philosophy but, unlike transformational grammar, also has a strong interest in matters that have traditionally been associated with anthropology—for example, the relation between language and culture, the development of human language from primate communication, and the like. For anyone working within the meaning-structure paradigm, therefore, the practice of normal science is certain to be quite different from what has been taken for granted in recent years.

The fact that a particular activity is emphasized during one era does not necessarily mean that the activity is abandoned entirely in subsequent eras. The interest in language teaching that dates from the era of traditional grammar has remained strong to the present day. Modern programs in foreign-language teaching are still indebted to traditional grammar, but the insights of structural grammar have also had a profound influence, particularly in the years since World War II. Traditional grammar remains the foundation on which all approaches to linguistics since the beginning of the nineteenth century have been based. Traditional grammar, in one version or another, is still the basis for language arts instruction in most school systems, although, to be sure, the presentation is often informed by the insights of other theoretical approaches.

Similarly, once it developed, historical linguistics has never been without its practitioners—even though the spotlight has shifted to synchronic studies in the present century. Structuralists have quietly continued their study of data even while the theoretical debates of transformationalists have held center stage. Transformationalists are likely to continue their study of syntax and formal systems even if younger linguists adopt a different paradigm. Ultimately, one hopes, linguists will be in a position to develop an eclectic theory of language that is adequate to the requirements of the subject matter itself.

11.6 REAL ISSUES AND PSEUDO-ISSUES

At professional meetings and in journal articles, scholars devote a great deal of energy to thoughtful discussions of what seem to be the crucial issues in their discipline. Such activity is part of normal science. Unfortunately, the issues of one generation often have a way of appearing pointless to a later generation approaching the subject with different assumptions. Thus, linguists no longer ask whether or not sound laws can admit exceptions, nor do they lose sleep when they discover a phone that seems to be an allophone of two different phonemes. Current issues focus instead on whether semantics should be generative or interpretive, what constraints should be imposed on transformations, whether transformations preserve meaning or change meaning, and the like. These questions are relevant of course only within a framework of certain assumptions about language and the role of transformational rules in language. If the underlying assumptions are rejected, the questions themselves become pseudo-issues.

We can easily think of topics that all linguists would reject as pseudo-issues. Questions dealing with the classification of language families that supposedly came into being at the Tower of Babel would fall into this category. So too would the question of how language differences are determined by racial differences. Other topics, for example, the ordering of linearization rules, are like questions relating to transformational rules: they are real issues only within a particular framework of theoretical assumptions that some may embrace and others reject.

Real issues, as distinct from pseudo-issues, are questions that, if answered, would have a bearing on the choice of one theory over another. Such issues are fairly easy to identify; the difficulty is that there is no way to deal with them in an atmosphere completely unbiased by the theoretical controversies they are supposed to resolve.

Thus, we might wish to ask whether semantics is essentially abstract or concrete. If abstract, we would expect to find meaning extremely vague and subjective. It would be elusive and variable from one person to the next, even within the same language community. If essentially concrete, we would expect meaning to be a structured system consisting of analyzable components arranged according to fixed patterns that would be shared by all speakers within a language community. Impartial investigators can answer such a question only by setting out to test the belief they have about language in the first place. And to do this they cannot really be impartial.

A number of similar issues can also be identified. Among these are questions relating to rule formalisms (§11.8), language and culture (§11.9), and rationalism as opposed to empiricism (§11.10). Each of these topics will be considered in detail, in hopes of bringing the real issues into focus. It seems reasonable to suggest that, even though these questions seem to be genuine issues today, they too may become pseudo-issues as a new consensus emerges among linguists.

11.7 ALTERNATIVE MODELS

The discussion thus far has centered on five theoretical models. These were chosen for several reasons. Each is a well-defined model enjoying enough support within the academic community that it must be taken seriously. Each has a body of literature available for further study. The five approaches cover the full range of interests that linguists have claimed as their field of study. And these approaches, taken together, represent a progression of thought from ancient times to the present. Several other approaches should be mentioned at this point, however, even though they will not be discussed in detail.

The development of American structuralism, which has continued without interruption since the emergence of transformational grammar, has often been termed **tagmemics.** The most prominent figure in this school has been Kenneth Pike, a scholar of broad interests whose writings have dealt with phonetics, phonemics, syntax, translation problems, and the integration of language study with the study of human behavior in general.

The **Prague School,** active in the 1930s, was a group of European scholars with wide-ranging interests. Prominent among them were the phonologist Nikolai Troubetzkoy and the versatile Roman Jakobson, whose interests have ranged from child language to the linguistic study of literature. Jakobson, who eventually settled in the United States, was instrumental in developing the theory of distinctive features in phonology. His work, and that of the Prague School in general, has had a strong influence on transformational theory.

The work of the Danish linguist Louis Hjelmslev built on the notions of Saussure and emphasized the formal structure of language. His work influenced European logicians and, through them, has had an indirect impact on transformational theory. A more direct influence has been on Sydney Lamb, whose **stratificational grammar** has been proposed as an alternative to transformational theory. Stratificational grammar is a formal system for describing language by means of several distinct strata including, among others, a semantic stratum and a phonetic stratum. The model has attracted less attention than transformational theory but nevertheless has a number of adherents and a growing body of literature.

A British school headed by J. R. Firth has developed an independent approach sometimes called **system-structure grammar.** Although Firth was influenced by the anthropologist Malinowski and a British phonetics tradition dating back to the nineteenth century, his approach is distinctly original and can be seen as an outgrowth of efforts to describe the varied languages of Africa and Asia that became part of the British Commonwealth. Firth's efforts were directed primarily to phonological description, but his associate M. A. K. Halliday has turned his attention to syntax as well and has had an influence on the work of Chafe and other American linguists.

The work of Soviet linguists has not gained wide circulation in the English-speaking world, largely because so few non-Soviet linguists are able to read Russian. Some of Sebastian K. Šaumjan's work, which he terms **applicative grammar,** is now available in translation. His writing, although criticized by American transformationalists, belongs in the library of any serious student of language.

Finally the **dependency grammar** of David Hays and his associates is an effort to develop a formal system emphasizing the dependency relations between verbs and nouns within a sentence and the dependency of other sentence elements on the nouns and verbs that make up the core of the sentence. Conceptually the approach is similar to meaning-structure grammar, but its quasi-mathematical formalizations are much closer to transformational theory.

11.8 LANGUAGE AND RULE FORMALISMS

Much of the recent work in linguistics has involved the analysis of language in terms of formal rules. This has had the advantage of stressing the occurrence of regular patterns in language, but it has also led to the introduction of extraneous issues. Chomsky (1972b) for example has dismissed case grammar and generative semantics as mere "notational variants" of his own theory. Whether this claim is a valid assertion or empty rhetoric cannot be determined in the absence of an explicit definition of notational equivalence, something that Chomsky has not provided. The real issue therefore seems to be whether or not a way can be found to determine when two systems are equivalent and, if not equivalent, to specify the differences.

Similarly the reliance on rule formalisms has led to the assumption that language learning is essentially a matter of learning rules and that language change is a matter of making changes in rules. To bring things into perspective, it should be emphasized that speakers of a language do not learn rules as such. Languages do not come in the form of rules to be learned. A language is a body of data. Speakers learn language data, and from this they abstract their own rules to account for the patterns in the data. Two speakers of the same language, who use much the same language patterns, will naturally abstract essentially the same rules from the data. And as language patterns change, the rules describing these patterns will also change. The rules themselves are not language but a description of language. The locus of the rule is the individual speaker—or linguist—not the language itself.

The real issue in this case is not the formal structure of rules or the reality of rules. The issue should be the relationship between rules and data—that is, an accurate description of surface structure and a reasonable set of rules to account for the observed data. The reality of the rules cannot be dealt with directly but can only be approached in terms of what one expects the rules to do. Should they describe competence or performance? Can they be applicable to both? Should they be an independent formal system, or should they be related to cognitive categories as well? These questions return us to the basic question of what one happens to believe language is.

11.9 LANGUAGE AND CULTURE

The assumption of linguists in recent years has been that formal grammars are in some way isomorphic with mental processes. For transformationalists this has involved the additional assumption that the formalisms of transformational grammar somehow reflect the inner workings of the mind. The approach has been to relate rule formalisms to presumed mental processes rather than trying first to identify mental processes and then devise rule statements to represent these processes.

Certainly language is related to cognition, and cognition in turn is related to the cultural setting. Language is a product of culture, but at the same time it is a system that is largely, if not fully, isomorphic with culture. The difficulties of separating language from culture become apparent as soon as we consider the complexities of teaching language to a computer. For the human language user (as noted in §10.5) the neural patterns that are presumably expressible as language are also related to sensory input—that is, to a knowledge of the world around us. This knowledge is built into the experience of every language user. Thus, any first-grader could read and understand the following passage (Winograd 1974:75):

> Tommy had just been given a new set of blocks. He was opening the box when he saw Jimmy coming in.

What was in the box? A computer would have no way of knowing because the passage does not specify the contents of the box or even indicate a connection between the new blocks of the first sentence and the box of the second sentence. But human language users assume they are dealing with a connected message. They know that new items often come in boxes and that one naturally opens a box to get at the contents. The answer has to be the blocks. A process of inference is involved, but the process is so dependent on previous experience that it is difficult to imagine programming a computer to reach a human level of understanding on the basis of responding to words alone.

A distinction between competence and performance is useful in the early stages of an investigation, when the observer must systematically disregard elements that are extraneous to the underlying pattern. But the distinction loses its usefulness when it begins to prevent rather than facilitate an account of how competence and performance are related. Such an account must of course be given a cultural setting and must eventually be related to a theory of cognition. Winograd's observation on the nature of understanding provides the proper framework for approaching the real issues: "A sentence does not 'convey' meaning the way a truck conveys cargo, complete and packaged. It is more like a blueprint that allows the hearer to reconstruct the meaning from his own knowledge" (1974:75).

11.10 RATIONALISM AND EMPIRICISM

The more language has been studied, the more linguists have marveled at its complexity. Yet language is so easily learned that small children master it within the first few years of life. Since mastery of a language involves a complex analytical feat that most adults (including linguists) find difficult, linguists in recent years have felt obligated to explain the language-learning facility of small children. The explanation that has gained favor among transformationalists holds that humans have an innate ability to use language—that is, an ability to use grammars having specified formal properties.

It has been pointed out by Chomsky and others that all natural languages make use of certain types of rules and never use other types (§10.4). For example, natural languages invariably form questions by modifying declarative statements in specific ways—either by inverting certain major sentence constituents, by adding a question particle, by changing the intonation pattern, or some combination of these. Questions are not formed in any language by permuting each odd-numbered word in the sentence with the following word, although this is an operation that would be simple for a computer. Facts such as this have been interpreted as an indication that humans are pre-programmed to master languages having rules of a highly specific type. Advocates of this viewpoint have argued that they are continuing the rationalist philosophy of Descartes and others (§10.8). They see themselves as diametrically opposed to the empiricist viewpoint of earlier philosophers such as Locke and represented today by behaviorists such as B. F. Skinner.

To consider the merits of the rationalist position, it is important to know what the claim actually means. At one extreme it can be interpreted as meaning that humans are born with an innate knowledge of transformational rules and that the task of learning a language is basically a problem of learning which transformational rules are actually operative in the language to be learned. This is a strong claim, but one that is inherently incapable of either confirmation or falsification. A much weaker claim would be simply that humans have certain biological equipment: organs capable of producing speech sounds and intellectual abilities of a very general sort that can form associations useful in the process of learning and using language. Such a claim is a self-evident truth, a mere triviality. But a theory that holds that the language learner starts with no genetically programmed abilities at all is equally absurd.

Any effort to look at all the facts requires us to acknowledge that humans are biological organisms and that their behavior must have points in common with the behavior of other organisms (§7.2). We would expect humans, in the course of evolution, to have developed certain genetic adaptations to their environment. We would expect them to engage in behavior that they find easy because of their physical make-up, and to avoid behavior that is physically difficult. We might also expect that certain behavior, even if difficult and even if imperfectly accomplished, might have been added to the human behavioral repertoire in the remote past because its usefulness offset its inherent difficulty.

Early humans were faced with a number of limitations. They were not physically endowed with teeth or claws that would make them natural hunters, but their ability to balance on two feet, manipulate objects in their hands, and work cooperatively with others of their species more than compensated for their physical shortcomings. For a creature adjusting to new surroundings, manual dexterity and cooperative behavior would be adaptive because such behavior would enhance one's ability to survive. In time these traits would be strengthened as individuals possessing the favorable traits matured and reproduced in greater numbers while individuals with less-favorable traits failed to survive. This is not to suggest that the traits themselves had to be transmitted genetically. It is enough that genes for a certain type of hand structure, or vocal tract structure, or neurological structure can be transmitted; the behavior exploiting the physical endowment remains largely a matter of social transmission. It must be learned anew by each generation.

What are the unique biological capacities of humans that enter into the use of language? A specialized foot and upright posture, while not directly related to speech production, are inseparable from our overall way of life. So is a hand with an opposable thumb and advanced manipulative ability. These specialized appendages were selectively developed as early humans established themselves in an ecological niche requiring a high degree of cooperative effort and problem-solving ability.

Upright posture and a manipulative hand do not develop in isolation from the neural mechanisms that control motor skills. Nor does a problem-solving ability develop apart from the development of the associative centers of the brain. It is pointless to ask whether an enlarged, complex brain led to expanded motor and symbolic skills or whether these skills led to increased brain size. The two developed together, each contributing to the further development of the other in a feedback relationship over long periods of time. The vocal tract too must have been involved in these changes. What began as a primate call system acquired greater phonetic flexibility as the vocal tract approached its present configuration. Along with these developments the signaling system itself had to expand to meet the needs of increased cooperation imposed by a new way of life.

We can imagine that the inventory of holistic signals increased and that some of these signals were combined with other signals to form messages of increased complexity. During this period, as the number of holistic signals (calls) increased, many calls must have contained phonetically similar sounds. With only a few calls to distinguish, a user of the system would not have to pay close attention to the individual parts of each call. But with an expanded number of calls, the sequential arrangement of component sounds would play an increasingly important part in differentiating signals. If a communication system that was more complex than that of other primates but less complex than that of modern languages had any social usefulness at all, it is natural that early humans would have incorporated it into their behavioral repertoire even if it required special effort at first. But it seems likely that the use of even a simple call system would have favored the transmission, genetically and socially, of traits that would predispose successive generations to make ever-increasing use of the system. Such a predisposition to behavioral patterns that later prove useful has been called **preadaptation.**

At some point—perhaps quite unconsciously—users of the system reanalyzed the holistic calls in terms of a duality: abstract components on one hand and patterns of arrangement on the other (§7.2–7.3). At this point users of a call system became speakers of a language. Reanalysis of a system is simply a matter of forming a new association. Prehumans must have been forming many new associations all the time. A stick could become a tool, a weapon, or part of a shelter. All that really is needed to give rise to language is a very general ability to form new associations, to recognize analogies, to classify two items as same or different—the very abilities that remain essential to the present day.

To argue that language is "innate" or that it is "learned" is to over-look the fact that it is an intricate combination of both innate and learned behavior. A full understanding of language behavior must in-clude an understanding of communicative behavior in general. Much remains to be done in clarifying the relationship between innate capacities and learned behavior as these relate to language. But seri-ous work cannot begin until we start asking the right questions. Lan-guage is admittedly complex; yet it is simple enough for a child to master in the first years of life. The complexities of modern language must certainly have sprung from a fairly simple system. Accounting for this curious blend of simplicity and complexity may prove to be more challenging and more productive than dealing with philosophical issues like rationalism and empiricism.

11.11 LANGUAGE AS COMMUNICATION

Once established, language must have had tremendous adaptive value for early humans. It facilitated cooperation, made possible the ac-cumulation and transmission of knowledge, and no doubt enhanced a human propensity to set problem-solving tasks for oneself. We need not speculate about the complexity of humankind's first "language" as distinct from earlier call systems. 'Me chase; you kill' is just as effective as 'I'll go chase the animals past you, and you kill one of them when it runs by.' The trappings of modern language are but a superficial addition to a call system that developed duality. The real breakthrough came with duality of patterning; everything else follows from that. It is unnecessary (and in principle impossible) to determine whether language originated in a single human community or in several communities simultaneously. We know it happened at least once; that is enough.

The question of just when language may have developed is one that we can come closer to answering. We have fairly extensive knowledge of the circumstances of life surrounding *Australopithecus* (3 million to 1 million years ago), *Homo erectus* (1 million to 250,000 years ago), and *Homo sapiens* (250,000 years ago to the present). Dates of course are approximations because of the many variables in classifying and interpreting fossil remains.

Homo erectus by about 500,000 years ago used fire, hunted, and had a culture roughly comparable to that of present-day hunting-and-gathering people. This type of life presupposes language as a tool for social organization. Language in turn presupposes a long develop-mental period during which auditory discrimination is developing, the phonetic range of vocal signals is expanding, and the neural ca-pacity for speech is developing. We assume that these physical changes developed slowly and that even when the physical changes accumulated to the point of speciation (e.g., from *Australopithecus* to *Homo erectus* to *Homo sapiens*) cultural changes were slow to follow. If cultural changes followed immediately on speciation, we would expect civilization to have emerged as soon as *Homo sapiens* replaced *Homo erectus*—and this was not the case.

Very likely *Homo sapiens* had language at the outset—that is, by transmission from *erectus* forbears—if the assumptions we have made about *erectus* are correct. *Homo erectus* in turn must have received at least an elaborate call system from their australopithecine ancestors. The most conservative estimate would place the development of duality (and true language) at 500,000 years ago, about midway through the era of *Homo erectus*. If we assume, less conservatively, that late australopithecines had a fully developed language, the development could still have taken place as recently as 1 million years ago. Such a chronology would attribute the developmental, prelanguage period to the earlier australopithecines and allow a developmental period of as much as 3 million years. To push the origin of language back much farther than 1.5 million years would require attribution of at least part of the developmental period to preaustralopithecines. While this is not impossible in itself, it might lead us to look for a somewhat earlier emergence of the social and technological complexities that language could be expected to facilitate—for example, coordinated hunting and the use of fire.

Until quite recently anthropologists have assumed that modern chimpanzees have a vocal apparatus suitable for speech production and lack only the requisite mental ability. Recent experimental work with chimpanzees suggests, however, that just the opposite may be true. Chimpanzees are able to manipulate nonverbal symbolic systems such as the sign language of the deaf or a syntactic code using plastic chips of different colors and shapes. The chimpanzees involved in these studies, Washoe and Sarah, have displayed communicative ability that might be compared to that of a three-year-old human child. Chimpanzees seem to have much more mental ability than has previously been supposed. But for some reason chimpanzees find it difficult to use vocalization as a communicative channel.

Chimpanzees in the wild are highly social animals, but their inventory of vocalizations is quite restricted. Their communication seemingly depends more on visual and physical contact than on vocalization as such. The success of Washoe and Sarah in learning to communicate with humans strongly suggests that chimpanzees have developed in such a way that they are preadapted to communication systems using a visual channel. But even though chimpanzees, of all primates, are closest to humans in physical make-up and mental ability, they have followed a way of life that did not require them to exploit this preadaptation. Nor did their way of life contain inducements to develop any other specialized communication channel.

Other primates, for example, vervet monkeys, a common African species, make rather extensive use of vocalization for communicative purposes. Their way of life, which includes foraging in trees where leaves may hide members of the group from one another, has evidently favored development of a vocal communication channel since this channel is not hindered by lack of visual contact. Struhsaker (1967) has identified thirty-six distinct signals, making the vervet system the most elaborate communication system of the living nonhuman primates. The system is organized like the animal communication system shown in Figure 7–1, which is reproduced in summary form as Figure 11–1. The diagram is not intended to represent the actual system of the vervet monkeys or any other animal. Rather, it is intended to represent the organization of the system itself. A conceptual unit (represented in capitals to the left of the arrow) is symbolized by a holistic unit of sound (represented in small letters to the right of the arrow). The arrow itself represents the process of symbolization. The system contains a finite number of conceptual units, each symbolized in a specified way. The sounds used for symbolization may be accompanied by postures, facial expressions, and gestures—features that accompany human language as well. These features, sometimes called body language, are quite important in animal communication systems, where both vocalizations and the accompanying postures are directed primarily at conveying information about the emotional state of the sender. Human language has elaborated the potential for transmitting nonemotive informational content and consequently has reduced the importance of body language. Body language continues to accompany language but is restricted to its original function of conveying information about the sender's emotional state.

A comment on the theory of sign systems seems appropriate in connection with posturing before we turn to a consideration of human language. Signs can be divided into three categories: icons, indexes, and symbols. An icon is a sign containing a point-by-point resemblance to the object it depicts. Thus, a statue or picture of a horse is an icon of the horse. An index involves a logical connection between the sign and the object it represents. Thus, a horseshoe or the tracks left by hoofprints are indexes of a horse. Symbols are arbitrary signs having no necessary connection with the object represented. Thus, the words *horse* (in English), *Pferd* (in German), or *uma* (in Japanese) qualify as symbols. In communication, degree of loudness is often iconic with degree of emotional intensity. A threatening posture may be an index of anger. But the line between an index and a symbol is not easily drawn. Thus, baring one's teeth is an index of readiness to attack when it precedes an actual attack. But if displaced from a genuine intent to attack, it becomes a symbol of the possible rather than an index of the inevitable. The development of human language has depended on the elaboration of symbols while deemphasizing the importance of icons and indexes. It is not difficult therefore to imagine how sounds that began as indexes of a particular action or emotion could become symbols once they came to be used apart from the circumstances that first motivated them.

A model of human language, presented originally in Figure 1–3, is repeated here in more detail as Figure 11–2. A comparison of Figure 11–2 with 11–1 reveals striking similarities in overall design despite differences in the internal structure of the two communication systems. In animal communication an emotive-experiential unit is symbolized by an arrangement of sounds—accompanied of course by posturing, as noted above. The system is largely indexical, and because of the one-to-one relationship between content units and units of expression, it can be described as a direct symbolization system. The human communication system is vastly more complex. Experience is related in a reasonably direct way to a semantic structure that in turn is converted into a syntactic structure. This is symbolized lexically and modified phonologically before it is actually expressed as sound, an element of the physical world that enters into the experience of others who use the same communication system. In Figure 11–2 each of the four components is identified and its operation described. The system as represented in Figure 11–2 may appear simpler than it really is. Postsemantic processes and phonological processes are not simple one-step processes but are actually a series of steps occurring within the component shown to the right of the respective arrows. The symbolization arrow, however, is analogous to the arrow in a direct symbolization system. Because of the many steps preceding and following symbolization in human language, we have referred to language as an indirect symbolization system.

We have attempted to survey the approaches that have been adopted in the formal study of language up to the present time. These approaches represent a continuity of thought, although there have been important shifts in emphasis as well. These shifts have involved, among other things, different ways of looking at language and different assumptions about the nature of language. The way of looking at language that has just been summarized has been urged throughout the book as an approach likely to prove fruitful in the study of language. But it should be emphasized that language is sufficiently complex that no single approach can claim to be "correct" while all others are "incorrect." If any approach can be called "correct," it is whatever approach examines the subject without preconceived answers, with an openness to use whatever method of inquiry is suitable, and with a determination to work out a description that is faithful to the data. There is no simple way to tell the linguist in advance how to do this. Much depends on the linguist's breadth of experience in dealing with languages of varied structural types. Much depends on an awareness of what other linguists have done in the past. A broad background offers the best assurance of grasping the concepts and mastering the techniques that can lead to the answers. Ultimately it is important to

FIGURE 11-1   The Structure of Animal Communication: Direct Symbolization

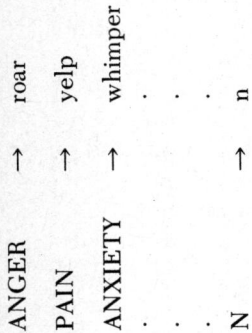

ANGER	→	roar
PAIN	→	yelp
ANXIETY	→	whimper
.	.	.
.	.	.
N	→	n

FIGURE 11-2   The Structure of Language: Indirect Symbolization

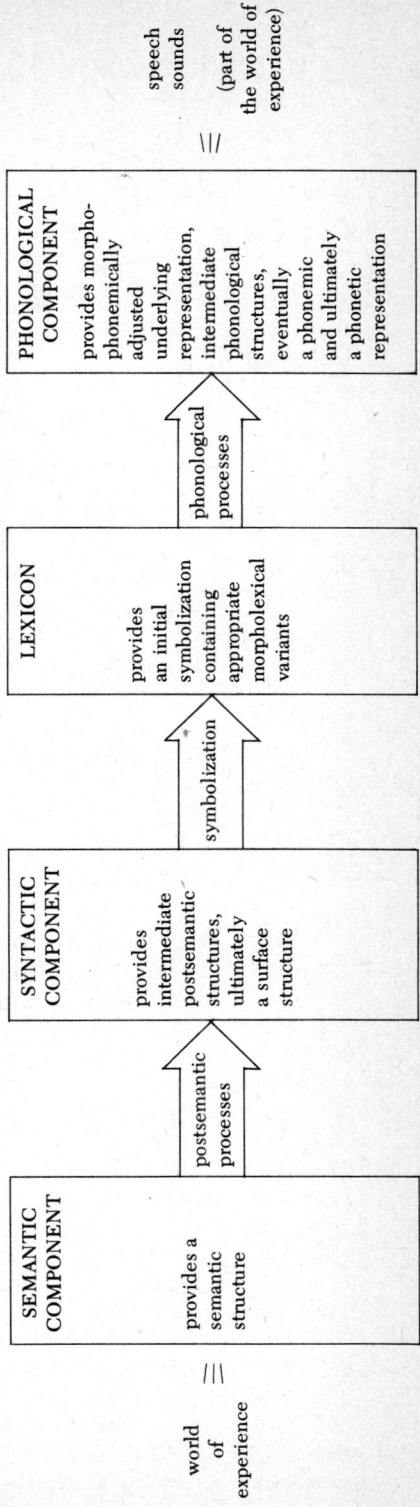

world
of
experience

≡

SEMANTIC COMPONENT		SYNTACTIC COMPONENT		LEXICON		PHONOLOGICAL COMPONENT
provides a semantic structure	postsemantic processes ⇨	provides intermediate postsemantic structures, ultimately a surface structure	symbolization ⇨	provides an initial symbolization containing appropriate morpholexical variants	phonological processes ⇨	provides morpho-phonemically adjusted underlying representation, intermediate phonological structures, eventually a phonemic and ultimately a phonetic representation

≡

speech
sounds

(part of
the world of
experience)

know what to look for. Insightful answers can come only by first asking the right questions.

summary

An adequate theory of language must be able to provide for synchronic description, diachronic description, cross-linguistic description, and the description of language acquisition. These goals have received different degrees of emphasis from the different schools of linguistics that have been considered in this book. But each of these schools—traditional grammar, historical grammar, structural grammar, transformational grammar, and meaning-structure grammar (as well as other schools)—must account for the totality of language. To do this a balance between theory and data is required. Language data must be analyzed in terms of the framework provided by a theory, but the adequacy of the theory to account for the data must undergo constant testing in the process. It is this interplay between theory and data that leads to progress in scientific investigations.

Real issues in linguistics, as distinct from pseudo-issues, are questions that, if answered, would have a bearing on the choice of one theory over another. Issues currently in need of clarification are the relationship between rules and data, the relationship between language and culture, and the relationship between innate and learned behavior in the process of learning one's native language. All of these questions have to do with language as an instrument of communication and with the relationship between human language and animal communication. More fundamentally, the real issues in linguistics call for an informed conception of what language, in its totality, is. Only by being well versed in a variety of theoretical approaches and having acquaintance with languages of varied structural types can linguists hope to advance their discipline.

further reading

General: Waterman 1963, Garvin 1970, Davis 1973, A. Makkai 1975, Hymes 1974. **11.2** Kuhn 1970, Percival 1976. **11.4** Pike 1947a, 1952. **11.6** Pap 1976. **11.7 General:** Parret 1974. **Tagmemics:** Waterhouse 1975, Pike 1967, Cook 1969, Brend 1973, Longacre 1964, Elson and Pickett 1960. **Prague School:** Vachek 1966. **Stratificational grammar:** Hjelmslev 1963, 1970, Lamb 1966, D. Lockwood 1972, Makkai and Lockwood 1973. **System-structure grammar:** Firth 1968, Halliday 1961, 1967–68, 1970. **Applicative grammar:** Šaumjan 1968, 1971, B. Hall 1964. **Dependency grammar:** Hays 1964, Robinson 1970. **11.9** Winograd 1972, 1974. **11.10** Langacker 1973 (Chaps. 2, 9), Chomsky 1966, 1972a. **11.11** Struhsaker 1967, Lancaster 1968, Gardner and Gardner 1969, Premack 1970, Kummer 1971, Holloway 1974, LeMay 1975, Fleming 1974, Linden 1974, Anttila 1972 (§1.10–1.15), Peirce 1955.

bibliography

Items in the bibliography are annotated as follows:

GENERAL   deals with matters of general interest in a nontechnical manner;

INTRODUCTORY   introduces technical concepts in a manner understandable to the beginning student;

ADVANCED   deals with relatively straightforward technical matters presupposing a background in basic linguistics;

TECHNICAL   covers fairly technical material intended for the advanced student or specialist.

A further comment, in brackets, will often follow the annotation. It gives some indication of the scope of the work, especially if this is not already clear from the title.

For works of major significance, the annotation is preceded by an asterisk (*).

All listings are presented by name of author and in order of year of publication. Bibliographic information includes title, place of publication, and name of publisher. Journal articles list the name of the journal, volume number, and inclusive pages. Thus a listing given as 1.56–72 means volume 1, pages 56 through 72. If two periods occur in a listing, the sequence is volume, number, page. Thus 1.3.8–16 indicates volume 1, number 3, pages 8 through 16.

Aarsleff, Hans. "The History of Linguistics and Professor Chomsky." *Language* (1970) 46.570–585. ADVANCED.

———. " 'Cartesian Linguistics': History or Fantasy?" *Language Sciences* (1971) 17.1–12. ADVANCED.

Abrahams, Roger D., and Troike, Rudolph C. *Language and Cultural Diversity in American Education.* Englewood Cliffs: Prentice-Hall, 1972. INTRODUCTORY.

Allen, Harold B. *Readings in Applied English Linguistics.* New York: Appleton-Century-Crofts, 1958. INTRODUCTORY.

———. *Linguistic Atlas of the Upper Midwest.* Minneapolis: University of Minnesota Press, 1973–76. ADVANCED.

Alston, William P. *Philosophy of Language.* Englewood Cliffs: Prentice-Hall, 1964. *INTRODUCTORY.

Anderson, Stephen R. *The Organization of Phonology.* New York: Academic Press, 1974. TECHNICAL.

Anttila, Raimo. *An Introduction to Historical and Comparative Linguistics.* New York: Macmillan, 1972. *ADVANCED.

Arbib, Michael. *Theories of Abstract Automata.* Englewood Cliffs: Prentice-Hall, 1969. TECHNICAL.

Arlotto, Anthony. *Introduction to Historical Linguistics.* New York: Houghton Mifflin, 1972. INTRODUCTORY.

Arthur, Bradford. *Teaching English to Speakers of English.* New York: Harcourt Brace Jovanovich, 1973. ADVANCED.

Bach, Emmon, and Harms, Robert T., eds. *Universals in Linguistic Theory.* New York: Holt, Rinehart and Winston, 1968a. TECHNICAL.

Bartsch, Renate, and Vennemann, Theo. *Linguistics and Neighboring Disciplines.* New York: American Elsevier, 1975. INTRODUCTORY.

Baugh, Albert C. *A History of the English Language.* New York: Appleton-Century-Crofts, 1957. GENERAL.

Bauman, Richard, and Sherzer, Joel. *Explorations in the Ethnography of Speaking.* London: Cambridge University Press, 1974. ADVANCED.

Beechhold, Henry F., and Behling, John L., Jr. *The Science of Language and the Art of Teaching.* New York: Scribner's, 1972. INTRODUCTORY.

Bentley, W. Holman. *Dictionary and Grammar of the Kongo Language.* London: Baptist Missionary Society, 1967. ADVANCED. [Originally published 1887.]

Berlin, Brent, and Kay, Paul. *Basic Color Terms: Their Universality and Evolution.* Berkeley and Los Angeles: University of California Press, 1969. ADVANCED.

Bloch, Bernard. "A Set of Postulates for Phonemic Analysis." *Language* (1948), 24.3–46 (Bobbs-Merrill Reprint L–5). TECHNICAL.

———, and Trager, George L. *Outline of Linguistic Analysis.* Baltimore: Linguistic Society of America, 1942. *ADVANCED.

Bloch, Jules. *The Grammatical Structure of the Dravidian Languages.* Poona: Deccan College, 1954. ADVANCED.

———. *Indo-Aryan from the Vedas to Modern Times.* Wiesbaden: International Publications Service, 1965. ADVANCED.

Bloomfield, Leonard. "On the Sound-System of Central Algonquian." *Language* (1925) 1.130–156. TECHNICAL.

———. *Language.* New York: Holt, 1933. *ADVANCED.

———. "Menomini Morphophonemics." *Travaux du cercle linguistique de Prague* (1939) 8.105–115. Reprinted in *A Leonard Bloomfield Anthology,* edited by Charles F. Hockett. Bloomington: Indiana University Press, 1970. *TECHNICAL.

———. "Algonquian." In *Linguistic Structures of Native America,* edited by Harry Hoijer. New York: Viking Fund Publications in Anthropology, no. 6, 1946. TECHNICAL.

———. *Eastern Ojibwa.* Ann Arbor: University of Michigan Press, 1957. ADVANCED.

———. *The Menomini Language.* New Haven: Yale University Press, 1962. ADVANCED.

———, and Barnhart, Clarence L. *Let's Read: A Linguistic Approach.* Detroit: Wayne State University Press, 1961. GENERAL.

Boas, Franz. "Introduction" to *Handbook of American Indian Languages.* Washington, D.C.: Bureau of American Ethnology, 1911. Reprinted by University of Nebraska Press, Lincoln, 1966. GENERAL.

Bolinger, Dwight L. "Adjectives in English: Attribution and Predication." *Lingua* (1967) 18.1–34. TECHNICAL.

———. "Ambient *It* Is Meaningful Too." *Journal of Linguistics* (1973) 9.261–290. ADVANCED.

———. *Aspects of Language.* 2d ed. New York: Harcourt Brace Jovanovich, 1975. INTRODUCTORY. [A comprehensive introduction to the study of language.]

Bowen, J. Donald, ed. *Beginning Tagalog.* Berkeley and Los Angeles: University of California Press, 1965. ADVANCED.

Boyle, J. A. *A Grammar of Modern Persian.* Neue Serie, 9. Wiesbaden: Porta Linguarum Orientalium, 1966. ADVANCED.

Braine, M. D. S. "The Ontogeny of English Phrase Structure: The First Phase." *Language* (1963) 39.1–13. TECHNICAL.

Brekle, Herbert H., ed. *Grammaire générale et raisonée, ou la grammaire du Port-Royal.* Stuttgart-Bad Cannstatt: Friedrich Fromann Verlag, 1966. TECHNICAL. [Facsimile of the third edition (1676), with notes by the editor.]

Brend, Ruth M., ed. *Advances in Tagmemics.* Amsterdam: North-Holland, 1973. ADVANCED.

Bright, William O., ed. *Studies in California Linguistics.* Berkeley and Los Angeles: University of California Press, 1964 (University of California Publications in Linguistics, 34). ADVANCED.

———. *Sociolinguistics.* The Hague: Mouton, 1966. ADVANCED.

Brown, Roger. *A First Language.* Cambridge, Mass.: Harvard University Press, 1973. ADVANCED.

Buck, Carl D. *The Greek Dialects.* Chicago: University of Chicago Press, 1955. ADVANCED. [A description of the language, emphasizing the ancient dialects.]

Burling, Robbins. *Man's Many Voices.* New York: Holt, Rinehart and Winston, 1970. INTRODUCTORY. [Presentation of anthropological linguistics.]

———. *English in Black and White.* New York: Holt, Rinehart and Winston, 1973. INTRODUCTORY. [Presentation of dialect differences between American blacks and whites.]

Burrow, Thomas. *The Sanskrit Language.* London: Faber & Faber, 1965. ADVANCED.

Campbell, Bernard. *Human Evolution.* Chicago: Aldine, 1974. INTRODUCTORY.

Chadwick, John. *The Decipherment of Linear B.* London: Cambridge University Press, 1958. INTRODUCTORY.

Chafe, Wallace L. "Internal Reconstruction in Seneca." *Language* (1959) 35.477–495. TECHNICAL.

———. "Language as Symbolization." *Language* (1967a) 43.57–91. TECHNICAL.

———. *Seneca Morphology and Dictionary.* Washington, D.C.: Smithsonian Contributions to Anthropology, no. 4, 1967b. ADVANCED.

———. "Idiomaticity as an Anomaly in the Chomskyan Paradigm." *Foundations of Language* (1968a) 4.109–127. *ADVANCED.

———. "The Ordering of Phonological Rules." *International Journal of American Linguistics* (1968b) 34.115–136. *TECHNICAL.

———. "A Semantically Based Sketch of Onondaga." *International Journal of American Linguistics* (1970a) 36.2. part 2 (Indiana University Publications in Anthropology and Linguistics, Memoir 25). ADVANCED.

———. *Meaning and the Structure of Language.* Chicago: University of Chicago Press, 1970b. *ADVANCED.

———. "Directionality and Paraphrase." *Language* (1971) 47.1–26. ADVANCED.

———. "Language and Memory." *Language* (1973a) 49.261–281. ADVANCED.

———. "Siouan, Iroquoian, and Caddoan." In *Current Trends in Linguistics,* vol. 10, edited by Thomas A. Sebeok. The Hague: Mouton, 1973b. ADVANCED.

———. "Language and Consciousness." *Language* (1974) 50.111–133. ADVANCED.

Chang, Kun, and Shefts, Betty. *A Manual of Spoken Tibetan.* Seattle: University of Washington Press, 1964. ADVANCED.

Chao, Yuen-Ren. "The Non-Uniqueness of Phonemic Solutions of Phonetic Systems," *Bulletin of the Institute of History and Philology,* Academia Sinica (1934) 4.4.363–397. Reprinted in *Readings in Linguistics,* edited by Martin Joos, 1958. ADVANCED.

Chatman, Seymour B., and Levin, Samuel R., eds. *Essays on the Language of Literature.* Boston: Houghton Mifflin, 1967. INTRODUCTORY.

Chomsky, Noam. "Morphophonemics of Modern Hebrew." Master's thesis, University of Pennsylvania, 1951. TECHNICAL.

———. *Syntactic Structures.* The Hague: Mouton, 1957. *ADVANCED.

———. "Review of B. F. Skinner, *Verbal Behavior.*" *Language* (1959) 35.26–58. Reprinted in *The Structure of Language,* edited by Jerry A. Fodor and Jerrold J. Katz, 1964. ADVANCED.

———. *Current Issues in Linguistic Theory.* The Hague: Mouton, 1964. Reprinted in *The Structure of Language,* edited by Jerry A. Fodor and Jerrold J. Katz, 1964. TECHNICAL.

———. *Aspects of the Theory of Syntax.* Cambridge, Mass.: MIT Press, 1965. *ADVANCED.

———. *Cartesian Linguistics.* New York: Harper & Row, 1966. ADVANCED.

———. "Remarks on Nominalization." In *Readings in English Transformational Grammar,* edited by Roderick A. Jacobs and Peter S. Rosenbaum. Waltham, Mass.: Ginn and Co., 1970. Reprinted in Noam Chomsky, *Studies on Semantics in Generative Grammar,* 1972. TECHNICAL.

———. *Language and Mind.* New York: Harcourt Brace Jovanovich, 1972a. ADVANCED.

———. *Studies on Semantics in Generative Grammar.* The Hague: Mouton, 1972b. ADVANCED.

———. *The Logical Structure of Linguistic Theory.* New York: Plenum, 1975. TECHNICAL. [Originally written 1955.]

———. *Reflections on Language.* New York: Pantheon, 1976. ADVANCED.

———, and Halle, Morris. "Some Controversial Questions in Phonological Theory." *Journal of Linguistics* (1965) 1.97–138. TECHNICAL.

———. *The Sound Pattern of English.* New York: Harper & Row, 1968. *TECHNICAL.

Chu, Yu-Kuang, and Nishimoto, Koji. *A Comparative Study of Language Reforms in China and Japan.* Saratoga Springs, N.Y.: Skidmore College, 1969. GENERAL.

Cole, Michael, and Scribner, Sylvia. *Culture and Thought.* New York: Wiley, 1974. INTRODUCTORY.

Collinder, Bjorn. *An Introduction to the Uralic Languages.* Berkeley and Los Angeles: University of California Press, 1965. ADVANCED.

Conklin, Harold C. "Hanunóo Color Categories." *Southwestern Journal of Anthro-*

pology (1955) 11.339–344 (Bobbs-Merrill Reprint A–42). ADVANCED.

Cook, Walter A. *Introduction to Tagmemic Analysis.* New York: Holt, Rinehart and Winston, 1969. ADVANCED.

———. "Case Grammar as a Deep Structure in Tagmemic Analysis." *Georgetown University Languages and Linguistics Working Papers* (1971a) 2.1–9. ADVANCED.

———. "Improvements in Case Grammar." *Georgetown University Languages and Linguistics Working Papers* (1971b) 2.10–22. ADVANCED.

———. "A Set of Postulates for Case Grammar Analysis." *Georgetown University Languages and Linguistics Working Papers* (1972) 4.35–49. ADVANCED.

———. "Covert Case Roles." *Georgetown University Languages and Linguistics Working Papers* (1973) 7.52–81. ADVANCED.

Comyn, William S. *Outline of Burmese Grammar.* Baltimore: Linguistic Society of America, Language Dissertation, no. 38, 1944. ADVANCED. [Supplement to *Language* 10.4.]

Cosmos, Spencer; Heny, Frank; Chafe, Wallace L.; and Long, Ralph B. "Chafe and Chomsky: A Reaction to a Review." *College English* (1973) 34.718–731. INTRODUCTORY.

Crowley, Thomas H. *Understanding Computers.* New York: McGraw-Hill, 1967. INTRODUCTORY.

Curme, George. *English Grammar.* New York: Barnes and Noble, 1947. ADVANCED.

Dale, Philip S. *Language Development: Structure and Function.* New York: Dryden Press, 1972. INTRODUCTORY.

Davis, Phillip W. *Modern Theories of Language.* Englewood Cliffs: Prentice-Hall, 1973. INTRODUCTORY.

DeFrancis, John. *Nationalism and Language Reform in China.* Princeton: Princeton University Press, 1950. INTRODUCTORY.

Denes, Peter B., and Pinson, Eliot N. *The Speech Chain.* New York: Garden State-Novo, 1963. INTRODUCTORY. [Detailed discussion of the physiological, neural, and acoustic bases of speech.]

De Saussure, Ferdinand. *See* Saussure, Ferdinand de

Diffloth, Gérard. "Austro-Asiatic Languages." In *Encyclopædia Britannica.* 15th ed., vol. 2. Chicago: Encyclopædia Britannica, 1974. GENERAL.

Dineen, Francis P. *An Introduction to General Linguistics.* New York: Holt, Rinehart and Winston, 1967. INTRODUCTORY.

Diringer, David. *The Alphabet: A Key to the History of Mankind.* New York: Philosophical Library, 1948. INTRODUCTORY.

Downing, John, ed. *The ITA Symposium.* Slough, Eng.: National Foundation for Educational Research in England and Wales, 1967. INTRODUCTORY.

Dyen, Isidore. "The Austronesian Languages and Proto-Austronesian." In *Current Trends in Linguistics,* vol. 8, edited by Thomas A. Sebeok. The Hague: Mouton, 1971. ADVANCED.

Elson, Benjamin, and Pickett, Velma B. *Beginning Morphology-Syntax.* Santa Ana, Calif.: Summer Institute of Linguistics, 1960. INTRODUCTORY.

Emeneau, Murray B. "India as a Linguistic Area." *Language* (1956) 32.3–16. ADVANCED.

Encyclopædia Britannica. 15th ed. Chicago: Encyclopædia Britannica, 1974. GENERAL. [Excellent articles on languages of the world and most of the language families discussed in Chapter 8.]

Entwistle, W. J., and Morrison, W. A., *Russian and the Slavonic Languages.* London: Faber & Faber, 1964. ADVANCED.

Farb, Peter. *Word Play: What Happens When People Talk.* New York: Alfred A. Knopf, 1974. GENERAL.

Fillmore, Charles J. "The Case for Case." In *Universals in Linguistic Theory,* edited by Emmon Bach and Robert T. Harms. New York: Holt, Rinehart and Winston, 1968. *ADVANCED.

———, and Langendoen, D. Terence, eds. *Studies in Linguistic Semantics.* New York: Holt, Rinehart and Winston, 1971. TECHNICAL.

Firth, John R., ed. *Studies in Linguistic Analysis.* Oxford: Basil Blackwell, 1968. ADVANCED.

Fischer, John L. "Social Influence in the Choice of a Linguistic Variant." *Word* (1958) 14.47–56. INTRODUCTORY.

———. Personal communication, 1975.

Fishman, Joshua A. *Readings in the Sociology of Language.* The Hague: Mouton, 1968. ADVANCED.

———. *Advances in the Sociology of Language.* The Hague: Mouton, 1972. ADVANCED.

Fleming, Joyce Dudney. "The State of the Apes." *Psychology Today* (1974) 7.8.31–38. GENERAL.

Fodor, Jerry A., and Katz, Jerrold J., eds. *The Structure of Language*. Englewood Cliffs: Prentice-Hall, 1964. TECHNICAL. [Readings in transformational theory.]

Forrest, R. A. D. *The Chinese Language*. London: Faber & Faber, 1948. ADVANCED.

Francis, Winthrop Nelson. *The Structure of American English*. New York: Ronald Press, 1958. INTRODUCTORY. [Presentation of structural grammar.]

Fraser, Bruce. "Idioms Within a Transformational Grammar." *Foundations of Language* (1970) 6.22–42. INTRODUCTORY.

Fries, Charles C. *The Structure of English*. New York: Harcourt, Brace and World, 1952. ADVANCED.

————. *Linguistics and Reading*. New York: Holt, Rinehart and Winston, 1962. ADVANCED.

Fromkin, Victoria A. "The Non-anomalous Nature of Anomalous Utterances." *Language* (1971) 47.27–52. ADVANCED.

————, and Rodman, Robert. *An Introduction to Language*. New York: Holt, Rinehart and Winston, 1974. INTRODUCTORY. [Introduction to linguistics and communication from the standpoint of transformational grammar.]

Gardner, A. R., and Gardner, B. T. "Teaching Sign Language to a Chimpanzee." *Science* (1969) 165.664–672. INTRODUCTORY.

Garvin, Paul L., ed. *Natural Language and the Computer*. New York: McGraw-Hill, 1963. ADVANCED.

————. "Moderation in Linguistic Theory." *Language Sciences* (1970) 9.1–3. INTRODUCTORY.

Gelb, I. J. *A Study of Writing*. Chicago: University of Chicago Press, 1952. ADVANCED.

Gleason, H. A., Jr. *An Introduction to Descriptive Linguistics*. New York: Holt, Rinehart and Winston, 1961. INTRODUCTORY. [Presentation of structural grammar.]

Goddard, Ives. "The Algonquian Independent Indicative." *National Museum of Canada Bulletin* (Ottawa) 214.66–106. TECHNICAL.

————. "Delaware Verbal Morphology." Doctoral dissertation, Harvard University, 1969. ADVANCED.

Greenberg, Joseph H. *Essays in Linguistics*. Chicago: University of Chicago Press, 1957. INTRODUCTORY.

————. "A Quantitative Approach to the Morphological Typology of Language." *International Journal of American Linguistics* (1960a) 26.178–194. ADVANCED.

————. "The General Classification of Central and South American Languages." In *Selected Papers of the Fifth International Congress of Anthropological and Ethnological Sciences*, edited by Anthony F. C. Wallace. Philadelphia: University of Pennsylvania Press, 1960b. INTRODUCTORY.

————. *The Languages of Africa*. The Hague: Mouton, 1966. ADVANCED.

————. *Anthropological Linguistics*. New York: Random House, 1968. INTRODUCTORY.

————. *Language, Culture, and Communication*. Stanford: Stanford University Press, 1971. INTRODUCTORY.

————., ed. *Universals of Language*. Cambridge, Mass.: MIT Press, 1963. TECHNICAL.

Grinder, John T., and Elgin, Suzette Haden. *Guide to Transformational Grammar*. New York: Holt, Rinehart and Winston, 1973. INTRODUCTORY.

Gruber, Jeffrey. "Studies in Lexical Relations." Doctoral dissertation, Massachusetts Institute of Technology, 1965. TECHNICAL.

————. *Functions of the Lexicon in Formal Descriptive Grammars*. Bloomington: Indiana University Linguistics Club, 1972. TECHNICAL.

Gunter, Richard. "Elliptical Sentences in American English." *Lingua* (1963) 12.137–150. Reprinted in *Sentences in Dialog*, edited by Richard Gunter, 1974. ADVANCED.

————. "On the Placement of Accent in Dialogue: A Feature of Context Grammar." *Journal of Linguistics* (1966) 2.159–179. Reprinted in *Sentences in Dialog*, edited by Richard Gunter, 1974. ADVANCED.

————. "English Derivation." *Journal of Linguistics* (1972) 8.1–19. ADVANCED.

————. *Sentences in Dialog*. Columbia, S.C.: Hornbeam Press, 1974. ADVANCED.

————. *Reading Poems*. Columbia, S.C.: Hornbeam Press, 1975. INTRODUCTORY.

Haas, Mary R. "The Classification of the Muskogean Languages." In *Language, Culture, and Personality*, edited by Leslie Spier, A. Irving Hallowell, and Stanley S. Newman. Menasha, Wis.: Sapir Memorial Fund, 1941. Reprinted by University of Utah Press, Salt Lake City, 1960. ADVANCED.

———. "Algonkian-Ritwan: The End of a Controversy." *International Journal of American Linguistics* (1958a) 24.159–173. ADVANCED.

———. "A New Linguistic Relåtionship in North America: Algonkian and the Gulf Languages." *Southwestern Journal of Anthropology* (1958b) 14.231–264. ADVANCED.

———. "Is Kutenai Related to Algonkian?" *Canadian Journal of Linguistics* (1965) 10.77–92. ADVANCED.

———. "Vowels and Semivowels in Algonkian." *Language* (1966) 42.479–488. ADVANCED.

———. *The Prehistory of Languages.* The Hague: Mouton, 1969. ADVANCED. [An earlier version appeared in *Current Trends in Linguistics*, vol. 3, edited by Thomas A. Sebeok.]

Hale, Kenneth. "A Note on a Walbiri Tradition of Antonymy." In *Semantics*, edited by Danny D. Steinberg and Leon A. Jakobovits. London: Cambridge University Press, 1971. ADVANCED.

Hall, Barbara. "Review of Šaumjan, S. K., and P. A. Soboleva, *Applikativnaja poroždajuščaja model' i isčislenie transformacij v russkom jazyke.*" *Language* (1964) 40.397–410. ADVANCED. *See also* Partee, Barbara Hall

Hall, Edward T. *The Silent Language.* Garden City: Doubleday, 1959. GENERAL.

Hall, Robert A., Jr. *Introductory Linguistics.* Philadelphia: Chilton, 1964. INTRODUCTORY.

———. *Pidgin and Creole Languages.* Ithaca: Cornell University Press, 1965. INTRODUCTORY.

———. *External History of the Romance Languages.* New York: American Elsevier, 1974. ADVANCED.

Halle, Morris. *The Sound Pattern of Russian.* The Hague: Mouton, 1959. TECHNICAL.

———. "Phonology in Generative Grammar." *Word* (1962) 18.54–72. Reprinted in *The Structure of Language*, edited by Jerry A. Fodor and Jerrold J. Katz, 1964. ADVANCED.

———. "On the Bases of Phonology." In *The Structure of Language*, edited by Jerry A. Fodor and Jerrold J. Katz. Englewood Cliffs: Prentice-Hall, 1964. ADVANCED.

Halliday, Michael A. K. "Categories of the Theory of Grammar." *Word* (1961) 17.241–292 (Bobbs-Merrill Reprint L-36). TECHNICAL.

———. "Notes on Transitivity and Theme in English." *Journal of Linguistics* (1967–68) Part 1 (3.37–81), Part 2 (3.199–244), Part 3 (4.179–215). TECHNICAL.

———. "Functional Diversity in Language as Seen from a Consideration of Modality and Mood in English." *Foundations of Language* (1970) 6.322–361. TECHNICAL.

Harms, Robert T. *Introduction to Phonological Theory.* Englewood Cliffs: Prentice-Hall, 1968. ADVANCED. [Now largely supplanted by Sanford A. Schane, *Generative Phonology*, 1973.]

Harris, Zellig S. "Morpheme Alternants in Linguistic Analysis." *Language* (1942) 18.169–180. Reprinted in *Readings in Linguistics*, edited by Martin Joos, 1958. TECHNICAL.

———. *Structural Linguistics.* Chicago: University of Chicago Press, 1951. TECHNICAL.

———. "Co-occurrence and Transformation in Linguistic Structure." *Language* (1957) 33.283–340. Reprinted in *The Structure of Language*, edited by Jerry A. Fodor and Jerrold J. Katz, 1964. TECHNICAL.

———. "Transformational Theory." *Language* (1965) 41.363–401. TECHNICAL.

Haugen, Einar, and Bloomfield, Morton, eds. *Language as a Human Problem.* New York: W. W. Norton, 1974. ADVANCED. [Essays on the functions of language in human affairs.]

Hays, David G. "Dependency Theory: A Formalism and Some Observations." *Language* (1964) 40.511–525. TECHNICAL.

Heny, Frank W. "Review of Wallace L. Chafe, *Meaning and the Structure of Language.*" *College English* (1972) 33.908–929. INTRODUCTORY.

Hertzler, Joyce O. *A Sociology of Language.* New York: Random House, 1965. INTRODUCTORY.

Hewes, Gordon. "Primate Communication and the Gestural Origin of Language." *Current Anthropology* (1972) 14.5–24. ADVANCED.

Hickerson, Nancy P. "Review of Brent Berlin and Paul Kay, *Basic Color Terms.*" *International Journal of American Linguistics* (1971) 37.257–270. ADVANCED.

Hill, Jane H. "On the Evolutionary Foundations of Language." *American Anthropologist* (1972) 74.308–317. ADVANCED.

———. "Possible Continuity Theories of Language." *Language* (1974) 50.134–150. ADVANCED.

Hjelmslev, Louis. *Prolegomena to a Theory of Language.* Translated by Francis J.

Whitfield. Madison: University of Wisconsin Press, 1963. TECHNICAL.

———. *Language: An Introduction.* Translated by Francis J. Whitfield. Madison: University of Wisconsin Press, 1970. TECHNICAL.

Hockett, Charles F. "Problems of Morphemic Analysis." *Language* (1947) 23.321–343. Reprinted in *Readings in Linguistics,* edited by Martin Joos, 1958. ADVANCED.

———. "Chinese Versus English: An Exploration of the Whorfian Theses." In *Language in Culture,* edited by Harry Hoijer. Chicago: University of Chicago Press, 1954a. INTRODUCTORY.

———. "Two Models of Grammatical Description." *Word* (1954b) 10.210–231. Reprinted in *Readings in Linguistics,* edited by Martin Joos, 1958. ADVANCED.

———. *A Manual of Phonology.* Bloomington: Indiana University Publications in Anthropology and Linguistics, no. 11, 1955. ADVANCED.

———. *A Course in Modern Linguistics.* New York: Macmillan, 1958. INTRODUCTORY.

———. "The Origin of Speech." *Scientific American* (1960) 203.3.89–96 (Freeman Reprint 603). GENERAL.

———, and Ascher, Robert. "The Human Revolution." *Current Anthropology* (1964) 5.135–147 (Bobbs-Merrill Reprint A–306). *ADVANCED.

Hoenigswald, Henry M. *Language Change and Linguistic Reconstruction.* Chicago: University of Chicago Press, 1960. TECHNICAL.

Hoijer, Harry, ed. *Linguistic Structures of Native America.* New York: Viking Fund Publications in Anthropology, no. 6, 1946. ADVANCED.

———. *Language in Culture.* Chicago: University of Chicago Press, 1954. ADVANCED.

Holloway, Ralph L. "The Casts of Fossil Hominid Brains." *Scientific American* (1974) 231.1.106–115. TECHNICAL.

House, Homer C., and Harmon, Susan Emolyn. *Descriptive English Grammar.* Englewood Cliffs: Prentice-Hall, 1950. *INTRODUCTORY.

Householder, Fred W. "On Some Recent Claims in Phonological Theory." *Journal of Linguistics* (1965) 1.13–34. ADVANCED.

Hughes, John P. *The Science of Language.* New York: Random House, 1968. GENERAL.

Hungerford, Harold; Robinson, Jay; and Sledd, James, eds. *English Linguistics: An Introductory Reader.* Glenview, Ill.: Scott, Foresman, 1970. INTRODUCTORY.

Hyman, Larry M. *Phonology: Theory and Analysis.* New York: Holt, Rinehart and Winston, 1975. TECHNICAL.

Hymes, Dell, ed. *Language in Culture and Society: A Reader in Linguistics and Anthropology.* New York: Harper & Row, 1964. ADVANCED.

———. *Studies in the History of Linguistics: Traditions and Paradigms.* Bloomington: Indiana University Press, 1974. ADVANCED.

International Phonetic Association. *The Principles of the International Phonetic Association.* London: Department of Phonetics, University College, 1949. INTRODUCTORY.

Jackendoff, Ray. *Semantic Interpretation in Generative Grammar.* Cambridge, Mass.: MIT Press, 1972. TECHNICAL.

Jacobs, Roderick A., and Rosenbaum, Peter S. *English Transformational Grammar.* Waltham, Mass.: Blaisdell, 1968. INTRODUCTORY.

———, eds. *Readings in English Transformational Grammar.* Waltham, Mass.: Ginn and Co., 1970. TECHNICAL.

Jakobson, Roman; Fant, Gunnar; and Halle, Morris. *Preliminaries to Speech Analysis.* Cambridge, Mass.: MIT Press, 1955. *ADVANCED.

Jakobson, Roman, and Halle, Morris. *Fundamentals of Language.* The Hague: Mouton, 1956. ADVANCED.

Jespersen, Otto. *Language: Its Nature, Development, and Origin.* London: Allen and Unwin, 1922. INTRODUCTORY.

———. *A Modern English Grammar on Historical Principles.* London: Allen and Unwin, 1954. ADVANCED.

Joos, Martin. *Acoustic Phonetics.* Baltimore: Linguistic Society of America, Language Monograph no. 23, 1948. ADVANCED.

———, ed. *Readings in Linguistics.* New York: American Council of Learned Societies, 1958. ADVANCED. [Subsequent editions issued as *Readings in Linguistics I* by University of Chicago Press.]

Kadokawa Kanwa Jiten. Tokyo: Kadokawa Shoten, 1956. TECHNICAL.

Karlgren, Bernhard. *Sound and Symbol in Chinese.* Hong Kong: Hong Kong University Press, 1962. INTRODUCTORY. [Originally published by Oxford University Press, London, 1923.]

Katz, Jerrold J. *The Philosophy of Language.* New York: Harper & Row, 1966. ADVANCED.

———. *Semantic Theory.* New York: Harper & Row, 1972. TECHNICAL.

———, and Fodor, Jerry A. "The Structure of a Semantic Theory." *Language* (1963) 39.170–210. Reprinted in *The Structure of Language,* edited by Jerry A. Fodor and Jerrold J. Katz, 1964. TECHNICAL.

———, and Postal, Paul M. *An Integrated Theory of Linguistic Descriptions.* Cambridge, Mass.: MIT Press, 1964. ADVANCED.

Keenan, Edward L. "On Semantically Based Grammar." *Linguistic Inquiry* (1972) 3.413–462. TECHNICAL.

Keiler, Allan R., ed. *A Reader in Historical and Comparative Linguistics.* New York: Holt, Rinehart and Winston, 1972. ADVANCED.

Kerr, Elizabeth M., and Aderman, Ralph M. *Aspects of American English.* New York: Harcourt Brace Jovanovich, 1971. INTRODUCTORY.

Kimball, John P. *The Formal Theory of Grammar.* Englewood Cliffs: Prentice-Hall, 1973. ADVANCED.

Kiparsky, Paul. "Phonological Change." Doctoral dissertation, Massachusetts Institute of Technology, 1965. TECHNICAL.

Krauss, Michael E. "Na-Dene." In *Current Trends in Linguistics,* vol. 10, edited by Thomas A. Sebeok. The Hague: Mouton, 1973b. ADVANCED.

———. "Eskimo-Aleut." In *Current Trends in Linguistics,* vol. 10, edited by Thomas A. Sebeok. The Hague: Mouton, 1973a. ADVANCED.

Kuhn, Thomas S. *The Structure of Scientific Revolutions.* 2d ed. Chicago: University of Chicago Press, 1970. INTRODUCTORY. [First edition 1962.]

Kuipers, A. H. "Caucasian." In *Current Trends in Linguistics,* vol. 1, edited by Thomas A. Sebeok. The Hague: Mouton, 1963. ADVANCED.

Kummer, Hans. *Primate Societies.* Chicago: Aldine-Atherton, 1971. INTRODUCTORY.

Kurath, Hans. *Studies in Area Linguistics.* Bloomington: Indiana University Press, 1972. ADVANCED.

———, and Bloch, Bernard, eds. *Linguistic Atlas of New England.* Providence: American Council of Learned Societies, 1939–

43. Reprinted by AMS Press, New York, 1972. ADVANCED.

———, and McDavid, Raven I., Jr. *The Pronunciation of English in the Atlantic States.* Ann Arbor: University of Michigan Press, 1961. ADVANCED.

Labov, William. "The Social Motivation of a Sound Change." *Word* (1963) 19.273–309. ADVANCED.

———. *The Social Stratification of English in New York City.* Washington, D.C.: Center for Applied Linguistics, 1966. ADVANCED.

———. *Language in the Inner City.* Philadelphia: University of Pennsylvania Press, 1972. ADVANCED.

Ladefoged, Peter. *Elements of Acoustic Phonetics.* Chicago: University of Chicago Press, 1962. ADVANCED.

———. *Linguistic Phonetics.* Los Angeles: UCLA Working Papers in Phonetics, no. 6, 1967. ADVANCED.

———. *A Course in Phonetics.* New York: Harcourt Brace Jovanovich, 1975. INTRODUCTORY.

Lado, Robert. *Linguistics Across Cultures.* Ann Arbor: University of Michigan Press, 1957. ADVANCED.

———. *Language Teaching.* New York: McGraw-Hill, 1964. ADVANCED.

Lafon, René. "The Basque Language." In *Current Trends in Linguistics,* vol. 9, edited by Thomas A. Sebeok. The Hague: Mouton, 1972. ADVANCED.

Laird, Charlton, and Gorrell, Robert M., eds. *Reading About Language.* New York: Harcourt Brace Jovanovich, 1971. INTRODUCTORY.

Lakoff, George. "Instrumental Adverbs and the Concept of Deep Structure." *Foundations of Language* (1968) 4.4–29. TECHNICAL.

———. "Global Rules." *Language* (1970) 46.627–639. TECHNICAL.

———. "On Generative Semantics." In *Semantics,* edited by Danny D. Steinberg and Leon A. Jakobovits. London: Cambridge University Press, 1971. TECHNICAL.

———. "The Arbitrary Nature of Transformational Grammar." *Language* (1972) 48.76–87. TECHNICAL.

Lakoff, Robin T. *Abstract Syntax and Latin Complementation.* Cambridge, Mass.: MIT Press, 1968. TECHNICAL.

———. "Review of *Grammaire générale et raisonée.*" *Language* (1969) 45.343–364. ADVANCED.

Lamb, Sydney M. *Outline of Stratificational Grammar.* Washington, D.C.: Georgetown University Press, 1966. ADVANCED.

Lancaster, Jane B. "Primitive Communication Systems and the Emergence of Human Language." In *Primates,* edited by Phyllis C. Jay. New York: Holt, Rinehart and Winston, 1968. INTRODUCTORY.

Landar, Herbert. *Language and Culture.* New York: Oxford University Press, 1966. INTRODUCTORY.

Langacker, Ronald W. "Review of Wallace L. Chafe, *Meaning and the Structure of Language.*" *Language* (1972a) 48.134–161. ADVANCED.

———. *Fundamentals of Linguistic Analysis.* New York: Harcourt Brace Jovanovich, 1972b. ADVANCED. [Good examples of data and data problems.]

———. *Language and Its Structure.* New York: Harcourt Brace Jovanovich, 1973. INTRODUCTORY. [Revision of first edition, 1967.]

Laycock, D. C., and Voorhoeve, C. L. "History of Research in Papuan Languages." In *Current Trends in Linguistics,* vol. 8, edited by Thomas A. Sebeok. The Hague: Mouton, 1971. ADVANCED.

Le Corbeiller, Philippe. *The Languages of Science.* New York: Basic Books, 1963. INTRODUCTORY.

Lees, Robert B. "Some Neglected Aspects of Parsing." *Language Learning* (1960a) 11.171–181. Also in *Readings in Applied English Linguistics,* edited by Harold B Allen, 1958. ADVANCED.

———. *The Grammar of English Nominalizations.* The Hague: Mouton, 1960b. TECHNICAL.

Lehmann, Winfred P. *Historical Linguistics: An Introduction.* New York: Holt, Rinehart and Winston, 1962. INTRODUCTORY.

———. *Descriptive Linguistics: An Introduction.* 2d ed. New York: Random House, 1976. INTRODUCTORY.

———, ed. *A Reader in Nineteenth-Century Historical Indo-European Linguistics.* Bloomington: Indiana University Press, 1967. ADVANCED.

Leichty, V. E. *Discovering English.* Englewood Cliffs: Prentice-Hall, 1964. INTRODUCTORY. [Presentation of structural grammar.]

LeMay, Marjorie. "The Language Capability of Neanderthal Man." *American Journal of Physical Anthropology* (1975) 42.9–14. ADVANCED.

Lenneberg, E. H. *Biological Foundations of Language.* New York: Wiley, 1967. ADVANCED.

Leopold, Werner F. *Speech Development of a Bilingual Child.* Evanston, Ill.: Northwestern University Press, 1939–49. ADVANCED.

Levin, Samuel R. *Linguistic Structures in Poetry.* The Hague: Mouton, 1964. ADVANCED.

Li, Fang-Kuei. "Tai Languages." In *Encyclopædia Britannica.* 15th ed., vol. 17. Chicago: Encyclopædia Britannica, 1974. INTRODUCTORY.

Lieberman, Philip. *On the Origins of Language: An Introduction to the Evolution of Human Speech.* New York: Macmillan, 1975. ADVANCED.

———, and Crelin, Edmund S. "On the Speech of Neanderthal Man." *Linguistic Inquiry* (1971) 2.203–222. ADVANCED.

Liles, Bruce L. *Linguistics and the English Language: A Transformational Approach.* Pacific Palisades, Calif.: Goodyear, 1972. INTRODUCTORY.

———. *An Introduction to Linguistics.* Englewood Cliffs: Prentice-Hall, 1975. INTRODUCTORY. [Presentation of transformational grammar.]

Linden, Eugene. *Apes, Men, and Language.* New York: Saturday Review Press/E. P. Dutton, 1974. GENERAL. [Presentation of recent work in chimpanzee-human communication.]

Lockwood, David G. *Introduction to Stratificational Grammars.* New York: Harcourt Brace Jovanovich, 1972. ADVANCED.

Lockwood, W. B. *Indo-European Philology.* London: Hutchinson University Library, 1969. INTRODUCTORY.

Long, Ralph B., and Long, Dorothy R. *The System of English Grammar.* Glenview, Ill.: Scott, Foresman, 1971. INTRODUCTORY.

Longacre, Robert E. *Grammar Discovery Procedures.* The Hague: Mouton, 1964. ADVANCED. [Methodology of structural grammar and tagmemics.]

Loukotka, Čestmír. *Classification of South American Indian Languages.* Los Angeles: UCLA Latin American Center, Reference Series, vol. 7, 1968. ADVANCED.

Lounsbury, Floyd G. *Oneida Verb Mor-*

phology. New Haven: Yale University Publications in Anthropology, no. 48, 1953. ADVANCED.

Lyons, John. *Chomsky*. London: Fontana, and New York: Viking, 1970a. GENERAL.

———. *New Horizons in Linguistics*. Harmondsworth, Eng.: Penguin Books, 1970b. TECHNICAL. [Readings in theoretical linguistics and the relation of linguistics to other disciplines.]

———. *Introduction to Theoretical Linguistics*. New York and London: Cambridge University Press, 1971. INTRODUCTORY.

Makkai, Adam. *Idiom Structure in English*. The Hague: Mouton, 1972. ADVANCED.

———. " 'Take One' on *take:* Lexo-Ecology Illustrated." *Language Sciences* (1974) 31.1–6. ADVANCED.

———, ed. *The First LACUS Forum 1974*. Columbia, S.C.: Hornbeam Press, 1975. ADVANCED.

———, and Lockwood, David G. *Readings in Stratificational Linguistics*. University: University of Alabama Press, 1973. ADVANCED.

Makkai, Valerie Becker, ed. *Phonological Theory*. New York: Holt, Rinehart and Winston, 1972. ADVANCED.

Malinowski, Bronislaw. "The Problem of Meaning in Primitive Languages." Supplement to C. K. Ogden and I. A. Richards, *The Meaning of Meaning*. London: Paul, Trench, Trubner and Co., 1923. INTRODUCTORY.

Mandelbaum, David G., ed. *Selected Writings of Edward Sapir in Language, Culture, and Personality*. Berkeley and Los Angeles: University of California Press, 1949. INTRODUCTORY.

Martin, Samuel E. "Lexical Evidence Relating Korean to Japanese." *Language* (1966) 42.185–251. TECHNICAL.

———; Ha Lee, Yang; and Chang, Sung-Un. *A Korean-English Dictionary*. New Haven: Yale University Press, 1967. INTRODUCTORY.

Matthews, G. H. "The Magical Number Seven, Plus or Minus Two: Some Limits on Our Capacity for Processing Information." *Psychological Review* (1965) 63.2.81–97. ADVANCED.

Matthews, P. H. *Morphology*. London: Cambridge University Press, 1974. ADVANCED.

Mazurkiewicz, Albert J. *The Initial Teaching Alphabet in Reading Instruction*. Bethlehem, Pa.: Lehigh University, 1967. INTRODUCTORY.

McCawley, James D. "The Role of Semantics in a Grammar." In *Universals in Linguistic Theory*, edited by Emmon Bach and Robert T. Harms. New York: Holt, Rinehart and Winston, 1968. TECHNICAL.

———. "English as a VSO Language." *Language* (1970) 46.286–299. TECHNICAL.

McDavid, Raven I., Jr. "Post-vocalic /-r/ in South Carolina: A Social Analysis." *American Speech* (1948) 23.194–203. GENERAL.

———, and McDavid, Virginia G. "The Relationship of the Speech of American Negroes to the Speech of Whites." *American Speech* (1951) 26.3–17. Reprinted with additional notes in *Black-White Speech Relationships*, edited by Walter A. Wolfram and Nona H. Clarke, 1971. GENERAL.

———, and O'Cain, Raymond. "Sociolinguistics and Linguistic Geography." *Kansas Journal of Sociology* (1973) 9.137–156. GENERAL.

McNeill, David. "Developmental Psycholinguistics." In *The Genesis of Language*, edited by Frank Smith and George A. Miller. Cambridge, Mass.: MIT Press, 1966. TECHNICAL.

Meillet, Antoine. *The Comparative Method in Historical Linguistics*. Translated by Gordon B. Ford, Jr. Paris: Champion, 1967. ADVANCED.

———, and Cohen, Marcel. *Les Langue du monde*. Paris: Centre National de la Recherche Scientifique, 1952. ADVANCED.

Mencken, Henry L. *The American Language*. Abridged edition, edited with new material by Raven I. McDavid, Jr. New York: Alfred A. Knopf, 1963. GENERAL.

Miller, George A., ed. *Communication, Language, and Meaning: Psychological Perspectives*. New York: Basic Books, 1973. ADVANCED.

Miller, Roy Andrew. *The Japanese Language*. Chicago: University of Chicago Press, 1967. ADVANCED.

Moore, Timothy E., ed. *Cognitive Development and the Acquisition of Language*. New York: Academic Press, 1973. ADVANCED.

Newman, Paul. "The Reality of Morphophonemes." *Language* (1968) 44.507–515. ADVANCED.

Nida, Eugene A. *Morphology: The Descrip-*

tive Analysis of Words. Ann Arbor: University of Michigan Press, 1946. INTRODUCTORY.

O'Conner, J. D. *Phonetics.* Harmondsworth, Eng.: Penguin Books, 1973. INTRODUCTORY.

Palmer, L. R. *The Latin Language.* London: Faber & Faber, 1954. ADVANCED.

Pap, Leo. "Linguistic Terminology as a Source of Verbal Fictions." *Language Sciences* (1976) 39.1–5. ADVANCED.

Parret, Herman, ed. *Discussing Language: Dialogues with Wallace L. Chafe, Noam Chomsky, Algirdas J. Greimas, M. A. K. Halliday, Peter Hartmann, George Lakoff, Sydney M. Lamb, André Martinet, James McCawley, Sebastian K. Šaumjan, and Jacques Bouveresse.* The Hague: Mouton, 1974. ADVANCED.

Partee, Barbara Hall. "Subject and Object in English." Doctoral dissertation, Massachusetts Institute of Technology, 1965. TECHNICAL. *See also* Hall, Barbara

Pears, David. *Wittgenstein.* London: Fontana, 1971. GENERAL.

Pearson, Bruce L. "A Grammar of Delaware: Semantics, Morpho-syntax, Lexicon, Phonology." Doctoral dissertation, University of California at Berkeley, 1972a. ADVANCED.

——. "Crazy Rules and Natural Rules in Japanese Phonology." *Papers in Japanese Linguistics* (1972b) 1.89–102. TECHNICAL.

——. "Savannah and Shawnee: Same or Different?" *Names in South Carolina* (1974) 21.19–22. GENERAL.

—— "Lexical Symbolization and Phonological Processes in Delaware." In *Papers of the Seventh Algonquian Conference, 1975,* edited by William Cowan. Ottawa, Can.: Carleton University, 1976. ADVANCED.

Pedersen, Holger. *The Discovery of Language.* Translated by John Webster Spargo. Bloomington: Indiana University Press, 1959. ADVANCED. [Originally published as *Linguistic Science in the Nineteenth Century* by Harvard University Press, Cambridge, 1931.]

Peirce, Charles Sanders. *Philosophical Writings of Peirce.* Edited by Justus Buchler. New York: Dover, 1955. ADVANCED.

Penfield, Wilder, and Roberts, L. *Speech and Brain Mechanisms.* Princeton: Princeton University Press, 1959. ADVANCED.

Percival, Keith. "A Reconsideration of Whorf's Hypothesis." *Anthropological Linguistics* (1966) 8.8.1–12. GENERAL.

——. "The Applicability of Kuhn's Paradigms to the History of Linguistics." *Language* (1976) 52.285–294. GENERAL.

Perlmutter, David M. *Deep and Surface Constraints in Syntax.* New York: Holt, Rinehart and Winston, 1971. TECHNICAL.

Peters, Stanley, ed. *Goals of Linguistic Theory.* Englewood Cliffs: Prentice-Hall, 1972. ADVANCED.

Peterson, Philip L. *Concepts and Language.* The Hague: Mouton, 1973. TECHNICAL. [An essay on generative semantics and the philosophy of language.]

Pike, Kenneth L. *Phonetics.* Ann Arbor: University of Michigan Press, 1943. *ADVANCED.

——. "Grammatical Prerequisites to Phonemic Analysis." *Word* (1947a) 3.155–172. *ADVANCED.

——. *Phonemics.* Ann Arbor: University of Michigan Press, 1947b. *INTRODUCTORY.

——. *Tone Languages.* Ann Arbor: University of Michigan Press, 1948. ADVANCED.

——. "More on Grammatical Prerequisites." *Word* (1952) 8.106–121. *ADVANCED.

——. *Language in Relation to a Unified Theory of the Structure of Human Behavior.* The Hague: Mouton, 1967. ADVANCED.

Politzer, Robert L., and Politzer, Frieda N. *Teaching English as a Second Language.* Lexington, Mass.: Xerox College Publishing, 1972. INTRODUCTORY.

Poppe, Nicholas. *Introduction to Altaic Linguistics.* Wiesbaden: International Publications Service, 1965. ADVANCED.

Postal, Paul. "Constituent Structure: A Study of Contemporary Models of Syntactic Description." *International Journal of American Linguistics* (1964) 30.1. part 2. Reprinted by Indiana University Research Center in Anthropology, Folklore, and Linguistics, Bloomington, 1967, and by Mouton, The Hague, 1967. ADVANCED.

——. "A Note on 'Understood Transitivity.'" *International Journal of American Linguistics* (1966) 32.90–93. ADVANCED.

——. *Aspects of Phonological Theory.* New York: Harper & Row, 1968. ADVANCED.

Poutsma, Hendrik. *A Grammar of Late Modern English.* Gronigen: P. Noordhoff, 1914–29. ADVANCED.

Premack, David. "The Education of Sarah." *Psychology Today* (1970) 4.5.54–58. GEN-

ERAL. [Chimpanzee-human communication.]

Pyles, Thomas. *The Origins and Development of the English Language.* New York: Harcourt Brace Jovanovich, 1964. INTRODUCTORY.

Quirk, Randolph; Greenbaum, Sidney; Leech, Geoffrey; and Svartvik, Jan. *A Grammar of Contemporary English.* New York and London: Academic Press, 1972. ADVANCED.

Reibel, David A., and Schane, Sanford A., eds. *Modern Studies in English.* Englewood Cliffs: Prentice-Hall, 1969. TECHNICAL. [Readings in transformational theory.]

Reich, Peter A., ed. *The Second LACUS Forum 1975.* Columbia, S.C.: Hornbeam Press, 1976. ADVANCED.

Révész, G. *The Orgins and Prehistory of Language.* London: Longmans, Green, 1956. ADVANCED.

Robins, R. H. *Ancient and Mediaeval Grammatical Theory in Europe.* London: G. Bell and Sons, 1951. ADVANCED.

————. *General Linguistics: An Introductory Survey.* Bloomington: Indiana University Press, 1964. INTRODUCTORY.

————. *A Short History of Linguistics.* Bloomington: Indiana University Press, 1967. *INTRODUCTORY.

Robinson, Jane J. "Dependency Structures and Transformational Rules." *Language* (1970) 46.259–285. ADVANCED.

Rosenbaum, Peter S. *The Grammar of English Predicate Complement Constructions.* Cambridge, Mass.: MIT Press, 1967. TECHNICAL.

Ross, John R. "Auxiliaries as Main Verbs." *Studies in Philosophical Linguistics* (1969) 1.77–102. TECHNICAL.

————. "On Declarative Sentences." In *Readings in English Transformational Grammar,* edited by Roderick A. Jacobs and Peter S. Rosenbaum. Waltham, Mass.: Ginn and Co., 1970. TECHNICAL.

Ruhlen, Merritt. *A Guide to the Languages of the World.* Stanford: Department of Linguistics, Stanford University, 1976. ADVANCED.

Rycenga, John A., and Schwartz, Joseph, eds. *Perspectives on Language.* New York: Ronald Press, 1963. INTRODUCTORY.

Sansom, George B. *An Historical Grammar of Japanese.* London: Oxford University Press, 1928. ADVANCED.

Sapir, Edward. *Time Perspective in Aboriginal American Culture.* Ottawa, Can.: Geological Survey, Department of Mines, Memoir 90, Anthropological Series, no. 13, 1919. Reprinted in *Selected Writings of Edward Sapir in Language, Culture, and Personality,* edited by David G. Mandelbaum, 1949. INTRODUCTORY.

————. *Language.* New York: Harcourt, Brace and World, 1921. *GENERAL.

————. "Sound Patterns in Language." *Language* (1925) 1.37–51. Reprinted in *Idiom Structure in English,* edited by Adam Makkai, 1972, and in *Readings in Linguistics,* edited by Martin Joos, 1958. ADVANCED.

————. "Central and North American Indian Languages." In *Encyclopædia Britannica.* 14th ed., vol. 5. Chicago: Encyclopædia Britannica, 1929. Reprinted in *Selected Writings of Edward Sapir in Language, Culture, and Personality,* edited by David G. Mandelbaum, 1949. GENERAL.

————. "The Psychological Reality of Phonemes." In *Selected Writings of Edward Sapir in Language, Culture, and Personality,* edited by David G. Mandelbaum. Berkeley and Los Angeles: University of California Press, 1949. Reprinted in *Idiom Structure in English,* edited by Adam Makkai, 1972. ADVANCED.

Sasaki, Tsuyoshi. "Case Grammar for Japanese." *Georgetown University Languages and Linguistics Working Papers* (1971) 2.61–76. ADVANCED.

Šaumjan, Sebastian K. *Problems of Theoretical Phonology.* Translated by Anthony L. Vanek. The Hague: Mouton, 1968. ADVANCED.

————. *Principles of Structural Linguistics.* Translated by J. Miller. The Hague: Mouton, 1971. ADVANCED.

Saussure, Ferdinand de. *Course in General Linguistics.* New York: Philosophical Library, 1959. *ADVANCED. [Translation by Wade Baskin of the 1916 original.]

Schane, Sanford A. "The Phoneme Revisited." *Language* (1971) 47.503–521. ADVANCED.

————. *Generative Phonology.* Englewood Cliffs: Prentice-Hall, 1973. ADVANCED.

Schank, Roger C., and Colby, Kenneth M. *Computer Models of Thought and Lan-*

guage. San Francisco: W. H. Freeman, 1973. ADVANCED.

Scott, John Paul. *Animal Behavior.* Chicago: University of Chicago Press, 1958. GENERAL.

Sebeok, Thomas A., ed. *Style in Language.* Cambridge, Mass.: MIT Press, 1960. ADVANCED.

———. *Current Trends in Linguistics.* The Hague: Mouton, 1963–75. ADVANCED.

———. *Animal Communication: Techniques of Study and Results of Research.* Bloomington: Indiana University Press, 1968. ADVANCED.

———. *Native Languages of the Americas.* New York: Plenum, 1976. ADVANCED.

Seropian, Hasmig. "A Simple Semantic Description of Negation." Paper read at First California Linguistics Conference, Berkeley, 1971. ADVANCED.

Sherzer, Joel. *An Areal-Typological Study of American Indian Languages North of Mexico.* New York: American Elsevier, 1975. ADVANCED.

Shibatani, Masayoshi. "The Non-cyclic Nature of Japanese Accentuation." *Language* (1972a) 48.584–595. TECHNICAL.

———. "Three Reasons for Not Deriving 'Kill' from 'Cause to Die' in Japanese." *Syntax and Semantics* (1972b) 1.125–137. TECHNICAL.

———. "Lexical Versus Periphrastic Causatives in Korean." *Journal of Linguistics* (1973a) 9.281–297. TECHNICAL.

———. "Semantics of Japanese Causativization." *Foundations of Language* (1973b) 9.327–373. TECHNICAL.

Shores, David L. *Contemporary English: Change and Variation.* Philadelphia: Lippincott, 1972. INTRODUCTORY.

Shuy, Roger W; Wolfram, Walter A.; and Riley, William K. *Field Techniques in an Urban Language Survey.* Washington, D.C.: Center for Applied Linguistics, 1968. ADVANCED.

Skinner, B. F. *Verbal Behavior.* New York: Appleton-Century-Crofts, 1957. ADVANCED.

Sledd, James H. *A Short Introduction to English Grammar.* Glenview, Ill.: Scott, Foresman, 1959. INTRODUCTORY.

Slobin, Dan I. *Psycholinguistics.* Glenview, Ill.: Scott, Foresman, 1971. INTRODUCTORY.

Slocum, Marianna C. "Tzeltal (Mayan) Noun and Verb Morphology." *International Journal of American Linguistics* (1948) 14.77–86. ADVANCED.

Smith, Frank, and Miller, George A., eds. *The Genesis of Language.* Cambridge, Mass.: MIT Press, 1966. ADVANCED. [Papers on child language acquisition.]

Starosta, Stanley. "The Faces of Case." *Language Sciences* (1973) 25.1–14. ADVANCED.

Steinberg, Danny D., and Jakobovits, Leon A., eds. *Semantics.* London: Cambridge University Press, 1971. TECHNICAL.

Stockwell, Robert P.; Schachter, Paul; and Partee, Barbara Hall. *Major Syntactic Structures of English.* New York: Holt, Rinehart and Winston, 1973. TECHNICAL. [Originally published as *Integration of Transformational Theories on English Syntax,* 1968.]

Struhsaker, Thomas T. "Auditory Communication Among Vervet Monkeys." In *Social Communication Among Primates,* edited by Stuart A. Altmann. Chicago: University of Chicago Press, 1967. ADVANCED.

Swadesh, Morris. *The Origin and Diversification of Language.* Chicago: Aldine, 1971. ADVANCED.

Teeter, Karl V. "Leonard Bloomfield's Linguistics." *Language Sciences* (1969) 7.1–6. ADVANCED.

———. "The Main Features of Malecite-Passamaquoddy Grammar." In *Studies in American Indian Languages,* edited by Jesse Sawyer. Berkeley and Los Angeles: University of California Press, 1971 (University of California Publications in Linguistics, 65). ADVANCED.

Thompson, Laurence C. "The Northwest." *Current Trends in Linguistics,* vol. 10, edited by Thomas A. Sebeok. The Hague: Mouton, 1973. ADVANCED.

Trager, George L. *Language and Languages.* San Francisco: Chandler, 1972. INTRODUCTORY. [Covers phonetics, English dialects, the comparative method, and writing systems.]

———, and Smith, Henry Lee. *An Outline of English Structure.* Norman, Okla.: Battenburg Press, 1951. *ADVANCED.

Trubetzkoy, Nikolai S. *Principles of Phonology.* Berkeley and Los Angeles: University of California Press, 1969. ADVANCED. [Translation by Christiane Baltaxe of the 1939 original.]

Twaddell, W. Freeman. *On Defining the Phoneme.* Baltimore: Linguistic Society of America, Language Monograph no. 16,

1935. Reprinted in *Readings in Linguistics*, edited by Martin Joos, 1958. ADVANCED.

Uitti, Karl D. *Linguistics and Literary Theory*. Englewood Cliffs: Prentice-Hall, 1969. ADVANCED.

Vachek, Josef. *The Linguistic School of Prague: An Introduction to Its Theory and Practice*. Bloomington: Indiana University Press, 1966. ADVANCED.

Voegelin, C. F., and Voegelin, F. M. *Hopi Domains: A Lexical Approach to the Problem of Selection*. Bloomington: Indiana University Publications in Anthropology and Linguistics, Memoir 14, 1957. ADVANCED. [A study of Hopi semantics.]

———, eds. *Languages of the World*. Twenty articles appearing in *Anthropological Linguistics*, vols. 6–8, covering Sino-Tibetan (five articles), Indo-Pacific (Austronesian) (eight), Native American, (two), Indo-European (one), African (one), Boreo-Oriental (i.e., Uralic, Altaic, Korean, Japanese, Ainu, Paleosiberian) (one), Ibero-Caucasian and Pidgin-Creole (one), Index (one), 1964–66. ADVANCED.

———. *Classification and Index of the World's Languages*. New York: American Elsevier, 1976. ADVANCED.

von Neumann, John. *The Computer and the Brain*. New Haven: Yale University Press, 1958. INTRODUCTORY.

Wall, Robert. *Introduction to Mathematical Linguistics*. Englewood Cliffs: Prentice-Hall, 1972. TECHNICAL.

Wardhaugh, Ronald. *Introduction to Linguistics*. New York: McGraw-Hill, 1972. INTRODUCTORY.

Waterman, John T. *Perspectives in Linguistics*. Chicago: University of Chicago Press, 1963. GENERAL. [Concise history of linguistics.]

Weir, Ruth Hirsch. *Language in the Crib*. The Hague: Mouton, 1962. ADVANCED.

Wells, Rulon S. "De Saussure's System of Linguistics," *Word* (1947a) 3.1–31 (Bobbs-Merrill Reprint L–95). ADVANCED.

———. "Immediate Constitutents." *Language* (1947b) 23.81–117. Reprinted in *Readings in Linguistics*, edited by Martin Joos, 1958. ADVANCED.

Westerman, D., and Ward, Ida C. *Practical Phonetics for Students of African Languages*. London: Oxford University Press, 1933. INTRODUCTORY.

Whitehall, Harold. *Structural Essentials of English*. New York: Harcourt, Brace, 1951. INTRODUCTORY.

Whorf, Benjamin Lee. *Language, Thought, and Reality*. Cambridge, Mass.: MIT Press, 1956. GENERAL.

Willis, Hulon. *Modern Descriptive English Grammar*. San Francisco: Chandler, 1972. INTRODUCTORY. [Presentation of traditional grammar but strongly influenced by structural grammar and transformational grammar.]

Winograd, Terry. *Understanding Natural Language*. New York: Academic Press, 1972. ADVANCED. [Description of a program for teaching computers to use natural language and logic.]

———. "Artificial Intelligence: When Will Computers Understand People?" *Psychology Today* (1974) 7.12.73–79. GENERAL.

Winter, Werner. "Transformations Without Kernels?" *Language* (1965) 41.484–489. ADVANCED.

Wolfram, Walter A. *A Sociolinguistic Description of Detroit Negro Speech*. Washington, D.C.: Center for Applied Linguistics, 1969. ADVANCED.

———, and Clarke, Nona H., eds. *Black-White Speech Relationships*. Washington, D.C.: Center for Applied Linguistics, 1971. ADVANCED.

Worth, Dean. "Paleosiberian." In *Current Trends in Linguistics*, vol. 1, edited by Thomas A. Sebeok. The Hague: Mouton, 1963. ADVANCED.

Wurm, Stephen A. *Languages of Australia and Tasmania*. The Hague: Mouton, 1971. ADVANCED.

Ziff, Paul. "The Number of English Sentences." Lecture at University of South Carolina, March 14, 1973, unpublished.

Ziza, Charles A. *American Indian Languages: Classifications and List*. Washington, D.C. Center for Applied Linguistics, 1970. ADVANCED.

Zvelebil, Kamil. *Comparative Dravidian Phonology*. The Hague: Mouton, 1970. ADVANCED.

symbols used

The following symbols, although explained in detail when first introduced in the text, are presented together at this point for ease of reference.

GENERAL

word	italic type in print ⎱ used for linguistic forms
<u>word</u>	underlining in manuscript ⎰ cited as such
un-	denotes a prefix or root that is not itself a free form but must be followed by some other unit
-iv-	denotes an affix or root that must be preceded and followed by other units
-er	denotes a suffix or root that must be preceded by other units
'meaning'	denotes the lexical meaning of a linguistic form
PLURAL	used to indicate the function of a linguistic form or the meaning of a semantic unit

PHONOLOGY

C	any consonant
V	any vowel
V́	a stressed vowel
V̄ ⎱ V· ⎰	a long vowel
C·	a long consonant
Ø	denotes a null element
⎡voiceless⎤ ⎢alveolar ⎢ ⎣stop ⎦	denotes simultaneously occurring elements in phonological descriptions

HISTORICAL GRAMMAR

*	precedes unattested forms whose existence is posited inferentially
x > y	x becomes y historically
x < y	x derives from y historically
x/y/z	in the comparative method, denotes members of a correspondence set
x/y	in internal reconstruction, denotes alternating sets
w > x / y__z	w changes historically to x in the environment depicted to the right of the slash, i.e., following y and preceding z

STRUCTURAL GRAMMAR

#word#	denotes word boundary
walk-er	marks morpheme boundary
[xyz]	denotes phonetic transcription, i.e., transcription of unclassified speech sounds (phones) or allophones of a phoneme
/xyz/	denotes phonemic transcription
{xyz}	denotes a morpheme; diagonals (shown immediately above) are frequently used for the same purpose, especially if the morph is being transcribed phonemically
x ∼ y	x alternates with y

TRANSFORMATIONAL GRAMMAR AND PHONOLOGY

*	precedes ungrammatical or nonoccurring forms
$x \rightarrow yz$	x is replaced by (or changes to) yz
$w \rightarrow x \, / \, y\_\_z$	w changes to x in the environment depicted to the right of the slash
$xy \Rightarrow yx$	xy is transformed into yx
$x \rightarrow (y)z$	x changes to z or optionally to yz
$x \rightarrow \left\{ \begin{matrix} y \\ z \end{matrix} \right\}$ *Select one*	x changes to either y or z
$\left[\begin{matrix} w \\ x \end{matrix} \right] \rightarrow \left[\begin{matrix} y \\ z \end{matrix} \right]$	w changes to y and x changes to z, i.e., the element on each line to the left of the arrow is replaced by the element on the corresponding line to the right of the arrow

MEANING–STRUCTURE GRAMMAR

$x \rightarrow y$	x is replaced by y
$x \dashrightarrow y$	x is *optionally* replaced by y
$x \rightarrow\!\!> y$	x is further specified as y
$x \dashrightarrow\!\!> y$	x is *optionally* further specified as y
$\left\{ \begin{matrix} x \\ y \end{matrix} \right\}$	either x or y (not both)
$\left(\begin{matrix} x \\ y \end{matrix} \right)$	either x or y *or both*
$\left[\begin{matrix} x \\ y \end{matrix} \right]$	if semantic units x and y are both present—note that this use of brackets differs from the use of brackets in phonetics and in transformational syntax, although it parallels the use of brackets in phonology
-x	if x is not present
|x|	denotes an underlying form in lexical entries; used in conjunction with conventions for phonemic and phonetic transcription

NAMES FOR SYMBOLS

ɨ	barred I
ʌ	wedge
ə	schwa
ɪ	small capital I
ɛ	epsilon
æ	digraph
ʊ	small capital U
ɔ	open O
č	C-wedge
ǰ	J-wedge
š	S-wedge
ž	Z-wedge
ð	eth
θ	theta
ŋ	eng; velar nasal

glossary-index

Listed are (1) all key terms, the most important of which are defined; (2) names of linguists mentioned in the text; (3) names of language families; and (4) names of languages mentioned in connection with data examples. Other languages, if mentioned in the text, will be found in Chapter 8 under the family to which the language belongs.

language (*continued*)
263, 265; isolating, 233; model of, 7–12, 151, 166–167, 224–227, 350–351; natural, 144, 293, 305, 308, 311, 344; number of, 231; origin of, 188–193, 346–350; phylum, 235; polysynthetic, 233; superfamily, 235; synthetic, 234; unclassified, 265; universals, 233, 265–266
lateral, 79
Latin, 16–23, 29–30, 37–45, 50, 69, 71–73, 75–76, 82, 91, 100, 175, 233–234, 238–239, 276–278, 316
lexical insertion, 130–131, 151, 157, 165–166
lexical specification, 211–215
lexicalist position, 183
lexicon *a list of words and word formatives available to symbolize meanings in a language,* 10–12, 131, 157, 161, 165–168, 184, 210, 212, 225–226, 328, 350–351; as filter, 210
linearity, 7–11, 178–179, 212, 271
linearization, 220–225; primary, 221; secondary, 221
linguistics: and area studies, 322–324; and history, 322–324; and language teaching, 317–322; and literature, 315–317; and mathematics, 143, 310–312; and philosophy, 312–315; as interdisciplinary science, 295–296; evidence used in, 334–338; goals of, 332–334; issues in, 340–347; normal practice of, 338–340
locative, 176–177, 201–205
Locke, John, 313, 345
logograph, 71, 271–272, 278–288, 290–292

macron, 17, 100
Malecite-Passamaquoddy, 107–108
Malinowski, Bronislaw, 296, 342
manuscripts, study of, 35–36
marking, 96, 136, 141, 206, 210–211, 215–216, 223, 241
matching *any matching of a sound or sounds from two or more languages,* 40, 51, 59
McCawley, James D., 169
McDavid, Raven I., Jr., 301
meaning and form, relation of, 16, 115, 117, 121, 149–151, 162–163
Meaning and the Structure of Language, 188
meaning-structure grammar *an approach to language study emphasizing the identification of semantic units and semantic relationships as the elements believed to underlie syntactic structures,* 173, 187–229, 306, 310, 314, 319, 331–334, 337–339, 342
merger, 53–54
metaphor, 227
Middle Ages, 15–16, 35–36, 312
Middle English, 95
minimal pair, 75, 82
modality, 27, 154–156, 216

morph *a unit associated with meaning,* 103
morpheme *a unit of meaning functioning as a structural unit in a language,* 102–112, 114–115, 123; bound, 18, 158; content, 103, 158; discontinuous, 103, 156, 256; free, 18, 158; function of, 103, 158
morphophoneme, 116, 119, 158
Muskogean, 257

nasal, 79
nasal cavity, 78
nasalization, 96
natural class, 105
negative raising, 171
neural linguistics, 306–308
new information, 220, 222–224
Nilo-Saharan, 254, 255
nonstandard, 85
nontense, 84
noun, 26; abstract, 26; case, *see* case, grammatical; common, 26; concrete, 26; count, 26; mass, 26; proper, 26
noun, semantic inflection of, 216–219; aggregate, 217; definite, 217; generic, 217; plural, 217
noun, semantic specification of, 206–215; animate, 208; anthropomorphic, 213–215; count, 207; feminine, 208; first, 209; human, 208; masculine, 214; place, 213–214; potent, 207; second, 209; unique, 210
noun phrase advancement, 139
noun-verb relations: agent, 195–206; beneficiary, 200–206; complement, 204–206; experiencer, 199–206; hierarchy of, 205; instrument, 202–206; locative, 201–206; patient, 195–206

object, 25, 130, 139–140, 175; direct, 25, 126; indirect, 25, 126, 175; inner, 222; of preposition, 28, 175; outer, 222
objective complement, 25, 126
O'Cain, Raymond, 301
Odyssey, 36
Old English, 65, 75, 95, 118, 277, 316
old information, 220, 222–224, 297
onomatopoeia, 105
oral cavity, 78
ordering: of sound changes, 56–62, 118; of synchronic rules, 119, 122, 124, 205–206
Origin of Species, 36
Oto-Manguean, 263

Paleosiberian, 256
Pano-Tacanan, 265
Papuan, 252
paradigm *a set of linguistic elements in which one part remains constant while another part varies,* 16; experiential-behavioral, 228, 334; scientific, 330; semantic, 211, 225

sentence, 24–25; embedded, 135; matrix, 135; transformational derivation of, 157; types of, 126–127
set theory, 20–21, 45–48, 309
Shawnee, 323
sign language, 5, 190, 348
Siouan, 258
Skinner, B. F., 345
Slavic, 239
slot, 32, 111–112, 129
sociolinguistics, 24, 300–304
Spanish, 5, 6, 8, 21, 37, 88, 137, 277–278, 289, 321
spelling, 88, 118, 273, 275, 289–292, 317
spirant (fricative), 78
split, 53–54
standard, 85–86
state, 194–197
stem *a content form capable of taking inflectional affixes,* 18, 29, 108, 111
Stoics, 15–16, 149
stop, 49, 78
stratificational grammar, 341–342
stress *increased prominence of a syllable,* 88–89; assignment of, 222–224
structural grammar *a twentieth-century approach to language study emphasizing the synchronic analysis of individual languages in terms of each language's characteristic structural systems,* 71–113, 119, 125, 134, 150–151, 153–154, 158–159, 184–185, 187, 223, 319, 327–328, 332, 333–334, 336–339, 341
subcategorization, 159–169
subject, 24, 126, 130, 140, 175
suffix *a word formative that follows a stem or root,* 18, 29
suppletive, 106
surface structure *an actually occurring form (in phonology) or arrangement (in syntax) derived from an underlying structure,* 132, 138, 162, 167
syllabary, 273–276
symbolization, 12, 187–188, 210, 225–227, 349–351; initial, 226; final, 226
symbolization arrow, 12, 349–351
synchronic *with reference to a single point in time,* 91, 102, 116–120, 149, 153
syntactic component, 9–12, 167–174, 225, 350–351
Syntactic Structures, 112, 150, 159, 167, 180
syntactic variable, 181–182
syntax *the arrangement of words or word formatives in linear order,* 9, 11
system-structure grammar, 342

Tagalog, 98–101
tagmeme, 111–112
tagmemics, 341
Tai, 250

tense (as phonetic feature), 84
tense (as verbal category), 27, 134, 154–156, 215
Thorndike, Edward, 304
Tibeto-Burman, 249
tone *a distinctive quality of pitch associated with individual words in Chinese and other languages,* 90, 233
trachea, 78
traditional grammar *an approach to language study that developed in Greece, was transmitted through Rome to Medieval Europe, and has remained influential in school programs to the present time; also called school grammar,* 14–34, 107, 125, 149, 160, 175, 319, 326, 331, 333–335, 338–339
transcription, 92, 100; broad, 92; narrow, 92
transformation: prelexical, 172; syntactic, 33, 131–148, 151, 156–158, 162–164, 166–167, 170–172, 178–185, 189
transformational grammar *an approach to language study emphasizing the analysis of syntax in terms of underlying structures and process rules that transform these into surface structures,* 101, 109–110, 112, 114–186, 188, 194, 205–206, 221–223, 225–227, 304–306, 309–310, 313–314, 319, 328–329, 332, 334–339, 341–344
transformationalist position, 183
translation, 12, 309–310; by machine, 310
Troubetzkoy, Nikolai, 341
Tucanoan, 264
Tupi-Guaraní, 264
Turkish, 233
Tzeltal, 108–109, 111–112

umlaut, 238
underlying form (structure) *a (possibly nonoccurring) variant, taken as the basic form, from which other variants can be derived,* 28, 33, 62, 72, 117–119, 121, 124–125, 132–134, 138–141, 162–163, 167, 170–173, 178–179, 225
universal grammar, 16, 312–323
universals, 233, 265–266
unmarked, 136, 206
Uralic, 244–245
Uto-Aztecan, 261–262

variation, 83; allophonic, 81, 227, 351; conditioned, 81; free, 81; geographical, 300; morpholexical, 158, 226, 351; morphophonemic, 109–111, 115–117, 151, 156–158, 226, 351; phonemic, 115, 351; phonological, 110, 158, 226, 351; situational, 300, 303–304; social, 300–301; syntactic, 131–134. *See also* alternation
velum, 77–78